Electronic Document Preparation and Management for CSEC examination

O'Neil Duncan

Acknowledgements

O'Neil would like to thank Charmaine Gordon for her contribution to unit 1 of this work.

Table of Contents

INTRODUCTION

Welcome to Electronic Document Preparation and Management for CSEC examination. This book covers the EDPM syllabus in its entirety.

The Electronic Document Preparation and Management (EDPM) syllabus is designed to equip students with knowledge and computer-related skills required to enhance the performance of clerical and administrative tasks. The EDPM syllabus will provide a holistic approach to acquisition of knowledge and the development of candidates' decision-making and problem-solving skills. It is suited for candidates pursing any discipline, as the competencies and skills developed in the preparation and management of electronic documents are interdisciplinary and imperative in the world of work or in the pursuit of further studies.

The syllabus is arranged in nine sections, sub-divided into specific objectives and corresponding content.

Section I	-	Fundamentals of Computing
Section II	-	Keyboarding Mastery
Section III	-	Introduction to Application Software
Section IV	-	Use of Application Software
Section V	-	Business Document Preparation
Section VI	-	Specialised Document Preparation
Section VII	-	Electronic Communication
Section VIII	-	Document Management
Section IX	-	Ethics

Unlike the CSEC Information Technology Syllabus, CSEC EDPM emphasizes computer applications related to the production, filing and retrieval of documents, skills that are crucial in today's office environment.

Chapter I

Fundamentals of Computing

Highlights:

- *Types of Computers*
- *Computer Hardware and software*
- *General use of computers*
- *Health ergonomics and safety*

L esson 1

Types of Computer

Objective

At the end of this chapter, the student should be able t:

➢ *define computer*
➢ *identify types of computers*
➢ *discuss the advantages and disadvantages of computer usage*

What is a computer?

A **comput**er is an electronic machine or device that accepts data, processes and produces information. They are used as tools in every part of society together with the Internet. They take input such as numbers, text, sound, image, animations, video, etc., and converts it, presenting the changed input (processed input) as output.

- The **data** consists of numbers, text, sound, images, animations, and video.

- The **process** converts numbers, text, sound, images, animations, and video (data) into usable data, which is called information.
- The **information** consists of numbers, text, sound, images, animations, and video that has been converted by the process

COMPONENTS OF A COMPUTER

HARDWARE refers to the tangible part of the computer or parts of the computer that you can touch.

SOFTWARE refers to the set of instructions or program codes that instruct hardware to perform the tasks example: Windows Operating System (OS), Android OS, MAC, OS, MS Office. It is the intangible part of the computer.

Generally, they are classified based on their speed, storage size or capacity, cost and many other capabilities. Look at the various types of computers with their corresponding features as shown below.

Types of Computers

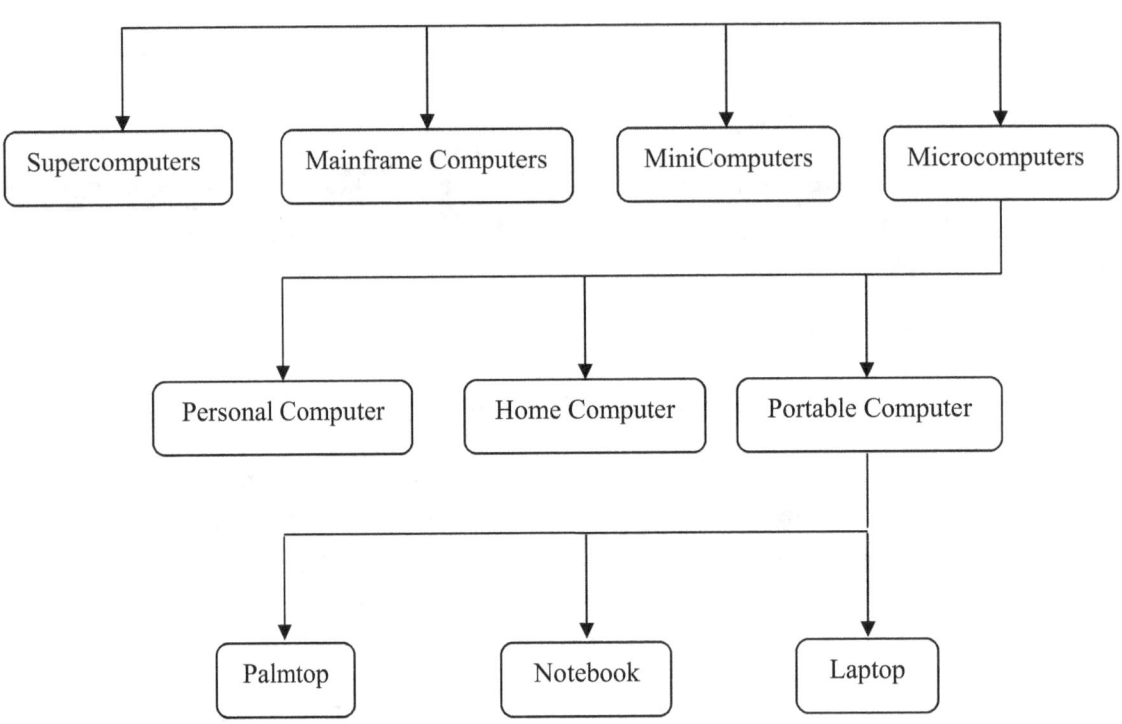

Supercomputers

The **supercomputers** are specially designed to perform faster and have larger storage capacity than other computers. They are military, space research and atomic study by various government organizations. They are also used in weather forecasting.

Mainframe Computers

Mainframe computer are large computer systems with the highest speed and biggest capacity. They perform tasks that include calculation of payroll. Keeping bank records, handling airline reservations and storing students records for a university. Mainframes are mainly used by large corporations, banks, government agencies and universities.

Minicomputers

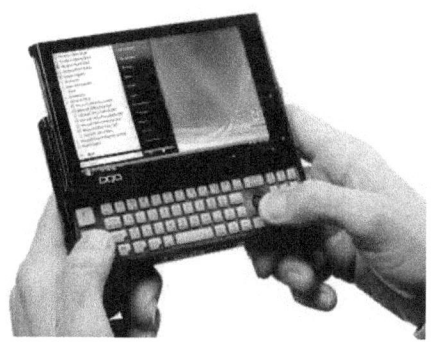

Minicomputers have lower speed and storage capacity than mainframe computers, but have larger capacity storage and speed than microcomputers. They are found in small industries, government offices, and universities.

Microcomputers

Microcomputers are considered the lowest in line of the computers. But today, they have almost the same computer power and storage capacity as the mainframes computers. **Microcomputers** uses a microprocessor which is sometimes called the "CPU" in a chip. It was first created for personal used even at home or in the office.

Personal Computer

A personal computer (PC) is the most popular and common microcomputer. It was first introduced by IBM (International Business Machine) Corporation. Personal computers are popular because they can be used by only one person at a time with different application software.

Home Computers

The home computers have lower capacity and are slower than personal computers. They are used for Playing games, for educational software and for management of personal budget. Other input devices and storage devices such as television and tape recorders can be used with these type of microcomputers.

Portable Computer

Portable computers are microcomputers that have different sizes, weight, screen color and can bring anywhere. These computers have all the basic parts of a regular computer such as keyboard, mouse, monitor, storage devices and other peripherals built into one. The three types of this are laptop, notebook and palmtop computer.

The *Laptop computer* is the largest and heavies portable computer. It is called laptop because you can use and keep it in your lap. They are commonly used by travellers or businessman who need to use computer while on trip. Laptop computers have the same memory capacity, speed and storage six of a personal computer.

A *notebook computer* is quite smaller than a laptop computer. It is called notebook because it has the size of a notebook. It can be easily placed in a small bag or briefcase while travelling. Though small, it has the same power and capacity of a personal computer.

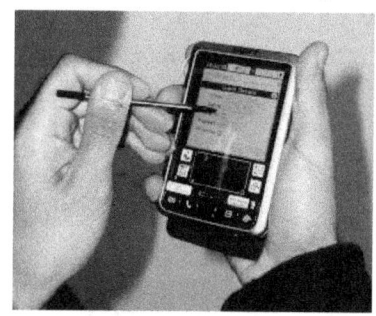

A *Palmtop computer* is the smallest portable computer. It is call palmtop because it is at most the size of a palm. It is larger than a regular calculator. Because of its size, it does not have a regular-size keyboard and monitor.

Advantages of computer usage

The main characteristics of a computer are the very high speed with which calculations and processes are carried out and also the very large amount of information and data that may be stored in a relatively small spaces called memory.

1 - Speed of Computing:

One of the main advantages in using computers is the possibility that a task that may take longer to do by hand may be done in a shorter period of time using a computer. Computers are designed to do tasks much faster and more accurately than humans. Numerical computations, creation and editing of documents, data organization and presentation, graphics are examples of tasks that are done efficiently when computers are used.

2 - Efficiency and Productivity:

It is perhaps easy to explain the efficiency of computers in comparing documents produced using a typewriter and a word processor (on a computer). Using a word processing makes it easy to make changes to letters, words, chapters or entire documents. There are possibilities to spell check words and therefore make changes. Deleting and inserting letters, words and paragraphs is done without leaving a trace. When all necessary changes are made, files may be saved, printed, edited as many times as is necessary, sent by e-mail to someone else in another continent within minutes. When using a typewriter, a simple typing error would be time consuming to fix. Several recent studies have shown a substantial increase in productivity due to the use of computers.

3 - Data Storage.

Computer storage or memory is measured in bytes. A byte correspond to 8 bits (binary digit). For example it takes 1 byte (or 8 bits) to represent (store) a character of the alphabet. A page of a book with 80 characters per line and 40 lines per page would need 80 * 40 = 3200 bytes of storage or 3 Kilobytes (1 Kilobyte = 1024 bytes). A book of 400 pages would need 400 * 3 Kilobytes = 1.2 Megabytes

(1 megabyte = 1000 Kilobytes)

Example 1: A CD has a storage capacity of 600 Megabytes and therefore can hold the contents of 600 / 1.2 = 500. Yes 500 books in ond CD!.

Now think about how much space and how much does it cost to store 4000 books!

Protect Your Eyes from Digital Eye Strain

<u>Disadvantages of using computer excessively</u>

1 - Impact on social life

Man is a social animal. His survival deems an interactive society. Sharing his ideas, thoughts and beliefs with others play a key role to his existence. Computers have locked him somewhere in the dark with no access to the outer world. He mostly remains to himself, secluded from the real world. He gets involved in a gradual transition to becoming nothing but a lifeless machine. He starts to perceive everything in terms of numbers and numerals. His metamorphosis into an emotionless animal arouses anti social tendencies that marks him as an alienated species. Computers might create wonders and help man to reach the acme of success. But, if not controlled it can also be the beginning of everything that requires a second thought.

2 - Strain to the eye

God created man as the guardian of his universe. He bestowed man with vision to savour the bounties of nature. While he has to provide them the greatest care, he strains them for passing pleasures. Exerting stress causes damage to the eye cells which can even impair one's eye sight. It necessitates the wearing of glasses, which of late though considered a beauty icon, is slowly eating our ability to see things. Moreover people can be rejected job offers due to poor vision. Loss of sight blinds us from worldly pleasures and we are destined to live with the nights. A dawn never comes visiting our thoughts.

3 - Effect on education

Every step to a developed nation is complete when the youth cooperates. There buds a symbiotic relationship insisting the youth to play its part. However technology has veiled his eyes from reality and the only thing that interests him is a computer. Gaming, chatting and other tempting software's are the apples in his eyes. This reduces the average study time of an individual, the result; a fruitless education. The effort he needs to devote himself to is literally nil. Reaping a negotiable output requires the sowing of proper inputs. Spending less time in learning life's lessons can affect you – socially, financially and mentally- in future.

4 - Prey to vicious crimes

The dominance a computer has over mankind is hypnotic. This can lead him to committing heinous crimes that has a negative impact on the environment. Tasting the spiciest food has been leisure to us. Adding to this, the belief man is invincible took him to places he is restricted entry. Watching the same movies and chatting with known friends for a very long period becomes a monotonous routine, prompting him to go for more entertainment. The tendency can be best acknowledged for the various cases of spamming, malwares and hacking, which under law are punishable offences. The dangers involved in chatting with strangers have ruined many a life over the past few years. It's high time we woke to the realization that the world needs not potential killers and criminals but a responsible bunch who can contribute the next leap to development.

5 - Tamper's your creativity

Most of us are used to the 'copy paste' method of writing assignments, projects and similar tasks. Carbon copies of ready information accessed from computers mostly make our homework. Technology has tampered our thoughts to an extent where we do not make an effort to do some extra research. Every individual is born with inbuilt creative skills. Proper channeling of our creativity can take us places. Intelligence is not about submitting a forged piece of work before some due date. It demands the exploitation of your thoughts to provide information that is new to the world and helps in structuring the proper foundation to success. May be your thoughts and insights could be of better aid to a developing country than the resources a computer donates. However, the present day influence is epidemic restricting the flow of free thoughts.

6- Susceptible to unproductive activities

A computer can be best considered as a resource that aids us in gathering information. This frame of reference moots gaming on computers as a form of recreation provided we do not over exploit the advantage. Gaming and chatting for an entire day leads to nothing constructive. While the competitive world demands productive outputs from individuals; sitting idly looking at a computer screen is not going to help. We accomplish nothing and get tagged as unsuccessful. The information the computer provides is the only knowledge we get exposed to. A responsible citizen should also be aware of his land and the various happenings in his society. Computer addicts are ignorant to every happening in his city. The joy of living among a group of people always helps in a spiritual learning which computers cannot provide. Life is an experience. It's a pity to remain inexperienced in an increasingly adept world.

7- Effect on health

An unhealthy individual can never bask in the glory of being healthy. Using computers for longer periods affect one's nervous system which in turn can hinder the proper functioning of your brain. This might even lead to short term/ long term memory losses. While a computer is useful in several ways, exposure to radiations emitted from them is the prime cause of various strain disorders. The key to a successful life is to remain healthy. A clear mind is the door to a clear vision. Proper planning and understanding of ideas always demand a healthy mind. On the contrary, an unhealthy individual is the owner of a clouded mind and disturbed soul.

8- Laziness: the pied wiper

Sitting for several hours in front of a PC suggest laziness. Being lazy reduces one to everything short of self respect. It wipes away the gentleman in you and people begin to spot defects that can be cancerous. Laziness prevents the realization and understanding of one's inherent skills. A slothful approach weakens the proper functioning of our body systems. The lazy man is the home of the useless. It carries one to the devil's workshop. Moving a chair can perhaps become a difficult task to be carried out by the laziest!

9- The addictive syndrome

Addiction demands a total resignation to forces that command your thoughts and actions. Ever since the universe saw its first light, man was considered the supreme force and every matter revolved around him. Today, man who called himself unbeatable has laid his weapons in defeat to a machine! He, who was the most powerful, is now a slave to some lifeless machinated box. As the situation deems to be pathetic, it's interesting how irony has played its wits on humans.

10- Reduce one's outlook

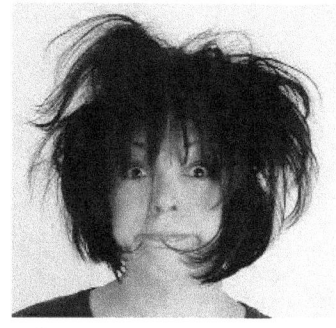

A prolonged usage of computers decimates your sense of conceiving knowledge to that obtainable within a computer frame. This calls for less participation in real life activities while you start perceiving everything as artificial. Man gets labeled as cynical and introverted. One is drained off his conceptions as he materializes himself to be auctioned. His life remains held on a string in a world, somewhere between the real and the unreal.

<u>Summary</u>

- **A compute**r is an electronic machine or device that accepts data, processes and produces information.
- The types of computers are supercomputers, mainframe, minicomputer, microcomputers to include laptop, desktop, notebook, tablet palmtop and other current devices.
- The Advantages and disadvantages of computer usage in terms of speed, accuracy, storage and other reliability.

 ## Exercise I.1.1

Name: _____   **Score:** ___ **/50**

Level/Section: _____   **Date:** _____

I. Answer the following questions.

1. What is a computer? (1 mark)

_____

2. What is the difference between hardware and software? (2 mark)

_____

3. How is data represented in the computer? (1 mark)

_____

4. What are the types of computers? Describe each. (10 marks)

_____

5. Why is the personal computer the most popular microcomputer today? (5 marks)

_____

6. Differentiate a laptop computer from a notebook computer. (5 marks)

_____

7. What are the types of microcomputers? (5 marks)

_____

8. Give the basic characteristics of each type of microcomputers. (10 marks)

_____

9. Give at least three advantages and disadvantages of using computers. (10 marks)

_____

10. It is the smallest portable computer (1 mark)

Lesson 2

Computer Hardware

System Unit   Screen   Monitor

Speaker

Speaker

Keyboard   Mouse   Microphone

Objective

At the end of this chapter, the student should be able t:

➢ *explain the functions of various input and output devices*
➢ *distinguish the use of a certain devices whether it is for input, output or storage data*
➢ *list various types of storage media and their practical applications*

Hardware

Like other machine, a personal computer is made up of different parts. These parts are connected to each other, which make up the computer system. The personnel computer (PC) comes in a rectangular case which contains important components, collectively called **hardware**. A basic knowledge of computer hardware components is important. Let us examine a few salient features of every **components of a simple computer system** works as shown below:

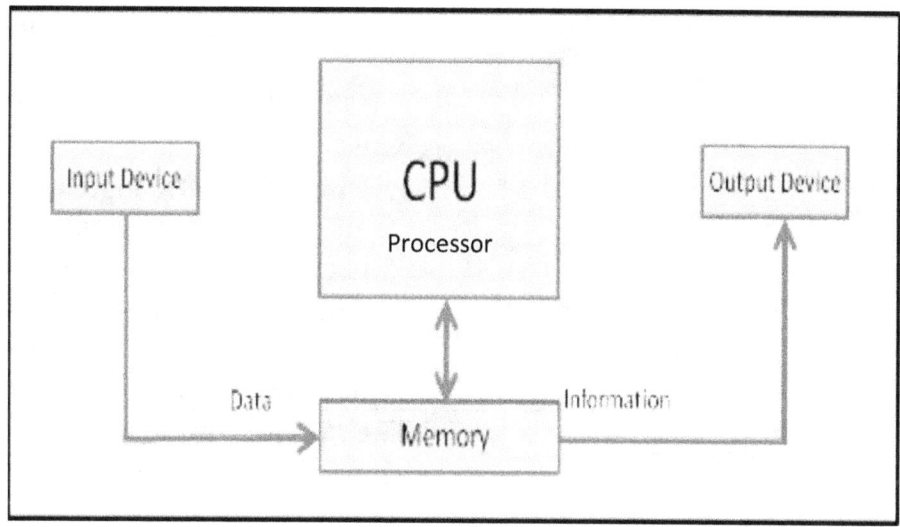

Data comes in through an *Input Device*, and is sent to the processor, the *Central Processing Unit (CPU) by Memory*.
The **Central Processing Unit (CPU)** *is the component that receives, interprets and carries out the basic instructions which is installed in the* **memory** *and manipulates the data to produce information.*

When the CPU has finished processing the data, it is presented through the **output device** *as information.* The **Central Processing Unit (CPU)** and **Memory** are put into a computer case/ housing.

Components of a Computer System

Central Processing Unit (CPU) or **processor** is the *brain* of the computer. It is the most important part of a computer system. The job of the CPU is to process data and carry out the programs or instructions given to it. It control the operations of all components of a computer such as the memory, input and output devices. The CPU checks all the works of all the components of a computer system.

The CPU incorporates three interrelated parts.
1. **The arithmetic logic unit** (ALU) performs all of the calculations and logic comparisons necessary for the computer to operate
2. **The control unit** (CU) which directs the flow of data through CPU and to and from other devices

The memory unit (MU) that holds all of the data and instructions that the computer uses to operate. There are **two types** of memory located within the MU:

• **Read only memory** (ROM) This memory cannot normally be changed – it is permanent. It is a secondary storage like Hard Disk Drive (HDD) or Compact Disk Drive (CDD) for long term memory.

• **Random access memory** (RAM) This memory can be changed instantly and is normally erased when the computer is turned off.

These *interrelated* parts use what is called 'procedures' which are a group of instructions that perform a specific task. They allow the user to operate the computers input processing and output.

Input devices

An input device is any hardware device that sends data to the computer.

Before a computer can do its work, the data and instruction must be fed into the computer. These data and instructions are given to the computer through the input devices. The common input devices are the following:

	A keyboard is the set of typewriter-like keys used to enter data into a computer. Keyboards are similar to typewriter keyboards but contain additional keys.
	TOUCH SCREEN – is an electronic visual display that the user can control through simple or multi-touch gestures by touching the screen with a special stylus/pen and-or one or more fingers.
	TABLET PEN (STYLUS) enables a user to hand-draw images, animations and graphics, similar to the way a person draws images with a pencil and paper.
	Mouse A device that controls the movement of the cursor or pointer on a display screen. A mouse is a small object you can roll along a hard, flat surface. The name comes from the small shape of the mouse, which you can move quickly back and forth on the mouse pad and the cord, which represents the mouse's tail. If you are using a wireless mouse, the analogy does not work so well. The term mouse is not an acronym. The mouse was invented by Douglas C. Engelbart around 1964 who named it for its resemblance to that rodent with its long tail. Yet some claim that mouse is an acronym for Manually-Operated User-Select Equipment.
	Scanners are used to capture incredibly detailed images.

	**Barcode readers and scanners** A barcode reader or scanner, also known as a **point of sale** (POS) scanner is a hardware device capable of reading a **barcode** and printing out the details of the product or logging that product into a database.

	**Optical Character Reader (OCR)**
	
	OCR recognizes letters, numerals, punctuation, and related communication symbols. Its main use is for getting printed **text** into a form that can be manipulated by a **word processor** or similar computer program.
	Advantages:
	  ✓ Quick method of inputting data.
	  ✓ Less labor needed to input data.
	Disadvantages:
	  ➢ Can misread characters not formed properly.
	  ➢ Not always accurate.

	**Optical Mark Reader (OMR)** is used for the evaluation of Mark sense forms (that require a number two pencil to fill in circles for answers, like those used for standardized testing and state lotteries). **OMR** recognizes the presence or absence of marks in pre-determined positions on a sheet of paper.
	This technology includes **digital image processing**. This software is very simple in working and it works with the help of a **scanner**.
	
	Advantages:
	  ✓ Quick method of inputting data.
	  ✓ Less labor needed to input data.
	Disadvantages:
	  ➢ Creased forms can jam the machine causing down time.
	  ➢ Damaged forms have to be keyed in manually or rewritten.

	**A joystick** is an input device consisting of a stick that pivots on a base and reports its angle or direction to the device it is controlling.

Output Devices

After the data is processed in the CPU, the computer will change it into useful information called Output. The processed data displays on the output devices such as the following:

	A computer **monitor** is the most commonly used output device, for the information processed by the CPU
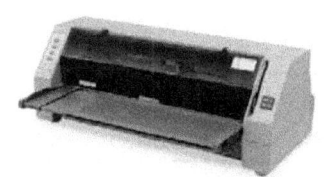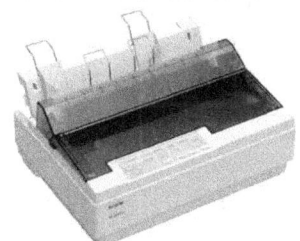	**A printer** is a device that accepts text and graphic output from a computer and transfers the information to paper, usually to standard size sheets of paper. The result produce by a printer is called hardcopy. **Categories of printer:** *daisy-wheel:* Similar to a ball-head typewriter, this type of printer has a plastic or metal wheel on which the shape of each character stands out in relief. A hammer presses the wheel against a ribbon, which in turn makes an ink stain in the shape of the character on the paper. Daisy-wheel printers produce letter quality print but cannot print graphics. **dot-matrix:** Creates characters by striking pins against an ink ribbon. Each pin makes a dot, and combinations of dots form characters and illustrations. **ink-jet:** Sprays ink at a sheet of paper. Ink-jet printers produce high-quality text and graphics. **laser:** Uses the same technology as copy achines. Laser printers produce very high quality text and graphics. **LCD & LED:** Similar to a laser printer, but uses liquid crystals or light-emitting diodes rather than a laser to produce an image on the drum.

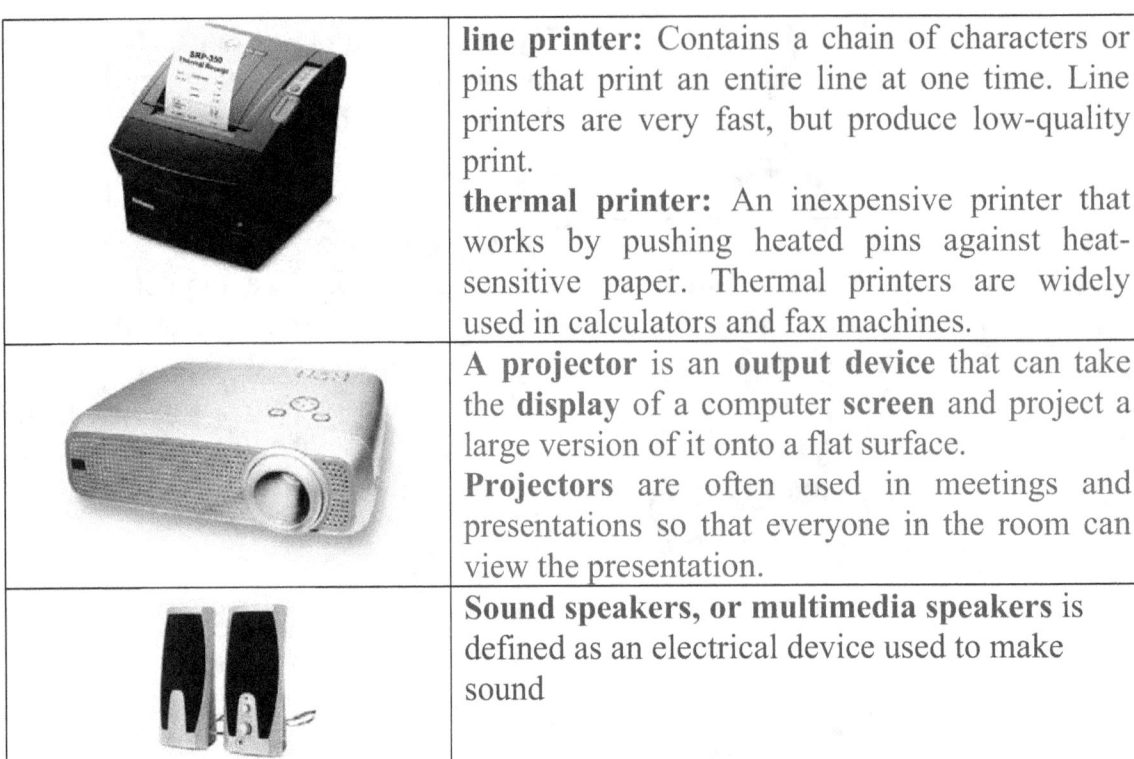

	line printer: Contains a chain of characters or pins that print an entire line at one time. Line printers are very fast, but produce low-quality print. **thermal printer:** An inexpensive printer that works by pushing heated pins against heat-sensitive paper. Thermal printers are widely used in calculators and fax machines.
	A projector is an **output device** that can take the **display** of a computer **screen** and project a large version of it onto a flat surface. **Projectors** are often used in meetings and presentations so that everyone in the room can view the presentation.
	Sound speakers, or multimedia speakers is defined as an electrical device used to make sound

STORAGE DEVICES

Storage of data can be done within the computer and on portable storage devices.

	HARD DISK is a magnetic disk use to store computer data. The term hard is used to distinguish it from a soft, or floppy, disk. Hard disks hold more data and are faster than floppy disks. A hard disk, for example, can store anywhere from 10 to more than 4 terabytes, whereas most floppies have a maximum storage capacity of 1.4 megabytes. It can be either internal or external to your computer.
	Compact Disc (CD) is a type of optical disk capable of storing large amounts of data -- up to 1GB, although the most common size is 650MB (megabytes). A single CD-ROM has the storage capacity of 700 floppy disks, enough memory to store about 300,000 text pages.

	**Digital Versatile Disc (DVD)** is a type of optical disk technology similar to the CD-ROM. A DVD holds a minimum of 4.7GB of data, enough for a full-length movie. DVDs are commonly used as a medium for digital representation of movies and other multimedia presentations that combine sound with graphics.
	**FLOPPY DISK** drives store information on floppy disks, also called floppies or diskettes. Compared to CDs and DVDs, floppy disks can store only a small amount of data. They also retrieve information more slowly and are more prone to damage. For these reasons, floppy disk drives are less popular than they used to be, although some computers still include them. They are called "floppy" disks because the outside is made of hard plastic and the disk inside is made of a thin, flexible vinyl material.
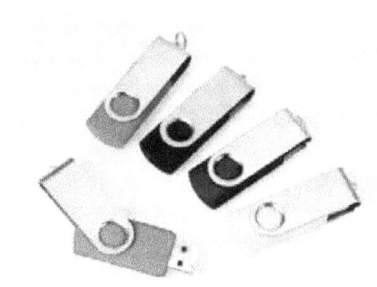	**USB FLASH DISK** is a data storage device that includes flash memory with an integrated *Universal Serial Bus (USB)* interface. It is typically removable and rewritable and physically much smaller than an optical disc. Most weigh less than 30 grams (1.1 oz). As of January 2013, drives of up to 512 gigabytes (GB) were available. A one-terabyte (TB) drive was unveiled at the 2013 Consumer Electronics Show and became available later that year.
	**Secure Digital (SD)** is a non-volatile memory card format developed by the SD Card Association for use in portable devices. It is widely used in digital cameras, cell phones, ebook readers, tablet computers, netbook computers, media players, GPS receivers, and video game consoles. The card has a rectangular design, but one edge is chipped off. This means that the cards cannot be inserted into the cameras (or other devices) the wrong way. It has been made of different capacities between 4 Megabytes and 32 gigabytes.

micro SD is a kind of removable flash memory card used for storing information. The cards are used in mobile phones, newer types of handheld GPS devices, portable media players, digital audio players, expandable USB flash drives, Nintendo DS flashcards, and digital camera. It is the smallest memory card that can be bought; at 15 mm × 11 mm × 1 mm (about the size of a fingernail), it is about a quarter of the size of a normal-sized SD card.

There are adapters that make the small microSD able to fit in devices that have slots for standard SD, minSD, Memory Stick Duo card, and even USB. TransFlash and microSD cards are the same and can be used in place of each other.

Summary

Components of a Computer System

An input device is any hardware device that sends data to the Computer. Before a computer can do its work, the data and instruction must be fed into the computer.

Central Processing Unit (CPU) or processor is the *brain* of the computer. It is the most important part of a computer system. The job of the CPU is to process data and carry out the programs or instructions given to it.

The memory unit (MU) that holds all of the data and instructions that the computer uses to operate. There are **two types** of memory located within the MU: **Read only memory** (ROM) and **Random access memory**(RAM).

An input device is the data processed in the CPU, the computer will change it into useful information.

Activity

1.   Identify the components of a computer system.

2.   Describe how a processor (Central Processing Unit) works.

Exercise I.2

Name: _____   Score: _____ /20

Level/Section: _____   Date: _____

I. *Identify the following pictures and distinguish the category? Write ID for input device and OD for output device and SD for Storage media before the label.* (2 marks each)

 1. _____	 2. _____
 3. _____	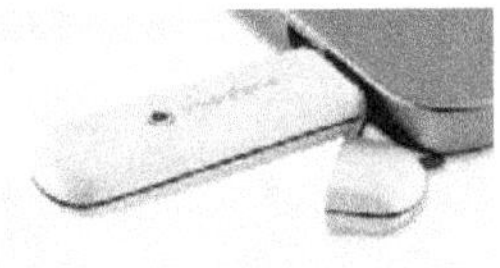 4. _____
 5. _____	 6. _____
 7. _____	 8. _____
9. 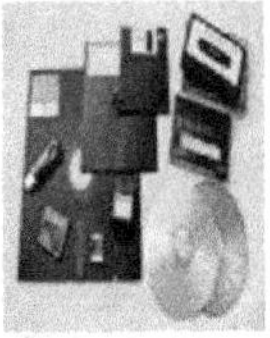 _____	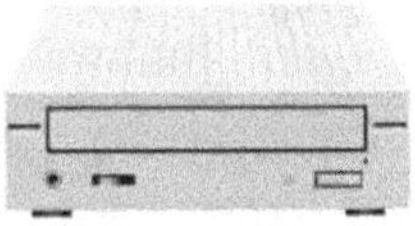 10. _____

II. Fill in the blanks using the word only once from the list as shown:

output	mouse	screen
programs	data	program
printer	instructions	keyboard
information	meaning	input

(a) Computers process _____ to produce _____.

(b) The sets of _____ that humans give computers are called

_____.

(c) The three basic stages of computing are _____, processing and

_____.

(d) A computer works through these stages by running a _____.

(e) The most commonly used input devices are the _____ and the

_____.

(f) The most commonly used output devices are the _____, or monitor,

and the _____.

(g) Information is data that has a _____.

L esson 3

Computer   Software

Objective

At the end of this chapter, the student should be able to:
- *define a computer software and its functions*
- *distinguish between operating system software and application software*
- *enumerate other programmes associated with the Operating system software and application software*

Software

A System Software is a set of one or more programs prepared to control the operation and increase the processing capability of a computer. It is capable of performing many different specific tasks, as opposed to hardware which only perform mechanical tasks that they are designed for. Without a soft ware, you cannot interact with the computer. Software enables computer hardware to perform specific tasks.

The software cannot be seen or touched. Only the action taken or task performed can be seen. All the information and instructions that make up a software can be compared to all the thoughts and ideas in your head. You can touch your head, but you cannot touch your thoughts.

Functions of system software:

> ➢ It makes the operation of a computer system more effective and efficient.

> ➢ It helps the hardware work components work together and assists in the development and execution of application software.

There are many computer software available today. As shown on the diagram below, they are mainly divided into two types: the System software and application software.

Major Types of Software:

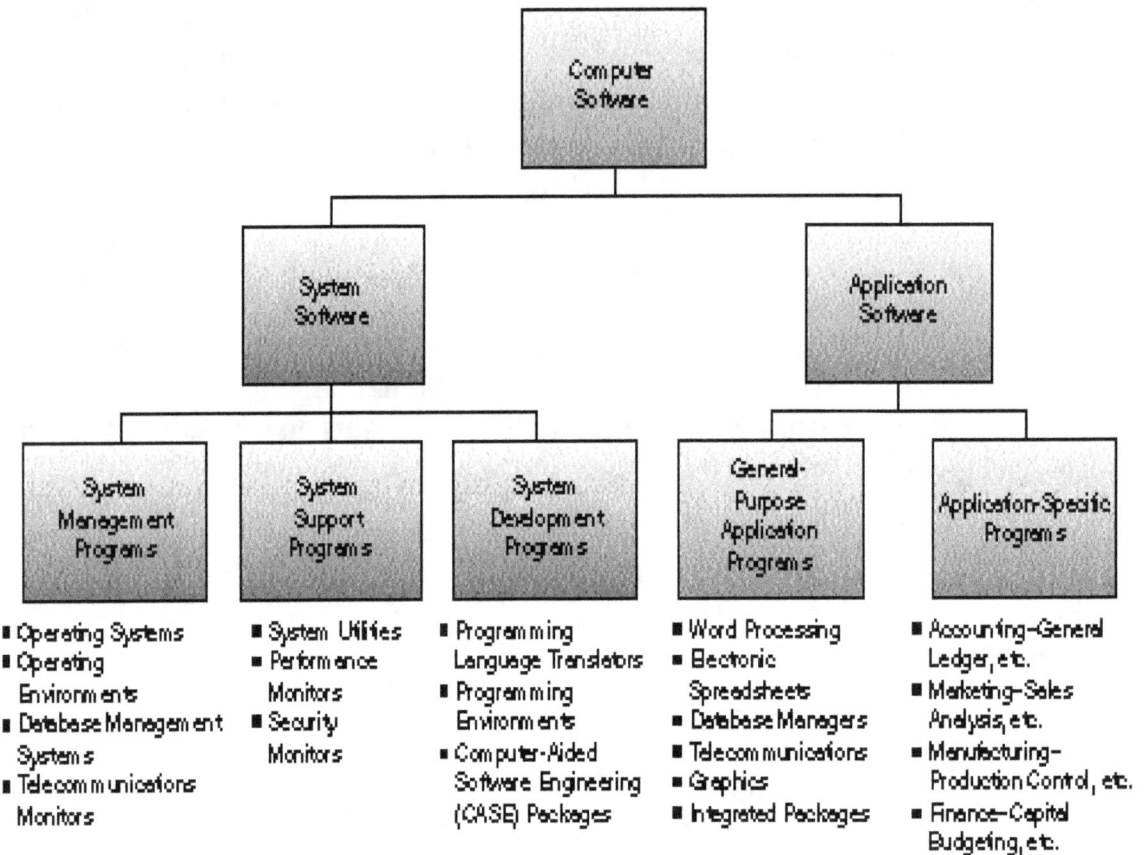

B. System software

System software is designed to operate the computer hardware, to provide basic functionality, and to provide a platform for running application software.

System software includes:

➢ **Operating systems** are essential collection of computer programs that manages resources and provides common services for other software. Supervisory programs, boot loaders, shells and window systems are core parts of operating systems. In practice, an operating system comes bundled with additional software (including application software) so that a user can potentially do some work with a computer that only has an operating system.

The most commonly used <u>operating systems</u> software are:

| Windows | MS DOS | Linux | Mac OS X |

> **Device drivers** are computer programs that operates or controls a particular type of device that is attached to a computer. Each device needs at least one corresponding device driver; thus a computer needs more than one device driver. Examples: video card and LAN card drivers

> Utilities are software designed to assist users in maintenance and care of their computers. Examples: Anti-virus, firewall, anti-spyware

C. *Application software:*

Application software is a set of one or more programs used to solve a specific problem or do a specific job. It Allows users to accomplish one or more tasks; browsing the internet or writing a text document.

Most application software are usually packed in a CD (compact disc) or floppy disks and come with instructional manual. Software, commonly known as programs or applications, consists of all the electronic instructions that tell the hardware how to perform a task.

Types of Application software
> **Word Processing Software** allows you to create, edit, store and retrieve documents. Documents can be letters, invitation, reports, files or essays. When a document is finished, you can store it in the computer's hard disk or external drives such as USB, DVD, CD and so on.

> **Spreadsheet Software** allows you to create tables, graphs and organize data into rows and columns. They are useful for predicting how much a business will profit (its income) and what it will spend in a year. Examples of spreadsheet software include Microsoft Excel, Lotus 123 and Quattro.

> **Database Management System Software** allows you to keep records electronically . It can be used to store, retrieve (get back) and manipulate large amount of data. Examples of database software include Microsoft Access, Database IV and Foxpro.

> **Graphics software** allows you to created many types of artwork like greeting cards, letterheads, signs, banners, pictures and many more. Examples of graphics software are Print Shop, Photoshop and Microsoft Paint.

> **Communication Software** is a program that will enable you to exchange information and messages with other computers in distant locations. Examples are Microsoft Outlook, Outlook Express and Yahoo and Yahoo! Messenger.

Summary

- **A System Software** is a set of one or more programs prepared to control the operation and increase the processing capability of a computer. **Operating system software**–programmes that coordinate the activities among computer devices. They contain instruction that allow the user to run application software

- **Application software**–programmes that perform specific tasks for users including word processing software, spreadsheet software, database management software, presentation software and anti-virus software

Exercise I.3.1

Name: _____   **Score:** _____ **/20**

Level/Section: _____   **Date:** _____

1. What is an Operating System?

2. Differentiate between the system software and application software? (2 marks each)

3. What type of instructions is given to the computer by systems software? (2 marks)

4. Give two examples of a system software and an application software.

5. As the editor for the school newsletter you are required to typeset and layout the next issue which is in color and which may include photographs. Name two types of application software that may be used for the task? Why? (2 marks each)

Lesson 4

General Care and Physical Protection

Objective

At the end of this chapter, the student should be able t:

➢ *describe ways of caring for computers and peripherals in the working environment*

➢ *discuss health and safety factors associated with computers*

General Care of Your Computer

Computer is one of the most important things in this life. All people sometimes need to finish doing their tasks by typing documents, look for any information by browsing on the internet, and enjoy using computer not only on playing games but also on doing an on-line jobs.

1.   Installing anti-virus software

Every computer should have anti-virus software inside because viruses sometimes turn up unexpectedly in your computer. You are not able to avoid getting viruses in your computer especially if you often browse on the internet using your computer. Keep in mind that you should always upgrade the latest version of your anti-virus software regularly.

2. Deleting unimportant files or uninstalling useless software

Your computer has limited storage which mightn't be able to save all your files inside. You have to delete unimportant files and folders in your computer because it can make your computer condition bad. Installing too many software can also make your computer damaged fast. Well, you should save your files like audios, videos, pictures, or other files in your computer by suiting them with your computer memory capacity.

3. Cleaning all hardware

Computer consists of many kinds of hardware, such as: monitor, mouse, CPU, keyboard, printer, etc. You should clean all hardware regularly by wiping the dusts. By the way, you need to use small brush for cleaning al dusts on the hardware. After cleaning all hardware, make sure that you arrange them well again.

Ways of Cleaning Computer and Peripherals

Keep your computer physically clean

When dealing with computers, dust isn't just unattractive—it can potentially destroy parts of your computer. By cleaning your computer regularly, you can help to **keep it working properly** and **avoid expensive repairs**.

Cleaning the keyboard

A dirty keyboard doesn't look nice and can cause your **keyboard** to **not work** properly. Dust, food, liquid, and other particles can get stuck underneath the keys, which can prevent them from working properly. Check your owner's manual to see if the manufacturer has provided you with instructions for your specific keyboard. If so, follow them. If not, the following steps are **basic cleaning tips** that can help keep your keyboard clean.

1. **Unplug** the keyboard from the USB or PS/2 port. If the keyboard is plugged into the PS/2 port, you will need to shut down the computer before unplugging it.
2. Turn the keyboard **upside down**, and gently shake it to remove dirt and dust.
3. Use a can of **compressed air** to clean between the keys.
4. Moisten a **cotton cloth** or **paper towel** with rubbing alcohol, and use it to clean the tops of the keys. Do not pour alcohol or any other liquid directly onto the keys.
5. **Reconnect** the keyboard to the computer once it is dry. If you are connecting it to a PS/2 port, you will need to connect it **before** turning on the computer.

Dealing with liquids

If you **spill liquid** on the keyboard, quickly shut down the computer and disconnect the keyboard and turn it upside down to allow the liquid to drain.

If the liquid is sticky, you will need to hold the keyboard on its side under running water to **rinse** the sticky liquid away. Then turn the keyboard upside down to drain for two days before reconnecting it. The keyboard may not be repairable at this point, but rinsing the sticky liquid off of it is the only chance for it to be usable again. The best way to avoid this situation is to keep drinks away from the computer area.

Cleaning the mouse

There are two main types of mice: **optical** and **mechanical**. Each is cleaned in basically the same way, although the mechanical mouse requires a bit more work.

- **Optical mice** require **no internal cleaning** because there aren't any rotating parts; however, they can get **sticky** over time as dust collects near the light emitter. This can cause erratic cursor movement or prevent the mouse from working properly.

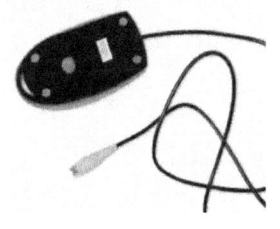

- **Mechanical mice** are especially susceptible to **dust** and **particles** that can accumulate inside the mouse, which can make it difficult to track—or move—properly. If the mouse pointer does not move smoothly, the mouse may need to be cleaned.

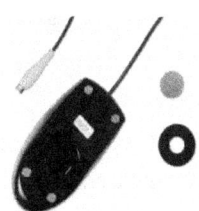

Before you clean your mouse, check the owner's manual to see if the manufacturer has provided you with instructions for your specific mouse. If so, follow those instructions. If not, the following steps are **basic cleaning tips** that will help keep your mouse clean.

1. **Unplug** the mouse from the USB or PS/2 port. If the mouse is plugged into the PS/2 port, you will need to shut down the computer before unplugging it.
2. Moisten a **cotton cloth** with rubbing alcohol, and use it to clean the top and bottom of the mouse.
3. If you have a **mechanical mouse**, remove the **tracking ball** by turning the **ball-cover ring** counterclockwise. Then clean the tracking ball and the inside of the mouse with a **cotton cloth** moistened with rubbing alcohol.

Cleaning the monitor

Dirt, fingerprints, and dust can make your computer screen difficult to read; however, it's easy to **clean your screen** when needed. Although there are monitor-cleaning kits you can buy, they may damage your monitor if they are designed for a different type of monitor. For example, a monitor cleaner that is designed for **glass screens** may not work with some **nonglass LCD screens**. The safest method is simply to use a **soft clean cloth** moistened with **water**.

Do not use glass cleaner to clean a monitor. Many screens have anti-glare coatings that can be damaged by glass cleaner.

1. **Turn off** the computer.
2. **Unplug** the monitor from the power. If you are using a laptop, unplug the laptop.
3. Use a **soft clean cloth** moistened with **water** to wipe the screen clean.

Do not spray any liquids directly onto the screen. The liquid could leak into the monitor and damage the internal components.

Tips for cleaning other computer surfaces

From time to time, you should clean your computer case and the sides and back of the monitor to avoid buildup of dust and dirt. Here are a few tips you can use when cleaning these surfaces.

- Dust is your computer's main enemy. Use an **antistatic** wipe to lightly dust your computer casing. **Don't use** furniture cleaners or strong solvents.
- Use a can of **compressed air** with a narrow nozzle to blow out debris from the air intake slots.
- Spray cleaning solution—like diluted ammonia cleaner or glass cleaner—on a **paper towel or antistatic** wipe. Clean the **monitor housing and case—not the monitor screen**—by wiping in a downward motion.
- A safe cleaning solution for **computer surfaces**—not computer screens—is **ammonia diluted** with water or **glass cleaner** comprised mostly of ammonia and water (check the label). The milder the solution, the better.

Keep it cool

Don't restrict airflow around your computer. A computer can generate a lot of heat, so the casing has **fans** that keep it from overheating. Avoid stacking papers, books, and other items around your computer.

Many computer desks have an **enclosed compartment** for the computer case. If you have this type of desk, you may want to position the case so it is not against the back side of the desk. If the compartment has a door, you may want to leave it open to improve airflow.

Setting up a Computer System

You have a **new computer** and are ready to set it up. While this may seem like an overwhelming and difficult task, it is actually quite simple. It doesn't matter what brand of computer you have because most computers are set up in a similar way.

If you're setting up a newly purchased computer that's still in the box, you'll probably find a **how-to guide** in the packaging that includes **step-by-step details**. However, even if it didn't include instructions you can still set up the computer in a **few easy steps**. In this lesson, we'll go through the different steps needed to set up a typical computer.

a) Setting up a laptop computer

If you have a laptop, setup should be easy: Just open it and press the **power** button. If the battery isn't charged, you'll need to plug in the **AC adapter**. You can continue using the laptop while it charges.

If your laptop has any **peripherals**, like **external speakers**, you may want to read the instructions below because laptops and desktops generally use the same types of connections.

b) In setting up a desktop computer, follow steps below:

Step 1

Unpack the **monitor** and **computer case** from the box. Remove any plastic covering or protective tape. Place the monitor and computer case where you want on a desk or work area.

Think about where you want your desk or work area to be located, and where you want your monitor, computer case, and other hardware to be. Be sure to place your computer case in an area that is **well ventilated** and that has good air flow. This will help to prevent overheating.

Step 2

Locate the **monitor cable**. There are several types of monitor cables, so the one on your computer may not look like the one in the image at the left. If you're having trouble finding your monitor cable, refer to the instruction manual for your computer. (If you have an **all-in-one** computer that's built into the monitor, you can skip to **Step 4**).

Step 3

Connect one end of the cable to the **monitor port** on the back of the **computer case** and the other end to the **monitor**. Hand tighten the plastic-covered screws on the monitor cable to secure it.

Many computer cables will only fit a specific way. If the cable doesn't fit, don't force it or you might damage the connectors. Make sure the plug aligns with the port, then connect it.

Step 4

Unpack the **keyboard** and determine whether it uses a **USB**(rectangular) connector or a **PS/2** (round) connector. If it uses a USB connector, plug it into any of the USB ports on the back of the computer. If it uses a PS/2 connector, plug it into the **purple** keyboard port on the back of the computer.

Step 5

Unpack the **mouse** and determine whether it uses a **USB** (rectangular) connector or a **PS/2** (round) connector. If it uses a USB connector, plug it into any of the USB ports on the back of the computer. If it uses a PS/2 connector, plug it into the **green** mouse port on the back of the computer.

If your keyboard has a **USB port**, you can connect your mouse to the keyboard instead of connecting it directly to your computer.

If you have a **wireless** mouse or keyboard, you may need to connect a Bluetooth **dongle** (USB adapter) to your computer. However, many computers have built-in Bluetooth, so a dongle may not be necessary.

Step 6

If you have **external speakers** or **headphones**, you can connect them to your computer's **audio port** (either on the front or the back of the computer case). Many computers have color-coded ports. **Speakers** or **headphones** connect to the **green** port, and a **microphone** connects to the **pink** port. The **blue** port is the **line in**, which can be used with other types of devices.

Some speakers, headphones, and microphones have **USB connectors** instead of the usual audio plug. These can be connected to any USB port. In addition, many computers have speakers or microphones built into the monitor.

Step 7

Locate the two **power supply cables** that came with your computer. Plug the first power supply cable into the back of the **computer case**, and then into a **surge protector**. Then, using the other cable, connect the **monitor** to the **surge protector**.

Step 8

Finally, plug the **surge protector** into a wall outlet. You may also need to turn on the **surge protector** if it has a power switch.

If you don't have a surge protector, you can plug the computer directly into the wall. However, this is **not recommended** because electrical surges can damage your computer.

Setup complete

Your basic computer hardware is now set up. Before you start it up, spend some time arranging your workspace. A workspace that is arranged well can **improve your productivity** and **promote health**.

Activity

1. If you have a desktop computer that is already set up at home, take a look at it.
2. Look at the **monitor cable**, and see where it connects to the computer case and monitor.
3. Locate the **power cords** for the monitor and computer case.
4. Locate the **audio ports**.
5. Does your computer have a **VGA monitor port**, or another kind?
6. Do you have a **USB** or **PS/2** mouse?
7. Do you have a **USB** or **PS/2** keyboard?
8. Is your computer plugged into a **surge protector**?

Exercise I.4.1

Name: _____   **Score:** _____ **/20**

Level/Section: _____   **Date:** _____

1. How do you care your computer and peripherals? Give at least two. (2 marks each)

   _____

2. Give at least two safety factors on using computers? (2 marks each)

   _____

Lesson 5

Health Ergonomics and Safety

Objective

At the end of this chapter, the student should be able t:
- ➤ *identify health and safety factors associated with computer use*
- ➤ *discuss the effects of extended use of computer, with inadequate lighting, inapprorpriate furniture and bad posture .*

Health Ergonomics

Why computer ergonomics? Many people spend hours a day in front of a computer without thinking about the impact on their bodies. They physically stress their bodies daily without realizing it by extending their wrists, slouching, sitting without foot support and straining to look at poorly placed monitors.

These practices can lead to cumulative trauma disorders or repetitive stress injuries, which create a life-long impact on health. Symptoms may include pain, muscle fatigue, loss of sensation, tingling and reduced performance.

Ergonomics is a science whose main purpose is to design workspaces arrangement and tools that help people do their jobs comfortably and safely.

A. Effects of extended use of computers

Many people who use computers for extended hours a day usually experienced discomfort and pain in different parts of the body pains that may interfere their creativity and productivity like the following:

- tendonitis in the elbow
- neck and back pain
- eye strain
- Musculoskeletal Disorders (MSD)

   signs & symptoms of prolonged and repetitive motions:
   - Numbness or a burning sensation in the hand and excessive force can cause
   - Reduced grip strength in the hand muscle and joint problems
   - Swelling or stiffness in the joints
   - Pain in wrists, forearms, elbows, neck, or back at risk
   - Reduced range of motion in the shoulder, neck
   - Dry, itchy, or sore eyes symptoms
   - Blurred or double vision
   - Carpal Tunnel Syndrome
   - Aching or tingling Repetitive Stress Injuries can be
   - Cramping debilitating
   - Weakness

Factors to Avoid strain and injury

I. Change your position!

No matter how good your working posture is, staying in the same posture or sitting still for long periods is not healthy. Change your position frequently throughout the work day in the following ways:

> ➤ Make small adjustments to your chair or backrest
> ➤ Stretch your fingers, hands, arms, and torso
> ➤ Stand up and walk around for a few minutes periodically.

II. Give Yourself a Break! Take a break! All Ergonomists agree that it's a good idea to take frequent, brief rest breaks such as the following:

> ➤ **Eye breaks**
> - Looking at a computer screen for a while causes some changes in how the eyes work, causes you to blink less often, and exposes more of the eye surface to the air.
> - Every 15 minutes you should Palming:
>   This teaches you to relax your briefly look away from the eyes, bringing healthy energy to your eyes. screen for a minute or two to a more distant scene, preferably
>   **First,** rub your hands together 15 to 20 something more than 20 feet seconds until they feel warm.
>   Place cupped away. This lets the muscles hands over your closed eyes - careful not to inside the eye relax.
>   Touch your eyes hands. Fingers should overlap and rest gently on the center of your forehead without unnecessary pressure on
>   Also, blink your eyes rapidly for a few seconds. This refreshes your face.
>   Rest your elbows on a table.
>   Do tear film and clears dust from this quietly for one to two.
>   As you relax, the eye surface, darkness will seem blacker.
>   *Natural Eye Care™ 2001-2008*
> ➤ **Micro-breaks**
> - Most typing is done in bursts rather than continuously. A Cornell University press release (Sept. 24, 1999) stated: Between these bursts of activity "When workers heed the you should rest your hands in a computer's reminder to relaxed, flat, straight posture. take a break, their productivity jumps."

- During a micro-break of < 2 minutes, you can briefly stretch, stand up, move around, or do a different work task.
- A micro-break isn't necessarily a break from work, but it's a break from the use of a particular set of muscles that's doing most of the work.

➤ **Rest breaks**
- Every 30 to 60 minutes you should take a brief rest break. During this break stand up, move around and do something else.
- Go and get a drink of water, soda, tea, coffee or whatever. This allows you to rest and exercise different muscles and you'll feel less tired.

➤ **Exercise breaks**
- There are many stretching and gentle exercises that you can do to help relieve muscle fatigue.
- You should do these every 1-2 hours. More stretches

Ergonomic Exercise For Hands

Wrist Rotation:

1. Stretch both arms straight to the front with closed fists.
2. Rotate both the fists together ten times in the clockwise direction and ten times in the anticlockwise direction.
3. Do ensure that only your fists are rotating and the rest of your arms are stationery.

Elbow Rotation:

1. Bend your hands towards the front and hold your shoulders with your palms.
2. Now, rotate your elbows ten times in the clockwise and ten times in the anticlockwise direction.

Whole hands, small circles:

1. Stretch both hands to the sides holding your palms straight up perpendicular to the hands.
2. Now, make small circles with both palms ten times in the clockwise and ten times in the anticlockwise direction.

3. Note that the smaller the circle, the better relaxation to your hands. This is an excellent Ergonomic Exercise for those who have to sit in front of the computer for very long hours.

Whole hands, big circles:

1. Stretch your hands to the sides. Make big circles (as big as possible) with both the hands ten times in the clockwise and ten times in the anticlockwise direction.
2. The number of times can be increased gradually as this becomes less strenuous.

All these Ergonomic Exercises can be done while you relax in your workstation seat. If you prefer doing them at home or in standing postures, you can stand in the 'attention' posture.

Ergonomic Exercises for Back

- *Backward:*
  1. Stand straight in the attention posture.
  2. Breath in while you bend gently back and come back to the normal position while you breathe out.
  3. While you bend back, try to bend as much as possible, but do not over extend your back. Try to do this ten times.
- *Forward:*
  1. Stand straight in the attention posture.
  2. Raise both hands up while you breath in and come down to touch your toes without bending your knees while you breath out.
  3. You might not be able to do it with perfection in the initial days, but can improve gradually day by day.
  4. Don't try to touch your toes in the beginning as it might hurt your back. Most users tend to increase their waist length on prolonged use with computers.

Ergonomic Exercises for Shoulders

1. Use a large bath towel and grasp it at opposite corners.
2. Sling it across the shoulder of tightness and bring both ends across to the opposite hip or waist.

3. With the arm on that side pull gently downward and then release slowly.

Apart from these Ergonomic Exercises, you can go for jogging, brisk walking, aerobics, swimming, outdoor games etc. to be in good shape and improve your stamina.

Remember that you don't get much Ergonomic Exercise the whole day when you are in front of your computer. So, sacrifice your time in the mornings or evening for your healthy body to have a healthy mind. *One to 1 ½ hours each day is recommended.*

➢ **Ergonomic software**
- Working at a computer can be rhythmic and time can pass quickly without realizing how long you've been working and how much you've been typing, mousing, and drawing.
- There are excellent ergonomic software programs that you can install on your computer. Free and purchased software is available.
- Most software will run in the background and will monitor how much you've been using the computer. Software will prompt you to take a rest break at appropriate intervals, and will suggest simple exercises.

B. Inadequate lighting

The level of light needs to be adjusted to suit the task. Glare from windows can cause problems with computer screens. Window shades, diffusers on overhead lighting and anti-glare filters are all available to assist with glare.

Brightness and contrast controls on computers should be adjusted to a comfortable level. Clean the screen regularly to assist in avoiding eye strain.

Regular eye examinations can be beneficial to those working with computers.

C. Inappropriate furniture

➢ Make sure that your chair is comfortable. Use chairs specially designed to support the lower back and promote good posture.

D. Effects of Bad posture

Effects of Bad posture	Solution
Neck and Upper Back o Forward head posture is a common cause of discomfort in the upper back and in the neck muscles. o It can compress the nerves that run from the neck into the arms, which may cause pain in the arms and hands.	o Maintain a neck posture by keeping aligned the ears with shoulders and hips. o This posture reduces the amount of work required of upper back and neck muscles.
Shoulder ▪ Sustained reaching forward with the shoulders can compress blood vessels and nerves that travel through the shoulder.	o Maintain a neutral shoulder position (relaxed, elbow at side, not over reaching). o This position allows proper circulation to arm and han
Forearm/Wrists o Wrists bent upward: extension o Wrists bent downward: flexion o Wrists bent to the side: deviation	o Maintain a neutral position: ▪ Elbow rests as your side, bent around 90 degrees. ▪ Wrist stays flat, with middle finger aligned with forearm ▪ May need to use split keyboard

Arrange Your Workstation: *Every time you work,* take time to adjust workstations that aren't quite right in order to minimize awkward and frequency performed movements.

A. Overloading electric sockets

The best way to protect your family starts with ensuring that your electrical systems and appliances are functioning properly and safely.

Since electrical malfunction can happen at any time and for many reasons, always check your Cords & Plugs regularly.

□ Check all cords, plugs, surge protectors and extension cords for frayed casing, exposed wire or broken components. Replace immediately.

□ Never run extension cords under carpets or over door thresholds.

□ Don't use an extension cord as a permanent fixture. If you need additional outlets, contact a licensed electrician to install some wherever you require.

- Always follow the manufacturer's instructions for plugging a device into the outlet.

- Do not overload one outlet with several high-wattage or heat-producing devices, for example a space heater or coffee maker.

- Plugs should fit snugly into outlets. If yours do not, contact a licensed electrician.

- Major appliances – washers, dryers, refrigerators, stoves, air conditioners, hot water heaters, etc. – should be plugged directly into a wall outlet. Do not use surge protectors, plug strips or extension cords.

- Only use water resistant extension cords in damp areas (like the basement).

B. Location of extension cords

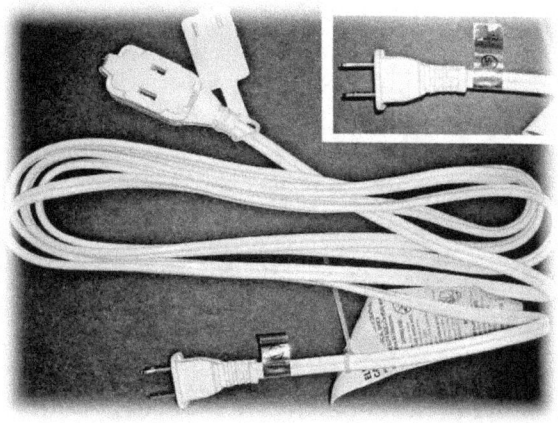

C. Position of work stations

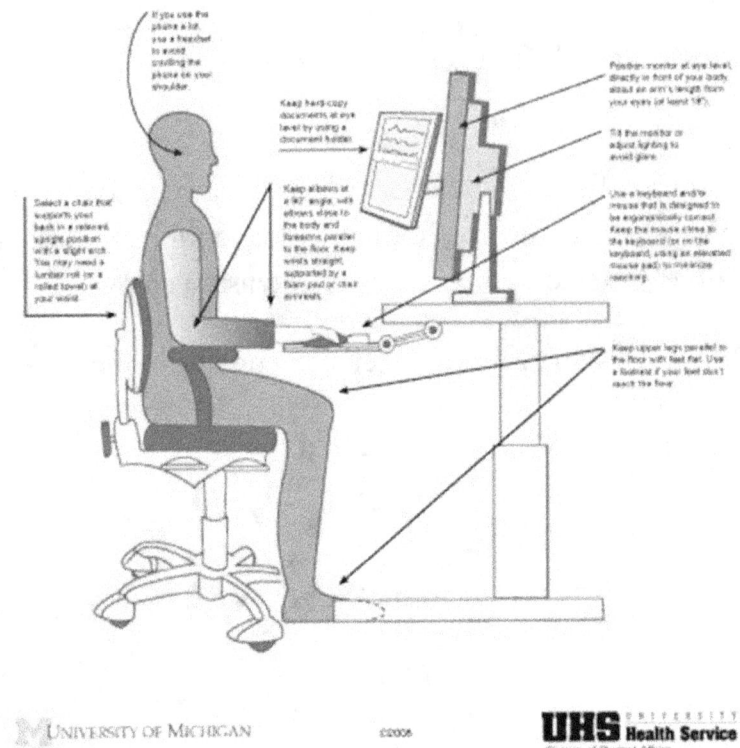

Arrange Your Workstation

Every time you work, take time to adjust workstations that aren't quite right in order to minimize awkward and frequently performed movements.

University of Michigan ©2006 **UHS** Health Service

Use your keyboard safely

Using your keyboard properly can help avoid distress or injury to your wrists, hands, and arms, particularly if you use your computer for long periods of time. Here are some tips to help you avoid problems:

- Place your keyboard at elbow level. Your upper arms should be relaxed at your sides.

- Center your keyboard in front of you. If your keyboard has a numeric keypad, you can use the spacebar as the centering point.

- Type with your hands and wrists floating above the keyboard, so that you can use your whole arm to reach for distant keys instead of stretching your fingers.

- Avoid resting your palms or wrists **on any type of surface while typing. If your keyboard has a palm rest, use it only during breaks from typing.**

- **While typing, use a light touch and keep your wrists straight.**

- **When you're not typing, relax your arms and hands.**

- **Take short breaks from computer use every** 15 to 20 minutes.

Summary

- General care and physical protection of the computer
- **Health Ergonomics**
  Effects of extended use, Inadequate lighting, inappropriate furniture and bad posture
- **Safety**
  Overloading electric sockets
  Position of work stations
  Location of extended cords

Activity

Place your hazard triangles on the danger areas in the picture or put a circle around them?

1 a. Examine the picture and carefully identify eight hazards? (10 marks)

1. .
2. .
3. .
4. .
5. .
6. .
7. .
8. .
9. .
10.

1 b. State what action you would take to prevent some of these hazards and bring order to this chaotic scene? (10 marks)

Exercise I.5

Name: _____   **Score:** _____ **/20**

Level/Section: _____   **Date:** _____

Instruction:

    1. Circle the hazards.

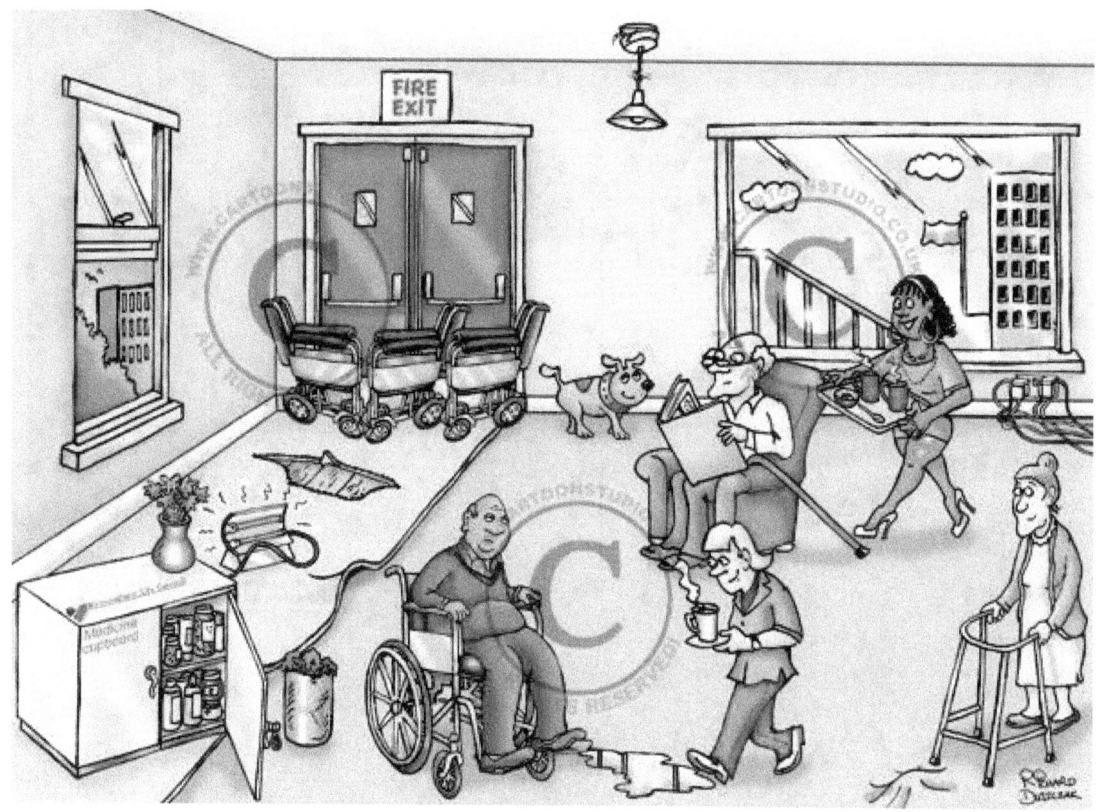

    2. What action would be needed to prevent these hazards

    3. Write a 5 step plan/procedure to maintain a proper environment in the work place

Chapter II

Keyboard Mastery

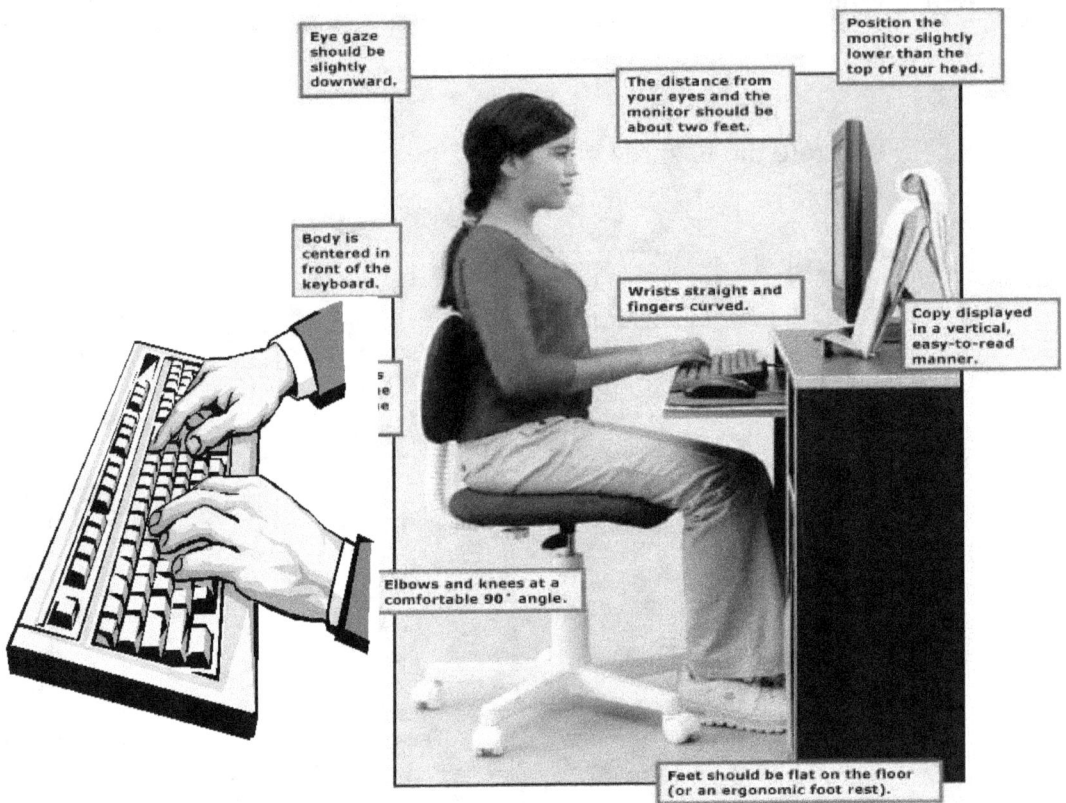

Eye gaze should be slightly downward.

The distance from your eyes and the monitor should be about two feet.

Position the monitor slightly lower than the top of your head.

Body is centered in front of the keyboard.

Wrists straight and fingers curved.

Copy displayed in a vertical, easy-to-read manner.

Elbows and knees at a comfortable 90° angle.

Feet should be flat on the floor (or an ergonomic foot rest).

Highlights:

- *Keyboarding Techniques*
- *Correct Posture*
- *Use of Special Keys*
- *Correct spacing after punctuation marks*
- *Manuscripts signs*
- *Types of Headings*
- *Manuscripts or type notes rules*
- *Documentation*
- *Minimum speed in typing*
-

Lesson 1

Keyboarding Techniques

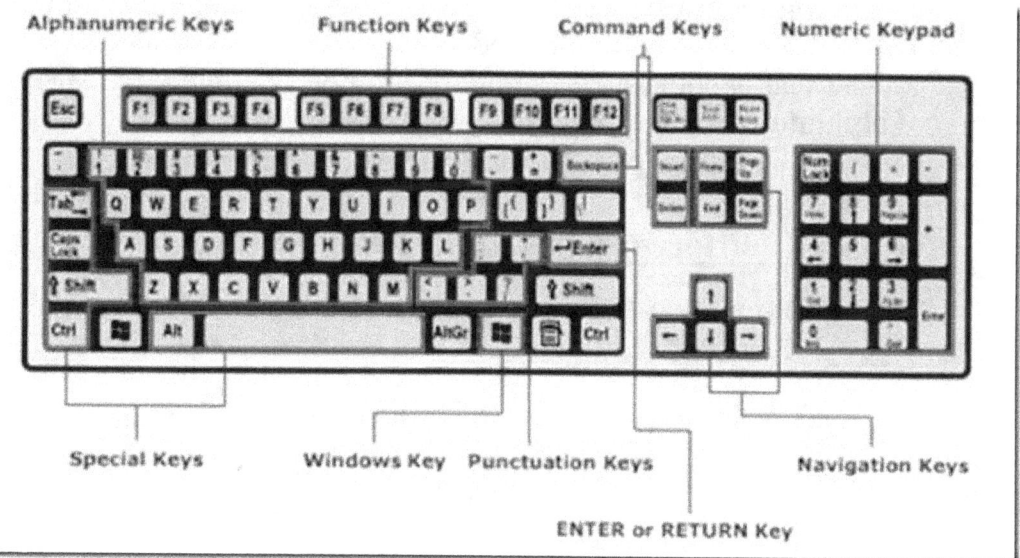

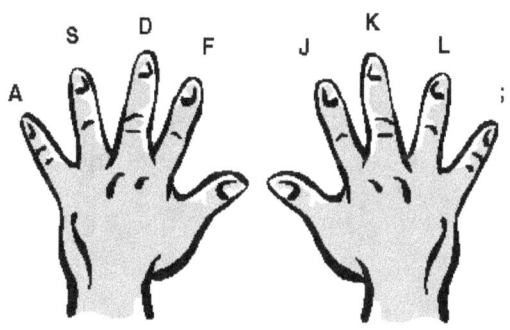

Objective

At the end of this chapter, the student should be able t:
➤ *demonstrate the proper touch of fingers on specific keys on the keyboard*
➤ *practice keyboarding techniques in typing with minimum errors*

KEYBOARDING

In this keyboarding lessons, you will learn how to use both hands on the keyboard. You also study the proper way of placing the fingers on the home keys. Keyboarding techniques on alphanumeric keys by proper touching can help develop your speed and accuracy.

Alphanumeric keys is commonly used to help explain the availability of text that can be entered or used in a field such as a password. Description of content that is both letters and numbers. For example, "1a2b3c" is a short string of **alphanumeric characters**.

Four (4) different parts of the keyboard

1. Alphanumeric Keys

These keys are used to type letters of the alphabet, numbers, and punctuation marks. The letters on these keys are in uppercase or capital letters. If you press a letter key, it will be displayed on the screen in lowercase or small letters. To type the letters in uppercase, press the Caps Lock key.

The number keys are used to display numbers on the screen. These keys have symbols above the numbers. These keys include symbols like !, +, %, and others.

2) Navigation Keys

These keys are used to navigate cursors from one place to another. There are ten keys on the Navigation keys. Eight of these are used to move the cursor around on the screen and the other two are used to insert and delete characters.

3) Numeric Keys

The Numeric keypad serves two purposes. When Num Lock is pressed it is a numeric keypad. It is a navigation keypad when Num Lock it is turned off.

4) Function Keys

Identified by the letter F and a number. Each key has a special purpose. This purpose varies according to the software program being used.

Home keys make up the center of the three rows of letters <?> the standard keyboard. At this time, you should be comfortable with the home keys. Home keys start with keys A, S, D, F, J, K, L, and; (semicolon).

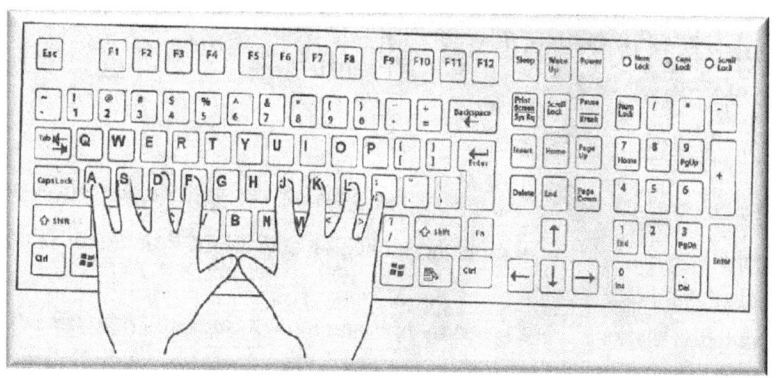

Before starting to type, always place your fingers on the home row. Now, let's learn how to type the keys above and below the home keys.

The W, Q, Z, X, P, (COMMA),• (PERIOD),? (question mark)

The letters Q, W, and P are located on top of the home row. While the letters

Z, X, and comma; period, and question mark are found below the home row.

The left hand is used to key the letters Q, Z, W, and X. The letter P, comma, period, and question mark are pressed with the right hand.

The keys and the proper fingers used to type them are the following:

Q and **Z** are pressed using the left pinky.

W and **X** are pressed with the left ring finger. P is typed with the right pinky.

? (question mark) is typed by pressing the left Shift key with the left pinky

. (period) is pressed with the right ring finger.

, (comma) is typed with the right middle finger.

. (period) is pressed with the right ring finger.

, (comma) is typed with the right middle finger.

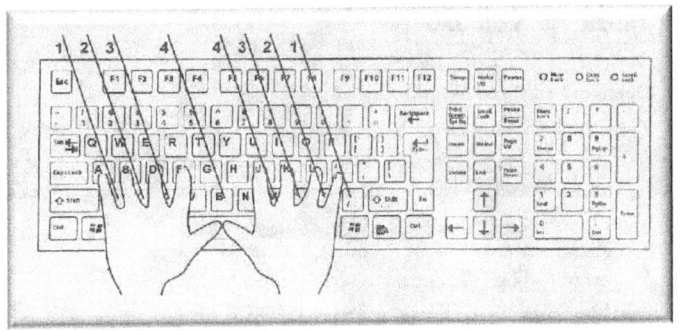

THE :, ", AND / KEyS

: The colon is typed by pressing the left Shift key with the left pinky

and typing the key :, which contains the semicolon and colon. Remember that a space always follows a colon.

" Quotation marks are typed by pressing the left Shift key with the left pinky and the key.

The slash (/) or division symbol key is typed using the right pinky.

THE TAB KEy

The **Tab** key is located on the upper left of the keyboard, right next to the **Q** key. Instead of pressing the **spacebar** key several times, the **Tab** key is used to indent paragraphs. It can also be used to begin lines that do not start at the left margin.

The top row of keys contains both numbers and symbols.

The right Shift key (It Shift) is used to type the symbols at the top of the keys from 1 to 5.

The left Shift key (t Shift)is used to type the symbols at the top of the keys from 6 to = (equal sign).

Follow the finger lines on the picture above to see which finger to use in typing the symbols.

Practice your fingers

The best and only proven technique to develop high speed in keyboarding is to implement **regular and frequent** practice. As you practice and practice regularly, this will develop speed and accuracy using proper touch keyboarding techniques on alphanumeric keys.

Now, observe the proper touch and position of your fingers on specific keys while practicing your typing skills.

Position your hands and fingers on the keyboard over the guide keys using the diagram below as a guide:

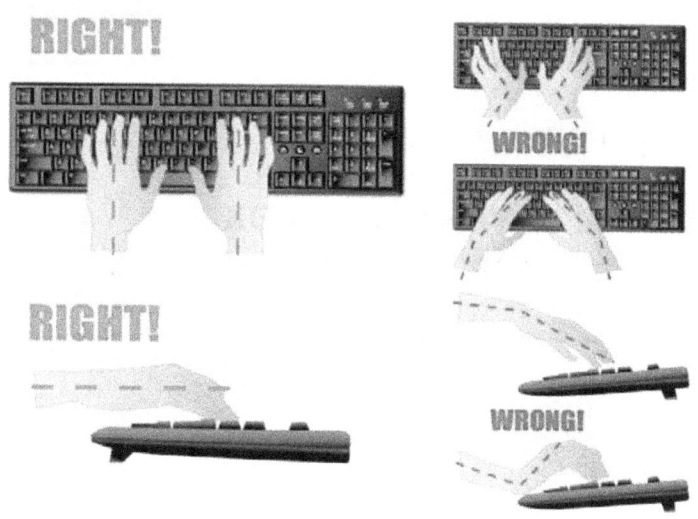

☐ *Feel the raised indicators under the F and J keys - they will help guide your fingers.*

☐ *Curl your fingers over the keys and lift your wrist up so that the fingers are coming down onto the keys.*

□ *Do not rest your wrists on the keyboard.*

You should aim to type at least 35 words per minute, then as you continue to practice your keyboarding skills regularly, your typing speed will be developed, likewise accuracy is being improved while minimizing such errors.

<u>Summary</u>

Alphanumeric keys is commonly used to help explain the availability of text that can be entered or used in a field such as a password.

Home keys make up the center of the three rows of letters <?> the standard keyboard.

The **Tab** key is located on the upper left of the keyboard, right next to the **Q** key. Instead of pressing the **spacebar** key several times, the **Tab** key is used to indent paragraphs.

<u>GOLDEN RULES TO KEEP IN MIND</u>

- ✓ **ALWAYS** keep your **FINGERS** positioned on the **GUIDE KEYS**.
- ✓ **ALWAYS** keep your **THUMBS** close the **SPACE BAR**
- ✓ **GUIDE KEYS** will help you **LOCATE ALL** other keys
- ✓ **RELAX** Arms and Wrists
- ✓ a **LIGHT SHARP STROKE**
- ✓ **RELEASE** the key **QUICKLY**

<u>Activity 1</u>

1. Open and start the Word program.

2. Place your fingers in a curved shape and tap them on the table as a finger strengthening exercise **1234 1234** (starting with the index or pointer finger and finishing with the little finger). Do one hand a few times, then the other.

3. Type the following pattern to the HOME KEYS on the keyboard as shown.

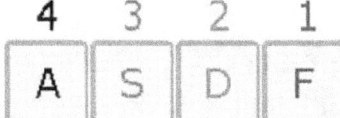

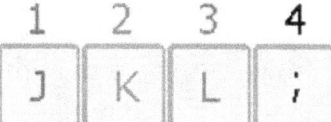

Left Hand

asdf asdf asdf asdf asdf asdf asdf asdf asdf asdf

fdsa fdsa fdsa fdsa fdsa fdsa fdsa fdsa fdsa fdsa

Right Hand

jkl; jkl; jkl; jkl; jkl; jkl; jkl; jkl; jkl; jkl; jkl; jkl

;lkj ;lkj ;lkj ;lkj ;lkj ;lkj ;lkj ;lkj ;lkj ;lkj ;lkj ;lkj ;lkj

Now, place your both hands on top of the keyboard. The index finger on 1F and your right index finger on 1J. Use your thumb to tap once on the space bar after each pattern/word or sentence as shown below.

Both Hands

fd fds fdsa jk jkl jkl; fd fds fdsa jk jkl jkl; fd fds fdsa jk jkl jkl;

fd fds fdsa jk jkl jkl; fd fds fdsa jk jkl jkl; fd fds fdsa jk jkl jkl;

4. After typing, save it using the filename KEYBOARD1 for checking.

<u>Activity 2</u>

1. Open and start the Word program.
2. Now, flex your fingers again and your shoulders. Tap the table drill **1234 1234**
3. Try typing the following by your both hands:

    juut jut jute kiit kit kite juut jut jute
     kiit kit kite juut jut jute kiit kit kite
    jud judder jug jugger judge judged
     juud judder jug jugger judge judged

    igh high thigh ight fight right fright
    igh high thigh ight fright right fright

     asdf asdf jkl; jkl; asdf asdf jkl; jkl;
     asdf asdf jkl; jkl; asdf asdf jkl; jkl;

4. Repeat each of the 2-3 word phrases (below) a few times or type whole lines   then   repeat.

5. Type the semi-colon with the right finger 4.

    red deer; tight fight; fool fight; the high kite; red deer; tight fight; fool fight; the high kite;

     free feed; red jug; right fight; the red kite; free feed; red jug; right fight; the red kite;

     free fight; right judge; higher kite; their fool fight; free fight; right judge; higher kite;

6. When finished, save your work with filename KEYBOARD2-2.

Activity 3

1. Open and start the Word program.
2. Type the following:

   Aaq   qqq   aqq   aqa sws wws ssw

   aqua, want; aqua. quart, extra, quilt.

   apple pops. Zero, quit? mixed fax.

   "abed" dibo   "what is that?" abclde

   "John is the best."   zyz/abc

   "What do you want?" rice, fish, or chicken?

   aql!   aql!   swz@ swz@ de3# d#3d

   fr4$ fr$f   fr5% f5%5 jy6 "jy6"

   ju78 ju78 ki8* ki8* I09 (l09)

   Jack and Jill went up the 3,450 m hill to fetch 12# of water.

3. When finished, save your work with filename KEYBOARD2,

4. Click on New Document button on the Standard toolbar. Type the paragraphs below. In this practice, you will press the Tab key with the left pinky to indent each paragraph.

   Once upon a time, there were three bears who lived in a little house in the woods. There was a great big Father Bear with a big voice, a middle-sized Mother Bear with a middle-sized voice, and a little Baby Bear with a tiny voice.

   While they were gone, along came a little girl named Goldilocks. Seeing the little house, she wondered who lived there. So she knocked at the door. No one answered, so Goldilocks opened the door and walked in.

5. After typing, save it using the filename KEYBOARD 2-3.

Exercise II.1

Name: _____   Score: _____ /___

Level/Section: _____   Date: _____

A.   Write Yes if the statement is correct and No if the sentence is not correct. (1 mark each)

1.   Before starting to type, always place your fingers on the home keys.

2.   The left hand is used to type letters P, the , (comma), . (period), and ? (question mark).

3.   Letters Q, Z, W, and X are typed with the left hand.

4.   The Shift key is used to indent paragraphs.

5.   'Quotation marks are typed by pressing the left hand

L esson 2

Correct Posture

Objective

> At the end of this chapter, the student should be able t:
> ➤ practice the position of fingers in order to develop their typing speed
> ➤ identify the basic techniques for enhancing and improving speed and accuracy

Posture

Correct posture is critical in an attempt to avoid any form of stress or strain on the body. The following diagram demonstrates how to sit comfortably and safely when using a computer.

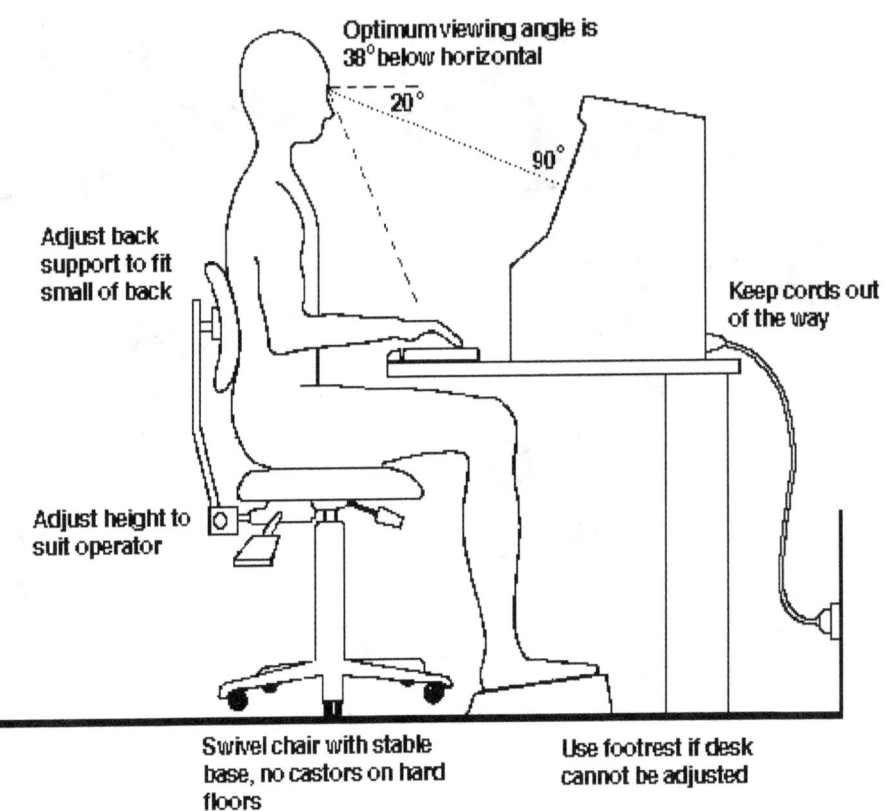

Once the workstation has been situated, then the user can adjust the office chair according to his or her physical proportions. Here are the most important guidelines - distilled into a quick checklist - to help make sure that you maintain **correct posture** while working at the computer:

1. **Elbow measure**

First, begin by sitting comfortably as close as possible to your desk so that your upper arms are parallel to your spine. Rest your hands on your work surface (e.g. desktop, computer keyboard). If your elbows are not at a 90-degree angle, adjust your office chair height either up or down.

2. Thigh measure

Check that you can easily slide your fingers under your thigh at the leading edge of the office chair. If it is too tight, you need to prop your feet up with an adjustable footrest. If you are unusually tall and there is more than a finger width between your thigh and the chair, you need to raise the desk or work surface so that you can raise the height of your office chair.

3. Calf measure

With your bottom pushed against the chair back, try to pass your clenched fist between the back of your calf and the front of your office chair. If you can't do that easily, then the office chair is too deep. You will need to adjust the backrest forward, insert a low back support (such as a lumbar support cushion, a pillow or rolled up towel), or get a new office chair.

4. Low back support

Your bottom should be pressed against the back of your chair, and there should be a cushion that causes your lower back to arch slightly so that you don't slump forward or slouch down in the chair as you tire over time. This low back support in the office chair is essential to minimize the load (strain) on your back. Never slump or slouch forward in the office chair, as that places extra stress on the structures in the low back, and in particular, on the lumbar discs.

5. Screen-to-eye level

Close your eyes while sitting comfortably with your head facing forward. Slowly open your eyes. Your gaze should be aimed at the center of your computer screen. If your computer screen is higher or lower than your gaze, you need to either raise or lower it to reduce strain on the upper spine.

6. Arm reach

Adjust the armrest of the office chair so that it just slightly lifts your arms to reach at the shoulders. Use of an armrest on your office chair is important to take some of the strain off your upper spine and shoulders, and it should make you less likely to slouch forward in your chair.

Stay Active To Reduce Back Pain in the Office

No matter how comfortable one is in an office chair, prolonged **static posture** is not good for the back and is a common contributor to back problems and **muscle strain**.

To avoid keeping the back in one position for a long period, remember to stand, stretch and walk for at least a minute or two every half hour. Even a quick stretch or some minimal movement – such as walking to the water cooler or bathroom - will help.

A twenty minute walk will help even more, promoting healthy blood flow that brings important nutrients to all the spinal structures.

In general, moving about and stretching on a regular basis throughout the day will help keep the joints, ligaments, muscles, and tendons loose, which in turn promotes an overall feeling of comfort, relaxation, and ability to focus productively.

Summary

Correct posture is critical in an attempt to avoid any form of stress or strain on the body.

Guidelines to maintain Correct posture while working at the computer considers **Elbow measure, Thigh measure, Calf measure, Low back support, Screen-to-eye level** and **Arm reach**.

Activity 1

1. Open and start the Word program.
2. Flex your fingers to loosen them.
3. Notice the two keys G and H in the centre of the keyboard. Sit properly so that these are in front of the centre of your body and use fingers as shown:

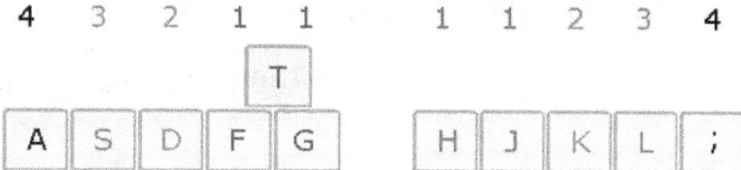

4. Keeping your fingers over the two sets of four keys we just practised - stretch your index fingers across to G & H (left hand for "G" and right hand for "H") and type the following:

   Both Hands
   gh gh gh gh gh gh gh gh gh gh gh gh gh
   gh gh gh gh gh gh gh gh gh gh gh gh gh

5. Stretch your Left index finger up/out to T (look on the keyboard) and type:
   th th th th th th th th ght ght ght ght ght ght ght
   th th th th th th th th ght ght ght ght ght ght ght

6. Follow the colours and finger numbers in the next chart to practise lines of each pattern or word of the following. Visualise where the letter keys are and use the fingers shown.

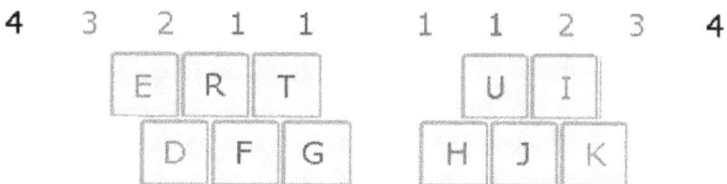

   Left Hand

   deed frrf deer reed red deed frrf deer reed red deed frrf deer reed red
   free freed fred feed fed free freed fred feed fed free freed fred feed fed

   Right Hand
   juuj kiik juj kik juuj kiik juj kik juuj kiik juj kik juuj kiik juj kik
   juuj kiik juj kik juuj kiik juj kik juuj kiik juj kik juuj kiik juj kik

7. After typing, save it using the filename KEYBOARD2 for checking.

Exercise II.2

Name: _____   Score: ___/____

Level/Section: _____   Date: _____

I. Answer the following questions.

1. What are the symbols on top row of the keyboard which also numbers from 1 up to 5?

2. What are the three (3) marks or symbols that are typed by pressing the left Shift key, together with numbers 6, 7 or 8?

L esson 3

Use of Special Keys

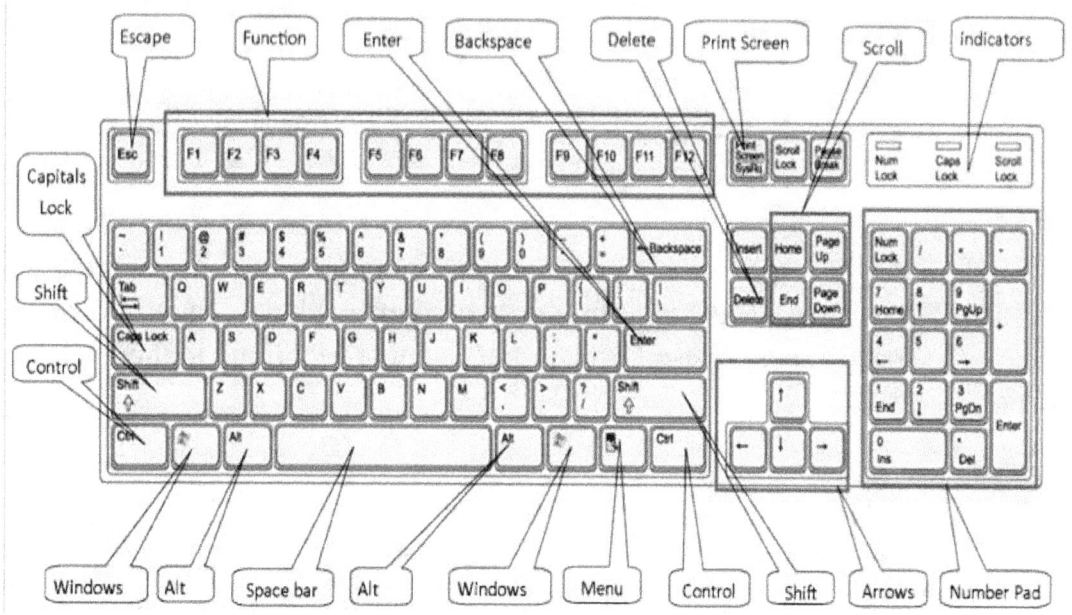

Objective

At the end of this chapter, the student should be able to:
  - ➢ *demonstrate competence in the use of special keys*
  - ➢ *Learn all the functions of Alphanumeric keys.*
  - ➢ *learn the use of function keys and other shortcut keys*

The Computer Keyboard

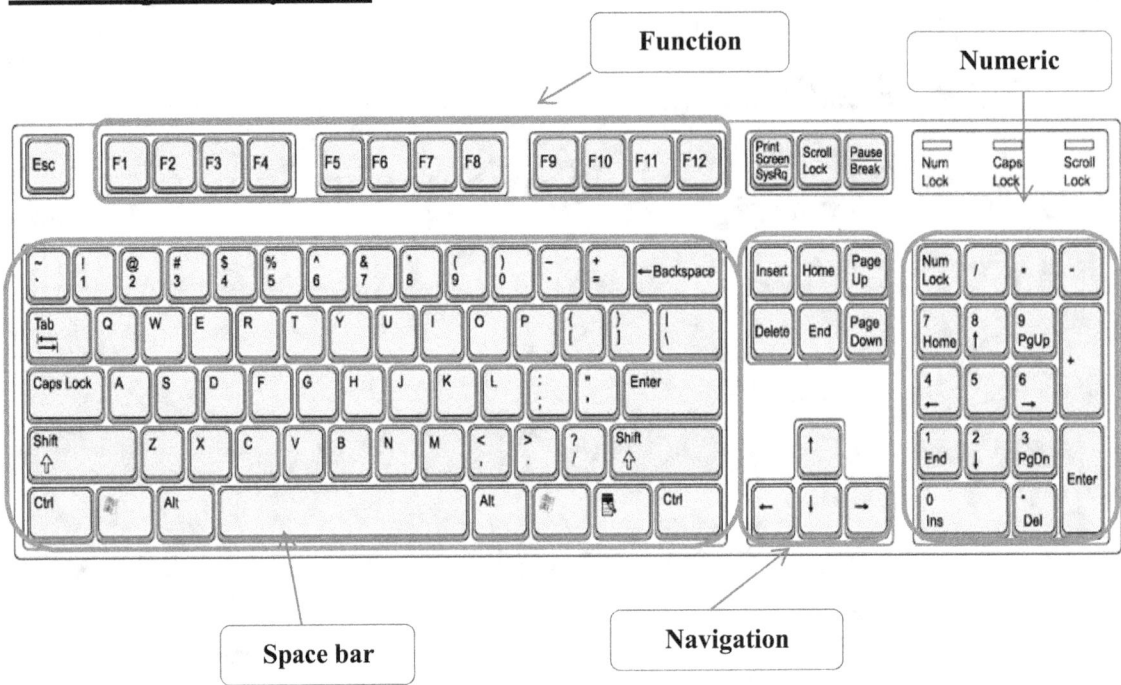

The keyboard is an input device used to enter data of instructions to the computer. The different parts are cursor keys, function keys, and some special keys. These keys are put together according to their works.

A **special key** or **media key** is a keyboard key that performs a special function not included with the traditional 104-key keyboard. *For example*, in the picture of this Logitech keyboard you can see that the first four buttons shown control the volume of your speakers and the brightness.

Keyboard Special Keys

Tip: Special keys are on keyboards often referred to as a **multimedia keyboard**. Some keyboards may also have special keys that require an **FN** key. With the second four buttons you can see that they are the function keys F9 to F12, but also have orange icons that perform the special functions of controlling music. In order to use special keys that have a dual purpose like these keys, press the FN key and a special key at the same time.

For example, if you wanted to press F12 you would press the F12 key. If you wanted to skip an audio track on the F12 key, you would press FN and F12 at the same time.

Tip: Toggle keys like the print screen and scroll lock are not special keys because they are on all keyboards.

Because these keys are special, they require software and drivers included with the keyboard. Typically the included software also allows you to choose how these keys on your keyboard work.

For example, if you have an e-mail special key maybe you want the key to open Mozilla Firefox instead of Microsoft Outlook. If you have an OEM computer such as a Hewlett Packard or Dell and the keyboard came with the computer, the software and drivers are on the computer companies website.

Other examples of special keys

There are dozens of different special keys found on keyboards with no standard to what special keys are required. Below is a list of some of the special keys and the functions they are intended to perform. In addition to this list, many special keyboards also allow you to program keys to perform any action.

- **Application** - Open applications such as calculator, Excel, or Word.
- **Audio controls** - Turn up and down the volume, mute, and open a media player and control it using play, pause, and skip tracks.
- **Folder control** - Open folders like the My Documents folder and My Pictures folder.
- **Internet controls** - Open Internet browser, home page, e-mail, favorites, or search.
- **Window control** - Show open windows, cascade windows, or switch between windows.

Shortcut keys help provide an easier and usually quicker method of navigating and using computer software programs. Shortcut keys are commonly accessed by using the Alt key (on IBM compatible computers), command key (on Apple computers), Ctrl key, or Shift key in conjunction with another key.

Shortcut keys that will work with almost all IBM compatible computers and software programs. It is highly recommended that all users keep a good reference of these shortcut keys or try to memorize them. Doing so will dramatically increase your productivity.

Top 10 keyboard shortcuts everyone should know

Using keyboard shortcuts can greatly increase your productivity, reduce repetitive strain, and help keep you focused. For example, highlighting text with the keyboard and pressing Ctrl + C is much faster than taking your hand from the keyboard, highlighting the text using the mouse, clicking copy from the file menu, and then putting your hand back in place on the keyboard. Below are our top 10 keyboard shortcuts we recommend everyone memorize and use.

Ctrl + C or Ctrl + Insert

Both **Ctrl + C** and **Ctrl + Insert** will copy the highlighted text or selected item. If you want to cut instead of copy press **Ctrl + X**.

Ctrl + V or Shift + Insert

Both the **Ctrl + V** and **Shift + Insert** will paste the text or object that's in the clipboard.

Ctrl + Z and Ctrl + Y

Undo any change. For example, if you cut text, pressing this will undo it. This can also often be pressed multiple times to undo multiple changes. Pressing Ctrl + Y would redo_the undo.

Ctrl + F

Pressing **Ctrl + F** opens the Find in any program. This includes your Internet browser to find text on the current page.

Alt + Tab or Ctrl + Tab

Quickly switch between open programs moving forward.

Tip: Press **Ctrl + Tab** to switch between tabs in a program.

Tip: Adding the **Shift key** to Alt + Tab or Ctrl + Tab will move backwards. For example, if you are pressing Alt + Tab and pass the program you want to switch to, press **Alt + Shift + Tab** to move backwards to that program.

Tip: Windows Vista and 7 users can also press the **Windows Key + Tab** to switch through open programs in a full screenshot of the Window.

Ctrl + Back space and Ctrl + Left or Right arrow

Pressing **Ctrl + Backspace** will delete a full word at a time instead of a single character.

Holding down the **Ctrl key** while pressing the **left or right arrow** will move the cursor one word at a time instead of one character at a time. If you wanted to highlight one word at a time, you can hold down **Ctrl + Shift** and then press the **left or right arrow** key to move one word at a time in that direction while highlighting each word.

Ctrl + S

While working on a document or other file in almost every program, pressing **Ctrl + S** saves that file. This shortcut key should be used frequently anytime you're working on anything important.

Ctrl + Home or Ctrl + End

Ctrl + Home will move the cursor to the beginning of the document and **Ctrl + End** will move the cursor to the end of a document. These shortcuts work with most documents, as well as web pages.

Ctrl + P

Open a print preview of the current page or document being viewed. For example, press **Ctrl + P** now to view a print preview of this page.

Page Up, Space bar, and Page Down

Pressing either the **page up** or **page down** key will move that page one page at a time in that direction. When browsing the Internet, pressing the **space bar** also moves the page down one page at a time.

Tip: If you are using the space bar to go down one page at a time, press the **Shift key** and **space bar** to go up one page at a time.

Ctrl + O

Allows you to select and open a file within the current software program. This works in most programs, including Internet browsers.

F2

After highlighting or selecting a file, pressing **F2** changes the file name to be editable, allowing you to rename the file.

PC shortcut keys for Special Characters

There are many special characters that can be created using keyboard shortcuts. Refer to INDEX part of this book Table I for more common and popular special characters and the keyboard shortcuts to create them.

Function keys

As you can see in the picture of the Saitek Gamers' keyboard below, the **function keys** are lined along the top of the keyboard; labeled F1 through F12. These keys act as shortcuts, performing certain functions like saving files or printing data.

In the past, earlier Apple Macintosh computers did not have function keys. Some early IBMcomputer keyboards had two rows of function keys, with the second row containing F13 - F24. For additional information, visit our page on the F1 through F12 keys and their individual functions.

Saitek Computer Keyboard

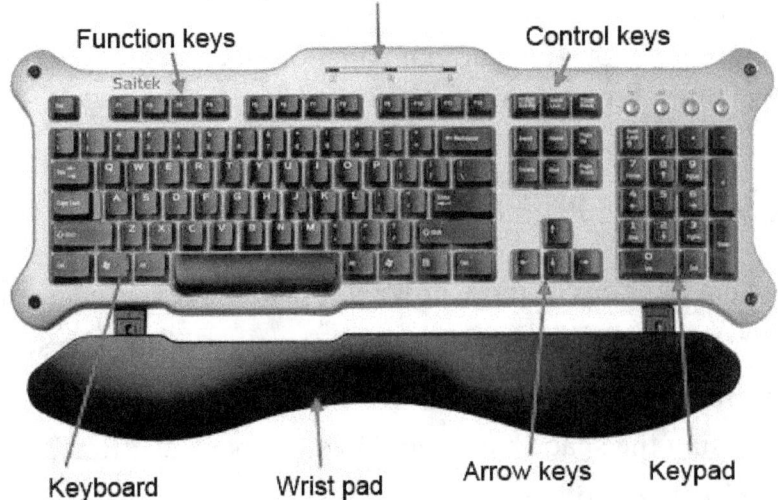

Esc Equivalent to clicking the **Cancel** button. In PowerPoint the Esc key will stop a running slide show. On a web page with animations, the Esc key will stop the animations. On a web page that is loading, the Esc key will stop the page from loading. The keyboard combination Ctrl + Esc will open the Start Menu. Return to Keyboard

Print Screen/SysRq

Usually located at the upper right hand corner of your keyboard next to the **Scroll Lock** and **Pause/Break** keys. Often abbreviated PrtScr, the **Print Screen** key is a useful key supported on most PCs. In DOS, pressing the **Print Screen** key causes the computer to send whatever images and text are currently on the display screen to the printer. Some graphics programs and **Windows**, use the **Print Screen**key to obtain **Screen Captures**. Return to Keyboard

Tab This key can be used to move forward through options in a dialog box.

Ctrl + Shift + Tab can be used to move backward through the options.

Ctrl + Tab allows movement from one open window to the next in an application with more than one open window.

Alt + Tab displays a list of open application windows. Keeping Alt depressed and selecting Tab cycles through the list. Releasing selects the highlighted application window.

Return to Keyboard

Caps Lock Locks the keyboard in "Capitals" mode (only applies to Alpha keys). The Caps Lock key should be used with caution. Using ALL CAPS is a usability no-no as many have difficulty scanning text that is ALL CAPS. Also, when sending email in ALL CAPS, THIS COULD BE MISCONSTRUED AS SHOUTING AT SOMEONE. Return to Keyboard

Shift The obvious use of this key is to allow selection of capital letters when depressing the alphabet characters, or selecting the characters above other non-alpha keys.

Control Key

Ctrl Depressing the Ctrl key while clicking allows multiple selections. Holding the Ctrl key down and pressing other key combinations will initiate quite a few actions. Some of the more common ones are listed below. Return to Keyboard

Ctrl + **A** Select **All** items then Return to Keyboard

Ctrl + **B** Add or remove **Bold** formatting then Return to Keyboard

Ctrl + **C** Copy, places the selected/highlighted copy on the clipboard.

Return to Keyboard

Ctrl + **C** + **C** Opens the clipboard. thenReturn to Keyboard

Ctrl + **F** Opens the **Find what:** dialog box. Great for finding references on a web page while using your favorite web browser. Then Return to Keyboard

Ctrl + **H** **Replace**, brings up the **Find and Replace** dialog box. Great for global find and replace routines while working in normal and html views in your favorite WYSIWYG editors like FrontPage. You can also use this to find and replace content within your Word Documents, Excel Spreadsheets, etc... Return to Keyboard

Ctrl + **I** Add or remove **Italic** formatting. Return to Keyboard

Ctrl + **N** **Window**, In Internet Explorer, opens a **New Window**. In Outlook, opens a **New Mail Message**. In most publishing programs like Word, opens a **New Document**. Return to Keyboard

Ctrl + **O** **Open**, brings up a browse dialog and allows you to select a file to open. Return to Keyboard

Ctrl + **P** Print **then** Return to Keyboard

Ctrl + **S** Save **then** Return to Keyboard

Ctrl + **U** Add or remove **Underline** formatting.

Ctrl + **V** **Paste**, inserts the copy on the clipboard into the area where your flashing cursor I is positioned or the area you have selected/highlighted.

Ctrl + **Z** **Undo** last command. Many software programs offer multiple Undo's by

+ **zc** Open the Start menu (or use the Windows Key if you have one).

Commonly known as **function keys** on a computer keyboard, F1 through F12 may have a variety of different uses or no use at all. The operating system installed on the computer and the software program currently open can change how each of these keys operate. A program is capable of not only using each of the function keys, but also combining the function keys with the ALT or CTRL key. For example, Microsoft Windows users can press ALT + F4 to close the program currently active.

Note: Some keyboards include additional functions on the function keys, which can be activated by pressing the FN key, usually located near the CTRL key, and the appropriate function key. The additional functions available with the use of the FN key will differ depending on the type and brand of keyboard being used. Please check your computer's documentation or manufacturer's website for specific details on which features are available on your keyboard function keys with the use of the FN key.

If your keyboard does not have a row of function keys, they are probably set up as secondary functions on other keys. Some laptop keyboards are set up this way to save space. They can be activated by pressing another key plus the key with the secondary F key functionality.

Below is a short-listing of some of the common functions of the functions keys. As mentioned above, not all programs support these function keys and the function keys on your keyboard may perform different tasks then those mentioned below.

Tip: If you are looking for specific shortcut keys and function key examples, please visit our shortcut key page.

F1

- Almost always used as the help key, almost every program opens a help screen when this key is pressed.
- Enter CMOS Setup.
- Windows Key + F1 would open the Microsoft Windows help and support center.
- Open the Task Pane.

F2

- In Windows renames a highlighted icon, file, or folder in all versions of Windows.
- Alt + Ctrl + F2 opens document window in Microsoft Word.
- Ctrl + F2 displays the print preview window in Microsoft Word.
- Quickly rename a selected file or folder.
- Enter CMOS Setup.

F3

- Often opens a search feature for many programs including Microsoft Windows when at the Windows Desktop..
- In MS-DOS or Windows command line F3 will repeat the last command.
- Shift + F3 will change the text in Microsoft Word from upper to lower case or a capital letter at the beginning of every word.
- Windows Key + F3 opens the Advanced find window in Microsoft Outlook.
- Open Mission Control on an Apple computer running Mac OS X.

F4

- Open find window in Windows 95 to XP.
- Open the address bar in Windows Explorer and Internet Explorer.
- Repeat the last action performed (Word 2000+)
- Alt + F4 closes the program window currently active in Microsoft Windows.

- Ctrl + F4 closes the open window within the current active window in Microsoft Windows.

F5

- In all modern Internet browsers, pressing F5 will refresh or reload the page or document window.
- Open the find, replace, and go to window in Microsoft Word.
- Starts a slideshow in PowerPoint.

F6

- Move the cursor to the Address bar in Internet Explorer, Mozilla Firefox, and most other Internet browsers.
- Ctrl + Shift + F6 opens to another open Microsoft Word document.
- Reduce laptop speaker volume (on some laptops)

F7

- Commonly used to spell check and grammar check a document in Microsoft programs such as Microsoft Word, Outlook, etc.
- Shift + F7 runs a Thesaurus check on the word highlighted.
- Turns on Caret browsing in Mozilla Firefox.
- Increase laptop speaker volume (on some laptops)

F8

- Function key used to enter the Windows startup menu, commonly used to access Windows Safe Mode.
- Used by some computers to access the Windows Recovery system, but may require a Windows installation CD
- Displays a thumbnail image for all workspaces in Mac OS

F9

- Refresh document in Microsoft Word.
- Send and receive e-mail in Microsoft Outlook.
- Opens the Measurements toolbar in Quark 5.0.
- Reduce laptop screen brightness (on some laptops)
- With Mac OS 10.3 or later, displays a thumbnail for each window in a single workspace.
- Using the Fn key and F9 at the same time opens Mission Control on an Apple computer running Mac OS X.

F10

- In Microsoft Windows activates the menu bar of an open application.
- Shift + F10 is the same as right-clicking on a highlighted icon, file, or Internet link.
- Access the hidden recovery partition on HP and Sony computers.
- Enter CMOS Setup.
- Increase laptop screen brightness (on some laptops)
- With Mac OS 10.3 or later, shows all open Windows for the active program.

F11

- Enter and exit full screen mode in all modern Internet browsers.
- Ctrl + F11 as computer is starting to access the hidden recovery partition on many Dell computers.
- Access the hidden recovery partition on eMachines, Gateway, and Lenovo computers.
- With Mac OS 10.4 or later, hides all open windows and shows the Desktop.

F12

- Open the Save as window in Microsoft Word.
- Ctrl + F12 opens a document In Word.
- Shift + F12 saves the Microsoft Word document (like Ctrl + S).
- Ctrl + Shift + F12 prints a document in Microsoft Word.
- Preview a page in Microsoft Expression Web.
- Open Firebug or browser debug tool.
- With an Apple running Mac OS 10.4 or later, F12 shows or hides the Dashboard.
- Access the list of bootable devices on a computer at startup, allowing you to select a different device to boot from (Hard drive, CD or DVD drive, Floppy drive, USB drive, Network)

F13 - F24

Early IBM computers also had keyboards with F13 through F24 keys. However, because these keyboards are no longer used, they are not listed on this page.

Summary

A special key or **media key** is a keyboard key that performs a special function not included with the traditional 104-key keyboard.

A Shortcut keys are combinations of keys that are pressed together to do special commands. It help provide an easier and usually quicker method of navigating and using computer software programs.

Function keys are lined along the top of the keyboard; labeled F1 through F12. These keys act as shortcuts, performing certain functions like saving files or printing data.

<u>Activity</u>

1. Open and start the MS Word program.

2. Type the following paragraphs:

Rice, an Important Food

Rice has grown in Asian countries for hundreds and hundreds of years. It is the main food for most people living in the East, including the Philippines. In some Eastern languages, the words for rice and for food are the same.

Rice is carefully planted by hand. Rice can only grow in hot, wet places.

The grains are hand-planted in muddy seedbeds. When the young plants are big enough, they are moved into a large, flooded fields called paddy fields. When the rice begins to ripen, the water is drainedoff. At the harvest time, the rice is gathered in and dried.

From: People and Faces; Childcraft

3. After typing, press CTRL and Home keys to move the cursor to the top of the paragraphs. Select the title, press CTRL and B keys to make the title bold.

4. Press CTRL and ~ arrow keys to move the cursor until it reaches the

   word "hot". Then insert and type the word "and'".

5. Now, move the cursor to the words "paddy fields" by pressing the CTRL and ~ (right arrow key). Select it, then press CTRL and J to make the words italics (slanted).

6. Press CTRL + Z keys together and notice that the last action you did was cancelled.

7. Save the whole document using the shortcut keys by pressing CTRL and S keys together. Name it SHORTCUT.

Exercise II.2.1

Name: _____   Date: _____

Grade and Section: ----------------------.   Score:_____

A. Answer the following questions:

1. What is the shortcut key to open a new document?

2. This key is used to move cursor to the end of the document?.

3. What is the shortcut key to erase one word to the left of the cursor?

4. This shortcut key is used to save a document.

5. What is the shortcut key for the Redo command?

B. Write how each of these shortcut keys works.

1. Ctrl + X

2. Ctrl + V

3. Ctrl + C

4. Ctrl + B

5. Ctrl + U

Lesson 4

Correct Spacing after Punctuation

't work on the Web , a fact that has been clear to usability research
ey are **contrary to the Web's basic imperative** , which is to let use
n needs instantly gratified.

so clear that this indictment of Web advertising had two exceptions:

e as far as users are concerned, they are **content** , not advertising:
h they are looking to buy. This explains the success of eBay, Monste
ority of Web classifieds portends dire times ahead for traditional prin
e source continues to migrate online.
cause search engines are the one type of website that people visit v

Objective

At the end of this chapter, the student should be able to:
  ➢ *use correct spacing after punctuation marks*
  ➢ *edit documents in relation to proper punctuation*

Punctuation means putting the right kind of little marks in the right place so as to show the exact length and meaning of sentences. Proper punctuation is essential in written English to enable the reader to understand what you are trying to say.

Common Rules of Correct Spacing when using Punctuation Marks

. full stop	, comma	' apostrophe
! exclamation mark	: colon	" " quotation marks
? question mark	; semi colon	- hyphen

Apostrophes [']

Apostrophes next to the letter ('s) indicate possession or belonging. No space is needed before or after the apostrophe.

For example: This is Paul's web site.

They are also used to show missing letters in shortened words, especially in informal writing. No space is needed before or after the apostrophe.

For example: It's a nice day today, isn't it? I've got an idea. Let's go out.

Exclamation marks [!]

Exclamation marks act as a full stop. An exclamation mark is most often used to show shock, surprise, horror or pleasure. As with full stops you do not put a space before an exclamation mark, but you do need at least one space after one (two spaces for purists).

There's an increasing tendency to overuse them on the internet. Shock horror!!!! Try to stick to the rule of one exclamation mark per sentence, otherwise they will lose their effect.

For example: Oh! Wow! Brilliant! etc... It was shocking!

Commas [,]

Commas point out brief pauses in a complex sentence or separate items in long lists. Commas are useful for breaking up long sentences, but only to show a natural break. You do not put a space before a comma, but you do need a pace after one.

For example:

There were a lot of people in the room, teachers, students, and parents. The teachers were sitting, the students were listening and the parents were just worrying.

Note - We don't always put a comma before the word 'and'

Colons [:]

Colons precede a list, an explanation or an example. You do not put a space before a colon, but you do need a space after one.

For example: "The main areas in Nottingham: Broadmarsh Centre and Victoria Centre."

Full stops [.]

Full stops (periods in the USA) go at the end of sentences that are statements. You do not put a space before a full stop, but you do need at least one space after one (two spaces for purists, but in these days of computers and e-mails one space is fine).

For example: My name is Jessie. I am a teacher.

Hyphens [-]

Hyphens are used to connect words or syllables, or to divide words into parts. You don't use a space on either side of a hyphen.

For example: There were ninety-nine red balloons.

Question marks [?]

Question marks go at the end of sentences that are questions. As with full stops you do not put a space before a question mark, but you do need at least one space after one (two spaces for purists).

For example: Is my name Lynne? Of course it is.

You need a question mark at the end of tag questions too.

For example: It's a nice day, isn't it?

Semicolons [;]

Semicolons are used to separate two sentences that would otherwise be joined with a word such as 'and', 'because', 'since', 'unless' or 'while'. You do not put a space before a semicolon, but you do need a space after one.

For example:

"I'm looking forward to our next lesson; I'm sure it will be a lot of fun."

Quotation marks (Speech marks) |Double quotes [" "] Single quotes [' ']

Quotation marks (single or double) are used to show words that are directly spoken (direct speech). Only the words actually being quoted are enclosed by speech marks. You need a space before the opening speech mark, but no space after it, and a space after the closing one, but no space before it.

For example: "Could everyone sit down please," said the teacher.

Another general rule is to use a comma after the introduction to quoted speech or writing.

For example: Jamie said, "I love you."

Sometimes when writing a spoken sentence it is split in two. The speech marks must then be placed at the beginning and end of each part of the sentence. Commas are used to separate the spoken part from the rest of the sentence.

For *example:-*

"I wonder," she said quietly, "whether people will ever truly understand each other."

However if you need a question mark or exclamation mark the markers that punctuate the quoted words are enclosed by the speech marks.

Rules on Correct spacing

:	1. Space twice after a colon.
. ? !	2. Space twice after the punctuation at the end of a sentence.
(	3. Space once before an open parenthesis but do not space after it.
)	4. Space once after a closed parenthesis but do not space before it.
#	5. Do not space between the number and the number sign. (The sign before a number means number and after a number it means pounds.)
&	6. Space before and after the ampersand (the and symbol).
$	7. Do not space between the dollar sign and the number.
@	8. Space once before and after the "at" symbol, except in e-mail addresses.
%	9. Do not space between the number and the percent sign.
/	10. Do not space before or after the forward slash.

<u>Summary</u>

Punctuation means putting the right kind of little marks in the right place so as to show the exact length and meaning of sentences.

Spacing with Punctuation: With a computer, use only one space following periods, commas, semicolons, colons, exclamation points, question marks, and quotation marks. The space needed after these punctuation marks is proportioned automatically. With some typewriters and word processors, follow ending punctuation with two spaces when using a fixed-pitch font.

Exercises

Observe the difference on using punctuation marks:

"I   don't   understand",   replied   Nathan.
Nathan   replied,   "I   don't   understand."

"Do   you   understand?"   asked   Nathan.
Nathan   asked,   "Do   you   understand?"

"I   don't   understand!"   shouted   Nathan.
Nathan shouted, "I don't understand!"

L esson 5

Manuscripts Signs

Objective

At the end of this chapter, the student should be able to:
 ➢ *interpret the edited document by the use of manuscript signs.*
 ➢ *modify such document accordingly when edited using signs.*

In order to avoid too much writing on your document, we usually use signs to convey the meaning of an edit. Different signs were created to easily interpret the editing of documents in relation to **Grammar & spelling, Formatting, Font Type Styles** and **Punctuation.**

Signs related to Grammar & spelling

Sign	Meaning	Example	Please change as follows
४ or ---	Delete	to err is ɣhuman to err is not human	to err is human
∧	Insert	to err ^is human	to err is human
/ or ---	Words change	to err in human (s) to err was human (is)	to err is human
⊓⊔	Word replacement	to err human is	to err is human
(stet)	Back before calibration	to err [is] human (stet)	to err is human
(sp)	No abbreviation	[3rd Flr] (sp)	third floor

Accepted abbreviations    [third floor]   3rd Flr

<u>Signs related to Formatting</u>

Sign	Meaning	Example	Please change as follows
#	Insert Space	to err̬is human	to err is human
◡	Remove Space	to err is hu‿man	to err is human
⌐< #	Insert line space	xxxxxxxxxx xxxxxxxxxx <#	xxxxxxxxxx xxxxxxxxxx
⌐<ɣ#	Remove line space	xxxxxxxxxx xxxxxxxxxx <ɣ#	xxxxxxxxxx xxxxxxxxxx
⌐	Left-justified alignment	⌐ abcdefghijklmnop	abcdefghijklmnop
⌐	Right-justified alignment	⌐abcdefghijklmnop	abcdefghijklmnop

|]...[| Centering |]Abcdefghijklmnop[| Abcdefghijklmnop |

| ¶ | Change paragraph | Xxxxx.¶Xxxxxxx xxxxxxx. | Xxxxx.

Xxxxxxxxxxxxxxx. |

| ⅄¶ | Paragraph need not change | Xxxxx. ⅄¶ Xxxxxxxxxxxxxx. | Xxxxx. Xxxxxx xxxxxxxx. |

Signs related to Font Type Styles

Sign	Meaning	Example	Please change as follows
(ital)	Italic	[abcdef] (ital)	*abcdef*
(bf)	Bold typeface	[abcdef] (bf)	**abcdef**
↗	Convert to uppercase	abcdef	Abcdef
↙	Convert to lower case	Abcdef	abcdef

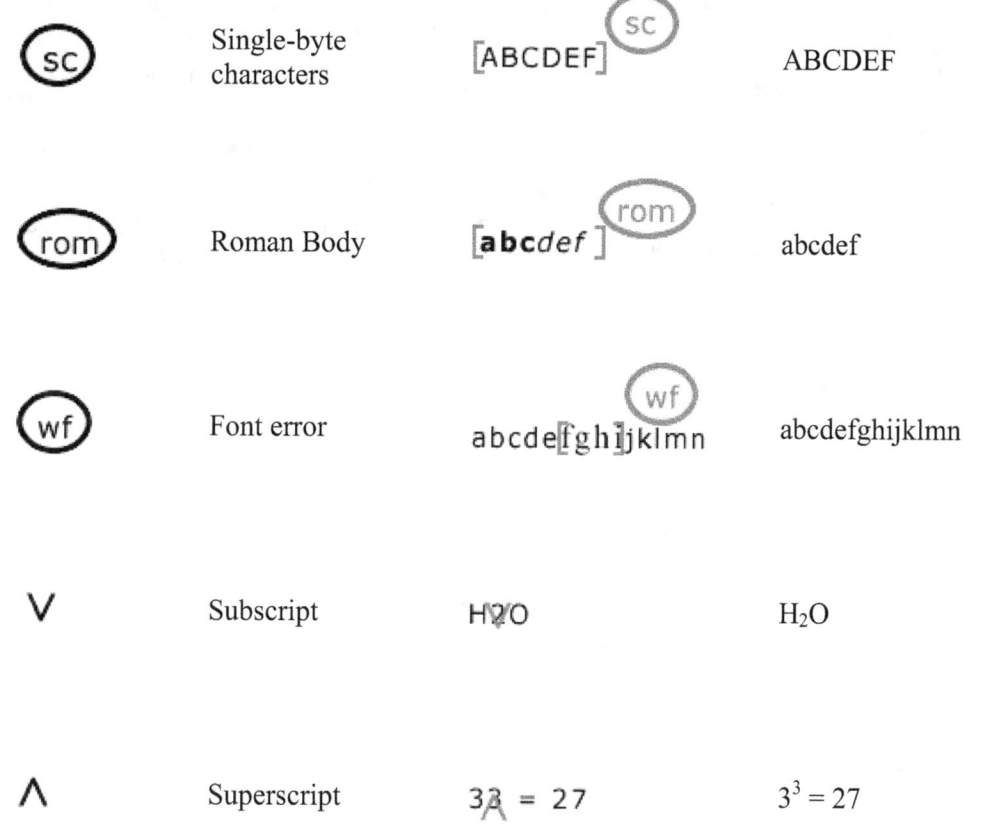

	Single-byte characters	[ABCDEF] ⟨sc⟩	ABCDEF
⟨sc⟩			
⟨rom⟩	Roman Body	[**abc**_def_] ⟨rom⟩	abcdef
⟨wf⟩	Font error	abcde[fghi]jklmn ⟨wf⟩	abcdefghijklmn
V	Subscript	H₂O	H_2O
Λ	Superscript	3³ = 27	$3^3 = 27$

<u>Signs related to Punctuation</u>

Sign	Meaning	Example	Please change as follows
⟨ . ⟩	Period	To err is human, to forgive divine.	To err is human, to forgive divine.
⟨ , ⟩	Comma	To err is human, to forgive divine.	To err is human, to forgive divine.

:	Colon	Hamlet:To be or not to be...	Hamlet: To be or not to be...
;	Semicolon	I got a cat;her name is Luca.	I got a cat; her name is Luca.
?	Question mark	Is it human to err?	Is it human to err?
!	Exclamation point	Wow!	Wow!
(-)	Hyphen	Nobody is error free.	Nobody is error-free.
,	Apostrophe	Abc's	Abc's
" ... "	Quote	"Superman"sighted	"Superman" sighted
$\frac{1}{N}$	En dash (Use Alt +0150 to enter en dash).	pages 10 20	pages 10–20
$\frac{1}{M}$	Em dash (Use Alt +0151 to enter em dash).	To err well, it's only human.	To err—well, it's only human.

/slash/	Slash	6 cells/meter	6 cells/meter
(…)	Parentheses	to err make a mistake is human	to err (make a mistake) is human
[…]	Square brackets	to err make a mistake is human	to err [make a mistake] is human

Samples:

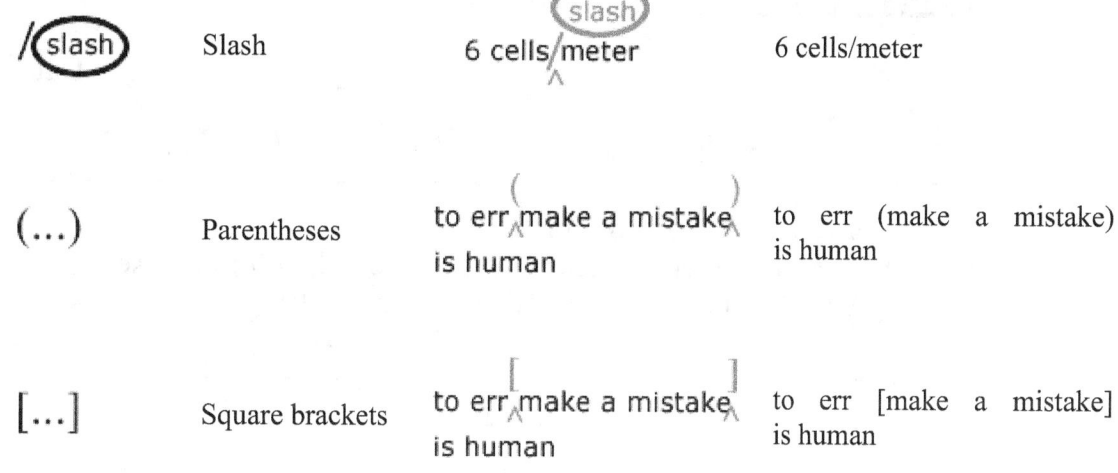

It is sometimes written equivalently as the 2-step recurrence relation

The [Lozi] map is a linear "tent map" version of the Hénon map is given by

Although not realistic as an approximation to a smooth flow, the Lozi map is a very helpful tool for developing guess on the topology of a whole class of maps of the Hénon type, so called once-folding maps.

The Hénon map is the simplest map that captures the "stretch & fold" dynamics of return maps such as the Rösslers. The Hénon map dynamics is conveniently plotted in the (x_n, x_{n+1}) plane an example is given in fig. 2.

Summary

Manuscript Signs are use for editing documents in relation to Grammar & spelling, Formatting, Font Type Styles and Punctuation.

Different signs were created to easily interpret the editing of documents in relation to *Grammar & spelling, Formatting, Font Type Styles* and **Punctuation.**

Exercise II.4.1

Name: _____ Date: _____

Grade and Section: ----------------------. Score: _____

1. Open and start the Word program.
2. Type the correct sentence to the second column based on the corrected sentence from the first column. (2 marks each)

Correction using signs	Corrected
covering the period of december 25 to 31, 2014 (ital)	
the leader of Maguddatu Group tagged as the No. 10 Most Wanted Person	
You've come to the right site.	
cruise tours for early bird discounts or last minute markdowns	
I just was discussing this yesterday	
: AC, DIDMD status of : Updates on Stephany Nicole Ella Case	

Exercise II.4.2

Name: _____   Date: _____

Grade and Section: _____.   Score: _____

1. Open and start the Word program.
2. Type the following in double line spacing with fonts of Tahoma , size 12

3. Make the Title with font size into 16, bold and format to the center.
4. Save the document as your lastname exercise 1 and make necessary corrections.
5. Print one copy then close the file.

Lesson 6

Types of Headings

Greener, cleaner living ← Main Heading is the title of the whole article

Singapore recently released its National Climate Change Strategy 2012. Let's look at what is being done to use energy more efficiently, reduce our carbon footprint and mitigate climate change effects.

Generating Power ← Sub-Headings are headings of the paragraphs

About 80 per cent of our electricity is generated by natural gas from Malaysia and Indonesia today, a marked increase from 19 per cent in 2000. Scheduled to open in 2013, Singapore's first liquefied natural gas terminal in Jurong Island will allow us to tap into global gas markets. We will explore ways of using solar energy. There are four large-scale solar PV installation in Singapore, including Resorts World Sentosa and the Building and Construction Authority's Zero Energy Building.

Waste and Water ← There is usually many sub-headings in an article but only one main heading.

Firstly, we will look into reducing direct methane emissions by incinerating sludge rather than disposing in landfills. Our target to reduce plastic incineration and increase recycling

Objective

At the end of this chapter, the student should be able to:
➢ *use the appropriate heading in a document*
➢ *differentiate between the paragraph, marginal, headings and others*

The main **heading** may be blocked at the left margin or centred in the **typing** line, and is usually **typed** in closed or spaced capitals. This may be *names, name/title combinations, uniform titles, chronological terms, topical terms, genre/form terms, subdivisions, extended subject headings, or node labels.*

▶ **Name heading** - A heading that is a personal, corporate, meeting, or jurisdiction (including geographic) name.

▶ **Name/title heading** - A heading consisting of both name and title portions. The name portion contains a personal, corporate, meeting, or jurisdiction name. The title portion contains the title by which an item or a series is identified for cataloging purposes and may be a uniform or conventional title, a title page title of a work, or a series title.

▶ **Uniform title heading** - A heading consisting of the title by which an item or a series is identified for cataloging purposes when the title is not entered under a personal, corporate, meeting, or jurisdiction name in a name/title heading construction.

▶ **Chronological term heading** - A heading consisting of a chronological subject term.

▶ **Topical term heading** - A heading consisting of a topical subject term.

▶ **Genre/form term heading** - A heading consisting of a genre/form subject term.

▶ **Subdivision heading** - A heading consisting of a general (topical or language), form, geographic, or chronological subject subdivision term. An *extended subdivision heading* contains more than one subject subdivision term (subfields $v, $x, $y, and $z).

▶ **Extended subject heading** - A name, name/title, uniform title, topical term, or genre/form term heading that includes one or more general, form, geographic, or chronological subject subdivision terms (subfields $v, $x, $y, or $z).

▶ **Node label heading** - A heading consisting of a term used in the systematic section of a thesaurus to indicate the logical basis on which a category is divided. paragraph

The machine reason is that search engines use headlines and subheads to help rank your content. The human reason is similar – using headlines makes your content more scannable – easier to read. Best practice is to include target keywords in tagged headings and subheads (note: this is not just making the standard copy bold, you have to actually use the heading style) when appropriate.

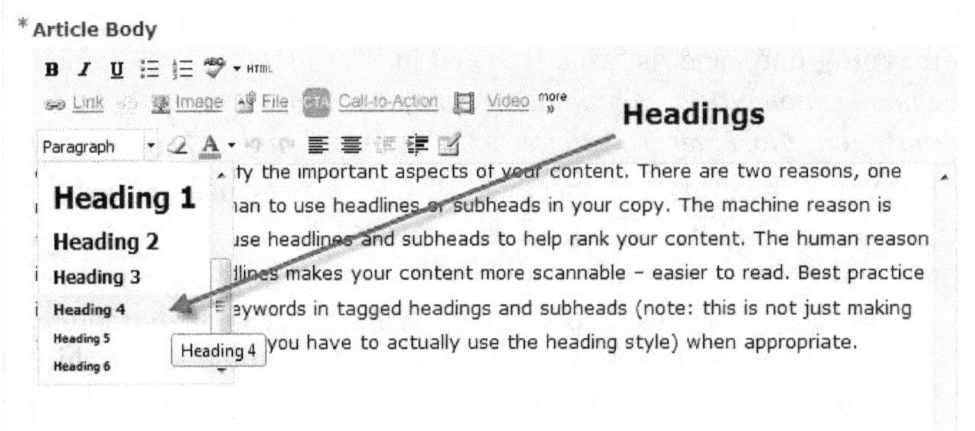

Styles save time and make your document look good

One of the great things about using a word processor is that you can create documents that look professionally typeset.

- Headings are in a font that contrasts with body text.
- Paragraphs are separated with just enough white space.
- Elements such as bulleted lists are indented.
- Emphasized text is in a contrasting color.

The document may even include special elements such as a table of contents.

Using direct formatting

Word provides several ways for you to achieve each of these effects in your document. For example, to format **headings**, you can select the text, apply bold formatting, and then apply a slightly larger font size than the size that you use for the body text.

Applying formatting in this manner is known as **direct formatting**. The process of applying direct formatting can be tedious. It's easy to make mistakes, and you might not get a good looking document. In the example in the previous paragraph, you must repeat the direct formatting process for each heading, and you must be careful to select the same font size every time.

If you want **subheadings**, you must decide how to differentiate the subheadings from the headings (smaller size? italicize?) and repeat the direct formatting process for each subheading. If you don't have expertise in design or typography, it may take some time before you create a look that you like.

Furthermore, documents that are formatted by direct formatting are difficult to update. If you want to change the look of the document, you must select each element and apply the new formatting choices.

PROFESSIONAL LOOKING DOCUMENTS

GALLERIES OF COORDINATED ITEMS

On the Insert tab, the galleries include items that are designed to coordinate with the overall look of your document. You can use these galleries to insert tables, headers, footers, lists, cover pages, and other document building blocks. When you create pictures, charts, or diagrams, they also coordinate with your current document look.

FLEXIBLE FORMATTING

You can easily change the formatting of selected text in the document text by choosing a look for the selected text from the Quick Styles gallery on the Home tab.

DIRECT FORMATTING

You can also format text directly by using the other controls on the Home tab.

THEMATIC LOOK

Most controls offer a choice of using the look from the current theme or using a format that you specify directly.

THEME ELEMENTS AND QUICK STYLE GALLERIES

To change the overall look of your document, choose new Theme elements on the Page Layout tab. To change the looks available in the Quick Style gallery, use the Change Current Quick Style Set command. Both the Themes gallery and the Quick Styles gallery provide reset commands so that you can always restore the look of your document to the original contained in your current template.

LOCATION OF GALLERIES

Gallery Name	Tab	Group
Tables	Insert	Tables
Headers	Insert	Header & Footer
Footers	Insert	Header & Footer
Cover pages	Insert	Pages
Themes	Page Layout	Themes
Quick Styles	Home	Styles

Using styles

By contrast, when you use styles to format your document, you can quickly and easily apply a set of formatting choices consistently throughout your document.

A style is a set of formatting characteristics, such as font name, size, color, paragraph alignment and spacing. Some styles even include borders and shading.

For example, instead of taking three separate steps to format your heading as 16-point, bold, Cambria, you can achieve the same result in one step by applying the built-in Heading 1 style. You do not need to remember the characteristics of the Heading 1 style. For each heading in your document, you just click in the heading (you don't even need to select all the text), and then click **Heading 1** in the gallery of styles.

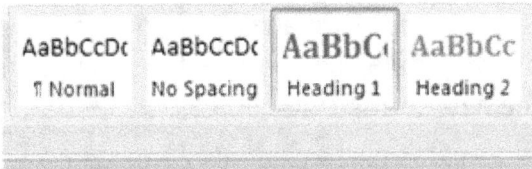

Galleries of coordinated items

On the Insert tab, the galleries include items tha
your document. You can use these galleries to ir
other document building blocks. When you crea
with your current document look.

If you decide that you want subheadings, you can use the built-in Heading 2 style, which was designed to look good with the Heading 1 style.

1. The Quick Styles that you see in the gallery of styles are designed to work together. For example, the Heading 2 Quick Style is designed to look subordinate to the Heading 1 Quick Style.

2. The body text of your document is automatically formatted with the Normal Quick Style.

3. Quick Styles can be applied to paragraphs, but you can also apply them to individual words and characters. For example, you can emphasize a phrase by applying the Emphasis Quick Style.

4. When you format text as part of a list, each item in the list is automatically formatted with the List Paragraph Quick Style.

If you later decide that you want headings to have a different look, you can change the Heading 1 and Heading 2 styles, and Word automatically updates all instances of them in the document. You can also apply a different Quick Style set or a different theme to change the look of the headings without making changes to the styles.

Built-in styles turn on timesaving features

The built-in styles (Heading 1, Heading 2, etc.) provide other benefits, too. If you use the built-in heading styles, Word can generate a table of contents automatically. Word also uses the built-in heading styles to make the Document Map, which is a convenient feature for moving through long documents.

TIP   Try it. If you have a document that uses the built-in heading styles, open it, and on the **View** tab, in the **Show/Hide** group, select the **Document Map** check box. Click a heading in the document map to jump to the corresponding part of the document.

Word provides several style types of heading:

- **Character and paragraph styles** determine the look of most of the text in a document. Some styles work as both character and paragraph types, and these styles are known as **linked styles.**
- **List styles** determine the look of lists, including characteristics such as bullet style or number scheme, indentation, and any label text.
- **Table styles** determine the look of tables, including characteristics such as the text formatting of the header row, gridlines, and accent colors for rows and columns.

I. Character, paragraph, and linked styles

Character, paragraph, and linked styles appear in the **Styles** group on the **Home** tab. You can quickly apply a style from the gallery of styles. To see more information about each style, click the **Styles** Dialog Box Launcher.

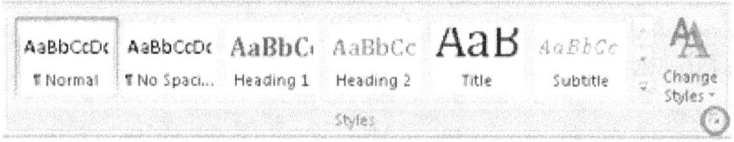

The **Styles** task pane opens.

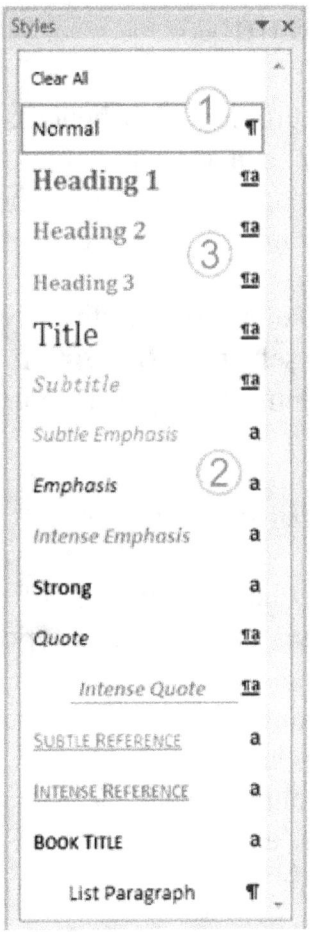

1. **Paragraph styles** *are marked with a paragraph symbol: You can see the paragraph symbol in the Quick Style gallery as well as in the Styles task pane. Click anywhere in a paragraph to apply the style to the entire paragraph.*

A paragraph style includes everything that a character style contains, but it also controls all aspects of a paragraph's appearance, such as text alignment, tab stops, line spacing, and borders.

For example, you can have a character style called Alert that formats text as bold and red. Additionally, you can have a paragraph style called Headline that formats text as bold and red. But the Headline paragraph style also centers the text horizontally and adds 24 points of space above the text.

In this scenario, if you select a paragraph and then apply the Alert style, all the text in the paragraph is formatted as bold and red, but nothing else about the paragraph changes. However, if you select the paragraph and then apply the Headline style, the text become bold and red, extra space is inserted before the paragraph, and the paragraph is centered between the left and right margins.

Word includes two built-in paragraph styles: Normal and List Paragraph. By default, Word automatically applies the Normal paragraph style to all text in a blank, new document. Similarly, Word automatically applies the List Paragraph paragraph style to items in a list — for example, when you use the **Bullets** command to create a bulleted list.

To apply a paragraph style, you select the paragraphs that you want to format, and then you click the paragraph style you want.

NOTE To select a single paragraph for applying a paragraph style, you can click anywhere in the paragraph. To select more than one paragraph, click anywhere in the first paragraph and drag to anywhere in the last paragraph that you want to select. You do not need to select the entire paragraph.

2. **Character styles** *are marked with a character symbol: **a**. Click anywhere in a word to apply the style to the entire word. Or you can select more than one word to apply the style to more than one word.*

Character styles contain formatting characteristics that can be applied to text, such as font name, size, color, bold, italic, underline, borders, and shading.

Character styles do not include formatting that affects paragraph characteristics, such as line spacing, text alignment, indentation, and tab stops.

Word includes several built-in character styles, such as Emphasis, Subtle Emphasis, and Intense Emphasis. Each of these built-in styles combines formatting, such as bold, italic, and accent color, to provide a coordinated set of typographic designs. For example, applying the Emphasis character style formats text as bold, italic, in an accent color.

To apply a character style, you select the text that you want to format, and then you click the character style that you want.

On the Insert tab, the galleries include items that coordinate with the overall look of your docum

On the Insert tab, the *galleries* include items that coordinate with the overall look of your docu

1. Click in the word you want to format.

2. Mouse over the Quick Styles to see a preview of the formatting in your document. When you point to a character style, only the word where you clicked is formatted. When you point to a paragraph style or a linked style, the entire paragraph is formatted. Click the character style that you want to use.

3. The word that you selected is formatted with the characteristics of the style that you chose.

3. **Linked styles** *are marked with both a paragraph symbol and a character symbol:* **a***. Click anywhere in a paragraph to apply the style to the entire paragraph. Or you can select one or more words to apply the style to the words that you selected.*

A linked style behaves as either a character style or a paragraph style, depending on what you select. If you click in a paragraph or select a paragraph and then apply a linked style, the style is applied as a paragraph style. However, if you select a word or phrase in the paragraph and then apply a linked style, the style is applied as a character style, with no effect on the paragraph as a whole.

For example, if you select (or click in) a paragraph and then apply the Heading 1 style, the whole paragraph is formatted with the Heading 1 text and paragraph characteristics. However, if you select a word or a phrase and then apply Heading 1, the text that you selected is formatted with the text characteristics of the Heading 1 style, but none of the paragraph characteristics are applied.

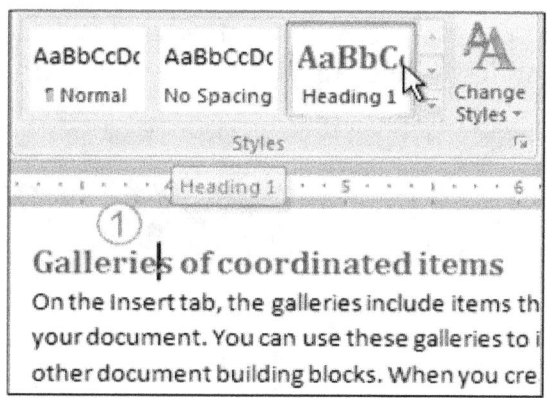

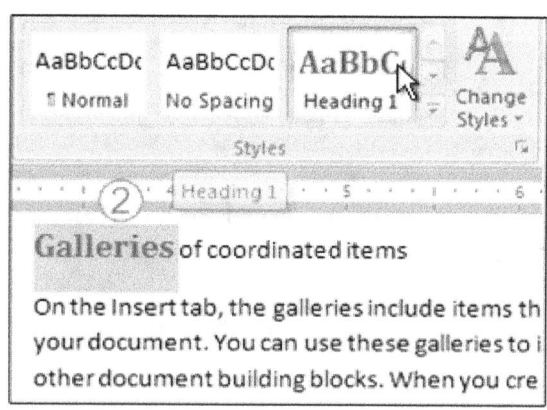

1. When you select or click in a paragraph and apply a linked style, the style is applied to the whole paragraph.

2. When you select a word or phrase and apply a linked style, the style is applied only to the selected text.

How is this useful? Consider the scenario above, in which an Alert character style and a Headline paragraph style each format text as bold and red. If the Headline style were a linked style instead of a paragraph style, you would not need a separate character style for formatting words and phrases. Wherever you wanted a headline in your document (bold, red, centered, with extra space above), you would select a paragraph and apply the linked style. Wherever you wanted an alert, you would select a word or phrase and apply the same linked style.

Word includes many built-in linked styles, notably the heading styles (Heading 1, Heading 2, and so on).

TIP   You might want the first few words of a paragraph to coordinate with the formatting of the headings in your document. This type of formatting, known as a run-in head or a side head, is easy to apply by using linked styles. Select the first few words of a paragraph, and then apply a heading style.

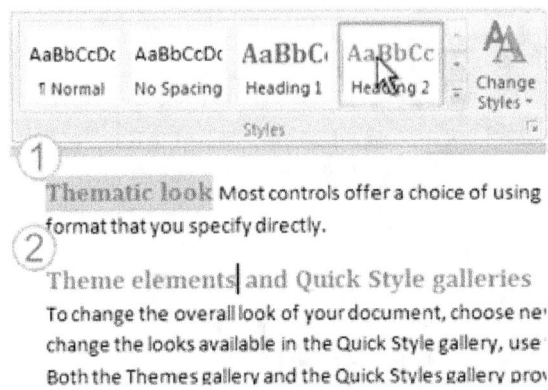

1. Select the first few words of a paragraph and then click a heading style to create a run-in head.

2. Click in a paragraph and then click a heading style to create a heading.

II. List styles

A list style applies characteristics for formatting a list. A list can include levels of hierarchy, like an outline, that can be indicated by indentation and numbering schemes. For example, level one in a multilevel list can be aligned against the margin and can begin with an Arabic numeral followed by a period. Level two can be indented slightly from the margin and can begin with a lowercase alphabetical character followed by a closing parenthesis. Here is an example of a multilevel list that is two levels deep:

1.   This   is   the   first   item   at   level   one.
  a) This is the first item at level two, within the first item at level one.
  b) This is the second item at level two, within the first item at level one.
2.   This   is   the   second   item   at   level   one.
  a) This is the first item at level two, within the second item at level one.
3.   This   is   the   third   item   at   level   one.
  a) This is the first item at level two, within the third item at level one.
  b) This is the second item at level two, within the third item at level one.
  c) This is the third item at level two, within the third item at level one.

A list style can define formatting for as many as nine levels of a list. The formatting scheme can include paragraph indentation for each level of the list, any label text (such as, "Item" or "Chapter"), and the numbering or bullet characters to use in the list.

Unlike the other types of styles (paragraph, character, linked, and table), predefined list styles are not available when you first create a document in Word.

NOTE   A document may contain list styles if you receive it from someone who created his or her own list styles. If your document contains list styles, they are listed under the **List Styles** heading in the gallery of multilevel lists. To see that gallery, click **Multilevel List** in the **Paragraph** group on the **Home** tab.

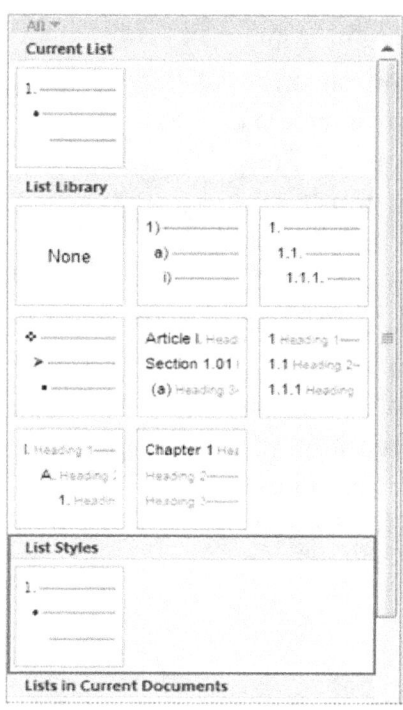

List Library: the starting point for list styles

Instead of predefined list styles, Word provides several multilevel list templates, which are displayed under the **List Library** heading in the gallery of multilevel lists. These preformatted designs can be applied to lists in your document, and they can also serve as a handy starting point for creating your own list styles.

Consider creating your own list style when you want to do the following:

- **Change list formatting consistently throughout your document**   After list styles are defined and applied, they can be changed. The changes affect all instances where the list style is used in the document.
- **Use complex list formatting that varies from one multilevel list design to another**   List styles provide great flexibility, and each one is named separately, which makes it easier to distinguish among them in the list of list styles.
- **Apply formatting to a multilevel list by using a keyboard shortcut**   You can assign keyboard shortcuts to list styles that you create, but not to the preformatted multilevel list templates.

TIP   If you use the built-in heading styles in your document (Heading 1, Heading 2, and so on), you can use multilevel list templates to apply a numbering scheme to your headings. For example, to number headings so that top-level headings (Heading 1 paragraphs) are numbered 1, 2, 3, second-level headings (Heading 2 paragraphs) are numbered 1.1, 1.2, 1.3, and so on, you click in the first Heading 1 paragraph, and then under **List Library** you click **1 Heading 1, 1.1 Heading 2, 1.1.1 Heading 3**. Multilevel list templates that number headings are marked in the list gallery with **Heading** in gray text.

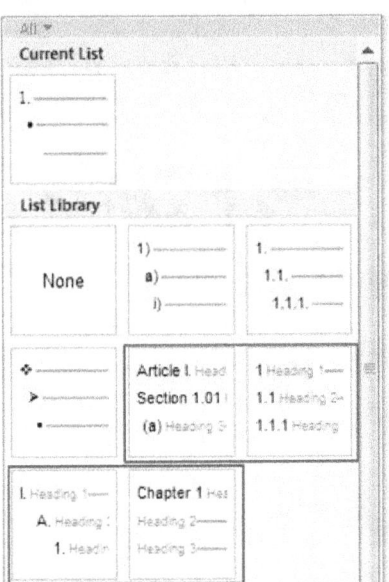

Create your own list style

The easiest way to create a list style is to start with one of the preformatted multilevel list templates.

1.   Select the list that you want to format.
2.   On the **Home** tab, in the **Paragraph** group, click the arrow next to **Multilevel List**.
3.   Under **List Library**, click the design that most closely matches how you want your list style to look.
4.   Click **Multilevel List** again, and then click **Define New List Style**.

5.   Make any modifications you want to the preformatted design.
6.   In the **Name** box, type a name for your list style.
7.   If you want your list style to be available for all new documents that you create, click **New documents based on this template**.

III. **Table styles**

A table style provides a consistent look to borders, shading, alignment and fonts in tables.

To apply a table style, you select the table that you want to format, and then you click a table style from the gallery of table styles on the **Design** tab, on the **Table Tools** contextual tab. Within a table cell, you can use styles and direct formatting to format the content of the cell. Formatting that you apply this way overrides the formatting that comes from the table style.

In other words, if you use a style or direct formatting to format the content of a table cell and then you switch to a different table style, the content that you formatted with the style or direct formatting is not updated to match the new table style.

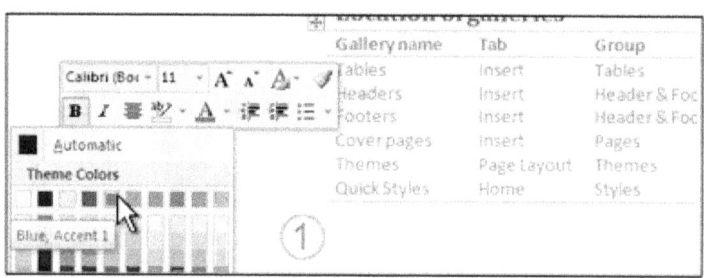

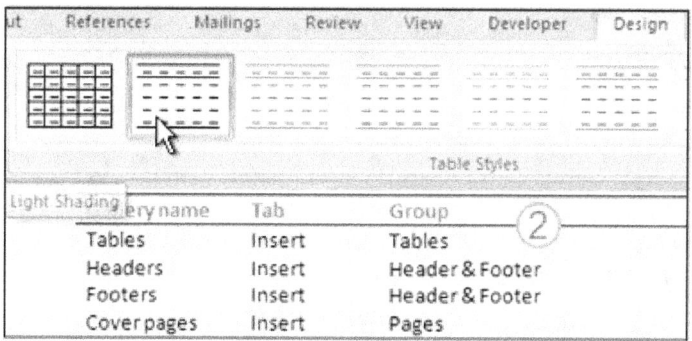

1. You can apply formatting to the content of a table, such as changing the header row to blue.

2. When you switch to a different table style, the header row remains blue.

TIP You can change the selection of table styles in the gallery by selecting or clearing check boxes in the **Table Style Options** section on the **Design** tab, before you open the gallery of table styles. For example, if your table has no header row, and you don't want rows to alternate shading, clear the **Header Row** and **Banded Rows** check boxes. When you open the gallery of table styles, you see previews that do not include formatting for header rows or banded rows.

Applying custom font choices

Applying a theme or a font scheme defines font choices for headings and body text that are designed to go together. The font choices stay in effect regardless of which Quick Style set you choose, until you switch to a different theme or font scheme.

If you want to specify that text be displayed in a particular font regardless of the theme or font scheme, create a custom style. Or you can use direct formatting by selecting the text and applying the font that you want.

NOTE If you don't want the font to update to reflect updates to the theme or font scheme, be sure to format the text with a font whose name is not followed by **(Headings)** or **(Body)**. These are listed as **Theme Fonts** in the gallery of fonts.

1. The fonts that you select among the **Theme Fonts** will be updated to a different font scheme if you apply a different theme or font scheme to the document.

2. Click a font among the **Recently Used Fonts** or **All Fonts** to quickly apply a font that is not subject to changing the theme or font scheme.

Applying custom color choices

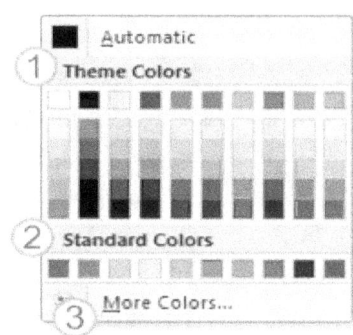

You can apply a color scheme that is designed as a coordinated set of colors. When you define the color of text, you can choose one of the theme colors, or you can select from a range of standard and custom colors.

If you choose a theme color, the color might change if you switch to a different color scheme or theme. However, if you choose a standard or custom color, text is displayed in that color regardless of the color scheme or theme that you apply to the document.

1. Colors that you select from the **Theme Colors** are updated to a different color scheme if you apply a different theme or color scheme to the document.

2. Colors that you select from the **Standard Colors** are not changed even if you apply a different theme or color scheme to the document.

3. Click **More Colors** to select from a wide array of color choices. These colors also are not changed even if you apply a different theme or color scheme to the document.

The bottom layer is the Normal paragraph style. Text formatted as Normal can automatically change its appearance when you switch themes or Quick Style sets. The top layer is direct formatting. If you select a word and apply the standard red color to it, the word remains red no matter what theme, Quick Style set, or style you apply to it.

NOTE   You can see the layers of formatting by using the Style Inspector. On the **Home** tab, in the **Styles** group, click the **Styles** Dialog Box

Launcher. At the bottom of the **Styles** task pane, click **Style Inspector**.

Using Marginal Heading

Closing a Document and Quitting Word

If you're ready to begin work on another document, you can close the active document's window and open another document, or if you're finished working, you can quit Word.

If a document has changes you haven't saved, Word asks if you want to save changes before closing the document or quitting Word. If you choose the Yes button, but haven't yet named the document, Word displays the Save As dialog box. For information on saving a document, see "Saving Your Work," earlier in this chapter.

This type of formatting is easily achieved by giving the heading style a negative left indent (see Figure 2). Be sure you have allowed a large enough left margin to accommodate this "outdent." In this example, with a 1.25″ negative indent, the default left margin of 1.25″ would obviously be inadequate.

In Most software programs

In general, the margins of any document are usually adjusted through the **properties**, **page properties**, or **page layout** of the document. Below are some more specific ways to adjust the margins in the program you may be using.

Microsoft Word and Excel (In Word and Excel 2007 and higher)

In the Microsoft Word or Microsoft Excel ribbon click the **Page Layout** tab and then click the Margins button. Select one of margins or click Custom Margins to specify the margins you want the document to have.

Microsoft Word 2003 and earlier versions

1. Click the **File** menu, then click **Page Setup...**
2. Under the **Margins** heading, enter the desired margin lengths or use the arrow buttons beside each margin to increase or decrease the margins.

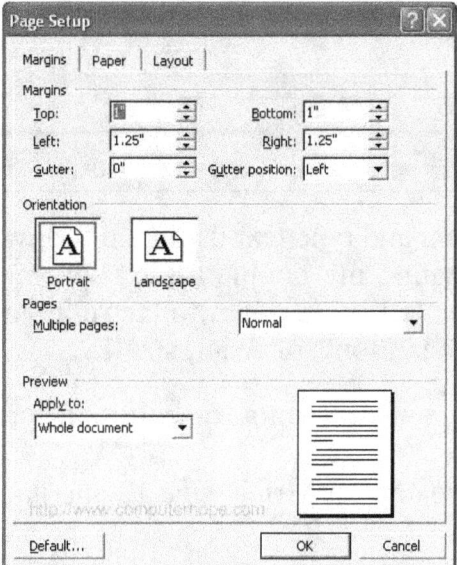

3. Click the **OK** button to set the selected margins.

OpenOffice Writer

To set margins for OpenOffice.org Writer, follow the steps below.

1. Click the **Format** menu, then click **Page**.
2. Under the **Margins** heading, enter the desired margin lengths or use the arrow buttons beside each margin to increase or decrease the margins.

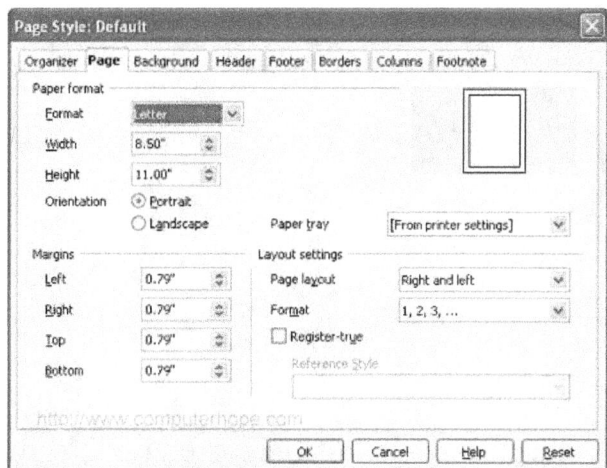

3. Click the **OK** button to set the selected margins.

Exercise II.5.1

Name: _____   Date: _____

Grade and Section: ----------------------.   Score: _____

1. Start the Word program and type text using the following instructions:
   a) Type the following in double line spacing with margins: 1.5"(3.81cm) to the left, 1" (2.54cm)to the right, top and bottom;
   b) The content must be in fonts of Ariel, size 12;

   c) Make the heading font size into 16, bold and format to the center; and
   d) Sub-head should be on Font Ariel , size 12 and italics.

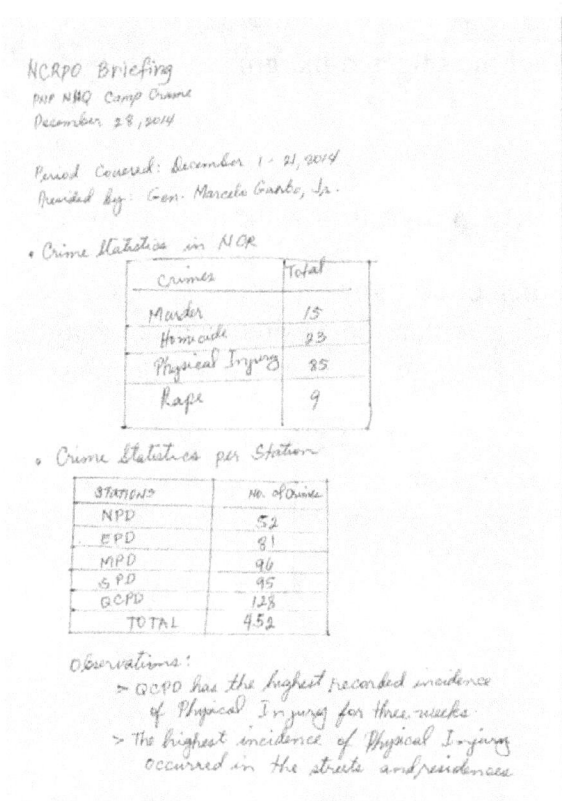

2. Save the document as your lastname exercise 2 and make necessary corrections.

3. Print one copy then close the file.

L esson 7

Manuscripts or Type Notes Rules

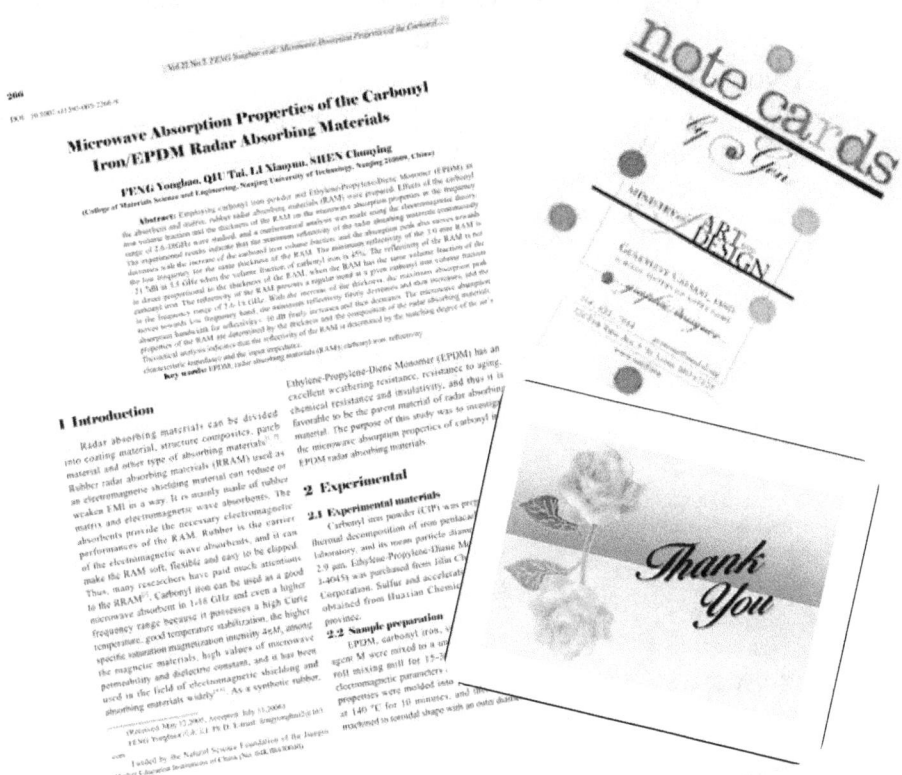

Objective

At the end of this chapter, the student should be able to:
- *prepare typescript based from manuscript or typed notes using accepted rules*
- *create a document in blocked, indented and hanging paragraphs*
- *interpret inset paragraph, abbreviations, typing figures and ellipses*

Application of rules governing paragraphing

For Blocked paragraphs

Tabs are often the best way to control exactly where text is placed. By default, each time you press the Tab key, the insertion point will move **1/2 inch** to the right. By adding **tab stops** to the **ruler**, you can change the size of the tabs, and you can even have more than one type of alignment in a single line. For example, you could **left-align** the beginning of the line and **right-align** the end of the line by adding a **right tab**.

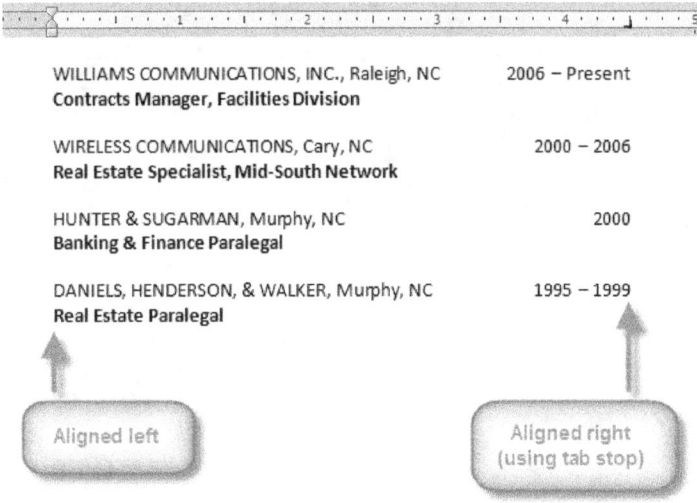

Pressing the Tab key can either add a **tab** or create a **first-line indent**, depending on where the insertion point is. Generally, if the insertion point is at the beginning of an existing paragraph it will create a first-line indent; otherwise, it will create a tab.

The tab selector

The **tab selector** is above the **vertical ruler** on the left. Hover over the tab selector to see the name of the type of **tab stop** that is active.

Types of tab stops include:

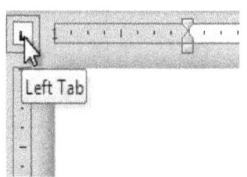

- **Left Tab** ⌊: Left-aligns the text at the tab stop
- **Center Tab** ⊥: Centers the text around the tab stop
- **Right Tab** ⌋: Right-aligns the text at the tab stop

- **Decimal Tab** ⬛: Aligns decimal numbers using the decimal point
- **Bar Tab** ⬛: Draws a vertical line on the document
- **First Line Indent** ⬛: Inserts the indent marker on the ruler and indents the first line of text in a paragraph
- **Hanging Indent** ⬛: Inserts the hanging indent marker and indents all lines other than the first line

Although **Bar Tab**, **First Line Indent**, and **Hanging Indent** appear on the **tab selector**, they're not technically tabs.

To add tab stops:

1. Select the paragraph or paragraphs you want to add tab stops to. If you don't select any paragraphs, the tab stops will apply to the **current paragraph** and any **new paragraphs** you type below it.
2. Click the **tab selector** until the tab stop you want to use appears.
3. Click the **location on the horizontal ruler** where you want your text to appear (it helps to click the **bottom edge** of the ruler). You can add as many tab stops as you want.

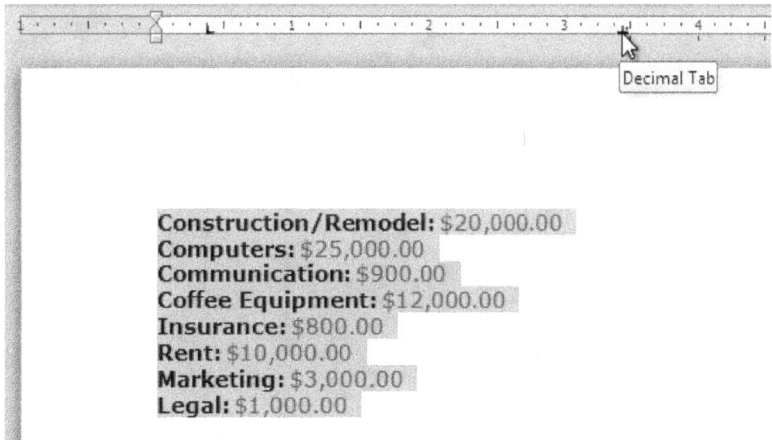

4. Place the **insertion point** where you want to add the tab, then press the **Tab** key. The text will jump to the next tab stop.

Construction/Remodel:	$20,000.00
Computers:	$25,000.00
Communication:	$900.00
Coffee Equipment:	$12,000.00
Insurance:	$800.00
Rent:	$10,000.00
Marketing:	$3,000.00
Legal:	$1,000.00

5. To remove a tab stop, drag it off of the Ruler.

Click the **Show/Hide ¶** command on the **Home** tab in the **Paragraph** group. This will allow you to see nonprinting characters such as the spacebar, paragraph (¶), and Tab key markings.

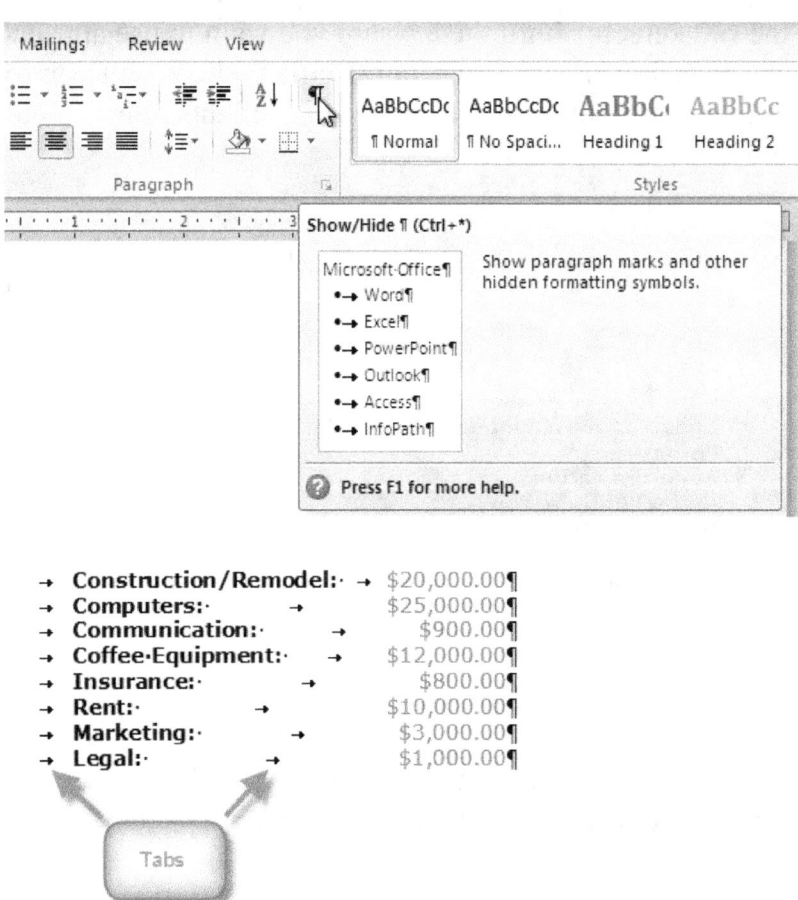

For Hanging Paragraph

Indents and **tabs** are useful tools for making your text more readable. Indenting text adds structure to your document by allowing you to separate information. Depending on your needs, you can use tabs and indents to move a single line or an entire paragraph.

In many types of documents, you may want to indent only the **first line** of each paragraph. This helps to **visually separate** paragraphs from one another. It's also possible to indent every line **except the first line**, which is known as a **hanging indent** or **a hanging paragraph**.

Dear Mr. Powell:

Thank you for taking the time to meet with me last Thursday abⅰ
enjoyed meeting with you and touring the facility. I was ⅰ
the showroom and with the competence of the staff at Qⅰ
chance to work in such a productive and supportive atm

As we talked about in our meeting, my fourteen years of sales exⅰ
floor sales and in the role of Sales Supervisor, would greⅰ
that time, I have learned many techniques that would inⅰ
satisfaction ratings at Quality Furnishings.

In addition, I wanted to let you know that I have recently receiveⅰ
Sales Training program at the National Business Instituteⅰ
program are sure to bolster sales. I look forward to havⅰ
Quality Furnishings.

To indent using the Tab key:

A quick way to indent is to use the **Tab** key. This will create a first-line indent of 1/2 inch.

1. Place the insertion point **at the very beginning** of the paragraph you want to indent.

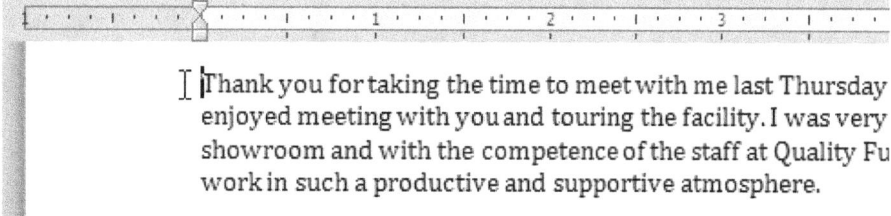

2. Press the **Tab** key. On the ruler, you should see the **first-line indent marker** move to the right by 1/2 inch.

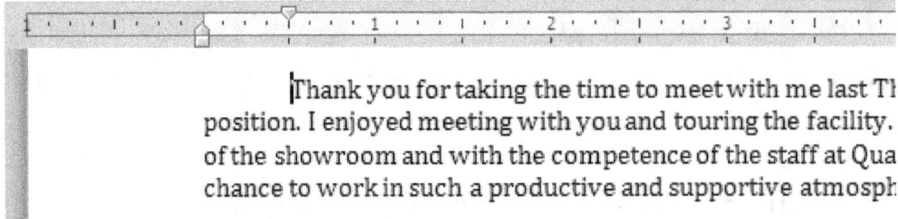

If you can't see the ruler, click the **View Ruler** icon over the scrollbar to display it.

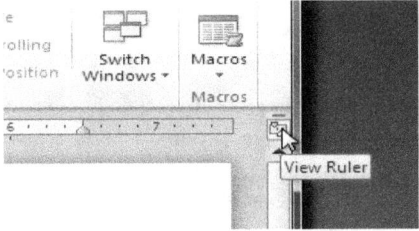

To create or adjust a first-line indent or hanging indent:

1. Place the **insertion point** anywhere in the paragraph you want to indent, or select one or more paragraphs.
2. To adjust the first-line indent, drag the **first-line indent marker** on the ruler.
3. To adjust the hanging indent, drag the **hanging indent marker**.
4. To move both markers at the same time, drag the **left indent marker**. This will indent all lines in the paragraph.

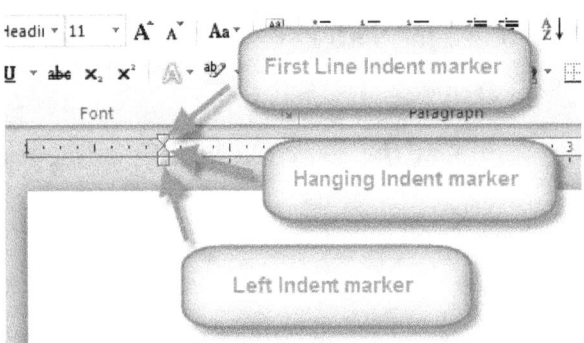

To use the Indent commands:

If you want to indent all lines in a paragraph, you can use the **Indent commands** on the Home tab.

1. Select the text you want to indent.
2. Make sure you are on the **Home** tab.
3. Click the **Increase Indent** command to **increase** the indent by increments of **1/4 inch**.

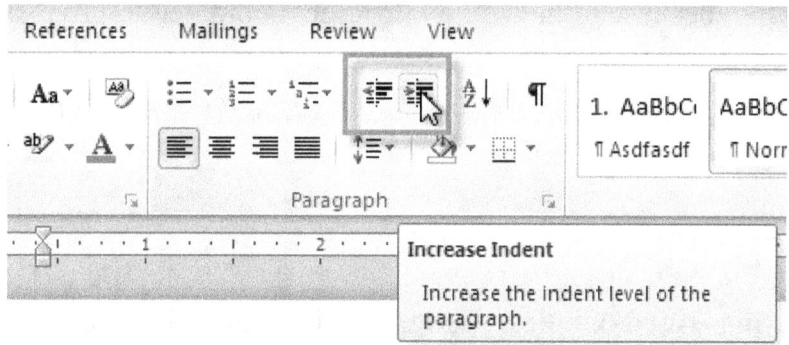

4. Click the **Decrease Indent** command to **decrease** the indent by increments of **1/2 inch**.

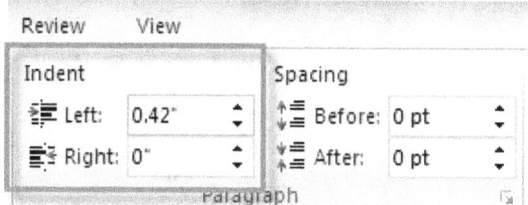

If you would prefer to type your indent amounts, you can use the **Indent fields** on the **Page Layout** tab.

Abbreviations are short forms of lengthy expressions. Abbreviations are in use in almost every discipline and area of life from commonly used abbreviations like names, place and so on.

Example:

Mr. for Mister

Sgt. for Sergeant

Acronyms

Short version of a word or phrase that contains parts of the full word. For example, the **acronym** PCMCIA is much easier to read and remember than "Personal Computer Memory Card International Association". The PCMCIA acronym is also referred to as "People Can't Memorize Computer Industry Acronyms" because of how many different computer acronyms there are

Refer to Index part of this book on Table 2 for the List of Commonly Used Abbreviations and acronyms.

Typing Figures

In Editing Hard Copies, Editors and proofreaders' marks are used in two different stages in the publishing process:

1. Before the copy (text) goes to the designer or typesetter. This is the copyediting stage, when your editor suggests corrections and revisions and asks about (or "queries") possible problems. If your editor requests hard copy, send a clean printout to the editor at the beginning of the project. Copyediting marks often go directly above the individual line or text being altered, so your document should be double-spaced with generous margins.

2. After the designer has finished laying out your text. At this stage you're given a proof – maybe a series of proofs - to check for mistakes and omissions. The symbols used to mark your changes are much the same as the ones used I the first stage. But since text in proofs is single-spaced, most of the symbols appear *in the margin* next to the line of text to be altered. The editors or proofreaders usually used common symbols for correction in editing.

Carets (∧) strikeouts, underlines circles and dots in the text itself show where each change is supposed to go. If there is more than 1 mistake in a line, separate the correction symbols in the margin with slash marks. If a necessary addition is longer than ten words or so, type it up as a double-spaced insert on a

Separate page.

Remember that this period is for catching errors, not for rewriting or revising. After marking text or proofs, reread your corrections to make sure they'll be clear to everyone who's working on the project.

Common Correction Symbols

INSERTIONS (*Note:* Put caret mark [ˌ] in text to show where insertion should go.)

⊙ insert period

⋀ insert comma

⋀ insert semicolon

⋀ insert colon

∨ or ∨ insert quotation mark

∨ or ∨ insert apostrophe or single quotation mark

? insert question mark

! insert exclamation mark

∨ or =/ insert hyphen

/ insert slash

(or) insert parenthesis

[or] insert square bracket

insert space between words

Insert 12a insert added text (more than 10 words or so) found on separate sheet. Put a caret in original text to show where insert goes; label insert by page number (e.g., first insert on p. 12 is "12A").

DELETIONS AND REPLACEMENTS

ℐ deletes the letter or word

⌒ close up (delete un⌒needed space)

ℐ delete and close up

ℐ delete and leave open

sp spell out circled text (or, if it's already spelled out, don't spell it out)

stet let stand all matter above dots

TYPE STYLE

lc lowercase letter

cap cAPITAL LETTER

clc LOWERCASE with initial capital

rom set in roman (plain) type

ital set in italic type

bf set in boldface type

bf ital set in boldface italic type

POSITION OF COPY

] move right

[move left

⊓ move up

⊔ move down

][center

‖ align vertically

= align horizontally

¶ Begin a new paragraph here *or:*

⌐Begin a new paragraph here

no ¶ No paragraph here. Run in.

∫ start next line here

or ∪ transpose: reorder marked or letters words

#⟩——— add a blank line ("line space")

Ellipses —those little dots in the middle of a sentence—can be mystifying. Their purpose is to let the reader know that some part of a quotation has been left out.

Sometimes, text is omitted from the middle of a sentence. The missing text is indicated with three ellipses:

Original: He came home, with dogs and parakeet in tow, just in time for supper.

With text omitted: He came home . . . just in time for supper.

Sometimes, the missing text occurs within two or more sentences. In that case, four dots are used—a period and three ellipses—to signal that the gap in text includes the end of one sentence and the beginning of another:

Original: He arrived just in time for dinner. Unbeknownst to the rest of the family, he had brought his roommates along.

With text omitted: He arrived just in time for dinner. . . . he had brought his roommates along.

Note that since the first dot is a period, there should be no space between the last word of the first sentence and the first dot. Some prefer to capitalize the first letter after the ellipses if what follows is an independent clause. So the example above would read as follows:

He arrived just in time for dinner. . . . He had brought his roommates along.

And what about punctuation other than a period? Other forms of punctuation can be included when doing so helps the reader understand the sentence. Whether it goes before or after the ellipses depends on whether it comes before or after the omitted text in the original quotation.

Here's an example where a semicolon is kept:

Original: He arrived just in time for a sumptuous dinner of broccoli and peanuts; his roommates didn't find the meal quite so appealing.

With text omitted and semicolon retained: He arrived just in time for a sumptuous dinner . . . ; his roommates didn't find the meal quite so appealing.

If instead, we insert ellipses for the missing text and don't retain the punctuation, we would be left with two independent clauses but no conjunction or punctuation to guide the reader.

Here's an example where a comma is retained—this time after the ellipses:

Original: He arrived in time to help out with dinner, but his sister had already assembled the casserole.

With text omitted and comma retained: He arrived in time . . . , but his sister had already assembled the casserole.

Sometimes, punctuation is retained so that the author's meaning isn't compromised:

Original: She found a cockroach in the stew!—much to her horror and hardly the impression she wanted to leave of her culinary skills.

With text omitted and exclamation point and em-dash retained: She found a cockroach in the stew!—hardly the impression she wanted to leave of her culinary skills.

It's usually clear on first reading whether retaining the punctuation makes sense.

Typically, *ellipses are used only within a quotation, not at the beginning or at the end of a quotation.* A rare exception would be an instance where the sentence could otherwise be misinterpreted

<u>Summary</u>

Application of rules governing paragraphing

<u>For Blocked paragraphs</u>

Tabs are often the best way to control exactly where text is placed. By default, each time you press the Tab key, the insertion point will move **1/2 inch** to the right. By adding **tab stops** to the **ruler**, you can change the size of the tabs, and you can even have more than one type of alignment in a single line. For example, you could **left-align** the beginning of the line and **right-align** the end of the line by adding a **right tab**.

<u>For Hanging Paragraph</u>

Indents and **tabs** are useful tools for making your text more readable. Indenting text adds structure to your document by allowing you to separate information. Depending on your needs, you can use tabs and indents to move a single line or an entire paragraph. In many types of documents, you may want to indent only the **first line** of each paragraph. This helps to **visually separate** paragraphs from one another. It's also possible to indent every line **except the first line**, which is known as a **hanging indent or a hanging paragraph**.

<u>**Abbreviations**</u> are short forms of lengthy expressions. Abbreviations are in use in almost every discipline and area of life from commonly used abbreviations like names, place and so on

<u>**Ellipses**</u> are those little dots in the middle of a sentence — can be mystifying. Their purpose is to let the reader know that some part of a quotation has been left out. They are used only within a quotation, not at the beginning or at the end of a quotation.

Activity

Type out the following document using the following instructions

1. Use letter size paper
2. Margins left 2cm right 2cm (top and bottom preset)
3. Spacing '0; - '0', Line spacing 1.5
4. Calibri font size 12
5. Your title for the document is 'Editing Hard Copies' type in Bold, font size 14 and center on paper. Leave two spaces before the following paragraph
6. On the other side of the paper are editing symbols and their meanings, please use these to help complete the task.
7. **Highlight all your corrections/changes using 15% gray shading**
8. Your name in the footer of the document
9. Save as 'Editing Hard Copies'
10. Print your work

Editors' and proofreaders marks are used in two different stages in the publishing process.

1. Before the copy (text) goes to the designer or typesetter. This is the copyediting stage, when your editor suggests corrections and revisions and asks about (or "queries" possible problems. If your editor requests hard copy, send a clean printout to the editor at the beginning of the project. Copyediting marks often go directly above the individual line of text being altered, so your document should be double-spaced with margins generous.

2. After the designer has finished laying out your text. At this stage you're given a proof—maybe a series of proofs to check for mistakes and omissions.

The symbols used to mark your changes are much the same as the ones used in the first stage. But since text in proofs is single-spaced, most of the symbols appear out in the margin next to the problem line, next to the line of text to be altered.

Carets (ʌ), strike outs, underlines, circles, and dots in the text itself show were each change is supposed to go. If there is more than 1 mistake in a line, separate the correction symbols in the margin with slash marks. if a necessary addition is longer than ten words or so, type it up as a double spaced insert on a separate page.

Remember that this period is for catching errors, not for making rewrites or revising. After marking text or proofs, reread your corrections to make sure they'll be clear to everyone who's working on the project.

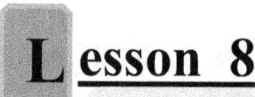

Lesson 8

Documentation

http://www.computerhope.com

Objective

At the end of this chapter, the student should be able to:

➢ *produce a professionally finished document*
➢ *to check the grammar and spelling of each document*
➢ *apply correct usage of punctuation and abbreviations*

Proper **punctuation** is an essential part of successful communication, remembering basic punctuation rules will make it easier for you to write clearly and effectively.

How to Use English Punctuation Correctly

With the dawn of the Internet, the birth of Internet slang, and the growing use of SMS, many of us are starting to forget the fundamental aspects of English punctuation. Proper punctuation usage is a must. Consider this article a crash course in English punctuation and See Step 1 below to get started!

Part 1: Using Proper Capitalization

Always start a sentence with a capital letter. Unless you're an avant-garde poet, you will need to capitalize the first letter of every sentence without exception. Usually, the capitalized form of a letter is just a bigger version of that letter, though there are exceptions (such as "q" and "Q").

- *Here is an example* of proper capitalization at the beginning of a sentence:
  She invited her friend over after school.

Use capital letters to start proper nouns and titles. In addition to starting sentences, capital letters should also be at the start of both proper nouns and titles. Proper nouns are the official names of specific people, places, and things. Titles, which are a type of proper noun, refer to the official names of works of art like books, movies, plays, and so on, and of institutions, geographical areas, and much more. Titles can also be honorifics (Her Majesty, Mr. President, etc.).

- Titles and proper nouns that are more than one word long should have every word capitalized, except for small words and articles like "the," "an," "and," etc. The first word of a title should be capitalized regardless of what it is.
- Here are a few examples of capital letters being used for proper nouns and titles:
  Genghis Khan quickly became the most powerful man in Asia, if not the world.
  In her opinion, Queen Roberta's favorite museum in the world is the Smithsonian, which she visited during her trip to Washington, D.C., last year.

Use capital letters for acronyms. An acronym is a word formed from the first letter of every word in a long proper noun or title. Acronyms are frequently used to shorten long proper nouns that would be awkward to reprint in their entirety every time they are mentioned. Sometimes the letters of an acronym are separated by periods, though this is not always the case.

- *Here is an example* of acronyms made from capital letters:
*The **CIA** and the **NSA** are just two of the **USA's** many intelligence agencies.*

Part 2: Using End-of-Sentence Punctuation Marks

Use a period (full stop) to end declarative sentences and statements. Every sentence contains at least one punctuation mark - the one at its end. The most common of these sentence-ending punctuation marks is the period (".", also called "full stop"). This simple dot is used to mark the end of a sentence that is *declarative*. The majority of sentences are declarative - any sentence that states a fact, explains an idea, or describes an idea, for instance, is declarative.

- *Here is an example* of a period (full stop) being used correctly at the end of a sentence:
The accessibility of the computer has increased tremendously over the past several years.

Use a question mark to end questions. The question mark ("?"), used at the end of a sentence, denotes that the sentence was an interrogative sentence - basically, a question. Use this punctuation mark at the end of all your questions, queries, and inquiries.

- *Here is an example* of a question mark being used correctly at the end of a sentence:
What has humanity done about the growing concern of global warming?

Use an exclamation point to end exclamatory sentences. The exclamation point ("!", also called an "exclamation mark" or "shout mark") suggests excitement or strong emphasis in the preceding sentence. The exclamation point is also used, appropriately, to end exclamations - short expressions of intense emotion that are often only one word long.

- *Here are two examples* of an exclamation point being used correctly at the end of a sentence:
I can't believe how difficult the exam was!
Eek! You scared me!

Part 3: Using Commas

Use a comma to indicate a break or pause within a sentence. The comma (",") is a very versatile punctuation mark - there are dozens of instances that might require you to use a comma in your writing. Perhaps the most frequent use of commas is to imply an appositive - a break within a sentence that supplements and adds information to the subject.

- *Here is an example* of commas being used to create a break in a sentence:
Bill Gates, CEO of Microsoft, is the developer of the operating system known as Windows.

Use the comma when listing items in a series. Another very common use for commas is to separate items that are being listed in sequence. Usually, commas are written between each of the items and between the second-to-last item and a conjunction.

- However, many writers omit the comma before the conjunction (called a Serial comma or "Oxford comma") as conjunctions like "and" can usually make the meaning of the list clear with or without the preceding comma.
- *Here are two examples* of commas used in listed series of items - one with an Oxford Comma and one without.
The fruit basket contained apples, bananas, and oranges.
The computer store was filled with video games, computer hardware and other electronic paraphernalia.

Use a comma to separate two or more adjectives describing a noun. Sometimes, multiple adjectives are used in a row to describe a single subject using multiple qualities. This usage of commas is somewhat similar to using commas to separate items in a series, with one exception - it is **incorrect** to place a comma after the final adjective.

- *Here are examples* of correct and incorrect comma usage when it comes to separating adjectives:
  CORRECT - *The powerful, resonating sound caught our attention.*
  INCORRECT - *The powerful, resonating, sound caught our attention.*

Use a comma to separate one geographical area from another that is located inside. Specific geographical places or areas are usually named by starting with the most precise location name and then proceeding outwards. For instance, you might refer to a specific city by naming the city itself, followed by the state it is in, followed by the country, and so on. Each geographic descriptor is followed by a comma. Note that commas are also used *after* the final geographical area if the sentence continues.

- *Here are two examples* of correct comma usage when it comes to naming geographical areas:
  I am originally from Hola, Tana River County, Kenya.
  Los Angeles, CA, is one of the largest cities in the United States.

Use a comma to separate an introductory phrase from the rest of the sentence. An introductory phrase (which is usually one or more prepositional phrases) briefly introduces the sentence and provides context, but is not part of the sentence's subject or predicate. Therefore, it should be separated from the main clause by a comma.

- *Here are two examples* of sentences with introductory phrases separated from the rest of the sentence by commas:
  After the show, John and I went out to dinner.
  On the back of my couch, my cat's claws have slowly been carving a large hole.

Use the comma to separate two independent clauses. Having two independent clauses in a sentence simply means that you can split the sentence into two separate ones while preserving the original meaning. If your sentence contains two independent clauses that are separated by a conjunction (such as *and, as, but, for, nor, so,* or *yet*), place a comma before the conjunction.

- *Here are two examples* of sentences containing independent clauses:
  Ryan went to the beach yesterday, but he forgot his sunscreen.
  Water bills usually rise during the summer, as people are thirstier during hot and humid days.

Use a comma when making a direct address. When calling one's attention by saying their name at the start of a sentence, separate the person's name and the rest of the statement with a comma. Note that this comma is somewhat rare to encounter in writing because this is something that is normally only done while speaking. In writing, it's more common for the writer to indicate who is speaking to whom via other methods.
Here is an example of a direct address:

Amber, could you come here for a moment?

Use a comma to separate direct quotations from the sentence introducing them. A comma should come after the last word *before* a quotation that is being introduced with via context or description provided by the rest of the sentence. On the other hand, it is **not** necessary to use a comma for an indirect quote - in other words, if you are paraphrasing a quote's meaning without recreating the precise wordage. Additionally, a comma is usually not necessary if you are not quoting an entire statement, but only a few words from it.

- *Here is an example* of a *direct* quotation that requires a comma:
  While I was at his house, John asked, "Do you want anything to eat?"
- *Here is an example* of an *indirect* quotation that does not require a comma:
  While I was at his house, John asked me if I wanted anything to eat.
- *Here is an example* of a *partial* direct quotation, which, due to its brevity and its use within the sentence, doesn't require a comma:

According to the client, the lawyer was "lazy and incompetent."

Part 3: Using Colons and Semicolons

Use a semicolon to separate two related but independent clauses. The proper use of a semicolon is similar, but not identical, to that of a period. The semicolon marks the end of one independent clause and the start of another within a single sentence. Note that, if the two clauses are very wordy or complex, it is better to use a **period (full stop)** instead.

- *Here's an example* of a semicolon being used correctly:
  People continue to worry about the future; our failure to conserve resources has put the world at risk.

Use a semicolon to separate a complex series of items. Usually, the items in a written list are separated by commas, but for lists in which one or more items require comment or explanation, semicolons can be used in conjunction with commas to keep the reader from becoming confused. Use semicolons to separate items and their explanations within the list from one another - to separate an item from its own explanation and vice versa, use a comma.

- *Here's an example* of semicolons being used correctly in a list whose meaning might otherwise be ambiguous:
  I went to the show with Jake, my close friend; his friend, Jane; and her best friend, Jenna.

Use the colon to introduce a list. Be careful, however, not to use a colon when stating an idea that requires naming a **series** of items. The two are similar, but distinct. Usually, the words *following* or "below" suggest the use of a colon. Use only after a full sentence which ends in a noun.

- *Here's an example* of a colon being used correctly in this fashion:
  The professor has given me three options: to retake the exam, to accept the extra credit assignment, or to fail the class.
- Here, on the other hand, is an **incorrect** example:
  The Easter basket contained: Easter eggs, chocolate rabbits, and other candy.

Use a colon to introduce a new concept or example. Colons can also be used after a descriptive phrase or explanation to imply that the next piece of information will be the thing being described or explained. It can help to think of this as *introducing a list containing only one item.*

- *Here's an example* of a colon being used properly in this way:
  There's only one person old enough to remember that wedding: grandma.

Use a colon to separate parts of a title. Some works of art, particularly books and movies, can have long, subdivided titles. In these cases, each title after the first is called a *subtitle.* Use colons at the end of each "part" of the title to separate each subtitle from the rest of the title.

- Here's an example of colons being used in this way to subdivide two lengthy titles:
  Fred's favorite movie was The Lord of the Rings: The Fellowship of the Ring, *though Stacy preferred its sequel,* The Lord of the Rings: The Two Towers.

Part 5 : Using Hyphens and Dashes

Use a hyphen when adding a prefix to some words. The purpose of this hyphen is to make the word easier to read. For instance, if you were to leave the hyphen out of a word like *re-examine,* it would be *reexamine,* which confuse readers. However, some words do not require a hyphen to separate the prefix from the word, such

as *restate, pretest,* and *undo.* Let a dictionary be your guide for when to use the hyphen after a prefix.

- *Here's an example* of good hyphen usage:
  Cara is his ex-girlfriend.

Use hyphens when creating compound words from several smaller words. If you've ever written about anything that's gold-plated, radar-equipped, or one-size-fits-all, you've used a hyphen in this way. To build a long, descriptive word out of two or more component words, use hyphens to separate the "pieces" from each other.

- *__Here's an example__* of a hyphen used to build a compound word:
  The up-to-date newspaper reporters were quick to jump on the latest scandal.

Use a hyphen when writing numbers out as words. Separate the two words of any number under one hundred with a hyphen. Be careful with spelling out numbers above one hundred — if the number is used as an adjective, it is completely hyphenated, since all compound adjectives are hyphenated (*This is the one-hundredth episode.*). Otherwise, a hyphen should only occur if a number lower than 100 occurs within the larger number, e.g., *He lived to be one hundred twenty-one.*

- Don't use "and" when writing numbers, as in "The amount is one hundred *and* eighty". This is a common error in the US and Canada, where the "and" is usually omitted. Elsewhere in the English-speaking world, however, the "and" can be included.
- Here are two examples of hyphens being used in numbers below and above one hundred, respectively:
  There are fifty-two playing cards in a deck.
  The packaging advertised one thousand two hundred twenty-four firecrackers, but it only contained one thousand.

Use a dash when making a brief interruption within a statement. The dash ("--" or "—") is slightly longer than the hyphen and is used to convey a sudden change of thought, an additional comment, or a dramatic qualification within a sentence. It can also be used to add a parenthetical statement, such as for further clarification, but this should still be relevant to the sentence. Otherwise, use parentheses. Keep in mind that the rest of the sentence should still flow naturally.

- To judge whether a dash is appropriate, try to remove the statement within the dash from the sentence. If the sentence appears disjointed or does not make sense, then you may need to revise, rather than using the dash.
- There should be spaces before and after the dash in British English.

- Here are two examples of proper dash usage:

An introductory clause is a brief phrase that comes — yes, you guessed it — at the beginning of a sentence.

This is the end of our sentence — or so we thought.

Use a hyphen to split a word between two lines. Though this use is not as common today, the hyphen ("-") was once a common punctuation mark on typewriters, used when a long word had to be split between two lines. This system is still seen in some books, though computer word processing programs have made this rarer.

Here's an example of a hyphen being used to split a word that's cut into two pieces by a line break:

No matter what else he tried, he just couldn't get the novel's elect- -rectifying surprise ending out of his head.

Part 6: Using Apostrophes

Use the apostrophe together with the letter *s* to indicate possession. **The apostrophe (" ' ") has a variety of uses for conveying the concept of possession. Be aware of the difference in using an apostrophe with singular or plural nouns. A singular noun will use the apostrophe before the "s" ('s), whereas the plural version of that singular noun will use the apostrophe after the "s" (s'). This use comes with several stipulations - see below.**

- Be mindful of nouns that are always considered to be plural, such as *children* and *people* — here, you should use **'s** even though the nouns are plural.

- Also be aware of pronouns that are already possessive and do not require apostrophes, such as *hers* and *its* (*it's* is used only for the contractions of *it is* and *it has*). *Their* is possessive without apostrophe or *s*, except as a predicate adjective, where it becomes *theirs*.

- *Example* of an apostrophe used for showing possession with a singular noun:
  The hamster's water tube needs to be refilled.

- *Example* of an apostrophe used for showing possession with a plural noun:
  In the pet store, the hamsters' bedding needed to be changed.

- *Example* of an apostrophe used for showing possession with a plural noun that doesn't end with "s":

These children's test scores are the highest in the nation.

Use the apostrophe to combine two words to make a contraction. Contractions are shortened combinations of two words. For example, *cannot* becomes *can't*, "it is" becomes "it's", *you are* becomes *you're*, and they have becomes *they've*. In every contraction, the apostrophe replaces the letters that are omitted from one or both words.

- Be sure to use the possessive pronoun *your* and the contraction *you're* for their distinct, separate uses — it is one of the **most common grammar mistakes** to confuse them!
- *Example* of apostrophes used for a contraction of *it is* and a singular noun with possession, while correctly being omitted for possessive pronouns (*hers, theirs, its*):
  *Friends of hers explained that **it's** her idea, not theirs, to refill the hamster's water tube and change its bedding.*

Use the single quotation mark within a regular quotation to indicate a quotation within a quotation. Single quotation marks, which look almost identical to apostrophes, are used to separate quotations from other quotations which surround them. Use these carefully - always make sure every quotation mark you use to start a quote in your sentence is paired with a corresponding one at the end of the quote.

- *Example* of a quote-within-a-quote:
  Ali said, "Anna told me, 'I wasn't sure if you wanted to come!'"

Don't use apostrophes with *s* to make a plural noun from a singular. This is a very common mistake and should be avoided. Remember that apostrophes are used to show possession - not that there are more than one of something.

- *Example* of correct and incorrect apostrophe usage:
  CORRECT - apple → apples
  INCORRECT - apple → apple's

Part 7: Using Slashes

Use the slash to separate *and* and *or*, when appropriate. Slashes (" / ") in phrases like *and/or* suggests the options described are not mutually exclusive.

- *Example* of good and/or usage:
  To register, you will need your driver's license and/or your birth certificate.

Use the slash when quoting lyrics and poetry to denote a line break. Slashes are especially useful when it is impractical to recreate the original formatting of a poem or song. When using slashes in this way, be sure to add spaces between your slashes.

- *Example* of slashes used to mark line breaks in a song:
  Row, row, row your boat / Gently down the stream. / Merrily, merrily, merrily, merrily, / Life is but a dream.

Also use the slash to replace the word *and* to join two nouns. By replacing *and* with a slash, you suggest that there is equal importance to both options listed. Use these replacements in moderation to place greater emphasis where *and* may not do so, as well as to avoid confusing the reader. You can also do the same for *or*, as in *his/her*. However, you should **not** use the slash to separate independent clauses.

- *Example* of how to use and how not to use a slash in this way:
  CORRECT
  "The student and part-time employee has very little free time." →
  "The student/part-time employee has very little free time."
  INCORRECT
  "Do you want to go to the grocery store, or would you prefer to go to the mall?" →
  "Do you want to go to the grocery store / would you prefer to go to the mall?"

Part 8: Using Miscellaneous Punctuation Marks

Use the double quotation mark (") to enclose a direct quotation, whether spoke by a person or taken from a written source. Generally speaking, quotation marks are used to denote that the information is a *quote*. In other words, whether you're recreating someone's verbal speech or simply re-writing something that they wrote elsewhere, you'll use quotation marks.

- *Example* of quotation mark usage:

"I can't wait to see him perform!" John exclaimed.
According to the article, the value of the dollar in developing nations is "strongly influenced by its aesthetic value, rather than its face value."

Use parentheses to clarify. Parentheses are often used to explain something that can't be deduced from the rest of the sentence. When using parentheses (" ( ) "), be sure to include the sentence's period *after* the closing parenthesis, except in the case that an entire sentence is within parentheses. Note that sometimes parentheses and commas can be used interchangeably.

- *Example* of parentheses used for clarification:

Steve Case (AOL's former CEO) resigned from the Time-Warner board of directors in 2005.

Use parentheses to denote an afterthought. Parentheses can also be used to contain information that is supplementary to the sentence they are part of. In this case, the line between when to use parentheses and when it is best to start a new sentence can be somewhat murky. A good general rule is to use parentheses for short additions and quips, not complex ideas.

- *Example* of parentheses used for an afterthought. Note that the period (full stop) follows the last parentheses — *not before the first*. Also note that replacing the parentheses with a comma may not be entirely suitable here, while a period or a semicolon may work:
You will need a flashlight for the camping trip (don't forget the batteries!).

Use parentheses for personal comments. One additional usage of parentheses is to contain the writer's direct comments to the reader. Usually, the comments contained in parentheses refer to the preceding sentence. As above, the shorter and simpler the better. If you have to expound at great length or reference several disparate pieces of your writing, it's usually best to start a new sentence.

- *Example* of parentheses used for a personal comment:
Most grammarians believe that parentheses and commas are always interchangeable (I disagree).

Use brackets to signify an editor's note in a regular piece of writing. You can also use brackets (" [ ] ") to clarify or to revise a direct quote so that it appeals to your own writing. Brackets are often used to encompass the word "sic" (Latin for *thus*), suggesting that the previous word or phrase was written "as is", with the error intended to be displayed.

- *Example* of brackets used for clarity in a direct quote. Note that, in this case, *"It was absolutely devastating!"*, for instance, might be the actual quote:
"[The blast] was absolutely devastating," said Susan Smith, a local bystander at the scene of the incident.

Use braces to denote a numeric set in mathematics. Though generally uncommon, braces (" { } ") can also be used in regular writing to indicate a set of equal, independent choices.

- Here are two examples of brace usage - note that the second is exceedingly rare:
The set of numbers in this problem are: { 1, 2, 5, 10, 20 }

Choose your favorite utensil { fork, knife, spoon } and bring it to me.

Using the wrong style of punctuation in the wrong context can cost you a job interview or credibility among your coworkers and peers. When you use correct punctuation in the right context, it signals that you have an eye for detail, care about professionalism and are capable of communicating effectively. There are two types of punctuation that are used in different contexts: open punctuation and closed punctuation. Knowing how and when to use each of these styles will prove useful in your personal and professional life.

Open Punctuation

Open punctuation uses fewer terminal punctuation marks -- periods and other marks that denote the end of a sentence -- as well as fewer commas than closed punctuation. When you think of open punctuation, "minimalism" is the name of the game. When using open style, don't use periods in abbreviations, acronyms or times of day. Avoid using commas where one is optional in a sentence, such as the Oxford comma -- the comma before the conjunction in a list. When in doubt, remove the comma.

When to Use

Most commonly, open punctuation is used for business and cover letters, but only when it is specifically indicated that open style is preferred. When writing such a letter, don't include commas in any of the addresses, dates or titles of individuals. Omit the comma after the salutary greeting -- as in "To Whom It May Concern" -- with no comma or colon afterward. If you're writing a business or cover letter in open style, use block style -- don't indent any of your paragraphs, but rather, your text should be left-justified.

Open Punctuation Examples

When writing in open punctuation style, omit periods and commas in several places where it may seem counterintuitive. Remember that when using open punctuation, you do not use punctuation in times of day or dates. Don't use periods in "am" or "pm." Don't use periods or commas in nicknames, addresses or a person's title. For example, you would say, "AJ Green PhD" instead of "A.J.

Green, Ph.D." When writing an address in an open style letterhead you would do so as follows: Apple grove Business LLC PO Box 58 SPRINGFIELD

Closed Punctuation

In contrast to open punctuation, **closed punctuation** uses commas and periods in a strict manner. Closed punctuation is what you'd typically learn and use in an English classroom. With abbreviations, introductory greetings or a letter closing, you use commas and periods. For example, when you write "Dear Mr. Jones," or sign a letter "Sincerely," you'd use a comma after both phrases, as opposed to open punctuation.

When to Use

Closed punctuation is used in everyday situations, scholarly writing and business writing, unless a posting or business specifically asks for letters to be written in open punctuation. When using closed punctuation, use periods in times of day such as "a.m." Use periods in abbreviations of degrees, a person's title or degree and when using acronyms. For example, you would use periods in instances such as "Ph.D." and "P.O. Box."

Closed Punctuation Examples

In contrast to open punctuation, closed punctuation calls for an abundance of periods and commas. When you denote times of day, use periods in "a.m." and "p.m." Likewise, when referring to nicknames, titles and degrees, use periods and commas. For example, you would say "A.J. Green, Ph.D." and not "AJ Green PhD." It's the exact opposite of open punctuation style. When writing an address for a letterhead, you would do so as follows: Applegrove Business, LLC P.O. Box 58 SPRINGFIELD.

A **grammar checker** is a software program or program feature sometimes found in a program such as a word processor that can be used to help check text for any improper grammar. An example of a software program that includes its own grammar checker is Microsoft Word, which underlines any grammar errors with a green squiggly underline as shown in the picture.

Reminder: Press the F7 function key to start the spelling and grammar checker in Microsoft Word and most word processors.

Spell checker

A software program or program feature designed to locate misspelled words and notify the user of the misspellings. Depending on the **spell checker**, the feature may either auto correct the word or allow the user to select from potential corrections on the misspelled word. In the picture, is an example of wavy red underlines and an example of how spelling errors in Microsoft Word are shown. When running a spell check on a document with red underlines, Word gives suggestions for each misspelled word. The red wavy underline can also be right-clicked to display corrections on the misspelled word.

The spell checker works by comparing every word typed with a list of thousands of correctly spelled words and then uses algorithms to determine the correct spellings. If a word, such as a name is correctly spelled you have the option of adding the word to the list of correctly spelled words.

Although spell checkers have become one of the most commonly used features in many programs, they have also become a hindrance. Some users have become so dependent on spell checkers that their spelling and grammar skills have declined, and they have a difficult time writing anything correctly without using a spell checker.

Tip: The F7 function key is the default key to start the spell check feature in Word and other programs that have spell checking features.

Tip: While spell checkers are a great feature, you should always proofread what you've written before hitting the send, print, or post button. A word may be spelt correctly but is not the word you intended to use

Below are the different methods of spell checking a document in some of the major text editors.

All versions of Microsoft Word have the ability to spell check a document. To spell check a document, follow the steps below.

1. Open Microsoft Word, FrontPage, or Outlook, and the document you want to edit.
2. Press the F7 key.

or

1. Open Microsoft Word, FrontPage, or Outlook, and the document you want to edit.
2. Click Tools
3. Click Spelling and Grammar

Following the above steps will start a spell check on the document you're viewing. Each found spelling error gives options to change the word to one of the available suggestions. If the word is spelled correctly, **Ignore** the word; if the word is misspelled and you believe that this spelling error is made throughout your document, **Change All**; and if you want to change the word to an alternate spelling, click one of the suggestions from the suggestion list and click **Change**.

Note: New versions of Microsoft products also automatically underline any misspelled word in a red squiggly underline, similar to what is shown in the picture. To correct these misspelled words right-click the word and choose the properly spelled word.

Microsoft Notepad and WordPad

Microsoft Notepad and Microsoft WordPad do not have any spell check solution. If you need to spell check a document that has been written in either of these programs, you need to either use one of the online solutions to spell check your document, or open the document in another program such as Microsoft Word.

Corel WordPerfect

All versions of Corel WordPerfect have the ability to spell check a document. To spell check a document, follow the steps below.

1. Open Corel WordPerfect and the document you want to edit.
2. Press Ctrl + F1

or
1. Open Corel WordPerfect and the document you want to edit.
2. Click Tools
3. Click Spell Checker

OpenOffice

You can spell check a document in OpenOffice writer by following the steps below.
1. Open OpenOffice writer and the document you want to edit.
2. Press the F7 key.

or
1. Open OpenOffice writer and the document you want to edit.
2. Click Tools
3. Click Spellcheck

Other text editors

If the text editor you're using is not listed above, try searching the program's online documentation for a spell check solution. You can open the online help for almost any program by pressing the F1 key. If searching the online help finds nothing relating to "spell check", it's likely the program you're using does not support the ability spell check and you should consider an alternate program.

Online solutions

There are several online solutions that users can use to spell check their documents online as well as add-ons that can be added to your web browser to enable you to spell check through your browser.

Summary

Proper punctuation is an essential part of successful communication, remembering basic punctuation rules will make it easier for you to write clearly and effectively.

Open punctuation uses fewer terminal punctuation marks -- periods and other marks that denote the end of a sentence -- as well as fewer commas than closed punctuation. When you think of open punctuation, "minimalism" is the name of the game. When using open style, don't use periods in abbreviations, acronyms or times of day. Avoid using commas where one is optional in a sentence, such as the Oxford comma -- the comma before the conjunction in a list. When in doubt, remove the comma.

Closed punctuation uses commas and periods in a strict manner. Closed punctuation is what you'd typically learn and use in an English classroom. With abbreviations, introductory greetings or a letter closing, you use commas and periods. For example, when you write "Dear Mr. Jones," or sign a letter "Sincerely," you'd use a comma after both phrases, as opposed to open punctuation.

A **grammar checker** is a software program or program feature sometimes found in a program such as a word processor that can be used to help check text for any improper grammar.

Activity

Type the following in double line spacing and shade correction in 25% gray.

(Handwritten manuscript with editing marks)

Margin marks: sp caps / A / A / stet / Authors: / close up / uc / close up # / # / # / o A uc / trs / NP / {} / A NP /NP / A NP / A NP / A

Definition of Copyright [←centre

Copyright is a statutory right to stop others copying or exploiting authors' works in various other ways without permission. Copyright typically lasts for the duration of the author's life plus another 70 years. The copyright, Designs and Patents Act creates several different ~~categories~~ classifications of 'work' in which copyright can exist, and different owners or of works. The principal categories of protected work are:

— Original literary, dramatic, musical or artistic works, including photographs.

• Sound recordings, such as tapes, CDs and digital files such as mp3s; films, television and sound broadcasts, and cable programmes.

• The typographical arrangements of published editions.

— Copyright does not exist in a literary, dramatic, musical or artistic work unless it is original. This means simply that some limited work or effort must have gone into the work by its creator and that it was not copied from another work. Even street directories or television schedules programme can attract copyright as literary works. [Owning the copyright in a work gives the owner the exclusive right to

Anyone who, with the consent of the owner copyright does any of the above acts, infringes the owner's copyright.

1. Copy the work 2. Issue copies to the public 3. Perform, show play the work in public 4. Make adaptation version of the work or do any of the above in relation to an adaptation 5. Broadcast the work or include it in a cable programme service

Place as last paragraph

Editing skills application:

1. Save document as Definition of copyright in your folder then make the following changes.
2. Make the heading font Bookman Old Style, size 16, bold and all uppercase.
3. Change font style of body to Microsoft Sans Serif size 14, Bold.
4. Perform an spelling and grammar check and make corrections.
5. Save changes as Definition of Copyrights 2. Put your name in the footer, print one copy then close the file.

Lesson 9

Typing Speed

Objective

At the end of this chapter, the student should be able t:

➢ *determine the number of words they can typed in every minute*
➢ *calculate their Gross typing speed*
➢ *calculate their accuracy in typing*

As mentioned from the beginning of this Chapter, our aim is to type at least 35 words per minute. To sum up all lessons, we need to put it into practice regularly in order to develop speed and accuracy in typing.

How can we improve typing?

There are different techniques you can do to improve your typing skills. Below is a short list of different ideas and recommendations you can do to help improve your typing. Keep in mind that most people are not going to be able to improve their typing speed overnight.

Proper placement

Learn to type the proper way (no typing with one or two fingers). This means your fingers should be on the home row keys A, S, D, and F with the left hand and J, K, L, and ; with the right hand. Of course if you're on a non-English keyboard or a non-QWERTY keyboard, this may change.

- What fingers are used for what keys on the keyboard?

Type more and practice

Starting off with the most obvious, practicing typing more will obviously help you improve your typing skills. The more you type, the more familiar you are going to become with the computer keyboard, position of the keys, and how your hands should be positioned.

When practicing, keep some of the below things in mind:

1. Try not to look at the keyboard while typing. This is usually the hardest for most people, but is definitely a skill that should be learned. Not having to look at where the keys are on a keyboard can dramatically improve the speed of your typing. If you need help learning to not look at your hands, try putting a large piece of paper over the keyboard that allows your hands to fit under it without you being able to see the keys, or put stickers on each of the keys.
2. Make sure your posture at the computer is good. For example, sit in the upright position with both feet flat on the floor and relax.

Chat

Online chat can be a great place to learn to type and is also usually fun at the same time. If you're really wanting to learn to type more efficiently while chatting, make sure to use proper capitalization, punctuation, and do not use chat slang.

E-mail, online bulletin boards and forums

Sending friends and family frequent e-mail letters can be another great way to learn to type and keep in touch with all your friends and family. In addition to sending e-mail messages, there are millions of online forums with every topic of conversation imaginable. Becoming a member of one of these forums and participating in talking about something you enjoy can also be fun and another great way to learn to type.

Run through online typing tests several times

Run through each of the online typing tests several times to improve your typing, catch errors, and review your progress.

Type pages of a book, letter, or any other page with lots of text

Although not an option that is as fun as some of the other suggestions listed in this document, taking any letter, page of a book, or document and typing everything on that page is a great way to help improve your typing. Not only will this help improve your typing of unfamiliar words, it is also a skill sometimes required for some jobs.

Create your own web page, blog, or online journal

Creating your own web page, blog, or online journal that you frequently update is another great way to practice your typing, while also doing something productive at the same time.

Typing games and programs

Typing games and programs are a great way to learn the position of all the keys on the keyboard and also help you practice your typing. Below is one game and one online typing tutorial that can help with your typing.

QWERTY Warriors

Fun and very addictive game, where you must defend yourself against other people, tanks, robots, and other vehicles by typing the word below it.

TypingWeb

A free online typing tutor program, TypingWeb allows users to learn how to type on their keyboard better and faster. The free tutorial teaches people how to place their hands on the keyboard, learn where keys are and how to type words more quickly. The typing tutorial is available for people of all ages and offers training for people at any level of typing skills.

Example:

www.typing.com

www.indiatyping.com

Below shows how to calculate typing speed and accuracy of your work.

Formula for calculating Typing Speed
Gross Word Per Minute (WPM)

$$\text{Gross WPM} = \frac{\left(\dfrac{\text{All Typed Entries}}{5}\right)}{\text{Time (min)}}$$

www.IndiaTyping.com

All typed entries = Total Key Strokes (or key depression)

Gross WPM is really the typing speed that you typed in one minute its getting by total key Stroke (Key depression) divided by 5 (One word = 5 character) and then divided by total minute to get word per minute speed.

If you type 200 character in 1 minute then your typing speed will be = 200/5 = 40 WPM
But GWPM is not your actual speed, actual speed is calculating by correct word you typed known as 'Net WPM'.
Note: delete, backspace, shift and other keys are not calculated in key stroke.
Net WPM Formula

Gross   typing   speed   is   calculated   as   follows:
1) Total keystrokes (=gross hits) is divided by duration, which gives gross speed in   characters/keystrokes   per   minute
2) Gross speed in CPM is divided by the standard word length to get typing speed in   WPM.

$$\text{Net WPM} = \text{Gross WPM} - \left(\frac{\text{Uncorrected Errors}}{\text{Time (min)}}\right)$$

$$= \frac{\left[\left(\dfrac{\text{All Typed Entries}}{5}\right) - \text{Uncorrected Errors}\right]}{\text{Time (min)}}$$

www.indiatyping.com

The international industrial standards counts typing speed in all English language. For written English, the commonly accepted standard is a 5-stroke standard word, including spaces and punctuation marks.

In result calculation this means that 5 keystrokes make one word and 5 keystrokes are deducted for each mistyped word. If needed, the word length can be changed on the Settings tab *(>Settings>Study settings>Word length)*.

Calculation of Net WPM

Net speed can be calculated by deducting errors in gross wpm.

For example if you typed 40 Word in 1 Minute but you typed 3 word wrong then your Net WPM = 40 - 3 = 37 WPM

Calculation of Errors

Errors are calculated by following two criteria

1. Errors that is corrected

If you correct wrong word that you typed then you will use backspace to delete that word will not calculated in WPM.

2. Errors that are incorrect

If you not correct the errors you made then you will penalize **5** character for each word error *(Regardless of how many character in this wrong word)*. So always try to type accurate and if mistake made then correct it.

Calculation of Accuracy

Accuracy is a ratio of GWPM and NWPM for example if your GWPM = 40 and NWPM = 37 then Accuracy =(37/40)*100 = 92.5%

Example   of   result   calculation:

A user completes a typing test with 1750 keystrokes in 5 minutes and 5 incorrectly typed words. The results are:
- 1750 gross hits, 25 error hits (5 mistakes * word length 5), 1725 net hits
-    Gross   typing   speed   is   70   WPM   (350   CPM)
-    Net   typing   speed   is   69   WPM   (345   CPM)
- Accuracy is 99% (1725/1750*100%)

How long does it take to become proficient at typing?

As with anything, the more you stick with it and practice good habits, the better you'll become. Best-selling author Malcolm Gladwell popularized the idea that 10,000 hours of appropriately guided practice was "the magic number of greatness." With enough practice, he claimed in his book "Outliers", anyone could achieve a level of proficiency that would rival that of a professional. It was just a matter of putting in the time.

Summary

To improve Typing skills, follow the following:

Proper placement
Type more and practice
Online Chat
E-mail, online bulletin boards and forums
Run through online typing tests several times
Type pages of a book, letter, or any other page with lots of text
Create your own web page, blog, or online journal
Typing games and programs
Typing games and programs

Formula for calculating Typing Speed
Gross Word Per Minute (WPM)

$$\text{Gross WPM} = \frac{\left(\dfrac{\text{All Typed Entries}}{5}\right)}{\text{Time (min)}}$$

Activity 1

1. Open and start the Word program.
2. Type exactly the following paragraph within one (1) minute only applying the shortcut keys and other special keys to test your speed and accuracy.

Planet of the Apes

Planet of the Apes is an American science fiction *media franchise* consisting of films, books, television series and other media about a world where humans and intelligent apes clash for control. The series began with French author **Pierre Boulle's** 1963 novel *La Planete des Singes*, translated into English as both *Planet of the Apes* and *Monkey Planet*. The 1968 film adaptation, *Planet of the Apes*, was a critical and commercial success, initiating a series of sequels, tie-ins, and derivative works. **Arthur P. Jacobs** produced the series under APJAC Productions until his death in 1973; since then 20th Century Fox has owned the franchise.

Four sequels followed the original film between 1970 and 1973: *Beneath the Planet of the Apes, Escape from the Planet of the Apes, Conquest of the Planet of the Apes*, and *Battle for the Planet of the Apes*. The series also spawned two television series: *Planet of the Apes* in 1974 and the animated *Return to the Planet of the Apes* in 1975. Plans for a film remake stalled in "development hell" for over ten years before **Tim Burton's** *Planet of the Apes* was released in 2001. A new reboot film series commenced in 2011 with *Rise of the Planet of the Apes*, which was followed by *Dawn of the Planet of the Apes* in 2014; another sequel is planned. All of these versions have in turn led to other media and merchandising tie-ins, including books, comics, video games, and toys.

Planet of the Apes has had a wide influence. It has impacted subsequent films, media and art, as well as popular culture and political discourse.

3. When one (1) minute is gone, save the whole document using the filename Typing2.
4. If you get more than 35 WPM and 80% than will consider as passed in typing test.

Activity 2

1. Open and start the Word program.
2. Type exactly the following paragraph within one (1) minute only applying the right position of your fingers on both hands and the correct posture to test your speed and accuracy.

Around the world today, there are an estimated 35.8 million men, women and children trapped in modern slavery. It is important to note that we are not asserting that there has been an increase in modern slavery around the world over the last year. We believe that this increase is due to the improved accuracy and precision of our measures and that we are uncovering modern slavery where it was not seen before. Five countries are appearing in the Global Slavery Index for the first time: Taiwan, South Sudan, North Korea, Kosovo and Cyprus.

A methodology was developed to measure how governments are responding to modern slavery in 167 countries. A team of researchers collected data against the following five objectives for each country: 1) Survivors are identified, supported to exit and remain out of modern slavery; 2) Criminal justice mechanisms address modern slavery; 3) Coordination and accountability mechanisms for the central government are in place; 4) Attitudes, social systems and institutions that enable modern slavery are addressed. and 5) Businesses and governments through their public procurement stop sourcing goods and services that use modern slavery. In April 2014, the Walk Free Foundation also conducted a survey of 167 governments; information from the 38 responses received was incorporated into relevant country research. Where possible, the Walk Free Foundation researchers verified data obtained through desk review with experts occurred in 60 countries.

A ranking of one in the Index indicates the most severely concentrated modern slavery situation; a ranking of 167 indicates the least severely concentrated modern slavery problem.

3. When one (1) minute is gone, save the whole document using the filename Typing1.
4. If you get more than 35 WPM and 80% than will consider as passed in typing test.

Chapter III

Introduction of Application Software

Highlights:

- Types of Application software
- Wordprocessing application
- Spreadsheet application
- Database application
- Presentation application
- Selection of appropriate software

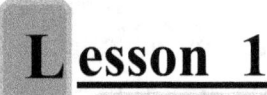

Lesson 1

Types of Application Software

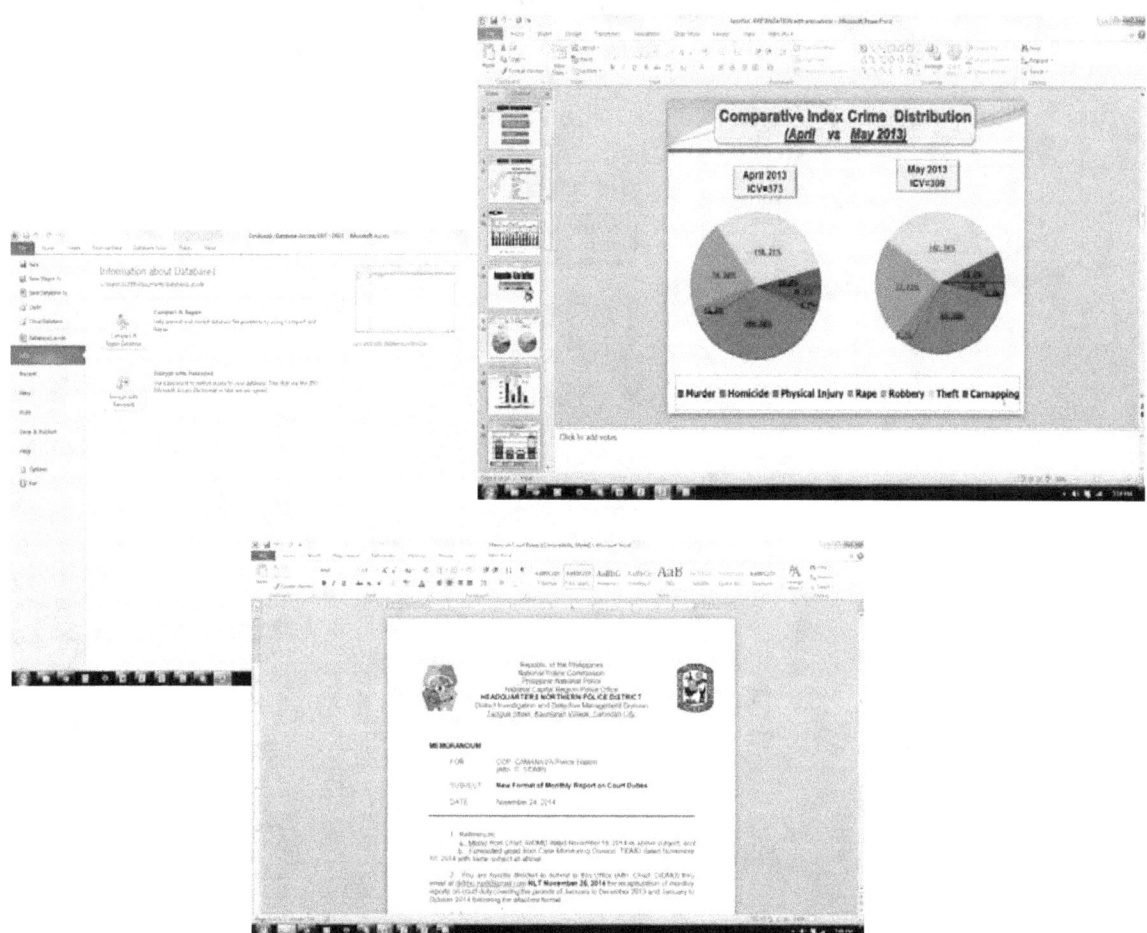

Objective

At the end of this chapter, the student should be able to:
> ➤ *Identify the four categories of application software*
> ➤ *Identify the type of application software use for productivity of documents*

In your previous application software lesson, you have learned the set of one or more programs used to solve a specific problem or do a specific job. You also learned that an application software often used for office productivity.

The diagram below shows how an application software interacts with other software. Microsoft Office is a productivity suite that's largely ubiquitous in work environments around the world that comprises word processing, spreadsheet, database management and many others.

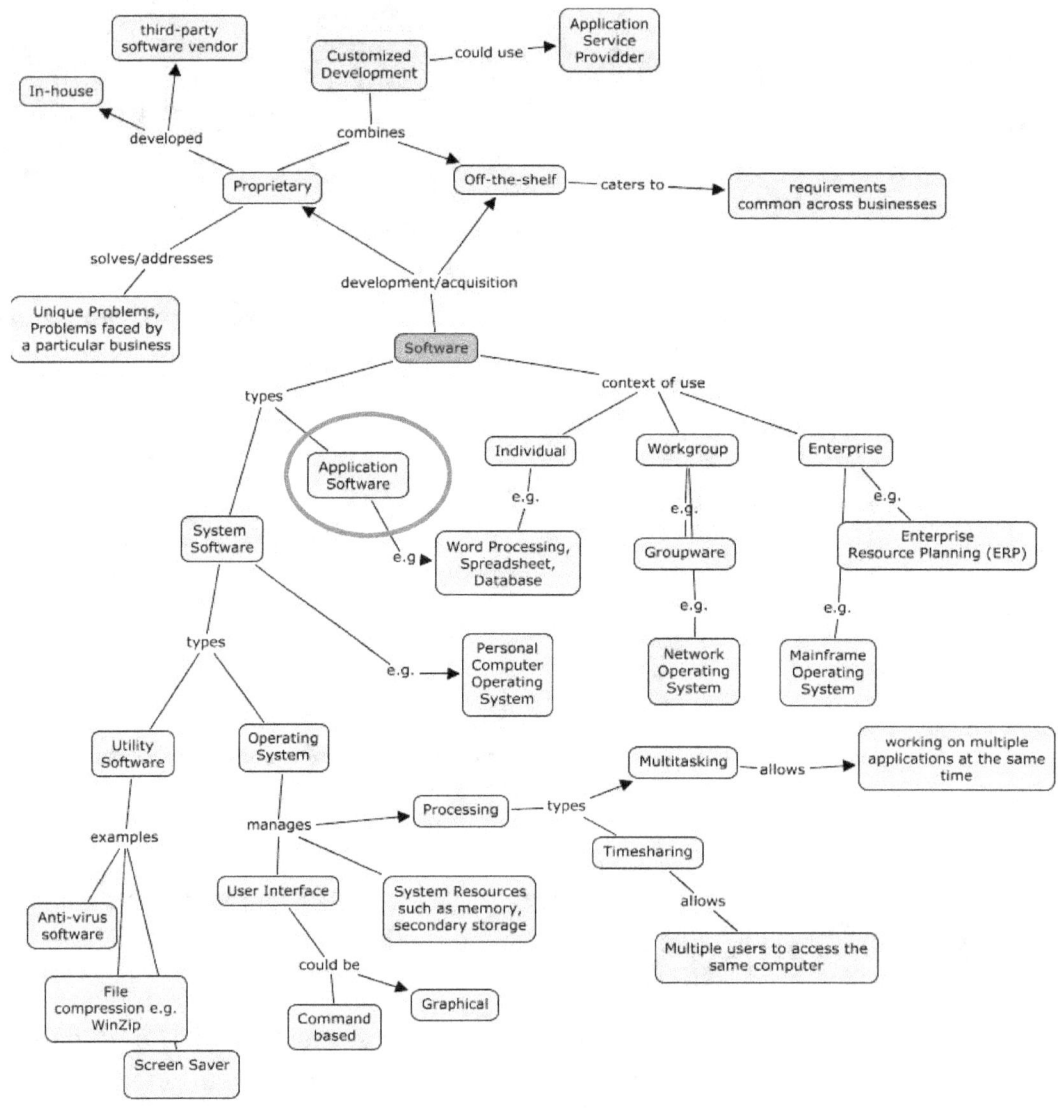

Applications software is written to improve our productivity. It can be classified under 3 main categories: General Purpose software, Specialist software and Tailor made (bespoke) software. The General Purpose applications can be used for a wide variety of tasks e.g. spreadsheets can be used for accounts, sales analysis, forecasting and many others while Specialist application software lacks the flexibility of generic software and is only capable of doing a single task. Accounting software is capable of doing only accounts and so is more restrictive than a spreadsheet.

The strategy, options, and issues are the most important to consider when making decisions for appropriate software choices in your organization. Common General Software includes: Word processing, Spreadsheets, Database management, Graphics, Desktop Publishing (DTP), Presentation, Web page authoring, Web browsing and Email.

Types of Application software

➢ **Word Processing Software** allows you to create, edit, store and retrieve documents. Documents can be letters, invitation, reports, files or essays. When a document is finished, you can store it in the computer's hard disk or external drives such as USB, DVD, CD and so on.

➢ **Spreadsheet Software** allows you to create tables, graphs and organize data into rows and columns. They are useful for predicting how much a business will profit (its income) and what it will spend in a year. Examples of spreadsheet software include Microsoft Excel, Lotus 123 and Quattro.

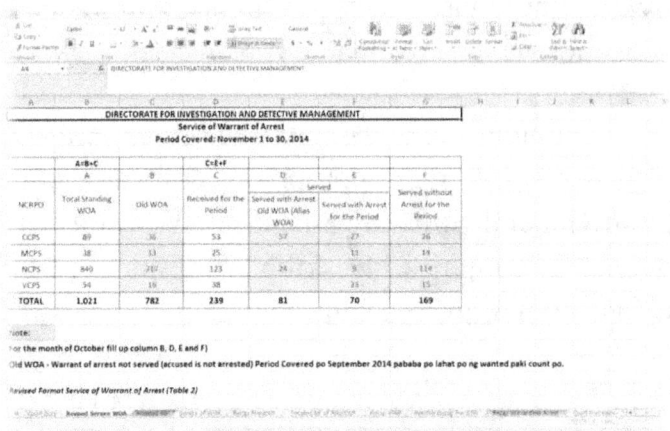

➢ **Presentation** software allows you to create many types of artwork like greeting cards, letterheads, signs, banners, pictures and many more. Examples of graphics software are Print Shop, Photoshop and Microsoft Paint.

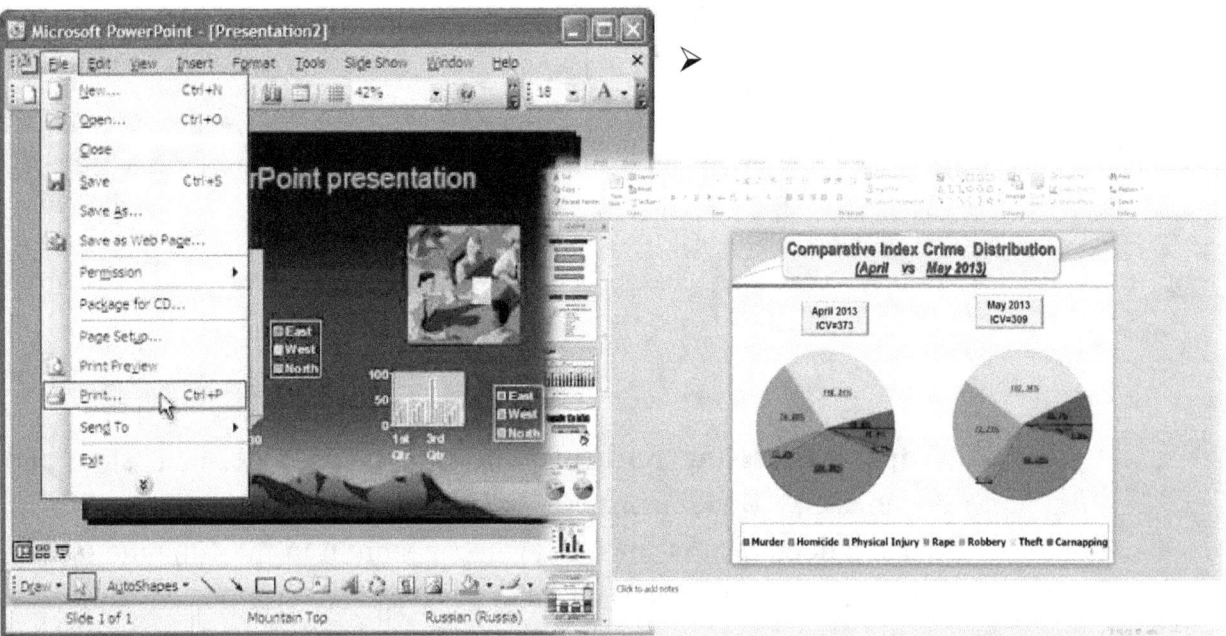

> **Database Management System Software** allows you to keep records electronically . It can be used to store, retrieve (get back) and manipulate large amount of data. Examples of database software include Microsoft Access, Database IV and Foxpro.

> **Communication Software** is a program that will enable you to exchange information and messages with other computers in distant locations. Examples are Microsoft Outlook, Outlook Express and Yahoo and Yahoo! Messenger.

> The communication software is basically the kind of software providing the user with the opportunity to exchange any kind of data through the internet.

Summary

<u>Types of Application software</u>

- **Word Processing Software** allows you to create, edit, store and retrieve documents. Documents can be letters, invitation, reports, files or essays.
- **Spreadsheet Software** allows you to create tables, graphs and organize data into rows and columns. They are useful for predicting how much a business will profit (its income) and what it will spend in a year.
- **Database Management System Software** allows you to keep records electronically . It can be used to store, retrieve (get back) and manipulate large amount of data.
- **Presentation Software** allows you to create many types of artwork like greeting cards, letterheads, signs, banners, pictures and many more.
- **Communication Software** is a program that will enable you to exchange information and messages with other computers in distant locations.

L esson 2

Wordprocessing Application

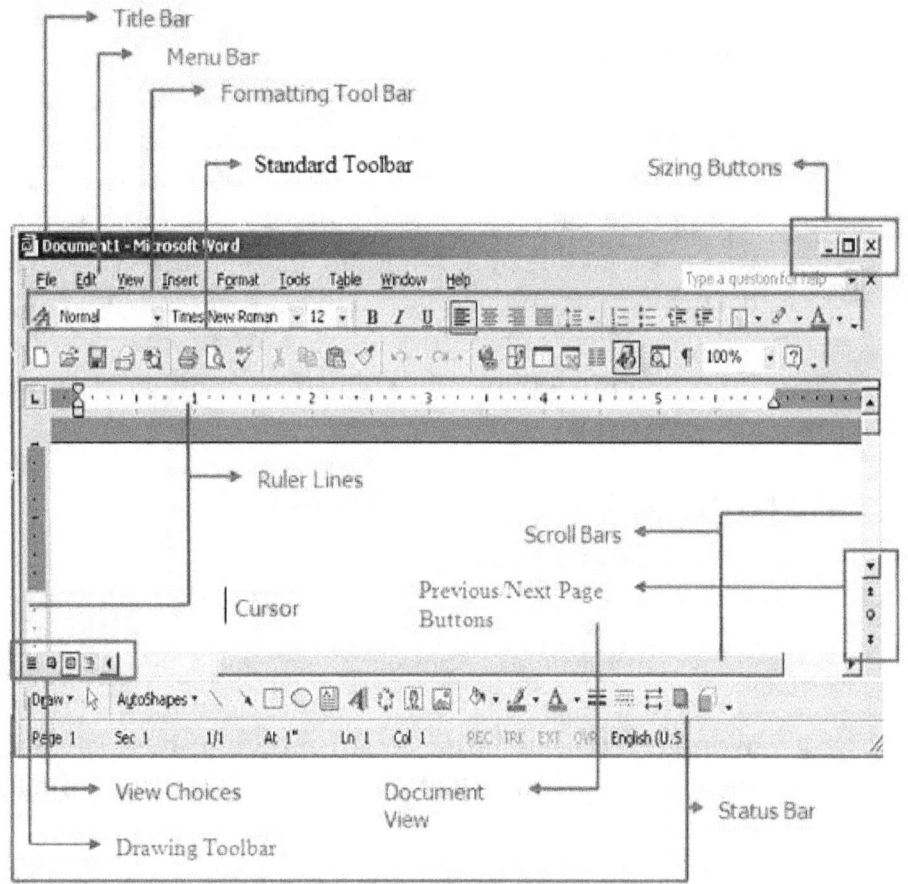

Objective

At the end of this chapter, the student should be able to:
➤ *explain the purpose of word processor.*
➤ *manipulation of data on using word processor.*
➤ *illustrate the features of a work processing application.*

Word-processing

A word processor is an application that allows you to type in, edit, format, save, and print text. The text shows on screen the same or very similar to how it will appear in hard copy format. Word processors are commonly used by students, writers, authors, desktop publishing professionals and layout artists.

Microsoft Word

- One of the most well-known and widely used word processing applications on the market is Microsoft Word. Word has more than 90 percent of the word processing market and more than 450 million users. Microsoft Corp. first released this program to the market in 1989, and since then there have been a number of upgrades to the software. Word can be purchased as part of the Microsoft Office suite of programs, which include Excel, PowerPoint, Outlook and Publisher. Word can be used to format text and build layout documents.

WordPerfect

- WordPerfect is a word processing application from Corel Corp.. WordPerfect was popular in the early 1990s. It is best for writing simple essays and articles. Though it isn't used as much today, WordPerfect is compatible with Microsoft Word, meaning that you can open and edit WordPerfect files in the Word program, then save them as WordPerfect files again. WordPerfect also can be used for formatting and laying out documents.

Lotus Word Pro

- If you use Lotus Notes or Lotus 1-2-3--common in corporate environments--Lotus Word Pro is an ideal program for your word processing needs. This program works in concert with Lotus applications to allow you to create and distribute formatted text documents. It is produced and distributed by IBM Corp. Lotus Word Pro is also compatible with Microsoft Word and ideal for writing reports, memos and proposals.

iWork Pages

- Pages is a word processing program offered by Apple Incorporated, so if you own a Mac computer this might be the ideal option for your needs. It is a part of Apple's iWork suite of programs. Pages allows you to perform basic word processing functions--writing and formatting--as well as more complex graphical layout actions. You can open and save Pages files in Microsoft Word.

And the Rest

- There are dozens of word processors on the market. Other lesser-known word processors include OpenOffice Writer, Adobe InCopy, AbiWord, Microsoft Works and Scrivener. A growing number of online word processors are available and include Google Docs and Microsoft Office Web Apps.

A word processor is a software application that creates, stores and prints documents. Word processors are categorized as application software created to accomplish specific tasks as needed by the user.

<u>Purpose of a word processor</u>

- Unlike an ordinary typewriter, a word processor enables the user to create a document and edit it multiple times before printing it or saving it on the computer. Furthermore, the saved document can be modified at a later date. In a networked setting, the saved document can be opened on another computer.
- Modern word processors offer a lot more functionality than simply creating, editing and storing documents. Some word processors come with tools for creating business documents, whereas others allow for rich text

formatting. A word processor is different from a text editor in that the latter only allows creating and editing of plain text documents. Notepad and WordPad are two popular text editors.

- There are a variety of word processors available, both commercial and free versions. Microsoft Word is a popular commercial word processor that's usually bundled with the Microsoft Office software suite. Other word processors include Corel WordPerfect, Apple iWork, Apple TextEdit, Microsoft Works and Sun Star Office, among others. Free word processors include OpenOffice, Lotus Symphony and AbiWorld.

Uses of Word Processing Programs

If you prefer to work with a red pen in hand, you can print a copy and edit that way. Above all, word processing programs offer you a wide range of control over every aspect of your documents. We can manipulate all text data by the following:

1. Document Input

- Whether you prefer to compose documents as you sit at your computer, or write longhand and input them later, word processing programs are a fact of modern life. In school, you might use them to type assignments and papers. At work, you might use them to type reports, letters, and other documents. If you learned to type on a typewriter, but haven't used a computer much, the keyboard layout is the same one that you've already learned -- the keys merely offer less resistance to your fingers as you type.

-

2. Document Formatting

- A big advantage that word processing programs have over typewriters is the ability to both compose and format your documents using the same program. Not only that, but you can do this and edit your work multiple times before printing a single page. This helps cut down on wasted paper. Line and paragraph spacing, margins, typeface, font size and alignment are just some of the formatting issues you can address via buttons and menus in word processing programs. Click menus along the top menu bar to drop down various options from which to choose. Typeface, font size and alignment are typically accessible just below the menu bar in most word processing programs.

3. Added Features

o Word processing programs allow you to add charts, graphs, tables and images to your documents to enliven the presentation. If your work involves aiming for a target word count, your word processing program offers "Word Count" as an option; this is usually located in the "Tools" menu. If you use an entire word processing suite, such as Microsoft Office, OpenOffice or Apple iWorks, you can usually import items from other in-suite programs, such as the spreadsheet program. Additionally, you can e-mail or share your documents with collaborators via most word processing programs.

4. Spelling and Grammar Checks

o It's unwise to rely on them completely, but spelling and grammar checks in word processing programs offer a second set of eyes -- albeit electronic ones -- to look over your important documents. Criticisms leveled at these checks say that they often leave or introduce errors while giving you a false sense of security in their abilities. Electronic spell-checks, for instance, don't understand context, so may offer incorrect options for synonyms like "there" and

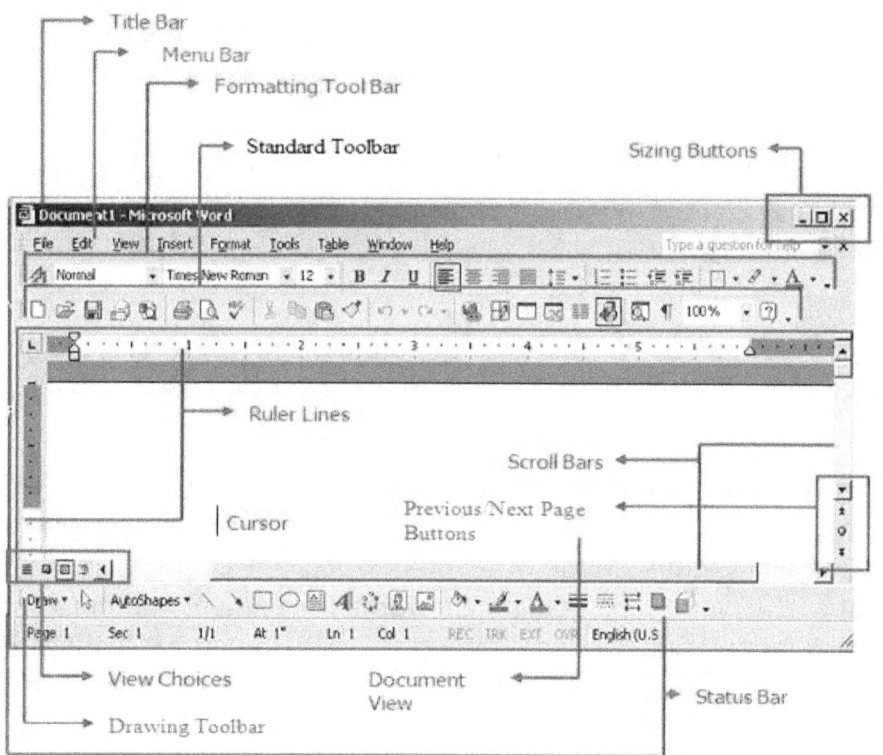

"their." Accuracy varies depending on your program, so keep reference books nearby to check it yourself, or ask your local spelling and grammar expert to check your documents.

Features of word processing

Word processors vary considerably, but all word processors support the following basic features:

Insert text: Allows you to insert text anywhere in the document.

Delete text: Allows you to erase characters, words, lines, or pages as easily as you can cross them out on paper.

Cut and paste: Allows you to remove (cut) a section of text from one place in a document and insert (paste) it somewhere else.

Copy: Allows you to duplicate a section of text.

Page size and margins: Allows you to define various page sizes and margins, and the word processor will automatically readjust the text so that it fits.

Search and replace: Allows you to direct the word processor to search for a particular word or phrase. You can also direct the word processor to replace one group of characters with another everywhere that the first group appears.

Word wrap: The word processor automatically moves to the next line when you have filled one line with text, and it will readjust text if you change the margins.

Print: Allows you to send a document to a printer to get hardcopy. Word processors that support only these features (and maybe a few others) are called text editors. Most word processors, however, support additional features that enable you to manipulate and format documents in more sophisticated ways. These more advanced word processors are sometimes called full-featured word processors. Full-featured word processors usually support the following features:

File management: Many word processors contain file management capabilities that allow you to create, delete, move, and search for files.

Font specifications: Allows you to change fonts within a document. For example, you can specify bold, italics, and underlining. Most word processors also let you change the font size and even the typeface.

Footnotes and cross-references: Automates the numbering and placement of footnotes and enables you to easily cross-reference other sections of the document.

Graphics: Allows you to embed illustrations and graphs into a document. Some word processors let you create the illustrations within the word processor; others let you insert an illustration produced by a different program.

Headers, footers, and page numbering: Allows you to specify customized headers and footers that the word processor will put at the top and bottom of every page. The word processor automatically keeps track of page numbers so that the correct number appears on each page.

Layout: Allows you to specify different margins within a single document and to specify various methods for indenting paragraphs.

Macros: A *macro* is a character or word that represents a series of keystrokes. The keystrokes can represent text or commands. The ability to define macros allows you to save yourself a lot of time by replacing common combinations of keystrokes.

Merges: Allows you to merge text from one file into another file. This is particularly useful for generating many files that have the same format but different data. Generating mailing labels is the classic example of using merges.

Spell checker: A utility that allows you to check the spelling of words. It will highlight any words that it does not recognize.

Tables of contents and indexes: Allows you to automatically create a table of contents and index based on special codes that you insert in the document.

Thesaurus: A built-in thesaurus that allows you to search for synonyms without leaving the word processor.

In Microsoft Office, the Mini Toolbar is a stripped down version of the Font group on the **Home** tab (with changes such as font, underline, bold, and italicize), as well as some other common tools from other groups.

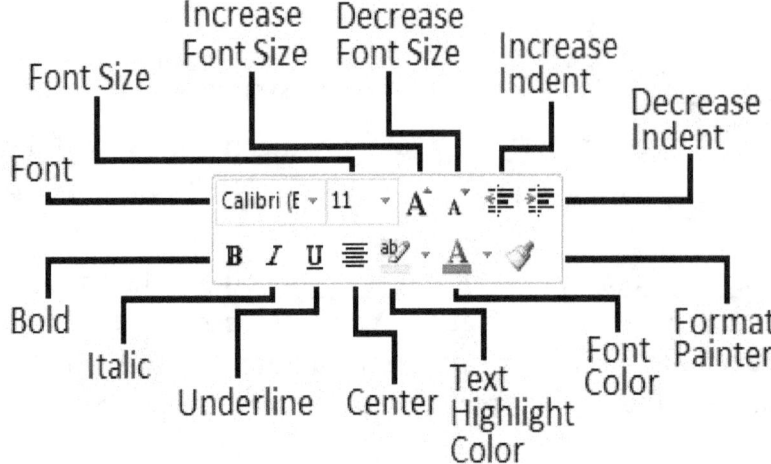

The Mini Toolbar for Microsoft Word 2010 features many options for editing the format of text.

To access the Mini Toolbar, [Right-Click] a section of a Word, Excel, Outlook or PowerPoint document. Or, select an area of text and hover your mouse over the selection. *(Note: The Mini Toolbar may look faint and transparent at first, but becomes solid and usable as you move the mouse over it.)*

You can see a description of each Mini Toolbar button by resting your pointer on it. If you wish to change the font or font size:

1. [Right-Click] the area of the document you want to edit.
2. [Click] FONT or FONT SIZE.
3. Browse the FONT or SIZE options, and select the one you want. *(Note: As you hover over different font and font size options, you'll see a live preview of how that selection will look if the change is made before you make the change.)*

Some users find the Mini Toolbar gets in the way or becomes annoying when it appears as you hover your mouse over a selection.

To disable the Mini Toolbar from popping up:

1. [Click] FILE, and select OPTIONS.
2. Choose the GENERAL tab.
3. Under USER INTERFACE OPTIONS, uncheck SHOW MINI TOOLBAR ON SELECTION, and [Click] OK.

<u>Summary</u>

- A word processor is an application that allows you to type in, edit, format, save, and print text. The text shows on screen the same or very similar to how it will appear in hard copy format.
- Manipulation of text data contains the document input, formatting, added features and spelling and grammar checks.
- Features of a word processing application-can insert, delete and copy text data anywhere in the document.

 L esson 3

Spreadsheet Applications

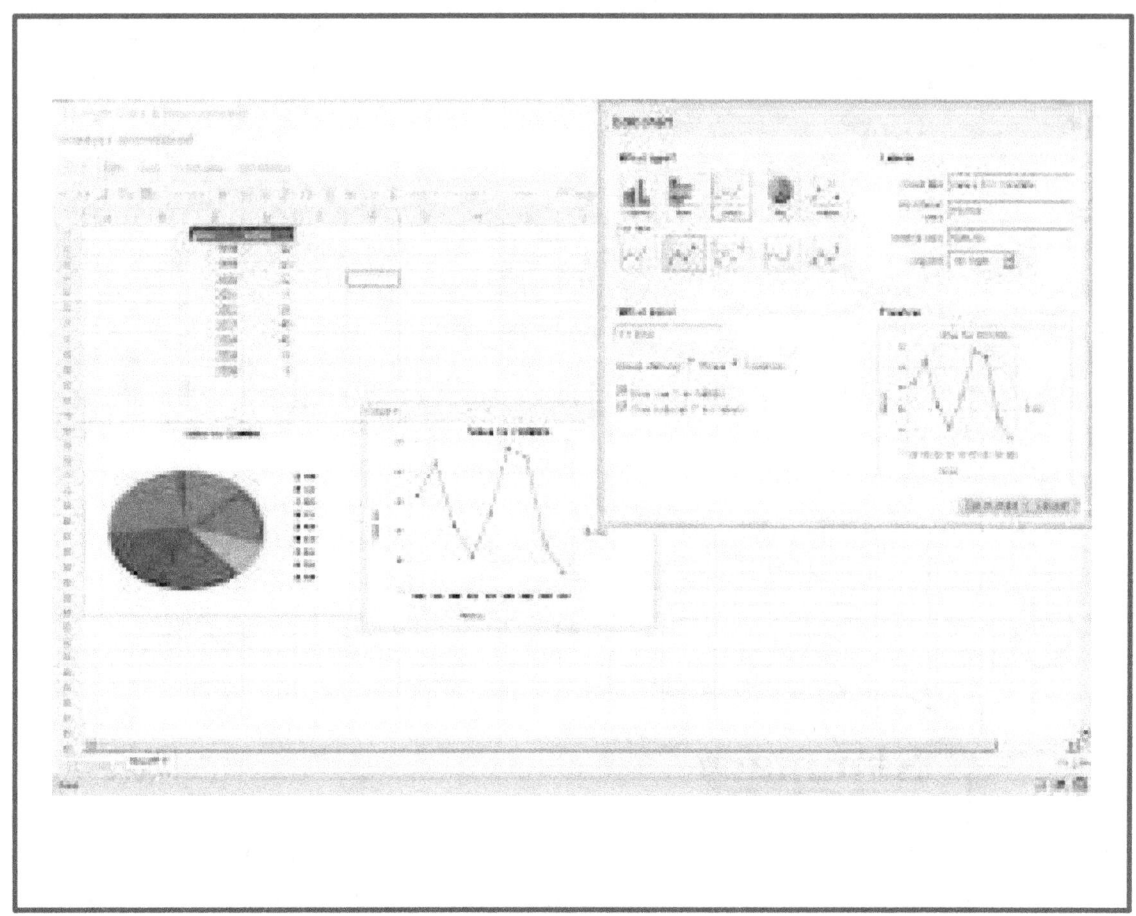

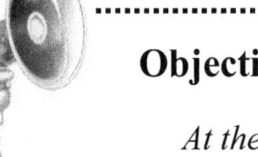 Objective

At the end of this chapter, the student should be able to:
- ➤ *Explain the purpose of a spreadsheet.*
- ➤ *Illustrate the features of a spreadsheet application.*
- ➤ *Manipulate formatting of a certain numeric data on spreadsheet.*

Spreadsheets also called worksheets, allow for the creation and organization of tables and data. Most spreadsheet editing is now performed using computer software, such as Microsoft Excel or Apple Numbers.

Types of Spreadsheets

Two-Dimensional Spreadsheets

- Two-dimension spreadsheets consist of "cells"-a box holding one piece of data-arranged in rows and columns like a table.

Three-Dimensional Spreadsheets

- Modern spreadsheet applications allow for more than one two-dimensional "sheet," effectively stacking related spreadsheets on top of each other and introducing a third dimension.

Arithmetic Spreadsheets

- Spreadsheets often utilize arithmetic functions, such as automatically adding up all the values of one particular column. These functions are necessary for budget and invoice spreadsheets, for example.

Logical Spreadsheets

- Some spreadsheets utilize logic functions, rather than arithmetic functions, to allow for deductive reasoning.

Object-Oriented Spreadsheets

- Instead of using two-dimensional cells, some spreadsheets are organized by objects, which are variables with a number of attributes attached. This allows the data to be viewed, analyzed and mapped in a number of different ways.

Instances of Spreadsheet Usage

By Carl Hose, eHow Contributor

Spreadsheets are typically used by business owners to keep track of expenses. The most well-known spreadsheets are Microsoft's Excel, Lotus 1-2-3 and Wordperfect's Quattro. Spreadsheets are one of the most underrated programs in an office suite. Their use goes far beyond creating simple expense sheets and employee time sheets, as spreadsheets are complex programs offering a range of powerful features, including game programming, text effects, graphing and graphics capabilities. Budget Planning.

- o **A spreadsheet** is an excellent budget planning tool, with calculation features that make keeping track of expenses and income easy, and calculating end-of-year data a breeze.

Inventory Tracking

- o You can use a spreadsheet to calculate sales percentages, help determine what products need to be ordered and keep track of stock.

Charts

- o Spreadsheets include graphic capabilities that allow you to calculate and compile information into visual representations. This is a great way to keep track of an employee's sales record or any other information that needs to be tracked and calculated on a regular basis.

Database and Address Books

- o A spreadsheet can be a versatile database, keeping track of important web pages and names, numbers and addresses of business contacts. It can even be used as a reference database for writers.

Surveys

- o You can use a spreadsheet to take surveys. Simply enter the survey results and use the calculation features to analyze and sort the information.

Different Spreadsheet Programs

1. Microsoft Excel

- o Microsoft Excel is available on its own or as part of the Microsoft Office suite of productivity applications.

With Excel, users input data into a seemingly limitless grid of cells. They can then perform arithmetic calculations such as totaling a column of numbers, sorting and filtering, and complex data manipulation. Excel can create charts in various formats from pie to scatter. It can format numbers as dates, currency, percentages and more--or in user-customizable formats. Each Excel spreadsheet begins with several "worksheets," called Sheet 1, Sheet 2 and Sheet 3. Users can add or delete worksheets.

The program provides contextual help with most functions, including formula entry, so users should not have to dip into the extensive help files. Start typing a formula and Excel will pop up tool tips to show you available formula names, then display the correct way to lay out the formula once you've finished typing the name. Excel also provides free downloads of hundreds of preformatted templates that are laid out logically for various tasks and functions, and in many cases, contain the formulas users are likely to need.

Excel is available for Windows and Mac OS and must be purchased. The application is at the expensive end of the spectrum for spreadsheet applications.

2. OpenOffice.org Calc

o Although OpenOffice.org--that's the name of the suite of productivity applications as well as its website address--is free, it's no lightweight. The spreadsheet module, Calc, performs standard spreadsheet functions such as organizing and crunching data. It can create various types of charts much like Excel's and employs a variety of number formats. Like Excel's, Calc's workspace is divided into multiple worksheets accessible by tabs at the bottom of the window. In fact, Calc and Excel have such similar feature sets that it's difficult to find much to differentiate between the two for the average user, except for price and platform availability.

Calc's interface is less slick, however, which may be a pro or a con, depending on your style. Calc's template offerings are far less intuitive to use than Excel's, and they're not all free. The program generally seems less focused on anticipating what you might want to do than Excel does, although it does provide contextual help for formula entry similar to Excel's. As with Excel, you can select cells to add to a formula by clicking and dragging to select with the mouse cursor.

The OpenOffice.org suite runs on Windows, Mac OS and Linux and is free.

3. Apple iWork Numbers

o Like many things Apple does, Numbers, part of the iWork for Mac OS X, has a slightly different approach than other applications. Although it includes the same basic functions--data entry, arithmetical functions, number formatting, charting and so forth--Numbers uses a canvas metaphor instead of one seemingly endless grid. Users opening the application to create a new spreadsheet will see a gray "canvas" with a small, blank spreadsheet grid. You can change the size of the grid, move it around and add more grids, which will appear in a list, table-of-contents style, in the window's left-hand pane. You can place a number of worksheets on a canvas, navigate among them and drag them around to reposition them.

Numbers promotes template use far more than the other spreadsheet programs do: They're part of the dialog users see each time they open the program. Besides selecting templates that affect an entire file, users see a subset of template choices whenever they add a new grid to their canvas. Numbers also uses a drag-and-drop method to help users build common formulas. You can select a group of cells, then drag over the "Sum" button to add them all together, for example. For more advanced functions, users can turn to the Function browser.

The iWork suite is available for Mac OS X and must be purchased. Though Numbers is not available separately from the rest of the suite, the suite's price is toward the low end of the spectrum.

4. Google Docs Spreadsheet

o   By now, Google's model of providing convenient and capable applications for free should be familiar. The spreadsheet application is continually enhanced, so it is difficult to name features or elements it lacks. The program is visually the simplest of the bunch, but the bare handful of buttons and spare menus hold a wealth of functions. With so few buttons and menu choices, everything is easy to find.

Like any other spreadsheet program, Google Docs Spreadsheet lets you enter numerical or other data in cells, perform arithmetical functions on the numbers and crunch all manner of data by sorting and filtering. The Web application includes some intriguing functions, such as the ability to run specifically formatted Google queries in a cell (for example, you can create a formula asking for the price of gold and the cell will display the current answer).

The Google Docs spreadsheet is available to anyone who signs up for a Google account and is accessible to anyone with an Internet connection and a browser.

Features of Spreadsheet

1. Data management:

Efficient data management facilities may include features for data entry with data validation, rearranging data (sorting), finding and/or extracting a part of the data depending upon the requirement, cutting and pasting, classification of data in the form of frequency tables etc.

2. Cell definition:

Cell is the intersection of a row and a column in the spreadsheet. The contents of a cell may be defined with the help of a value (number), label (text), formula, date or time. In case of the need to enter a series of data, electronic spreadsheets facilitate automatic filling of a range of cells within the series. The user has to define the starting value, the incremental value, the 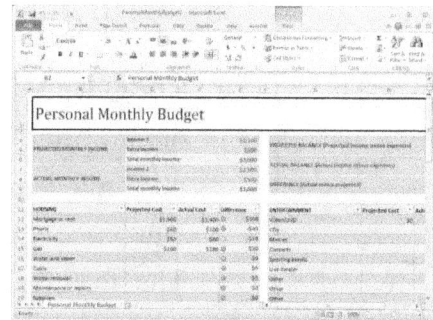 terminal value and the range of cells that are to be filled with the series of values.

The electronic spreadsheets have facilities for Copying, Deleting, Moving, Erasing, and Inserting data. These facilities are available for all types of data including labels and formula and are similar to those available in word processors.

3. Display of data:

Most electronic spreadsheets maintain two layers of data. The first layer contains the data the way they were entered and modified. The other layer of data is for display of values. The display of data is done on the basis of the formatting specifications made by the user.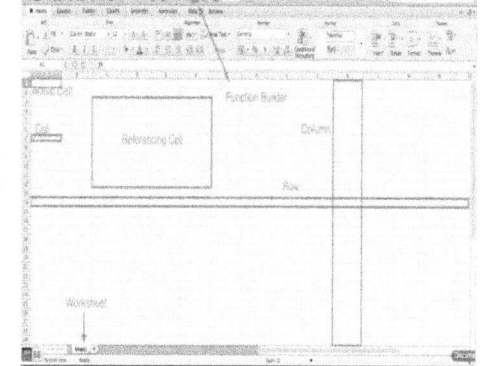

Once the data is ready, the predefined display format can be prescribed. For the purposes of computing values, the electronic spreadsheet uses the first layer.

For example, the values of sales for different branches of a company were specified to be displayed as rounded off to nearest thousands of rupees. However, while computing the sum of these sales values, the electronic spreadsheet shall use the values as they were originally entered.

<u>Summary</u>

- **Spreadsheets** also called worksheets, allow for the creation and organization of tables and data. Most spreadsheet editing is now performed using computer software, such as Microsoft Excel or Apple Numbers.
- The features of a spreadsheet application contains data management wherein the insert, delete and copy text data anywhere on a certain cell, cell definition and displaying of data.

L esson 4

Database Management Application

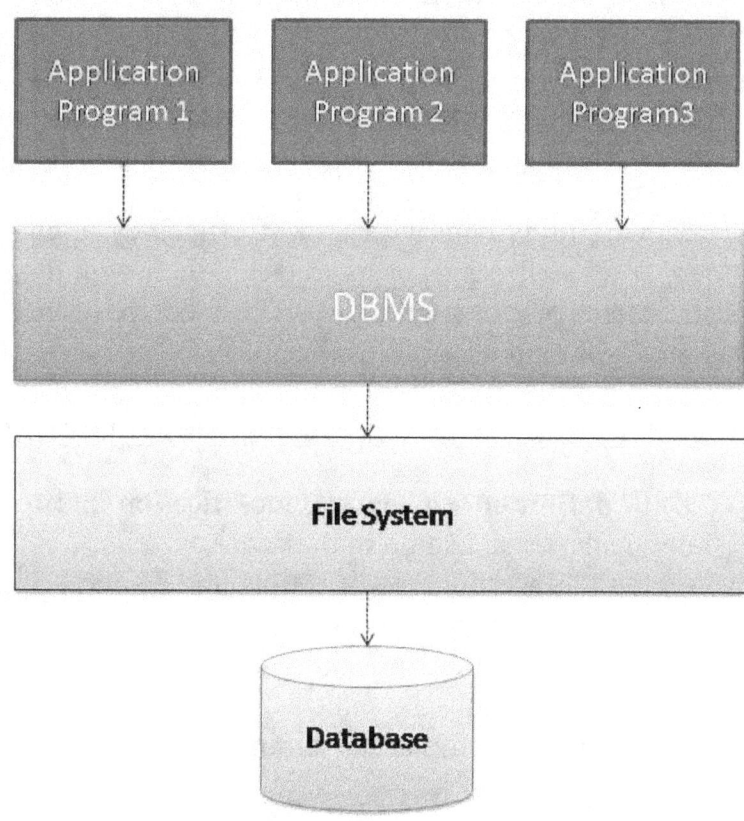

Objective

At the end of this chapter, the student should be able to:
- *explain the purpose of database management system*
- *determine instance in which database should be used*
- *illustrate the features of a database application*
- *manipulate data on tables for easy approval*

A **database** is an <u>application</u> that manages data and allows fast storage and retrieval of that data.

A **Database Application** - keeping customer records, sales records, appointments system. It includes reporting, sorting, filtering, querying data, Relational databases (many tables).

A **database management system (DBMS)** is a collection of <u>programs</u> that enables you to <u>store</u>, modify, and extract information from a <u>database</u>. There are many different types of DBMSs, ranging from small <u>systems</u> that <u>run</u> on <u>personal computers</u> to huge systems that run on <u>mainframes</u>.

Database Management System (DBMS) refers to the technology of storing and retrieving users data with utmost efficiency along with safety and security features. DBMS allows its users to create their own databases which are relevant with the nature of work they want. These databases are highly configurable and offers bunch of options.

The main purpose of database management system (DBMS):

- **Data definition** – Creation, modification and removal of definitions that define the organization of the data.
- **Update** – Insertion, modification, and deletion of the actual data.
- **Retrieval** – Providing information in a form directly usable or for further processing by other applications. The retrieved data may be made available in a form basically the same as it is stored in the database or in a new form obtained by altering or combining existing data from the database.
- **Administration** – Registering and monitoring users, enforcing data security, monitoring performance, maintaining data integrity, dealing with concurrency control, and recovering information that has been corrupted by some event such as an unexpected system failure.

Examples:

> ➢ computerized library systems
> ➢ automated teller machines
> ➢ flight reservation systems
> ➢ computerized parts inventory systems

Models of Database

o   Relational databases: *Most commercial systems are based on this model.*

o   Object Oriented database: *This model allows the users to create their own objects and specify how they are related to each other.*

▪   Object Relational databases: *This model manipulates data in the form of objects providing them with a relational interface.*

▪   Distributed databases: *This model is used to create databases that are shared by several systems in a network.*

▪   Multimedia databases: *This model produces a database that can store different types of files, that is text, graphics, sound, video etc.*

▪   Network databases: *This model organizes data in a network by linking the records.*

▪   Hierarchical databases: *This model organizes data in a hierarchy.*

o   Flat databases: *This model stores data in a single file that does not interact with any other data file.*

Databases consist of four objects:

1. *Tables* store data in rows and columns
2. *Queries* retrieve and process data
3. *Forms* control data entry and data views. It customized manner of inputting data into a database or presenting data on a screen
4. *Reports* summarize and print data

The key features of a database:

1. *Databases store data or information in tables*

The table allows you to see all of the records stored in the database. Table scan store and organize many records, from a few dozen for a small database up to millions for a large company database.   Tables are essential building blocks of any database that contain Rows called Records and Columns called Fields .

Components of a Database Table

1. **Record** – A group of related fields of information. Everything on one row is a record

1. **Field** – One item or bit of information in a record; represented by a COLUMN . Comprised of entries

2. **Entry** – Data typed into a field. Made up of characters. Example: John Doe is an entry in the name field. Also known as **data**.

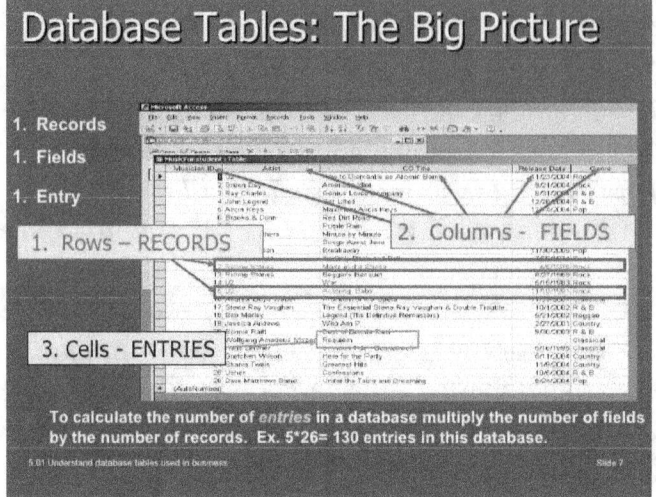

2. A database should have a separate table for every major subject. Example for employee records or customer orders

3. Each table contains a lot of record.

A record is made up of lots of individual pieces of information. Data should not be duplicated in multiple tables.

Look at Wonder Womans record: it stores her first name, last name, address, city and age. Each of these individual pieces of information in a record is called a field.

A field is one piece of data or information about a person or thing.

3. Every single record in a database has something to uniquely identify it

Each record in a table contains a unique field is known as primary key or sometimes the Key Field.

A Primary Key is a data item which is unique and can be used to identify a record with certainty.

AutoCounter data items are often used to provide a primary key.

• When you started school, you were given a student ID or an office number (primary key).This enables all of the girls called Charlotte Smith to be recognized.

• When patients go into hospital, they are given a patient number (primary key). This means that any treatment can be recorded on their record and they will be given the right operation.

A File is a collection of related records, that has a particular name. Or we can say in another way this unique name is called a filename.

Contents of a file (or a file may store): Data, Programs, Documents, Pictures, Sound or Other information.

A record is all of the data or information about one person or one thing.

A Field is an item of information consisting of number of characters, bytes or words that are treated together.

- o *Examples:-*
  - To form a Name
  - To form a Date
  - To form a Number

Field Name : *A Unique name that defines a field in a database*

Ex.: DOB, emp_name, add, phone, mob etc.

Attribute : *In relational database, a field is equivalent to a column*

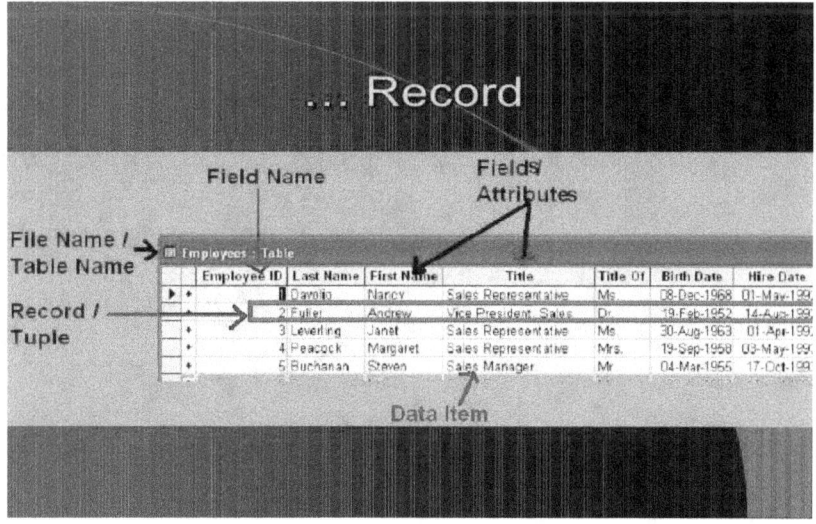

Manipulating a Database
HOW TO MAKE CHANGES TO THE STRUCTURE OF THE DATABASE?

1. Modifying the Columns

The Columns or fields in a database table can be easily modified using the 'alter table' command, which comes under DDL(Data Definition Language)

What are the changes that can be made to a field?

- Add a new field
- Edit an existing field
- Remove a field from table
- Add a constraint on the data that a field can hold (will be dealt with later)

2. Modifying an existing field

The Data contained in the field that is to be modified must be compatible with the destination data-type. Other-wise, conversion cannot be carried out

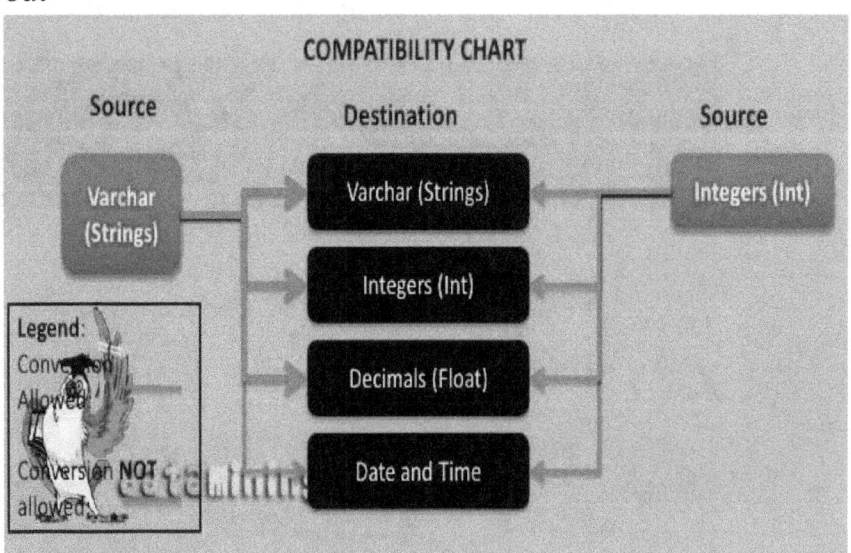

3. Remove a column from table

The DDL command 'alter table' in conjunction with the 'drop column' is used to delete a column/field from a user table. The Syntax is:

alter table <table_name> drop column <column_name>

For example, consider the follwingDreamTable. Suppose the User wishes to remove the DreamType field…

alter table DreamTable drop column DreamType

4. Deleting a Row

A Record is a row in a table.

For deleting a row, it must be identified using a 'distinguishing' attribute which lets the computer tell it apart from other records.

Consider a fish database maintained by a 'Eden-Lake Ecology farm'. Now, suppose the people go on a shark-mania and the sharp population vanished from the lake, it is meaningful for the Eco farm to remove its entry from the database.

Fish ID	Fish name	Diet	Mean Weight (Kg)	Market Value ($)
10D	Bass	Algae	2	1
23F	Yellow Perch	Worms, Algae	3	2
34B	Cat fish	Algae	1	4
23H	Shark	Smaller fishes	300	50

For the above example, the record can be identified using: The Primary key (FishID) Or any other special attribute (like Fish Name).
In general, always use the Primary Key, as it is best suited for uniquely identifying a record in a database table.

Summary

A Database Application - keeping customer records, sales records, appointments system. It includes reporting, sorting, filtering, querying data, Relational databases (many tables).

A database management system (DBMS) is a collection of <u>programs</u> that enables you to <u>store</u>, modify, and extract information from a <u>database</u>. There are many different types of DBMSs, ranging from small <u>systems</u> that <u>run</u> on <u>personal computers</u> to huge systems that run on <u>mainframes</u>.

Lesson 5

Presentation Application

Objective

At the end of this chapter, the student should be able to:

➢ *Explain the uses of presentation software*
➢ *Determine instance in which presentations should be used including delivery of reports, lectures and speeches*
➢ *Illustrate the features of a presentation application*

Presentation software (sometimes called "presentation graphics") is a category of <u>application</u> program used to create sequences of words and pictures that tell a story or help support a speech or public presentation of information.

A **presentation program** is a <u>software</u> program that helps create a slideshow that addresses a topic. Presentation programs can be used in businesses and schools for discussing a topic or for teaching. Many times, the presenter uses a <u>projector</u> to project the slideshow up on to screen that everyone can see. Below is an example of Microsoft Power Point, a commonly used program that creates presentations.

Presentation software can be divided into *business presentation software* and more *general multimedia* authoring tools, with some products having characteristics of both. Business presentation software emphasizes ease- and quickness-of-learning and use. Multimedia authoring software enables you to create a more sophisticated presentation that includes audio and video sequences. Business presentation software usually enables you to include images and sometimes audio and video developed with other tools.

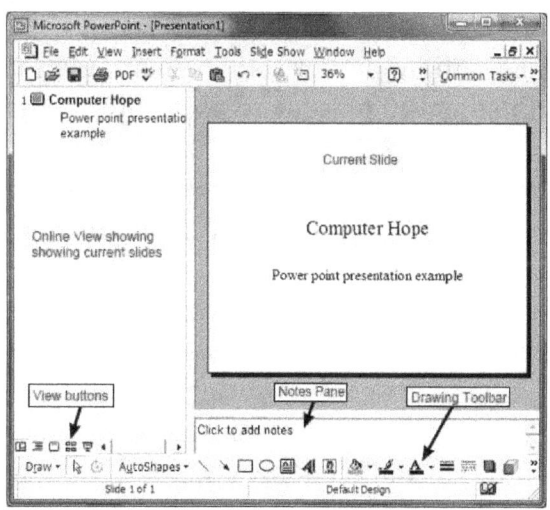

Presentation software is used to display information, normally in the form of a slide. It typically include three major functions:

1. An Editor - Allows text to be inserted and formatted
2. Method for inserting and manipulating graphic images, or animations with these objects
3. Slide show system (Slide Show Engine) to display the designed slide content

Once created, a person or group of people stand in front of other people and present the **presentation**. Presentations are presented one slide show at a time explaining the topics or bullet points of the slide and then moving to the next slide until all slides are shown. For example, in a business presentation a co-worker may go through slides that illustrate how well the company is doing, its profits, sales, and other important information.

Basic Presentation Software features are:

1. Insert Slide Feature: Allows you to inset slide anywhere in the presentation, at the beginning, middle or end.
2. Deletion of Inserted slides: Any slide of the presentation can be removed.
3. Allows cut and paste slides in any order.
4. Allows duplication content or slide
5. Allows you to display the presentation designed in a slide show system. (View Slide Feature)
6. Allows animations and/or sounds manipulations on objects in the slide.
7. Simple Find and Replace, and text editor features.

Full Featured Presentation software need more features than that above;
8. Good font specifications - Allows you to change and use different font faces, styles, and effects
9. Additional features for slide: footnotes, cross references, advanced navigation system, headers, footers
10. Good layout management system: Presets or Customized layout designing
11. Macros - for add interactive features
12. Spell checkers and dictionary support

Other than Microsoft Power Point; Corel Presentations, KPresenter, OpenOffice.org Impress are full-featured presentation software.

Summary

Presentation software can be divided into *business presentation software* and more *gener* A **presentation program** is a software program that helps create a slideshow that addresses a topic. Presentation programs can be used in businesses and schools for discussing a topic or for teaching. Many times, the presenter uses a **projector** to project the slideshow up on to screen that everyone can see. Below is an example of Microsoft Power Point, a commonly used program that creates presentations.

L esson 6

Selection of Application software

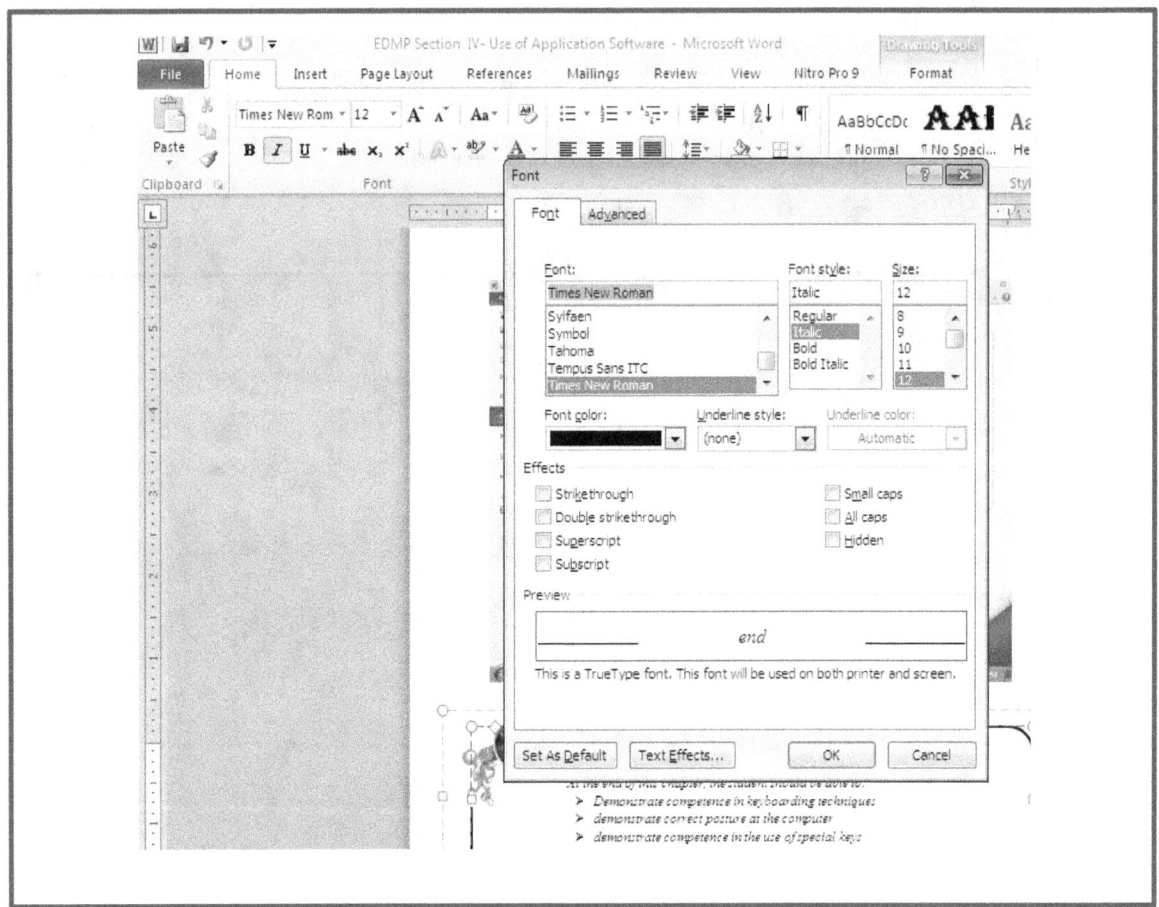

Objective

At the end of this chapter, the student should be able to:
- ➤ *Categorize a certain document supported by its application software*
- ➤ *determine the appropriate application software for office productivity*
  determine features and purpose of every type of application software

An application software is classified into Categories such as General Purpose software and specific software.

Categories of Application Software

I. **General Purpose Software** can be used for a wide variety of tasks e.g. spreadsheets can be used for accounts, sales analysis, forecasting and many others.

II. **Specialist Software**
This type of software lacks the flexibility of generic software and is only capable of doing a single task. Accounting software is capable of doing only accounts and so is more restrictive than a spreadsheet.

Appropriate uses of General Application Software

To improve our productivity, we must consider the kind of document we create before selecting the right Application software.

Word Processing Applications - Writing reports, memos, letter to customers. The features includes Mail Merge, Spell Check, Find and Replace, Dictionary, Thesauraus and many others.

Spreadsheet Applications - Keeping simple company accounts, calculating employee payments, simple stock control, modelling, simple invoice system. Its features includes Conditional Formatting, creating graphs, charts and tables, Absolute and Relative cell referencing.

Database Application - Keeping customer records, sales records, appointments system. It includes reporting, sorting, filtering, querying data, Relational databases (many tables).

Desktop Publishing Application - Creating leaflets, posters, business cards. This application features Templates for popular documents, change page size and orientation, WordArt, shapes and objects.

Presentation Software - Creating presentations to show customers or staff.

Graphics Application - Manipulating images that can be used at home, school or business Web Design (authoring) Application - Creating, maintaining personal or business websites

<u>Summary</u>

An application software is classified into Categories such as General Purpose software and specialist software.

Selection of appropriate General Application Software are the following:

Word Processing Applications
Spreadsheet Applications
Database Application
Desktop Publishing Application
Presentation Software
Graphics Application

Chapter IV

Use of Application Software

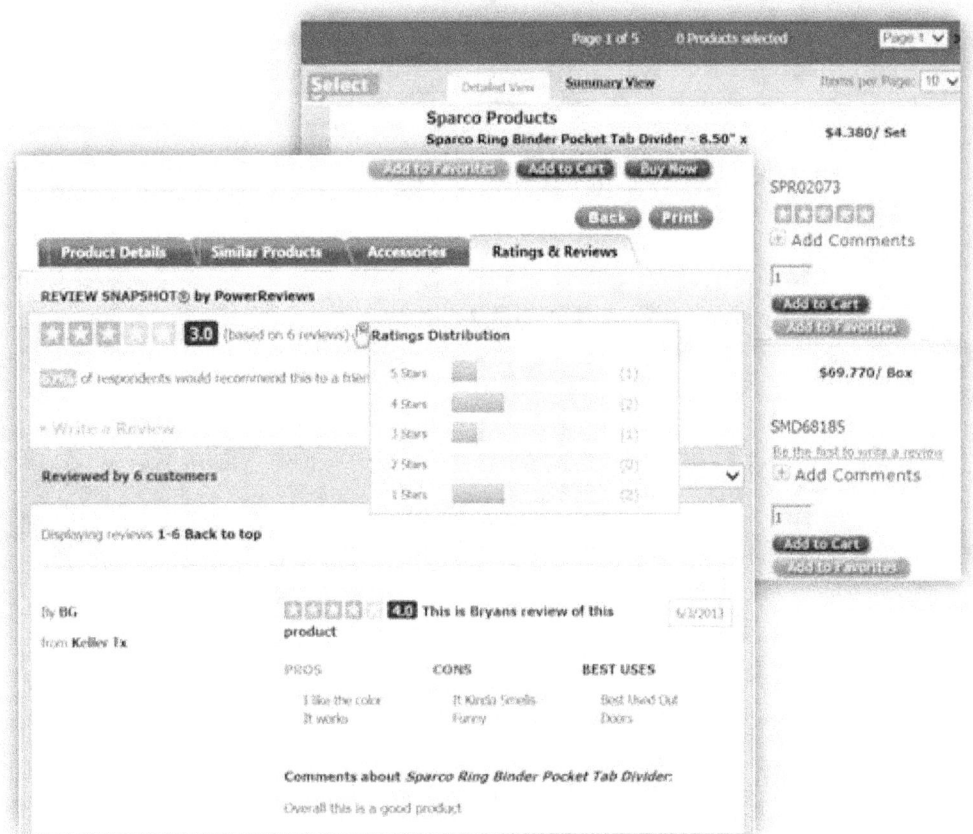

Highlights:

- *Formatting features on Word Processing*
- *Various Types of Documents*
- *Documents with Tabulations*
- *Creating Database*
- *Creating Simple Presentation*

L esson1

Features of Formatting

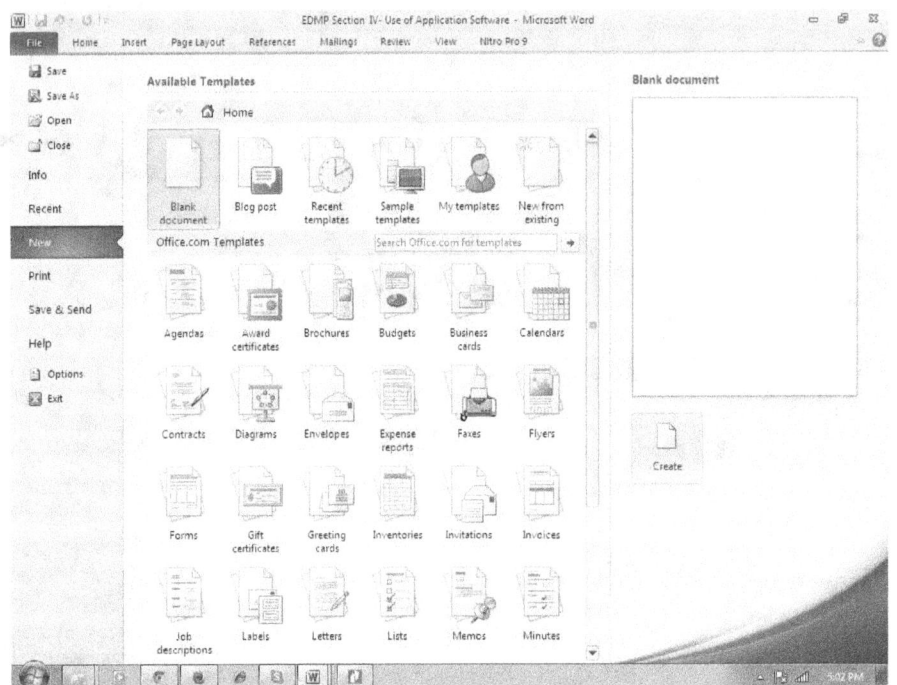

Objectives

At the end of this chapter, the student should be able to:

➢ *create and modify a document with exact margins, spacing and alignments*

➢ *applyappropriateformatting features toenhancespecificdocuments*

➢ *insert endnotes, footnotes, headers and the use of footers format a paragraph and save to a certain filename*

Guidelines on formatting documents

Creating a New Document

- Switch on the computer

- Windows displays a desktop screen with many icons on it.

- Search for Microsoft Word icon, point it with the help of the mouse and double click to select the application.

- If MSWord icon is not on the desktop screen then Click StartAll Programs àMicrosoft Word as shown below:

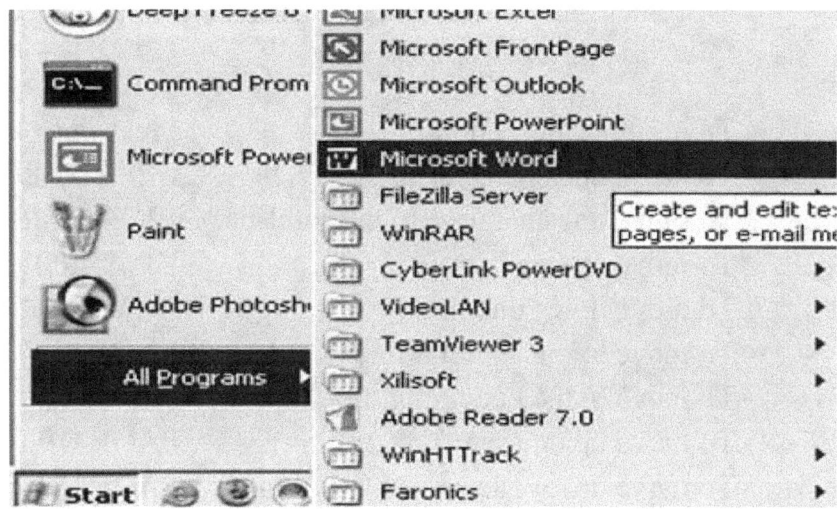

- The opening word screen will get displayed as shown below. The opening screen of word will automatically open a new document and the default name of that document will be Document1.

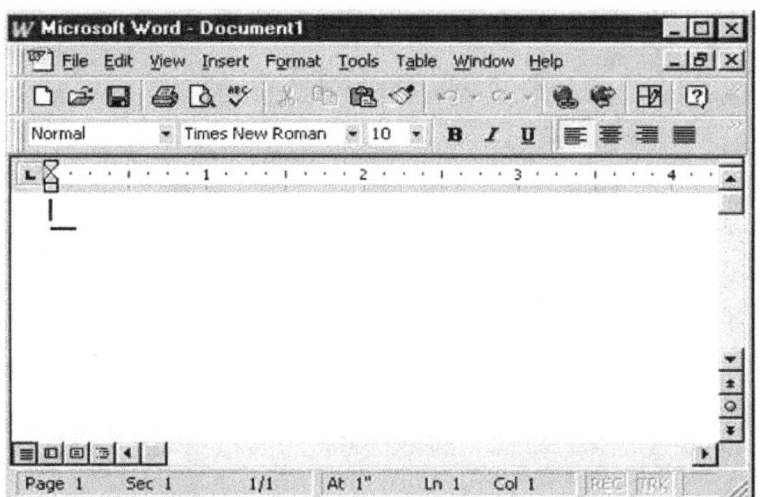

- If you've already started Word, you create a new document by clicking New on the File menu. In the New Document task pane that opens, click Blank document.

- In the upper-left corner of the document, or page, is the insertion point, a blinking vertical line. Typed content will appear there.
- Keep typing continuously even if the end of the line encountered. With the help of the word wrap property the lines will be automatically displayed in the next consecutive lines.
- Press ENTER to start another paragraph.

Navigating Through Document

- Movement around the created document is achieved with the help of the following operations:

To perform this action...	Press...
To move one character to the left	LEFT ARROW
To move one character to the right	RIGHT ARROW
To move up one line	UP ARROW
To move down one line	DOWN ARROW
To move to the end of a line	END
To move to the beginning of a line	HOME
To move up one screen (scrolling)	PAGE UP
To move down one screen (scrolling)	PAGE DOWN
To move to the end of a document	CTRL+END
To move to the beginning of a document	CTRL+HOME

Selecting the text in the document

- To select the document in the text the following operations can be performed:

To perform this action...	Press...
To select one character to the right	SHIFT+RIGHT ARROW
To select one character to the left	SHIFT+LEFT ARROW
To select to the beginning of a word	CTRL+SHIFT+LEFT ARROW
To select to the end of a line	SHIFT+END
To select to the beginning of a line	SHIFT+HOME
To select the entire document	CTRL+A

Formatting the Document

- ○ **Font**
  - ▪ Font change font style, size, color and a large number of other features.
  - ▪ To change the font style, size of a selected text go to format menu and select Font option or click the font icon (**A**) in the format toolbar.
  - ▪ The Font dialog box will get displayed.

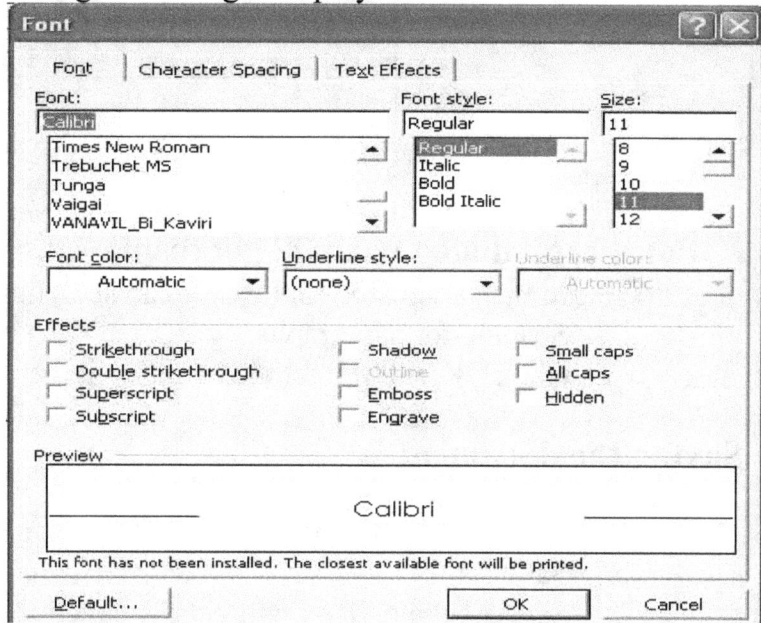

  - ▪ In the Font dialog box choose font face, font style, font size, font color etc.
  - ▪ Click OK button then the applied font effects will get reflected in the document.
    - ○ Bold, Italic and Underline
  - ▪ Bold, Italic, Underline - Format selected text: **Bold**, *Italic*, or Underlined
  - ▪ To bold the text press Ctrl + B or click the bold icon (**B**) on the toolbar
  - ▪ To underline the text press Ctrl + U or click the underline icon (*I*) on the toolbar
  - ▪ To italics the text press Ctrl + I or click the italic icon (U) on the toolbar

Paragraph

- ▪ Paragraph under format menu indents a paragraph using either margin or place some chosen amount of space before or after the paragraph.
- ▪ Select the paragraph if already entered or simply go Format menu and choose Paragraph option or click the paragraph icon (≣¶) in the toolbar.

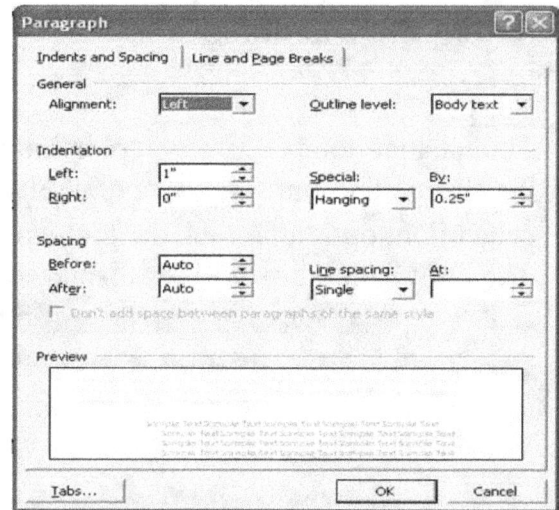

- **Paragraph dialog box will get displayed.**
  - o In the paragraph window we can set Alignment, Indentation and Spacing for paragraphs.
  - o Click OK will reflect the changes in the document accordingly.

Saving the document

  - o To save the document for the first time click File Menu→Choose Save As
  - o Save As dialog Box will get displayed.
  - o Select the directory where you want to save or create a new folder by clicking New Folder icon.
  - o Enter the file name in the File name box.

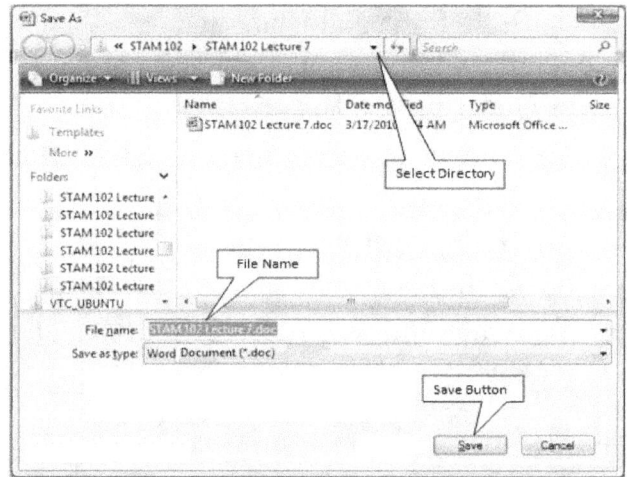

- Click Save. The file is saved under the new name.
- To save subsequently click on Save from File Menu.
- Or hold the Ctrl. Key and press S from keyboard.
- Or click Save button ( ) in the standard toolbar

BULLETS AND NUMBERING

InMicrosoftWord   2010,
bulletsandnumberedlistsareusedtoseparateinformationfromoneanother.
Theyarealsousedtogivemoreattentiontocertainpartsofadocument.Numbers
areusedtoshoworderinadocument.Youcancreatea   bulletedoranumbered
listusingeitertheFormattingtoolbarortheMenubar.

HowtoCreateaBulletedListUsing the,Home Menu Bar

- R i g h t   Clickwhereyouwantthebulletedlisttostart.
- Drag to Bullets then Click design of the bullet you
  want;ontheFormattingtoolbar, typethetext.Whenyou
  presstheEnterkey,anotherbulletisdisplayedonthenextline.
- Toendthebulletedlist,click:=again.

HowtoCreateaBulleted ListUsingtheHomeMenu Bar

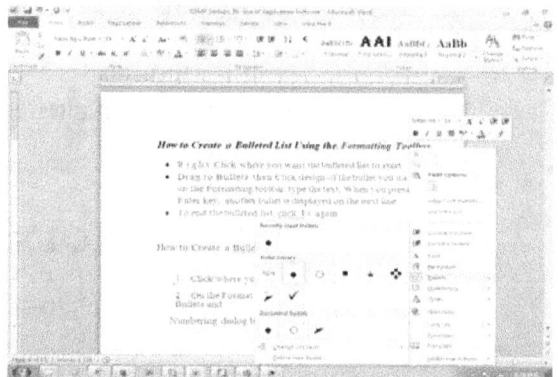

1.Clickwhereyouwantthebullettostart.
2. OntheHomemenu,click onBullets orNumbering tab.
3 . You may change design of bullets or Numbers in the Bullets or
     numbering library.
4. Whenyou presstheEnterkey,anotherbullet or
   numberingisdisplayedonthenextline.

5. Toendthebulleted or numberedlist,clickt a b   :=again.

SETTING TABSANDMARGINS

SETTING TABS

Tabsareusedwhenyouwanttoplaceinformation inyourdocumentinto columns.Withtheuseoftabs,yourdocumentscanbereadeasilybecausethere arespacesbetweencolumns.InMSWord,therearefour(4)typesoftabs.

Symbol	L			
Type	Left	Right	Center	Decimal

HowtoSettheTabStops

- Selecttheparagraph/syouwanttosettabsfor.

- Click(Tab)buttonatthefarleftofthehorizontalruleruntilitshows thetabthatyouwanttouse.

- Clickonthehorizontalrulerwhereyouwanttosetatabstop.

ToClearaTabStop

- Dragthetabmarkeroffthehorizontalrulerandreleasethemousebutton.

ToMoveaTabStop

- Dragthetabmarkertothelocationwhereyouwanttoplacethetabstop alongthehorizontalruler.

SETTING   MARGINS

MarginsinyourdocumentcanbesetusingthePageSetupoptionintheFilemenu.
HowtoChangeMargins

- ChoosePageSetupfromtheFile menu.ThePageSetupdialogbox appearsonthescreen.ThenclickonMarginstab.

- •Typethe measurementsyouwanttouseforthemarginsintheboxesofthePageSetupdialogbo x.Orclick   theup-anddown-arrowkeysto   choosethemeasurementsyouwant touse.

To insert References, footnotes, and endnotes

	Shortcut keys
Mark a table of contents entry.	ALT+SHIFT+O
Mark a table of authorities	ALT+SHIFT+I

entry (citation).	
Mark an index entry.	ALT+SHIFT+X
Insert a footnote.	ALT+CTRL+F
Insert an endnote.	ALT+CTRL+D

Summary

Guidelines for selection of formatting

- Creating a New Document
- Navigating Through Document
- Selecting the text in the document
- Formatting the Document
- Bullets and numbering
- **Setting Tabs and Margins**

Activity 1

1. OpenandstarttheMSWordprogram. Then typethefollowingandsetthetabstopstoplacetheinformationincolumns.

Adjective	Synonym	Antonym
fast	quick	Slow
happy	glad	sad
big	large	small
angry	mad	calm
old	ancient	new
little	small	big .,
tall	high	short

3. Whenfinished,saveitusingthefilenameTABS.

4.   ClickonNewDocumentin theFile.menu.Typetheparagraphsbelow.PresstheTabkeyonceatthestartofeach paragraph .indent.

TheCrowandtheP itcher

Averythirstycrowcameupona   pitcherthathadoncefullofwater.   But whenthecrowputhisbillintothepitcher,hefoundthattherewas onlyalittlewaterleftinit.Hcouldnotreachfar enoughdowntogetadrink.

Thenathoughtcametohim.Hetookapebbleanddroppeditintothepitcher.Thenhetoo kanotherpebble,andanother,anddroppedtheminto thepitcher.Beforelong,hecouldseethewaterrisinghigherandhigherThemoralofthisstor yisthat littlebylittledoesthetrick.

6. ChangethemarginsbyclickingFile·ontheMenubarandchoosingPage. Setup.InPageSetupdialogbox,clickonMargins.

7. Changethefollowingmarginsto:

top:	2"	left:	1.5"
bottom:	1" .	right:	1.25"

8. Whenfinished,saveyourworkusingthefilename MARGINS.

Exercises

Name _____   Date: _____

GradeandSection: _____   Score: _____

A. Directions: Fillin theblanks.

1. There aretypes of tab in MS Word, namely, _____ and_____ .

2. To atabstop,dragthetabmarkeroffthehorizontalruler.

3. The   optionin theFilemenuallowsyoutosetthepaper size,pageorientation,andmarginsofyourdocument.

4. YoucanchoosethepageOrientationbyclickingeither   or orientationbutton.

5. To _____ atabstop,dragthetabmarkertothelocationwhere youwantto placethetabstoponthehorizontalruler.

B. Answerthesequestions.

1. Howdoyouchangethemarginsofadocumentsothattheleftmarginis 0.5 andtherightmarginis3"?

2. Whataretabsusedfor?

Lesson 2

Various Types of Documents

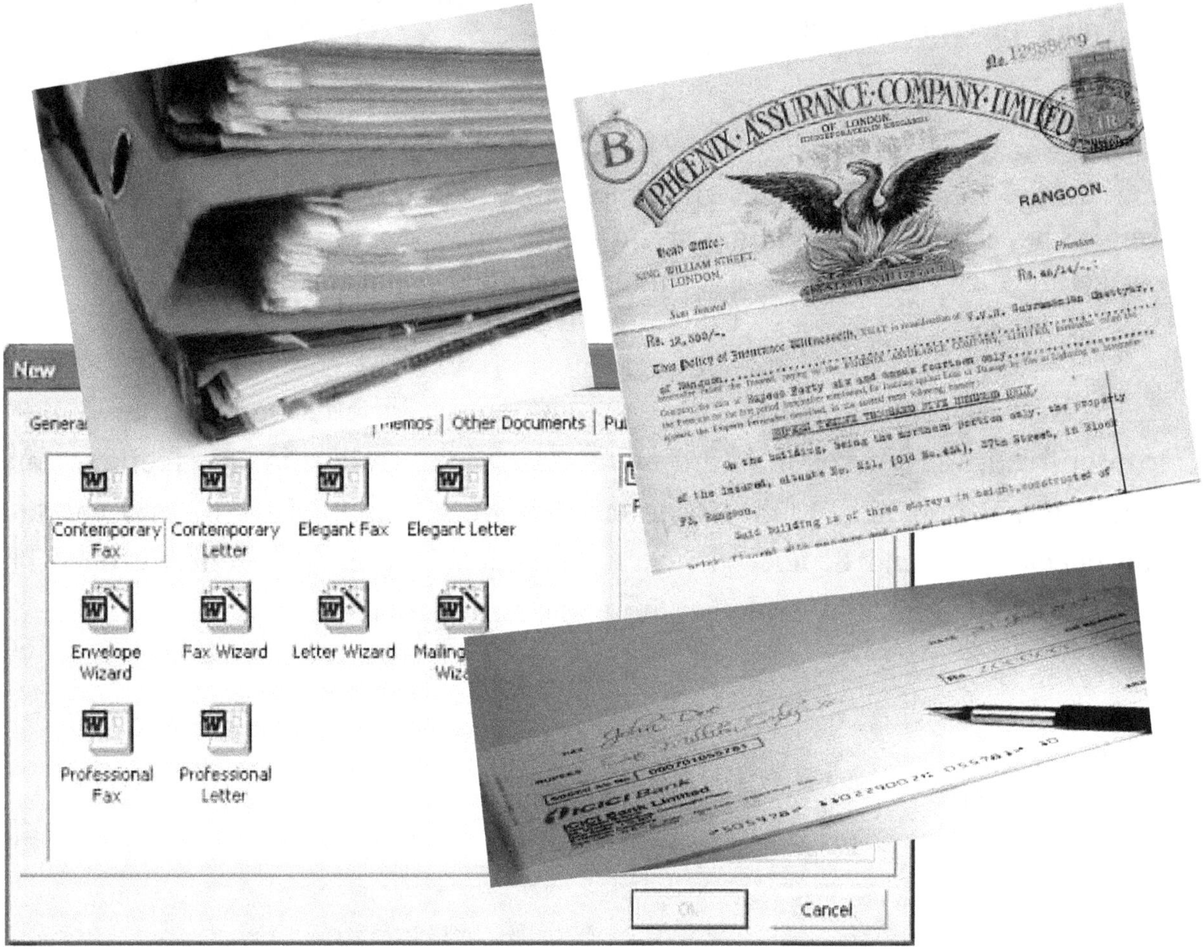

Objective

At the end of this chapter, the student should be able t:

➢ *technically edit various types of documents*
➢ *check the spelling and grammar of any business document automatically*
➢ *Proofread and correct any kind of documents suitable for mailing*

The students should be able to distinguish between Communication devices and communication media.

Proof-reading of documents and correcting errors

Proofreading is the reading of a galley proof or an electronic copy of a publication to detect and correct production errors of text or art. Proofreaders are expected to be consistently accurate by default because they occupy the last stage of typographic production before publication.

In using MS Word 2007 or 2010, **Proof-reading** includes the checking of text for the right spelling and grammar, punctuation and unclear sentences or too long. The errors are highlighted into red lines on screen, for you to decide correcting such errors of the text suitable for mail or publication.

Now, if you have a document, assignment or dissertation that you would like to proofread, the Microsoft Word's Track Changes feature is an excellent option. You can make changes to the document that are highlighted so the original author can check them and decide whether to accept or reject them one by one. Thus, retaining total control over his/her thoughts, arguments or experiences.

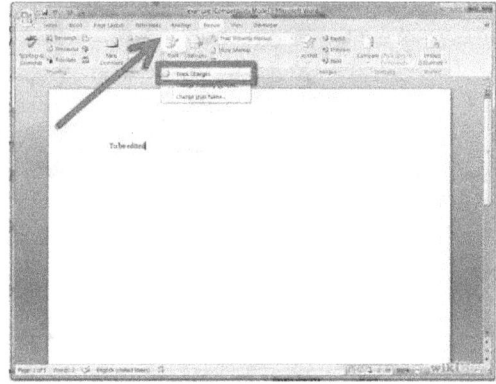

First, Enable Track Changes and save the document with a new file name.

Open the document to be edited with Microsoft Word (version 2007 or 2010), select the Review menu tab in the upper toolbar and then enable Track Changes by clicking the tab so it is highlighted. Then save the document with a new file name, for example filename1.docx, so that you now have two copies of the file (the original filename.docx for reference & filename1.docx which you will work with).

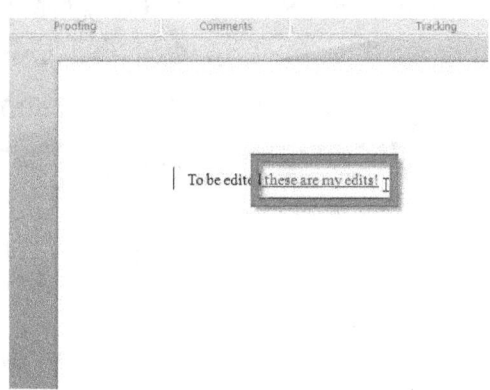

Second, Edit the document, inserting or deleting letters, words, punctuation

Inserted characters will be highlighted and underlined, while deleted characters will be highlighted and struck horizontally through the middle. Comments can be added by highlighting the word or section of text with the cursor (hold left click down and drag to select), in the place where you would like the suggestion to refer to, and then selecting the New Comment tab from the upper Review menu toolbar. A comment window will appear where you can write in feedback for the author about the specific area of text.

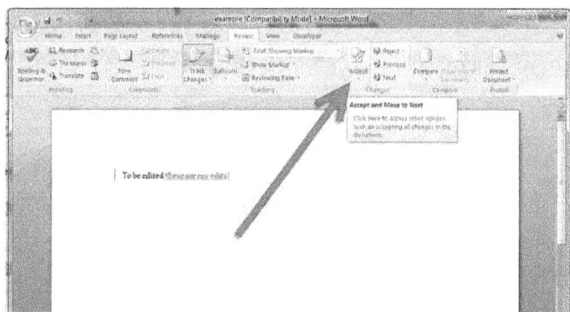

Third, When you have completed all the editing, save the document you are working with (filename1.docx)

One final time, then select the Accept tab from the Review menu toolbar, and click Select All Changes in Document. Now all the highlighted text will be accepted, the deletions will vanish and the insertions will be accepted. Only the comments remain to be deleted by the author after viewing them (right click over comment box and select Delete Comment). Now, very carefully (!!) go to the File menu and select Save As. Then save as a NEW DOCUMENT with all the changes accepted using the file name filename2.docx. Now you have three documents. Filename.docx (the original unedited document), filename1.docx (the proofread document with all the edits highlighted) and filename2.docx (the edited document with all the changes accepted).

Note: *Individual changes can be accepted and rejected by highlighting the area of text and selecting Accept-Accept Change / Reject-Reject Change from the Review toolbar.*

Application of techniques in editing the document

InMicrosoftWord,youcanmakechangesin yourdocumentbyfollowingsome steps.Youmustselectfirstthetextthatyouwanttochange.Textcanbeaword, groupofwords,.sentences,orparagraphs.

HowtoHighlightText

1. Holddownthemousebuttonat thebeginningofthetext you wanttoselect.

2. Dragthemousetotheendof thetextandrelease eituntilthe completetextishighlighted. Theselectedtextwillbe displayedin reversedcolor (whiteletteronblack background).

HowtoMoveText

MSWordallowsyoutomovetexttoanotherplaceinyourdocument.this processissometimescalled*"cutandpaste."*

Cut *operation removes the selection from the active document and places it on the clipboard.*

Steps on how tocutandpastetext:

1. Selectthetextyou wantto movebyhighlightingit.

2. ClickonEditmenuthenchoose Cutcommand.Oryoucanjust clickthe***Cutbutton***onthetoolbar.Youcanalsodothis by pressingCtrl +Xkeystogether.

3. Theselectedtextis   removed   fromthedocument.Itisstored   ina temporarystorageplaceor aclipboard.Theclipboardisusedforstoringtexttemporarily.

4. Placethecursortotheplacewhereyouwanttomovetheselectedtextin yourdocument.

5. ClickontheEditmenuthen   clickonPaste   command.   Or youcanjustclickthe***Pastebutton***onthetoolbarorpressthe Ctrl +Vkeystogether. The textwillthenappear onitsnew location.

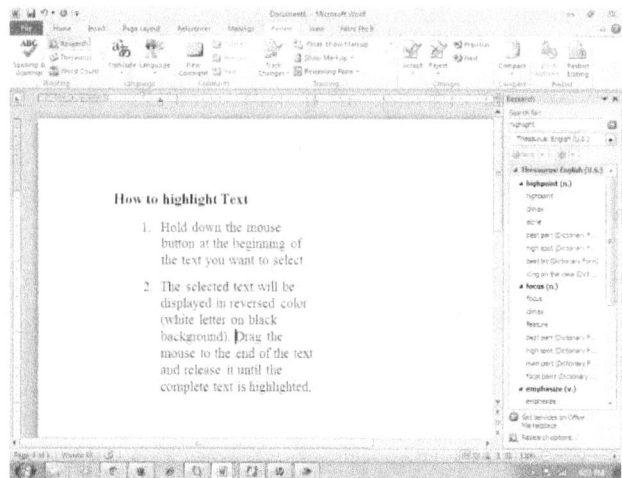

How to Copy Text

There aretimes when youneedtocopytextinadocument.   Youcandothis byfollowingthesestepscarefully:

1. Selectthetextyouwanttocopy.
2.   FromtheEditmenu,   choose   Copycommand   orclicktheCopy buttononthetoolbar orclicktheCtrl +Ckeystogether.
3. Putthecursortotheplacewhereyouwanttocopythetextinyourdocument.
4.   Click ontheEditmenuandchoose Paste command orclickthe**Paste** button onthetoolbar orpress theCtrl +Vkeystogether.

How to Delete (Erase) Text

Sometimes, youcannot avoidmaking mistakes whiletyping yourdocument. Youneedtocorrect itbyerasingordeleting itfromyourdocument.

Three (3)waystodeleteorerase text:
1. Putthecursor attheleftofthecharacters youwanttodelete. Pressthe ***Delete key***inthekeyboard.
2.   Putthecursor totherightofthecharacters youwanttodelete, thenpress theBackspace key.
3. Selectthetextyouwanttodeletethenpress theDelete**(Del)**key.

Another methodofdeleting text:
1. Selectthetextthatyouwanttodeletebyhighlighting it.
2. OntheEditmenu, clickCutorclick ⬐ button ontheStandard toolbar or press theCtrl +Xkeys.

How to Find a certain text and Replace it

Find *searches for specified text in the active document.*

- *To find a specified text in the document go to Edit menu choose find option or click the find icon (ᛘ) on the toolbar or make use of the shortcut key combination Ctrl+F.*
- ***The Find and Replace dialog box will get displayed.***

- Enter the text to be searched in the Find what tab.

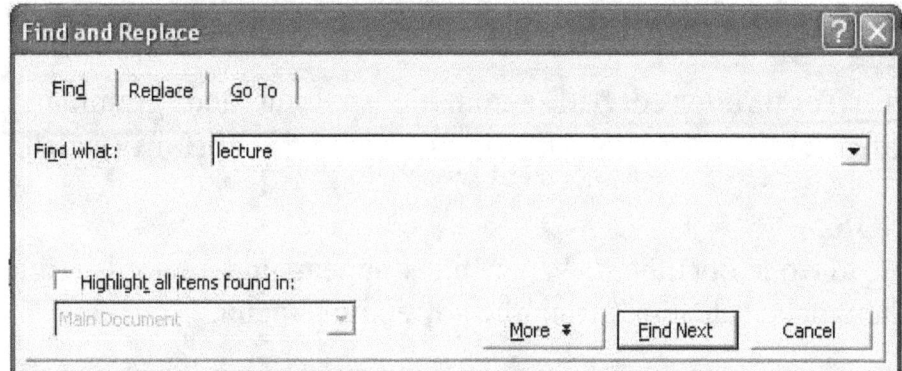

- Clicking the Find Next button the specified text will be located in the document.
  - Replace searches for and replaces specified text.
  - To replace go to edit menu and select Replace option or click the replace icon in the toolbar or make use of the shortcut key combination Ctrl+H.

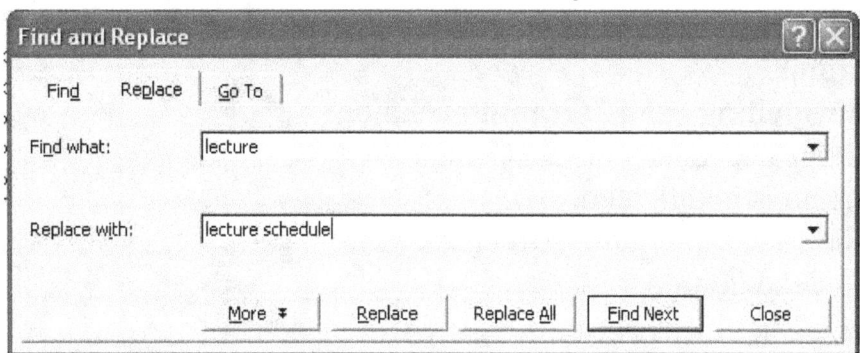

  - Find and Replace dialog will get displayed.
- Clicking Find Next and Replace buttons the specified text will be replaced.
- To replace all the instance of the text lecture with the text lecture schedule click Replace All button in the Find and Replace window.
- Then every instance of the text lecture in the document will get replaced with the text lecture schedule.

Spelling andgrammar   check, thesaurus, font type;

Turn on or off the red lines that appear under misspelled words

1. On the top-left corner, click the **Microsoft Office Button** .
2. At the bottom of the menu, click **Word Options**.
3. In the **Word Options** dialog box that appears, click **Proofing**.
4. In the **Exceptions for** list, click the currently-open document name.

5. Select or clear the **Hide spelling errors in this document only** and **Hide grammar errors in this document only** check boxes.

NOTE To turn on or off automatic spelling and grammar checking for all documents, select **All New Documents** in the **Exceptions for** list.

6. Click **OK**.
7. Return to your document. When lines appear under words, right-click the word, and then make selections from the corrections menu.

To Check spelling and grammar

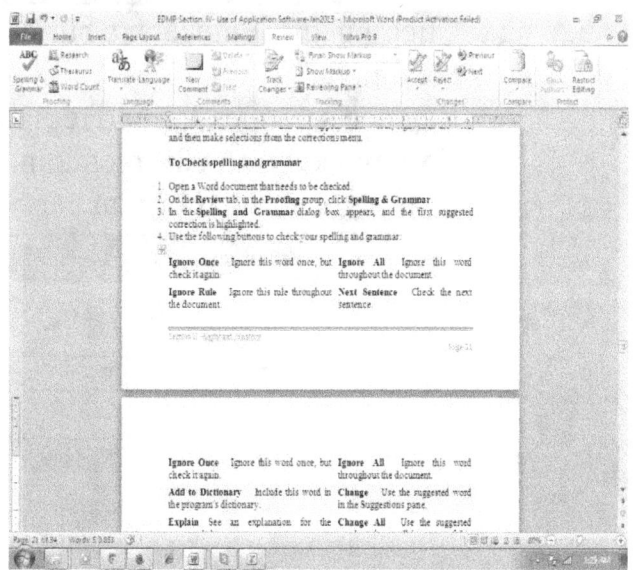

1. Open a Word document that needs to be checked.
2. On the **Review** tab, in the **Proofing** group, click **Spelling & Grammar**.
3. In the **Spelling and Grammar** dialog box appears, and the first suggested correction is highlighted.
4. Use the following buttons to check your spelling and grammar:

Ignore Once Ignore this word once, but check it again.

Ignore All Ignore this word throughout the document.

Ignore Rule Ignore this rule throughout the document.

Next Sentence Check the next sentence.

Add to Dictionary Include this word in the program's dictionary.

Change Use the suggested word in the Suggestions pane.

Explain See an explanation for the suggested change.

Change All Use the suggested word to change all instances of this word.

Change All Use the suggested word to change all instances of this word.

AutoCorrect Use the first suggested word each time you click AutoCorrect.

Check grammar Select to correct the grammar in this document.

Undo Undo the change. Continue clicking for previous corrections.

Recheck the words and grammar that you previously checked and chose to ignore

1. Open the document that you want to recheck.
2. On the top-left corner, click the **Microsoft Office Button** .
3. At the bottom of the menu, click **Word Options**.
4. In the **Word Options** dialog box that appears, click **Proofing**.
5. Under **Correcting spelling and grammar in Word**, click **Recheck Document**.
6. To recheck the spelling and grammar, click **Yes** when you see the following message: **This operation resets the spelling checker and the grammar checker so that Word will recheck words and grammar you previously checked and chose to ignore. Do you want to continue?**
7. In the **Word Options** dialog box, click **OK** to go back to the document.
8. On the **Review** tab, in the **Proofing** group, click **Spelling & Grammar**.

Look up words in the thesaurus

Using the thesaurus, you can look up synonyms (different words with the same meaning) and antonyms (words with the opposite meaning).

NOTE: In Microsoft Office Word, Microsoft Office PowerPoint, and Microsoft Office Outlook, you can look up a word quickly if you right-click anywhere in the document, presentation, open message, or previewed message in the Reading Pane, and then click **Synonym** on the shortcut menu.

Summary

- **Proofreading** is the reading of a galley proof or an electronic copy of a publication to detect and correct production errors of text or art. Proofreaders are expected to be consistently accurate by default because they occupy the last stage of typographic production before publication.

Lesson3

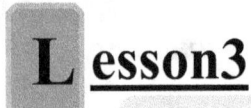

Documents using tabulations

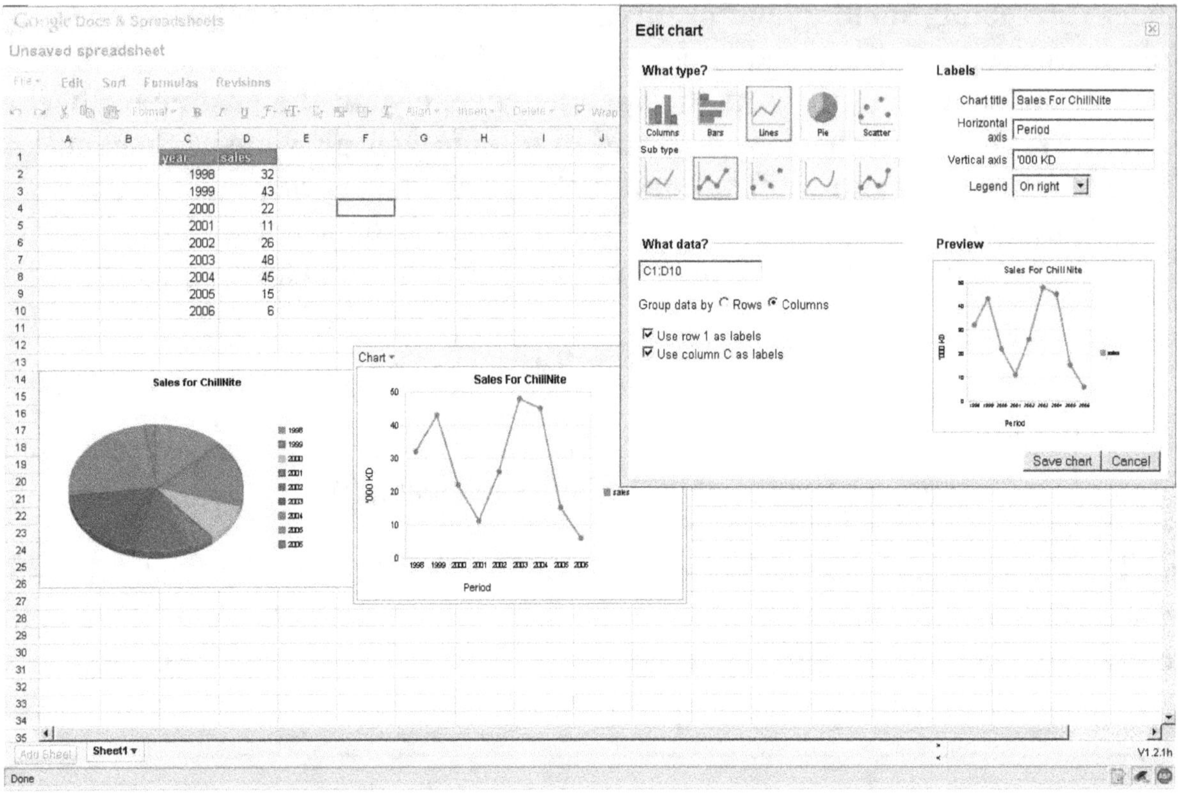

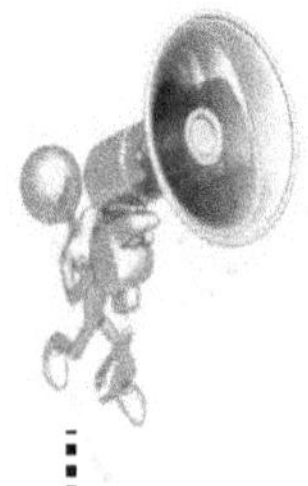

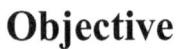

Objective

At the end of this chapter, the student should be able to:

- *define spreadsheet and identifythe differentpartsofMSExcel*:
- *manage several groups of data in various table*
- *create several kinds of charts in the calculated data of a certain table*

You have learned word processing from your previous classes wherein you type, edit, and format text. However, when you deal with numeric data, perform calculations; and manipulate them, you need to use a spreadsheet software like MS Excel. It handles work-related numeric data efficiency and information can be represented in chart or graph forms.

Before you work with MS Excel, you need to 'understand some of the fundamentals of spreadsheets.

A spreadsheet is composed of rows represented by numbers, and columns represented by letters. The intersection of a row and column forms the cell. A cell is a rectangular box where data are being entered. These data can be *labels, values (numeric, alphabetic, or combination), formula or functions.*

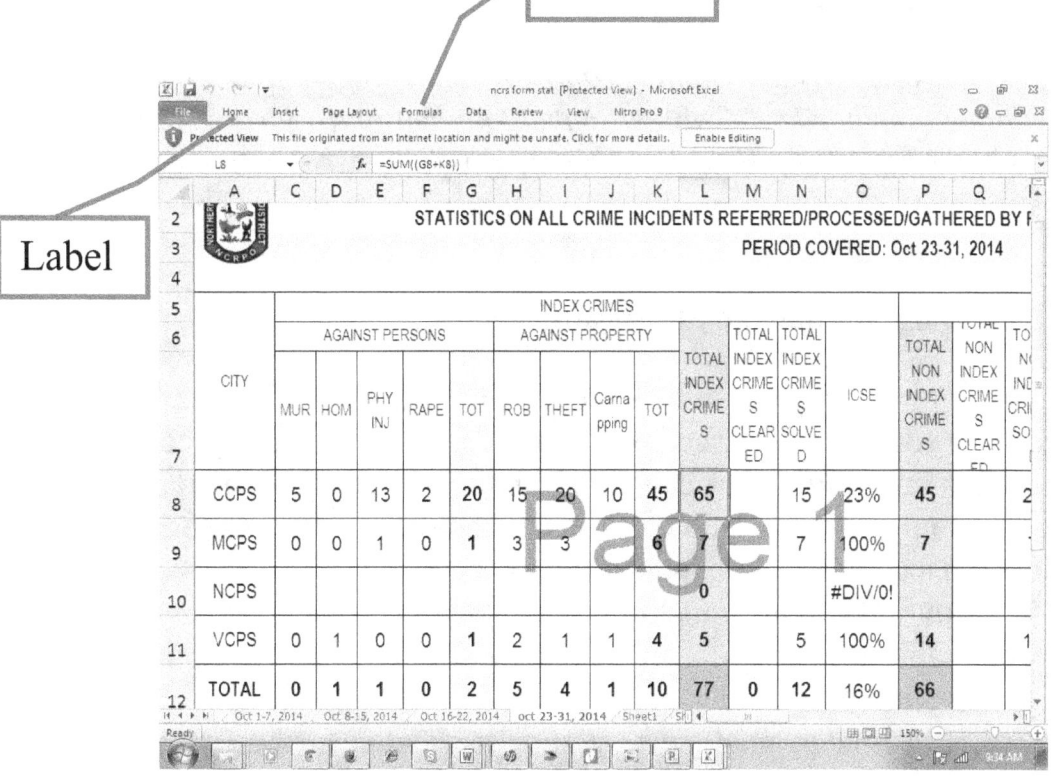

For Simple Tabulations, you can make managing and analyzing a group of related data easier, you can turn a range of cells into a Microsoft Office Excel table (previously known as an Excel list). A table typically contains related data in a series of worksheet rows and columns that have been formatted as a table. By using the table features, you can then manage the data in the table rows and columns independently from the data in other rows and columns on the worksheet.

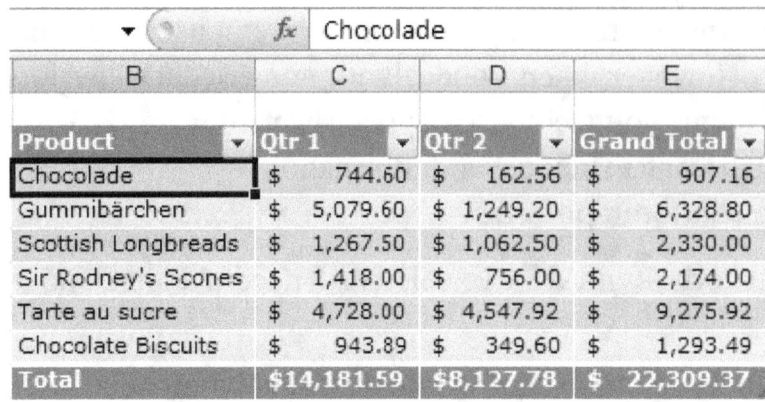

NOTE   Excel tables should not be confused with the data tables that are part of a suite of what-if analysis commands.

Managing data in an Excel table

In a table, you can *createcolumn androw headings and oblique andverticalheadings;applyborders, Tablealignmentonpage and Sorting ofdata.* You can also use one table to manage your data, but if you want to manage several groups of data, you can insert more than one table in the same worksheet.

Features that you can use to manage table data:

- **Sorting and filtering**   Filter drop-down lists are automatically added in the header row of a table. You can sort tables in ascending or descending order or by color, or you can create a custom sort order. You can filter tables to show only the data that meets the criteria that you specify, or you can filter by color. For more information on how to filter or sort data, see Filter data or Sort data.
- **Formatting table data**   You can quickly format table data by applying a predefined or custom table style. You can also choose Table Styles options to display a table with or without a header or a totals row, to apply row or column banding to make a table easier to read, or to distinguish between the first or last columns and other columns in the table. For more information on how to format table data, see Format an Excel table.
- **Inserting and deleting table rows and columns**   You can use one of several ways to add rows and columns to a table. You can quickly add a blank row at the end of the table, include adjacent worksheet rows or worksheet columns in the table, or insert table rows and table columns anywhere that you want. You can delete rows and columns as needed. You can also quickly remove rows that contain duplicate

data from a table. For more information about adding and deleting table rows and columns, see Add or remove Excel table rows and columns.

- **Using a calculated column**   To use a single formula that adjusts for each row in a table, you can create a calculated column. A calculated column automatically expands to include additional rows so that the formula is immediately extended to those rows. For more information on how to create a calculated column, see Create, edit, or remove a calculated column in an Excel table.
- **Displaying and calculating table data totals**   You can quickly total the data in a table by displaying a totals row at the end of the table and then using the functions that are provided in drop-down lists for each totals row cell. For more information on how to display and calculate table data totals, see Total the data in an Excel table.
- **Using structured references**   Instead of using cell references, such as A1 and R1C1, you can use structured references that reference table names in a formula.
- **Ensuring data integrity**   For tables that are not linked to SharePoint lists, you can use the built-in data validation features in Excel. For example, you may choose to allow only numbers or dates in a column of a table. For more information on how to ensure data integrity, see Prevent invalid data entry on a worksheet.
- **Exporting to a SharePoint list**   You can export a table to a SharePoint list so that other people can view, edit, and update the table data.

For many small business owners, Microsoft Excel 2010 is not only a powerful tool for internal tracking and bookkeeping, but it can also be used to prepare documents for distribution to partners or customers. When creating a spreadsheet for distribution, controlling the spreadsheet's appearance ensures it appears professional.

To *createcolumn androw headings*

Excel 2010 offers two types of column headings; the letters the Excel assigns to each column, which you can toggle in both view and print modes, or the headings that you create yourself and place in the spreadsheet's first row, which you can then freeze in place.

1. Create a Table in Any of Several Ways

You can create a table from the Insert tab or (as here) from the Home tab, where you can choose a style at the same time.

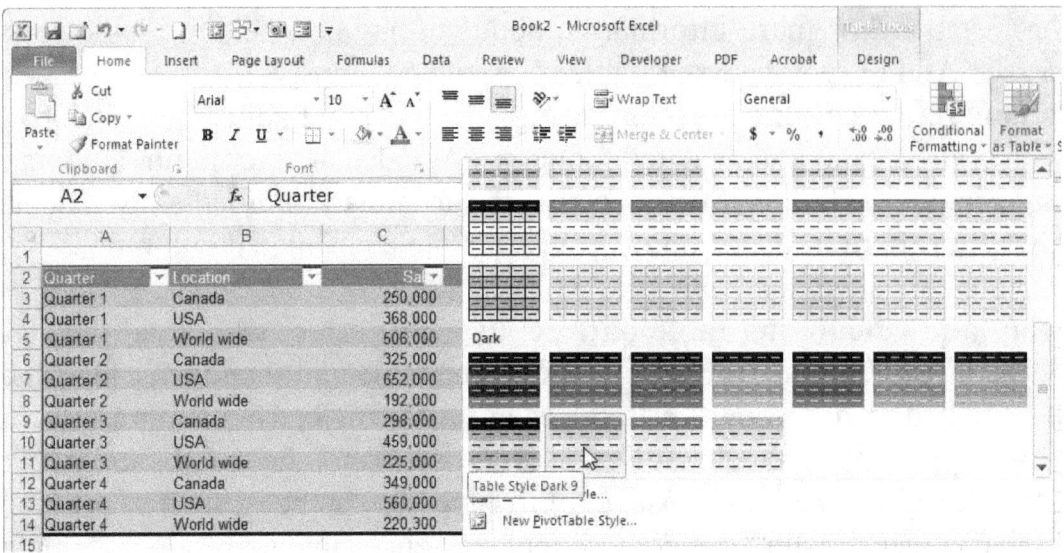

The first step in learning how to work with Excel's Tables features is to use the program to create a table. You'll need a list with column headings and (if you wish) row headings. Select the data, including the heading rows and columns, and click *Insert > Table*. Visually confirm that the range you've selected is correct, click the *My table has headers* checkbox, and click *OK*. Excel will then create a formatted table for you. If you would prefer to choose a particular table format, select the same data area and click *Home* (instead of Insert); then choose a table style from the Table Styles gallery.

2. Remove the Filter Arrows

Click the Filter option to toggle the display of the filter arrows on or off.

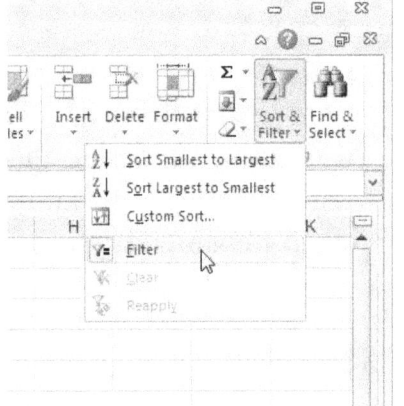

When you want to use some features of an Excel table, but you don't plan to filter or sort your data, you can hide the filter arrows. To do this, click somewhere inside the table and then click *Data > Sort & Filter > Filter*. Now you can toggle between hiding the arrows with one click and revealing them with the next. The shortcut keystroke combination **Shift-Ctrl-L** accomplishes the same thing.

3. Take the Format but Ditch the Table

Formatting data as an Excel table is the quickest way to achieve a neatly formatted range of cells in Excel. The only potential problem is that it may seem that you can't get the formatting without getting all the unwanted table features as well. But while this limitation is technically true, you don't have to keep the table features if you don't want them. To borrow a table style for any worksheet, first create the data as a table, making sure to choose your preferred table style for formatting it.

Next, click inside the table and then click *Table Tools > Design > Convert to Range*. Click *Yes* when Excel prompts you with 'Do you want to convert the table to a normal range?' and the table will revert to being a regular range--but with its attractive formatting intact.

4. Fix Ugly Column Headings

Use the Increase Indent option with right-aligned column headings to push them to the left of the filter arrows.

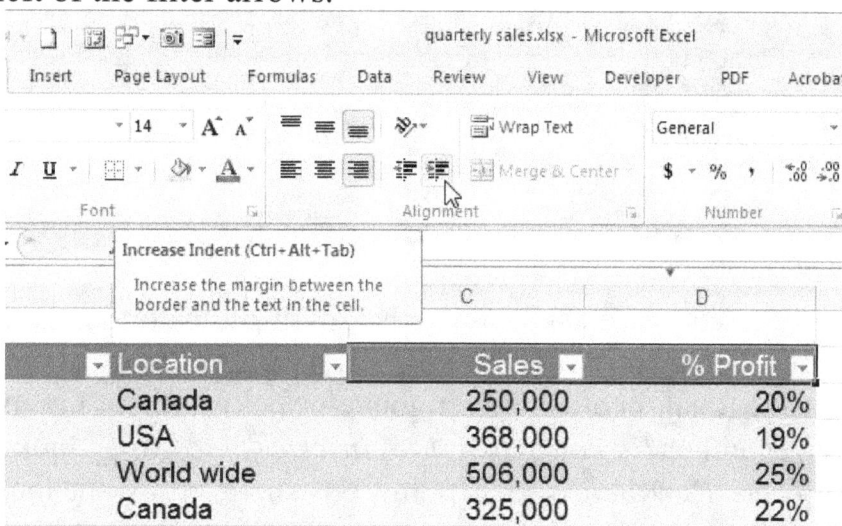

The filter arrows in an Excel table's column headings look downright ugly when those headings are right-justified. The arrows cover the rightmost characters in the headings, and there is no obvious way to fix the problem. The workaround is to indent the content from the right side of the cell. To do this, select the cells containing the headings that are partly hidden and click *Home > Increase Indent*.If the cell contents respond by jumping to the left edge of the cell, click *Home > Align Right* to return them to right justification. Click *Increase Indent*more than once as necessary to position the heading text well clear of the filter arrows.

5. Add New Rows to a Table

Rows in a table behave a little differently from rows in a regular worksheet. If you need to add a new row to a table, and if the Totals row is not visible, click in the bottom right cell in the table and press the **Tab** key. This simple procedure adds a new row to the table, just as it would if you were working with a Word table.

To add a new row inside a table, use the special insert options that appear only when you've selected a cell inside a table.

To add rows to the end of a table, drag the small indicator in the bottom right corner of the table to add more rows and more adjacent columns, if desired. To add a row inside a table, click in a cell either above or below where the row should be inserted and click either *Home > Insert > Insert Table Row Above* or *Home > Insert >Insert Table Row Below*, depending on where you want the new row to appear. The table's formatting will automatically adjust so that the new row is correctly formatted.

To *createvertical and obliqueheadings*

Vertical headings identify data listed in Microsoft Excel columns. When you have numerous columns, you may be unable to view all data without scrolling sideways. However, if the column data is numeric, the headings are probably the widest text in the column. Making these headings vertical conserves space and allows you to view more columns without scrolling. Vertical headings can be rotated 90 degrees to conserves vertical space as well, but this format forces you to tilt your head to read the headings easily. Alternatively, you can have each character in the vertical text printed normally, which improves readability at the expense of vertical space. However, you may change vertical heading into oblique heading automatically through the following steps:

Step 1 -Open your spreadsheet in Microsoft Excel.

Step 2 -Click the cell containing the column heading. Alternatively, click the gray row number that corresponds to the heading to select all cells in that row.

Step 3 -Click the "Home" tab and click the "Orientation" button in the Alignment group. This button is graphically depicted with the angled text "ab."

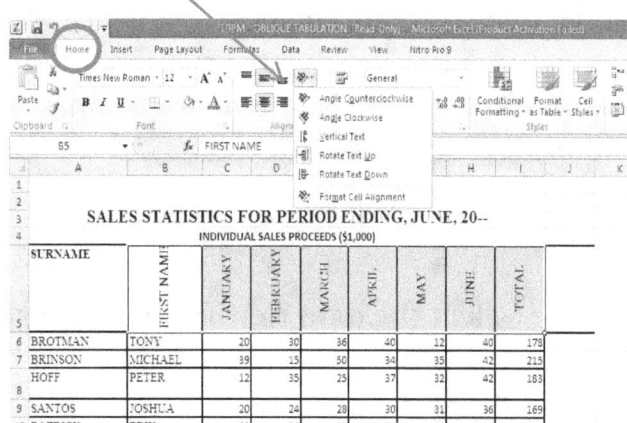

Step 4 -Click "Vertical Text" from the Orientation drop-down menu. This selection keeps the letters angled normally, but lists the text vertically. Alternatively, select "Rotate Text Up" or "Rotate Text Down," which rotates the entire header up or down.

Step 5 -Click the gray column letter that corresponds to the column header. Alternatively, hold the "Ctrl" key and press "A" to select all columns.

Step 6 -Double-click the gray divider to the right of the selected column, or double-click any gray column divider if you previously selected all columns. Doing so automatically resizes the columns to match the widest text currently entered. If the headings were previously the widest text, this will significantly reduce space requirements.

Step 7 –To obtain the oblique headings, highlight the selected column, then on the "Orientation" button in the Alignment group graphically depicted with the angled text "ab." , click "Format Cell Alignment".

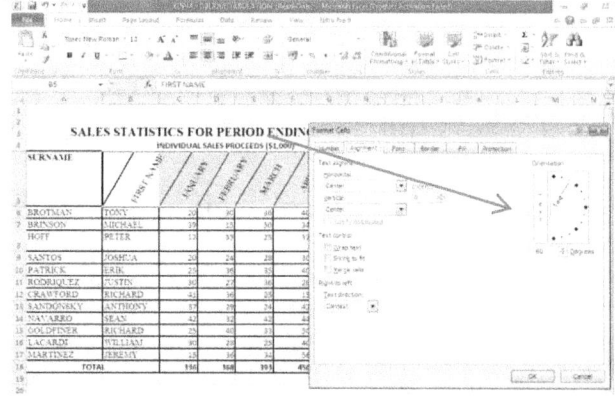

Step 8 –At the right side of the "Format Cell" as you click the alignment tab, choose the number of degrees or angle you want your oblique headings to be at. You may design your text alignment of your choice and control such as to wrap, shrink or merge the text.

For Table Alignment on page

How to Sort data in a table

When you sort information in a table, you can see data the way you want and find values quickly. You can sort a range or table of data on one or more columns of data; *for example, you can sort employees first by department and then by last name.*

How?

1 **Select the data that you want to sort**

Select a range of data, such as A5:H17 (multiple rows and columns) or A6:A17 (a single column). The range can include titles that you created to identify columns or rows.

	SURNAME	FIRST NAME	JANUARY	FEBRUARY	MARCH	APRIL	MAY	JUNE	TOTAL
5									
6	BROTMAN	TONY	20	30	36	40	12	40	178
7	BRINSON	MICHAEL	39	15	50	34	35	42	215
8	HOFF	PETER	12	35	25	37	32	42	183
9	SANTOS	JOSHUA	20	24	28	30	31	36	169
10	PATRICK	ERIK	25	36	35	40	53	15	204
11	RODRIQUEZ	JUSTIN	30	27	36	28	41	43	205
12	CRAWFORD	RICHARD	41	36	25	15	45	40	202
13	SANDONSKY	ANTHONY	37	29	24	42	56	45	233
14	NAVARRO	SEAN	42	32	42	44	35	30	225
15	GOLDFINER	RICHARD	25	40	33	50	45	52	245
16	LACARDI	WILLIAM	30	28	25	40	44	50	217
17	MARTINEZ	JEREMY	15	36	34	56	48	54	243

2 **Sort quickly**

1. Select a single cell in the column on which you want to sort.
2. Click to perform an ascending sort (A to Z or smallest number to largest) or
3. Click to perform a descending sort (Z to A or largest number to smallest).

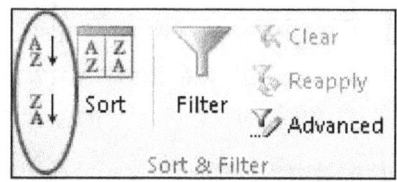

4. Click the button "Continue with the current Selection" then Sort to perform the requested sorting.

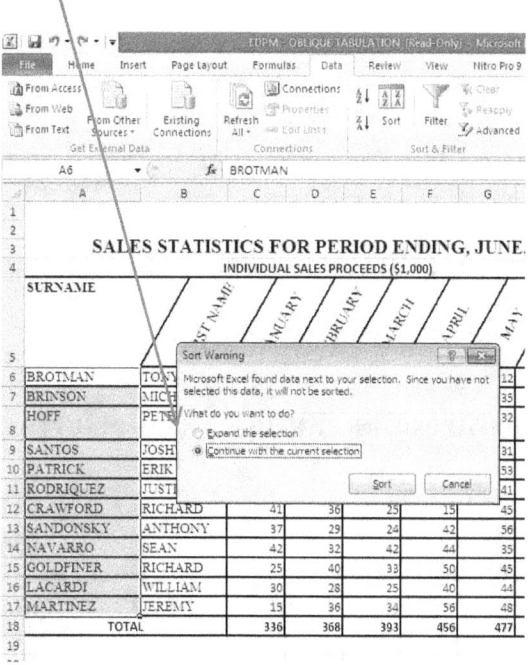

③ Sort by specifying criteria

You can choose the columns on which to sort by clicking the **Sort** command in the **Sort & Filter** group on the **Data** tab.

1. Select a single cell anywhere in the range that you want to sort.
2. On the **Data** tab, in the **Sort & Filter** group, click **Sort**.
3. The **Sort** dialog box appears.

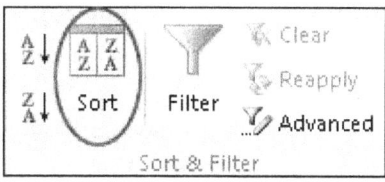

4. In the **Sort by** list, select the first column on which you want to sort.
5. In the **Sort On** list, select either **Values**, **Cell Color**, **Font Color**, or **Cell Icon**.

6. In the **Order** list, select the order that you want to apply to the sort operation — alphabetically or numerically ascending or descending (that is, A to Z or Z to A for text or lower to higher or higher to lower for numbers).

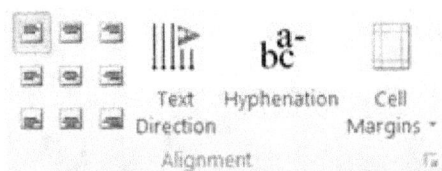

An advanced tabulationsbasicallydealswith largenumeric data rather thantext. Itiswidelyusedto preparebudgets,payrolls,andothercalculationsinbusinessesandotherorganizations.

Thefollowingfeaturesmakeitanidealchoicefortheseorganizations.

- **Calculation**

   Itisapowerfulprogramforcalculations,evenforlargenumericdatathatrequire several types of computation. It also has built-in functionslike sum, Average, Max, and so on.

- **Recalculation**

   Ifyouchangeacertainvalueinthe worksheet,itwillbeautomaticallyrecalculated onthegivenformulausingthenewvalue.

- **Intelligent Addressing**

   Supposeyouhavetocomputeforthetotalvalueoftwocolumnswithonehundred ofrows.Doingitmanually,youwillhavetodoitonehundredtimesbutbecauseofits intelligentaddressing, youjusthavetodo itonceandcopytheformulatotherestofthe rows.

A table can include the following elements:

- **Header row** By default, a table has a header row. Every table column has filtering enabled in the header row so that you can filter or sort your table data quickly.

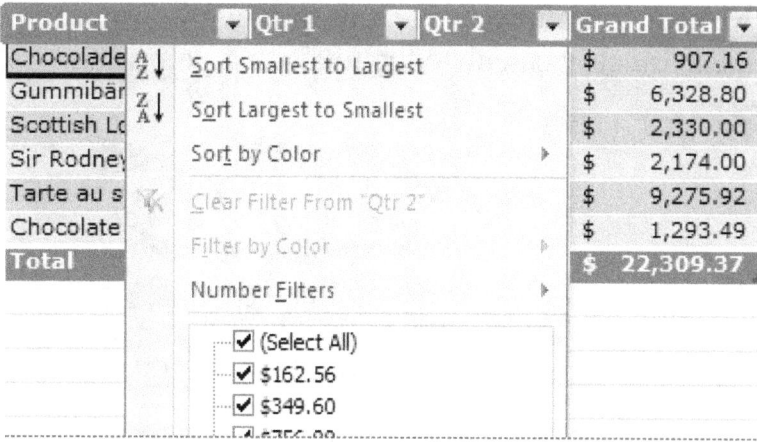

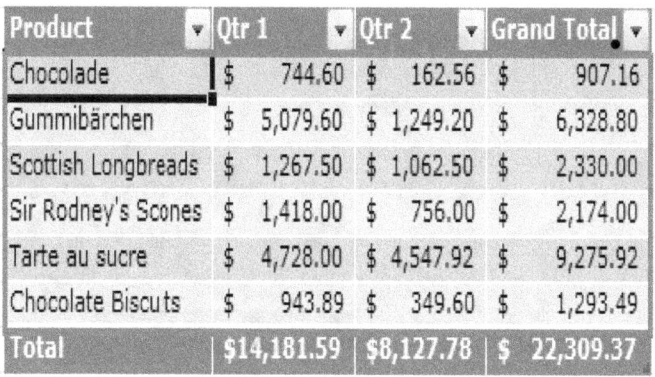

Banded rows By default, alternate shading or banding has been applied to the rows in a table to better distinguish the data.

- **Calculated columns** By entering a formula in one cell in a table column, you can create a calculated column in which that formula is instantly applied to all other cells in that table column.

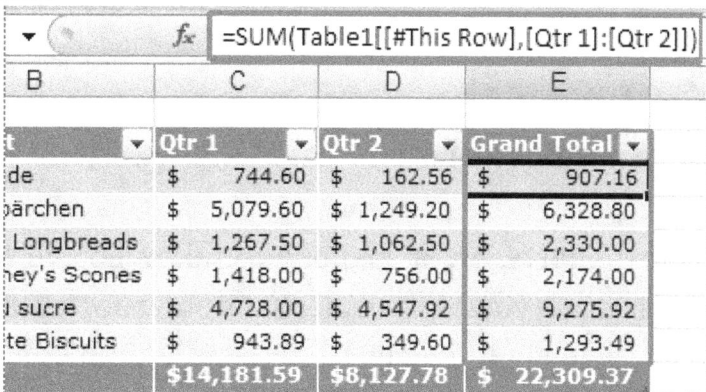

Total row   You can add a total row to your table that provides access to summary functions such as theAVERAGE, COUNT, SUM, MINIMUM or MAXIMUM functions). A drop-down list appears in each total row cell so that you can quickly calculate the totals that you want.

Product	Qtr 1	Qtr 2	Grand Total
Chocolade	$ 744.60	$ 162.56	$ 907.16
Gummibärchen	$ 5,079.60	$ 1,249.20	$ 6,328.80
Scottish Longbreads	$ 1,267.50	$ 1,062.50	$ 2,330.00
Sir Rodney's Scones	$ 1,418.00	$ 756.00	$ 2,174.00
Tarte au sucre	$ 4,728.00	$ 4,547.92	$ 9,275.92
Chocolate Biscuits	$ 943.89	$ 349.60	$ 1,293.49
Total	$14,181.59	3,127.78	$ 22,309.37

None
Average
Count
Count Numbers
Max
Min
Sum
StdDev
Var
More Functions...

- **Sizing handle**   A sizing handle in the lower-right corner of the table allows you to drag the table to the size that you want.

Grand Total
$ 907.16
$ 6,328.80
$ 2,330.00
$ 2,174.00
$ 9,275.92
$ 1,293.49
$ 22,309.37

Inserting charts and graphs

Graphs, also called **charts**, are incredibly useful tools, and Excel makes it quick and easy to add them to your spreadsheets in order to tell a visual presentation, story, and so on. Although graphs can seem intimidating, they are actually incredibly easy to make on Excel. In fact, Excel makes graphs so efficiently that it is considered a basic feature of the program.

How to insert charts and graphs:

1. Enter your data into the Excel spreadsheet in table format. Your data should have column headers, row headers and data in the middle to make the most out of your graph.

   In Excel, "columns" refer to vertical depth. If you look at the above pictures, the columns are labeled with letters, and go from top to bottom: "A," "B," "C," and so on."Rows," on the other hand, refer to horizontal distance. They are labeled with numbers, and go from left to right: "1," "2," "3," and so on.

T24			fx				
A	B	C	D	E	F	G	H
Area/ Day	Mon	Tues	Wed	Thurs	Fri	Sat	Sun
A	50	35	20	12	100	533	606
B	20	28	10	8	132	451	540
C	30	66	35	66	152	300	450
D	45	23	65	35	101	623	661
E	30	32	45	45	88	800	268
F	10	12	85	52	63	211	365
G	25	45	35	22	26	112	347

2. With your cursor, highlight the cells that contain the information that you want to appear in your graph. If you want the column labels and the row labels to show up in the graph, ensure that those are selected also.

8R x 8C			fx	Area/ Day			
	A	B	C	D	E	F	G	H
1	Area/ Day	Mon	Tues	Wed	Thurs	Fri	Sat	Sun
2	A	50	35	20	12	100	533	606
3	B	20	28	10	8	132	451	540
4	C	30	66	35	66	152	300	450
5	D	45	23	65	35	101	623	661
6	E	30	32	45	45	88	800	268
7	F	10	12	85	52	63	211	365
8	G	25	45	35	22	26	112	347
9								
10								
11								
12								

3. With the text selected, click Insert → Chart. In some versions of Excel, you can also try navigating to the Charts tab in the Ribbon tab and selecting the specific kind of graph you'd like to use. This will create your a graph on a "chart sheet." A chart sheet is basically a spreadsheet page within a workbook that is totally

dedicated to displaying your graph.For Windows users, you can create a graph with a shortcut by hitting the F11 button on your keyboard.

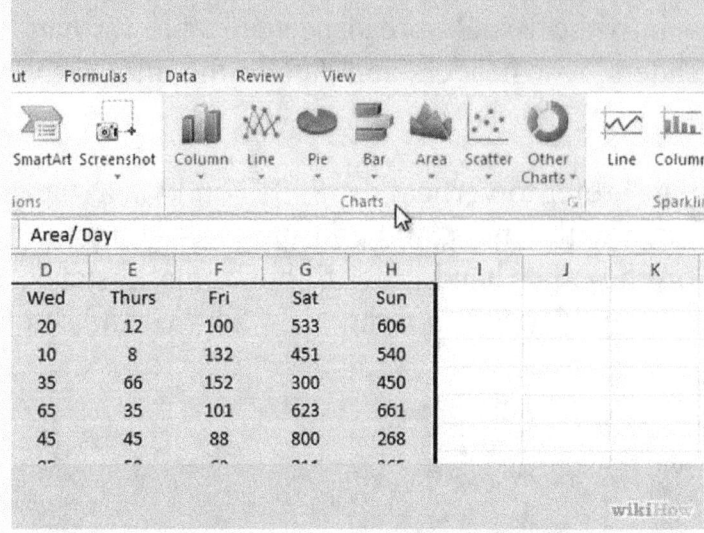

4. Change your graph to fit your needs. Select the perfect kind of graph depending on what information you have and how you want to present it — don't just settle for any old one. Different versions of Excel allow you to change the chart type in various different ways:

Change your chart on the Chart toolbar, which appears after your chart is created. Click on the arrow next to the Chart Type button and click on the whatever type of chart you'd like.

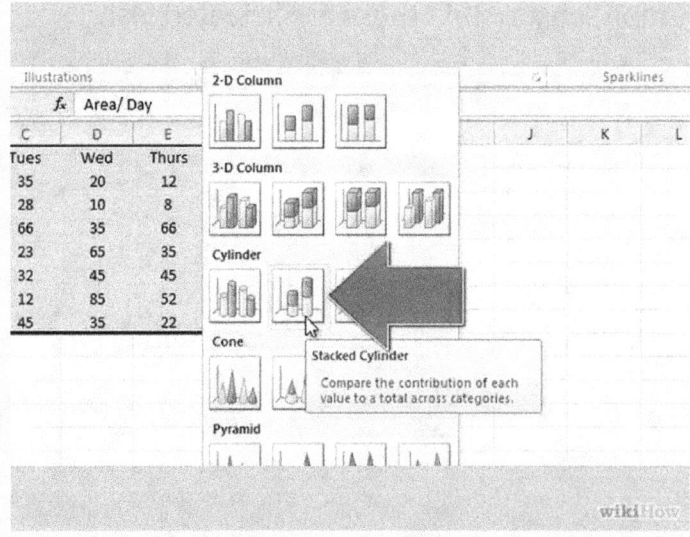

Manipulate the chart types in the Chart Layout tab in the Ribbon tab. Some versions of Excel won't have a "Chart Toolbar," but instead will keep the same basic information in a whole tab devoted to charts.

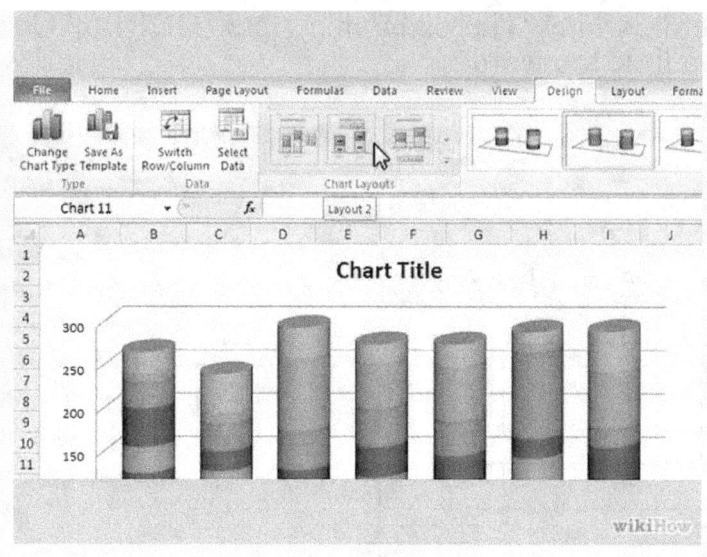

After inserting such charts or graphs, we need to enrich it into a more professional looking presentation in order to emphasize the real message of the graphs. Excel has an embarrassment of riches when it comes to charts and graphs. This is usually a great thing, but it can also paralyze the user with choice. Which graph should I choose? the user asks herself.

First:*Here's a breakdown of the basic kinds of graphs or charts you can use in Excel:*

Column charts *-These charts compare values across categories. Great for comparing sales and expenditures, for example, during a period of time.*

Bar chart *-These charts compare multiple values. They're similar to column charts, except their "columns" are twisted 90° and stick out to the side instead of up and down.*

Line chart. *-These charts display trends over time. Use a line chart to track global production of steel from 1930 to present, for example.*

Pie chart *-These charts depict the contribution of each value to a whole. Use these charts to display the percentage breakdown of ethnicity in a given population, for example.*

Area chart *-These charts display differences in data sets over time. Use these charts to show how revenue and profit are linked for a year, for example.*

Scatter plot *-These charts compare pairs of values. Use these charts to plot the relationship between a person's weight and their height.*

Second:Give your chart a title. Click on the "Chart Title" button in the Ribbon tab and select whether you want your title to overlap the graph or to sit solidly above it. Give your graph a useful name while still keeping it pithy. "GDP in Cuba,

1901-1945" is useful, while "The economic state (GDP) of Cuba, from 1901 to 1945" is probably a little too wordy.

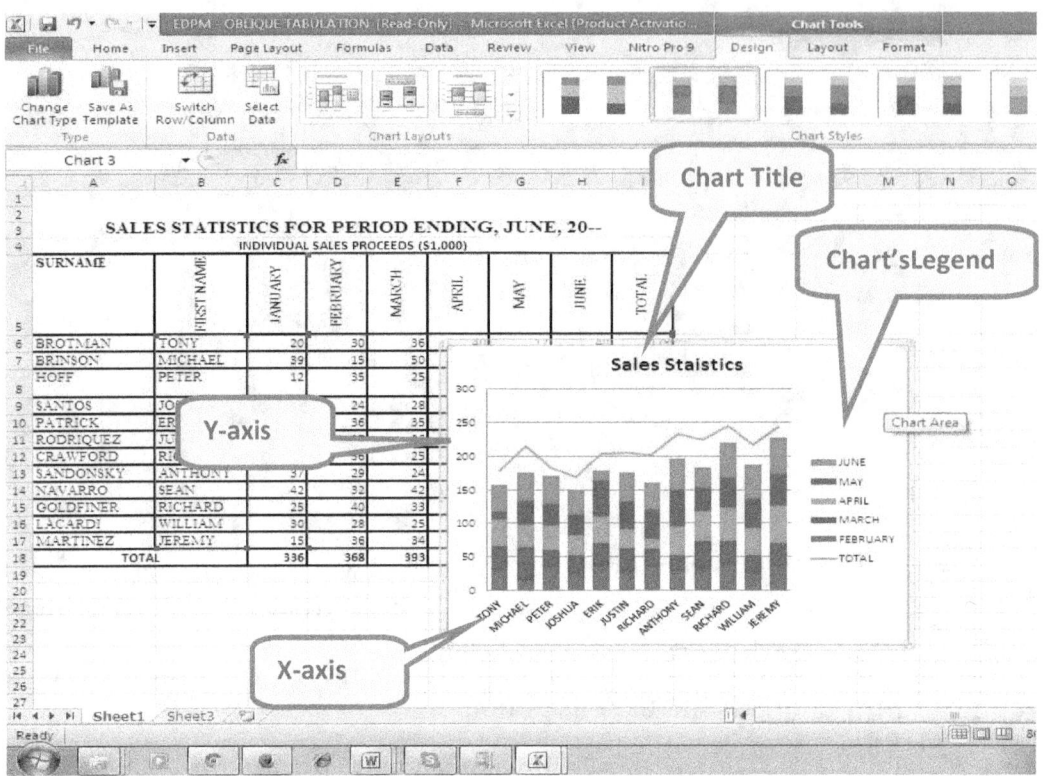

Third: Pay attention to axis titles. What does your x-axis represent, and how about your y-axis? If you don't pay attention to labeling your chart's axes, it's like you're creating a novel without chapters or an instruction manual without pictures. Either way, it will be very hard to interpret your graph.

Fourth: Pay attention to the chart's legend. The legend is the sort of glue that holds a chart together. Without a legend, you're unlikely to know what the graph means because you won't know what information is plotted on the graph.

➢ When you create a chart, Excel creates a legend by default, unless you specify not to. Your legend will be the column and row headers that you highlighted in the beginning while creating your graph.
➢ Changing any column and row headers in their cells automatically changes their representation in the legend.

Fifth: Learn how to change your graph by switching the plotting. Maybe you've accidentally input your information into the cells wrong, and your rows are mixed up with your columns. Instead of inputting the information all over again, simply find the "Data" subsection in the Charts tab (in the Ribbon tab) and press either "plot series by row" or "plot series by column."

<u>Summary</u>

- **SimpleTabulations**
- *Createcolumn androw headings and oblique andverticalheadings;applyborders.Tablealignmento npage. Sortingdataintables.*

-

- **Advanced Tabulations**
  Usingsimple formulae; using spreadsheet or *database software to perform predefined functions: Sum, Average, Minimum, Maximum;* inserting charts and graphs, formatting oftables using %and $;invoices, debit notes and credit notes

esson 4

Creating Database

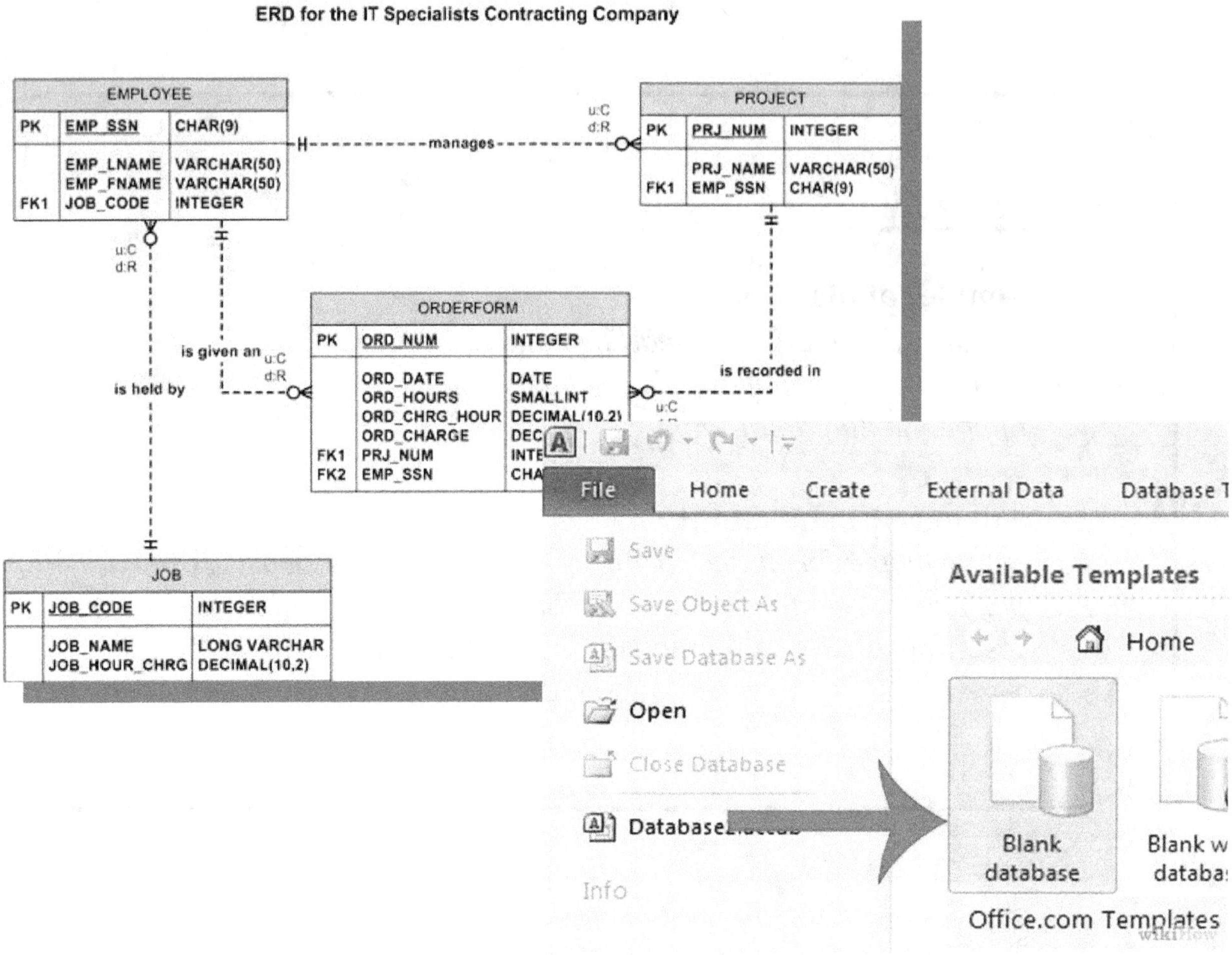

ERD for the IT Specialists Contracting Company

EMPLOYEE		
PK	EMP_SSN	CHAR(9)
	EMP_LNAME	VARCHAR(50)
	EMP_FNAME	VARCHAR(50)
FK1	JOB_CODE	INTEGER

u:C
d:R

---- manages ----

u:C
d:R

PROJECT		
PK	PRJ_NUM	INTEGER
	PRJ_NAME	VARCHAR(50)
FK1	EMP_SSN	CHAR(9)

u:C
d:R

is given an
u:C
d:R

is held by

ORDERFORM		
PK	ORD_NUM	INTEGER
	ORD_DATE	DATE
	ORD_HOURS	SMALLINT
	ORD_CHRG_HOUR	DECIMAL(10,2)
	ORD_CHARGE	DEC
FK1	PRJ_NUM	INTE
FK2	EMP_SSN	CHA

is recorded in

u:C

JOB		
PK	JOB_CODE	INTEGER
	JOB_NAME	LONG VARCHAR
	JOB_HOUR_CHRG	DECIMAL(10,2)

File Home Create External Data Database T

Save

Save Object As

Save Database As

Open

Close Database

Database

Info

Available Templates

← → 🏠 Home

Blank
database

Blank w
databas

Office.com Templates

Objective

At the end of this chapter, the student should be able to:
> *create a database using a single table*
> *perform a simple query using one or two fields*

Access 2010 is a relational database application in the Microsoft 2010 Office suite that lets you enter, manage, and run reports on large amounts of data. You will learn the essential skills needed to create a database, including on how to populate database using tables, running queries to search data, and producing meaningful reports. To understand Access 2010, you must first understand **databases.**

What is a database?

A **database** is a collection of data that is stored in a computer system. Databases allow their users to **enter**, **access**, and **analyse**their data quickly and easily.

The easiest way to understand a database is to think of it as a **collection of lists**. Think about one of the databases we mentioned above—the database of patient information at a doctor's office. What lists are contained in a database like that? Well, to start with, there's a list of patient names. Then there's a list of past appointments, a list with medical history for each patient, a list of contact information ... and so on.

This is true of all databases, from the simplest to the most complex. For instance, if you like to bake you might decide to keep a database containing the types of cookies you know how to make and the friends you give those cookies to. This is one of the simplest databases imaginable. It contains two lists: a list of your friends, and a list of cookies.

However, if you were a professional baker you would have many more lists to keep track of: a list of customers, a list of products sold, a list of prices, a list of orders ... it goes on and on. The more lists you add, the more **complex** the database will be.

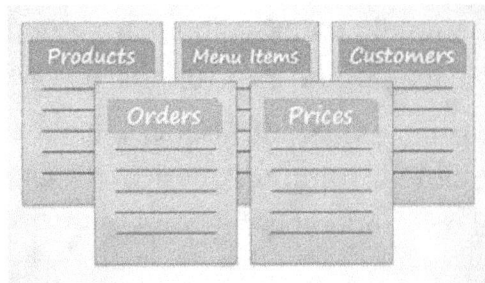

In Access, lists are a little more complex than the ones you write on paper. Access stores its lists of data in **tables**, which allow you to store even more detailed information. In the table below, the "People" list in the amateur baker's database has been expanded to include other relevant information about the baker's friends.

ID ▾	Name ▾	Cell Phone ▾	Birthday ▾	Nut Allergy?
1	Dad	555-0404	June 3	Yes
2	Aunt Aida	555-9890	July 8	No
3	Joakim	555-0462	September 19	No
4	Dwane	555-9975	January 5	No
5	Allegra	555-0099	January 14	Yes

Why use a database?

The thing that really sets databases apart from any other way of storing data is **connectivity**. We call a database like the ones you'll work with in Access a **relational database**. A relational database is able to understand how lists and the objects within them **relate** to one another.

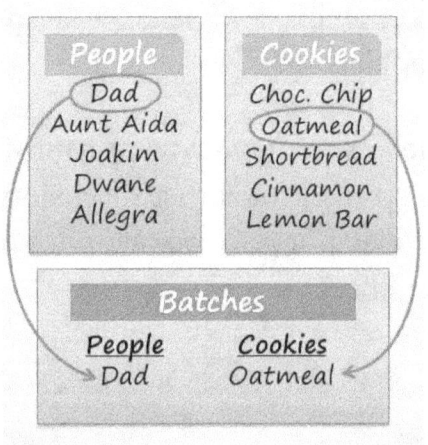

See how the third list uses words that appeared in the first two lists? A database is capable of understanding that the "Dad" and "Oatmeal" cookies in the "Batches" list are the same things as the "Dad" and "Oatmeal" in the first two lists. This relationship seems obvious, and a person would understand it right away. However, an Excel workbook wouldn't.

The fact that relational databases can handle information this way allows you to **enter**, **search**, and **analyze** data in more than one table at a time. All of these things would be difficult to do in Excel, but in Access even complicated tasks can be simplified and made fairly user friendly.

In Access 2010, **tables** are arguably the most important. Even when you're using forms, queries, and reports, you're still working with tables, since that's where all your **data** is stored. Tables are at the heart of any database, so it's important to understand how to use them.

How to populate database using no more than 5 fields:

In this lesson, you will learn how to **open tables**, create and edit **records**, and **modify the appearance** of your table to make it easier to view and work with.

I. **To open an existing table:**

1. **Open** your database, and locate the **Navigation Pane**.
2. In the **Navigation Pane**, locate the table you would like to open. Tables are marked with the ⊞ icon.
3. **Double-click** the name of the table. It will open and appear as a **tab** in the **Document Tabs bar**.

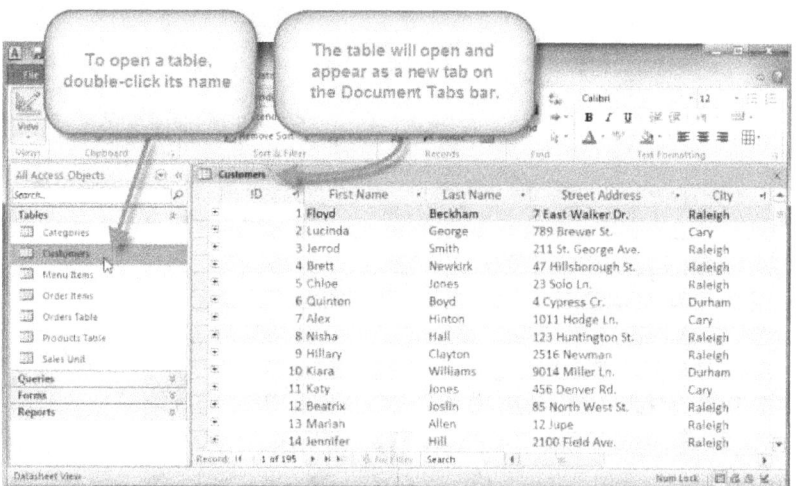

II. Understanding tables

All tables are composed of horizontal **rows** and vertical **columns**, with small rectangles called **cells** in the places where rows and columns intersect. In Access, rows and columns are referred to as **records** and **fields**.

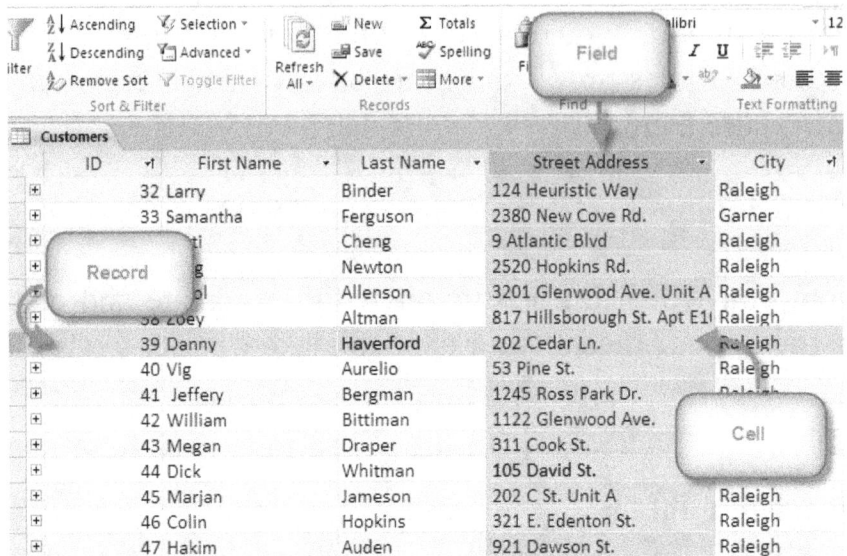

A **field** is a way of organizing information by type. Think of the **field name** as a question, and every cell within that field as a response to that question.

A **record** is one unit of information. Every cell on a given row is part of that row's record. Each record has its own **ID number**. Within a table, each ID number is unique to its record and refers to all of the information within that record. The ID number for a record cannot be changed.

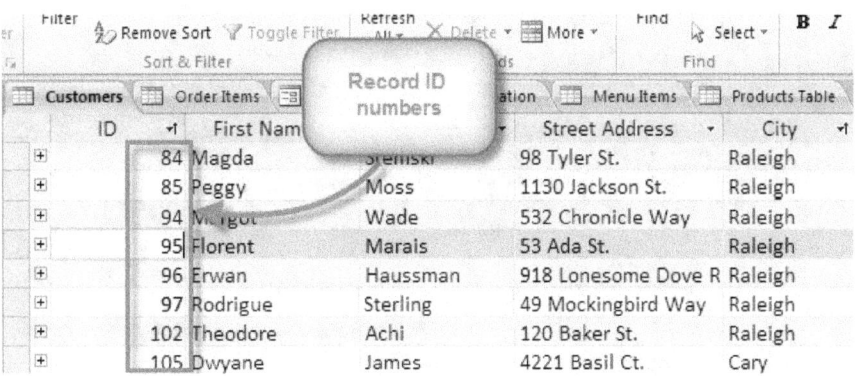

Each cell of data in your table is part of both a **field** and a **record**. For instance, if you had a table of names and contact information, each person would be represented by a record, and each piece of information about each person—name, phone number, address, and so on—would be contained within a distinct field on that record's row.

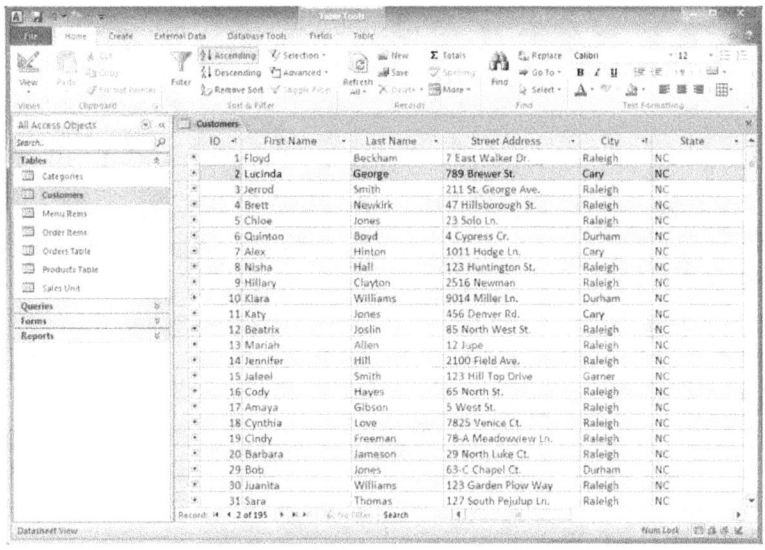

III. Navigating within tables

To navigate through records in a table, you can use the **up and down arrow keys**, **scroll up and down**, or use the arrows in the **record navigation bar** located at the bottom of your table. You can also find any record in the currently open table by **searching** for it using the **record search box**. Simply place your cursor in the search box, type any word that appears in the record you would like to find, and press **Enter**. To view additional records that match your search, press Enter again.

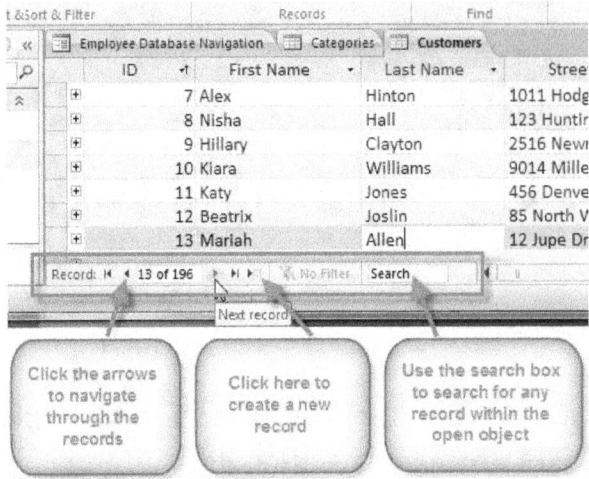

To navigate between fields, you can use the **left and right arrow keys** or **scroll left and right**.

IV. *Adding records and entering data*

Entering data into tables in Access is similar to entering data in Excel. To work with records, you'll have to enter data into **cells**

To add a new record:

There are three ways to add a new record to a table:

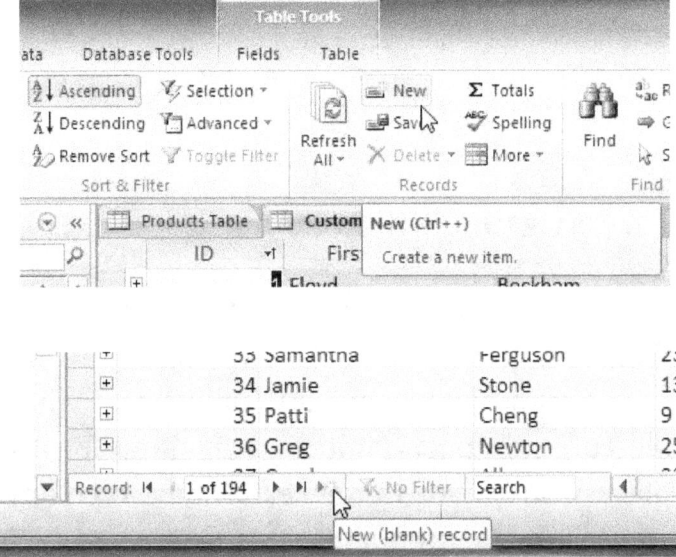

- In the **Records** group on the **Home** tab, click the **New** command.

- On the **Record Navigation bar** at the bottom of the window, click the **New Record** button.

- Simply begin **typing** in the row below your last added record.

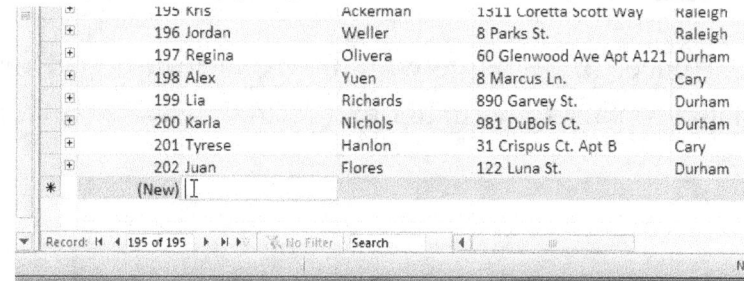

Occasionally when you enter information into a record, a window will pop up to tell you the information you've entered is invalid. This means the field you're working with has a **validation rule**, which is a rule about the type of data that can appear in that field. Click **OK**, then follow the instructions in the pop-up window to **re-enter** your data.

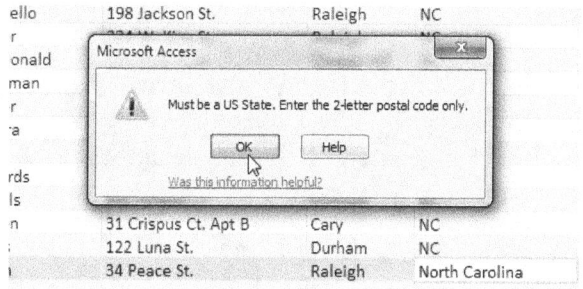

To save a record:

1. Select the **Home** tab, and locate the **Records** group.
2. Click the **Save** command.

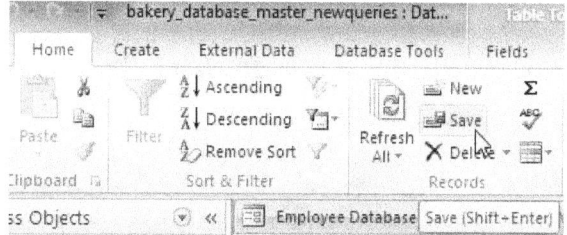

Be sure to save any unsaved records before closing a table. Access will not prompt you to save them when you close the table.

Editing records

To quickly edit any record within a table, simply click on it and type in your changes. However, Access also offers you the ability to **find and replace** a word within multiple records and to **delete** records entirely.

To replace a word within a record:

You can edit multiple occurrences of the same word by using **Find and Replace**, which searches for a term and replaces it with another term.

1. Select the **Home** tab, and locate the **Find** group.
2. Select the **Replace** command. The **Find and Replace** dialog box will appear.

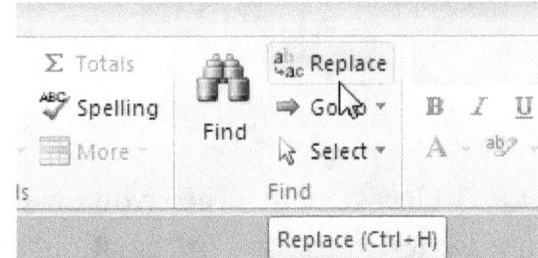

3. Click the **Find What:** box, and type the word you would like to find.

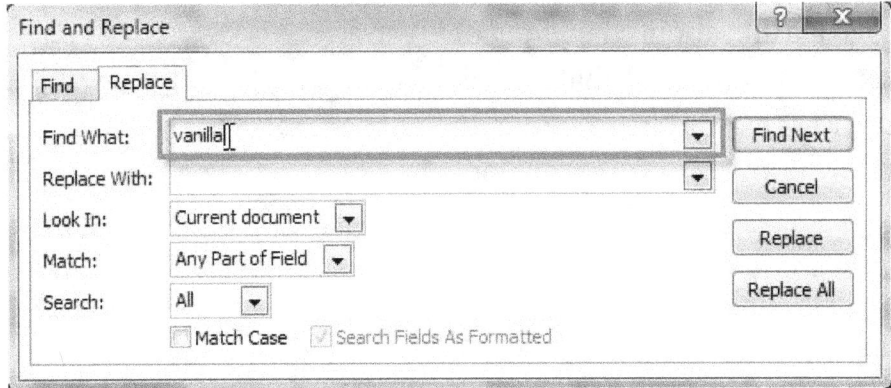

4. Click the **Replace With:** box, and type the word you would like to replace the original word.

5. Click the **Look In:** drop-down arrow to select the area you would like to search.
   - Select **Current Field** to limit your search to the currently selected field.
   - Select **Current Document** to search within the entire table.

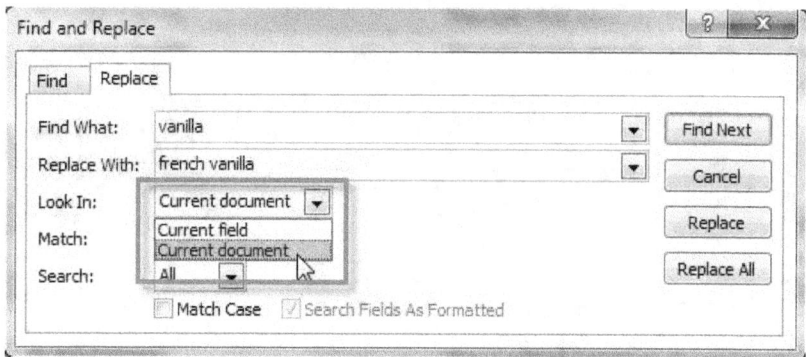

6. Click the **Match:** drop-down arrow to select how closely you'd like results to match your search.

   o Select **Any Part of Field** to search for your search term in any part of a cell.

   o Select **Whole Field** to search only for cells that match your search term exactly.

   o Select **Beginning of Field** to search only for cells that start with your search term.

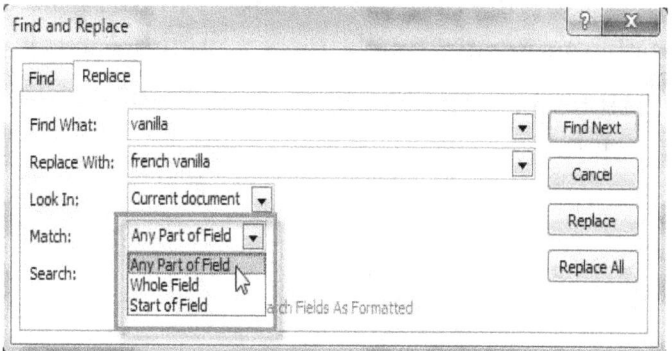

7. Click **Find Next** to find the next occurrence of your search term.

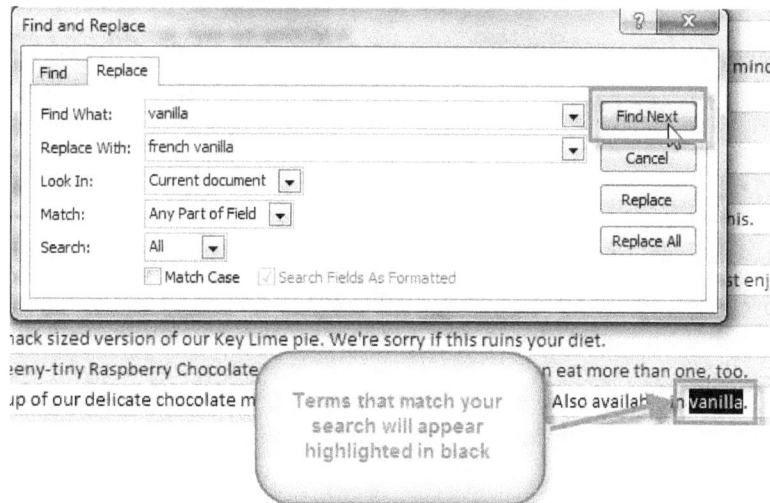

8. Click **Replace** to replace the original word with the new one.

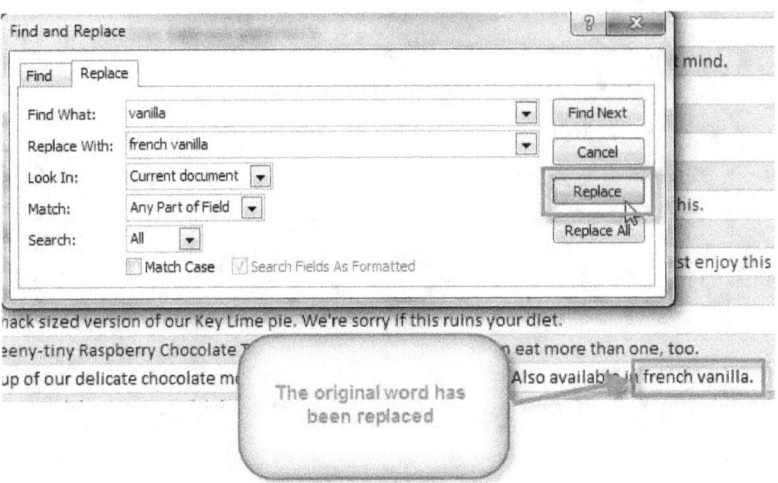

The original word has
been replaced

While you can use **Replace All** to replace every instance of a term, replacing them one at a time allows you to be absolutely certain that you edit only the data you want. Replacing data unintentionally can have a negative impact on your database.

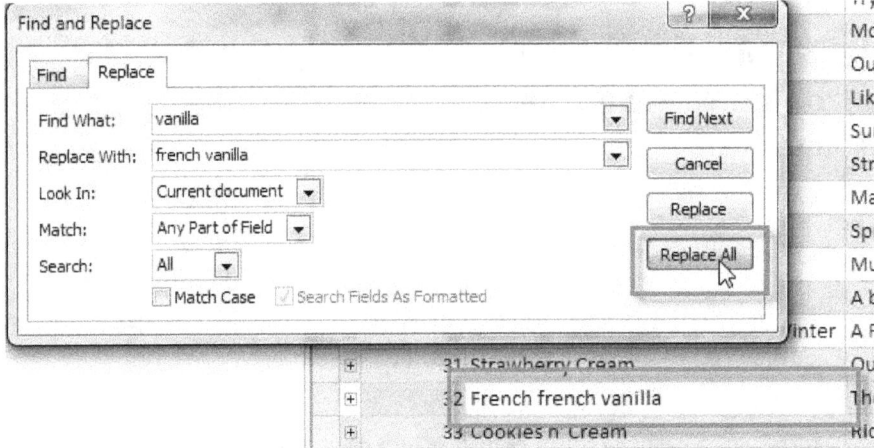

To delete a record:

1. Select the entire record by clicking the **gray border** at the left side of the record.

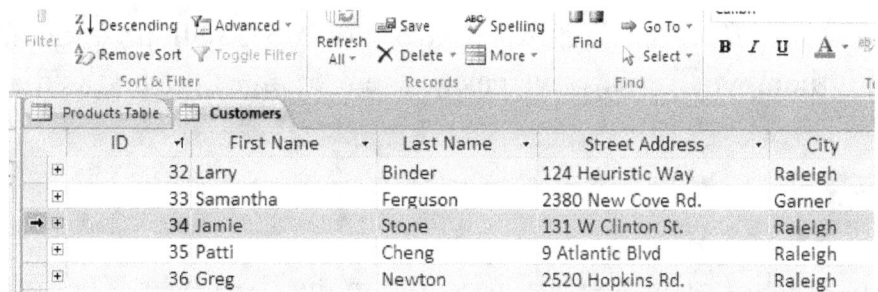

2. Select the **Home** tab, and locate the **Records** group.

3. Click the **Delete** command. The record will be permanently deleted.

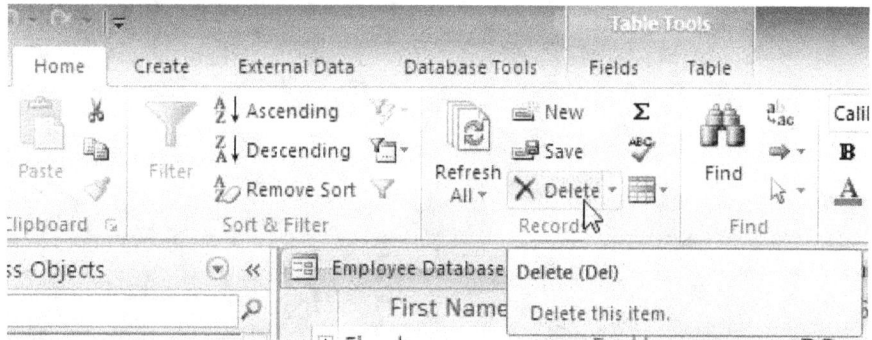

The ID numbers assigned to records stay the same even after you delete a record. For example, if you delete the 34th record in a table, the sequence of record ID numbers will read "...32, 33, **35**, 36..." rather than "...32, 33, **34**, 35, 36...".

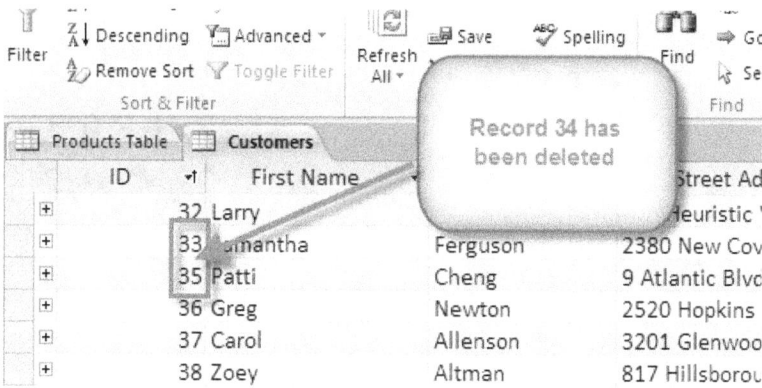

Modifying table appearance

Access 2010 offers several ways to modify the appearance of tables. These changes aren't just about making your table look nice—they can make the table easier to read too. If your fields and rows are too small or large for the data contained with them, you can always **resize** them so all of the text is displayed.

To resize a field:

1. Place your cursor over the **right gridline** in the **field title**. Your mouse will become a **double arrow ✛**.

2. **Click and drag** the gridline to the right to increase the field width or to the left to decrease the field width.

3. **Release** the mouse. The field width will be changed.

To resize a row:

1. Place your cursor over the **bottom gridline** in the **gray area** to the left of the row. Your mouse will become a **doublearrow ✛**.

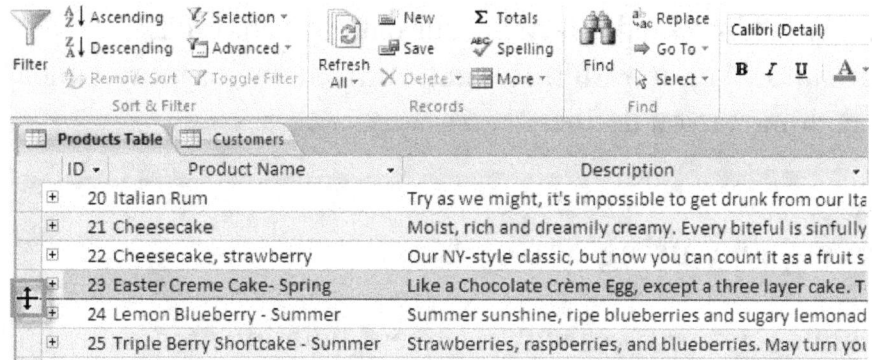

2. **Click and drag** the gridline downward to increase the row height or upward to decrease the row height.

3. **Release** the mouse. The row height will be changed.

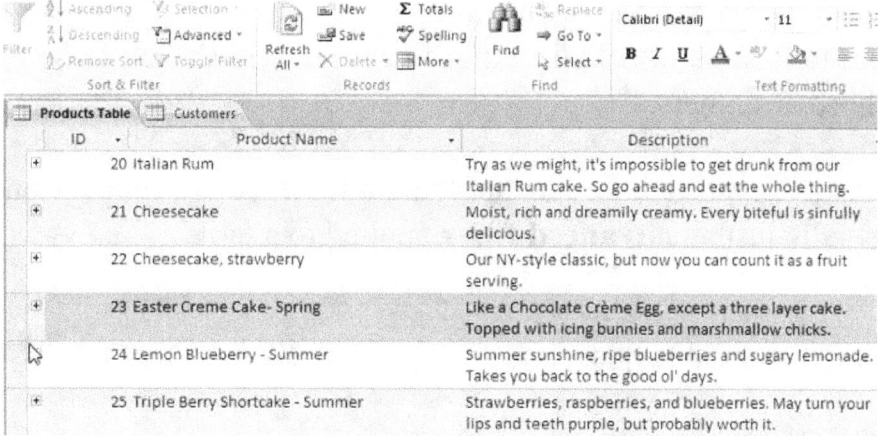

If you have a field you don't plan on editing or don't want other people to edit, you can **hide** it. A hidden field is invisible but is still part of your database. Data within a hidden field can still be accessed from forms, queries, reports, and any related tables.

To hide a field:

1. Right-click the **field title**.

2. From the drop-down menu, select **Hide Fields**.

3. The field will be hidden.

The real power of a relational database lies in its

ability to quickly **retrieve** and **analyze** your data by running a query. **Queries** allow you to **pull information** from one or more tables based on a set of search conditions you define.

To perform a query using one or two fields:

Let's familiarize ourselves with the query-building process by building the **simplest** query possible: a one-table query.

We will run a query on the **Customers** table of our bakery database. Let's imagine that our bakery is having a special event, and we want to invite our customers who live nearby since they are the most likely to come. This means we need to see a list of all of the customers who live close by, and **only** those customers.

If you think this sounds a little like applying a filter, you're right. A one-table query is actually just an **advanced filter** applied to a table.

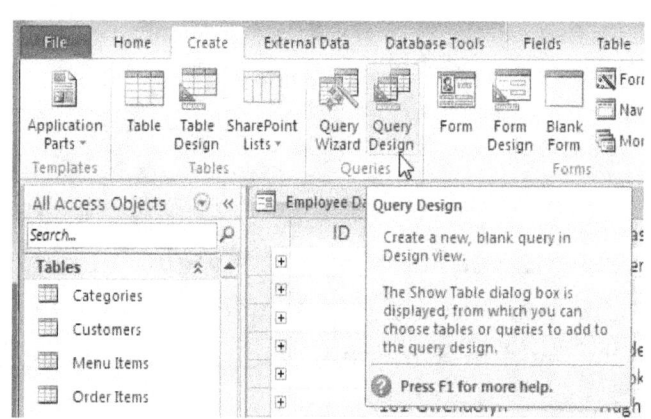

To apply a simple one-table query:

1. Select the **Create** tab on the Ribbon, and locate the **Queries** group.
2. Select the **Query Design** command.

3. Access will switch to **Query Design view**. In the **Show Table** dialog box that appears, select the table you would like to run a query on. Click **Add**, then click **Close**. We are running a query about our customers, so we will add the **Customers** table.

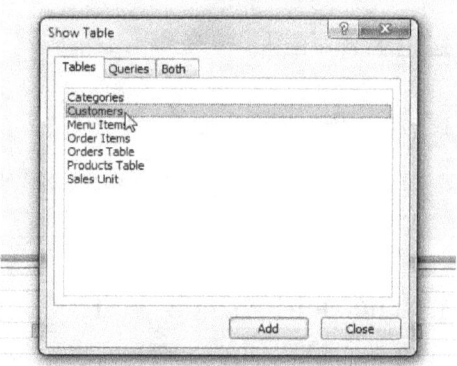

4. The selected table will appear as a small window in the **Object Relationship Pane**. In the table window, double-click the **field names** you would like to include in your query. They will be added to the **Design Grid** in the bottom part of the screen.

5. In our example, we want to mail invitations to customers who live in a certain area, so we'll include the **first** and **last name**, **street address**, **city**, **state**, and **zip code** fields. We aren't planning on calling or emailing our customers, so we don't have to include the **telephone** or **email** fields.

6. Set the **search criteria** by clicking on the cell in the **Criteria: row** of each **field** you would like to filter. Typing criteria into more than one field in the Criteria: row will set your query to include only results that meet all the criteria. If you want to set multiple criteria but don't need the records shown in your results to meet them all, type the first criteria in the Criteria: row and additional criteria in the **Or: row** and the rows beneath it.

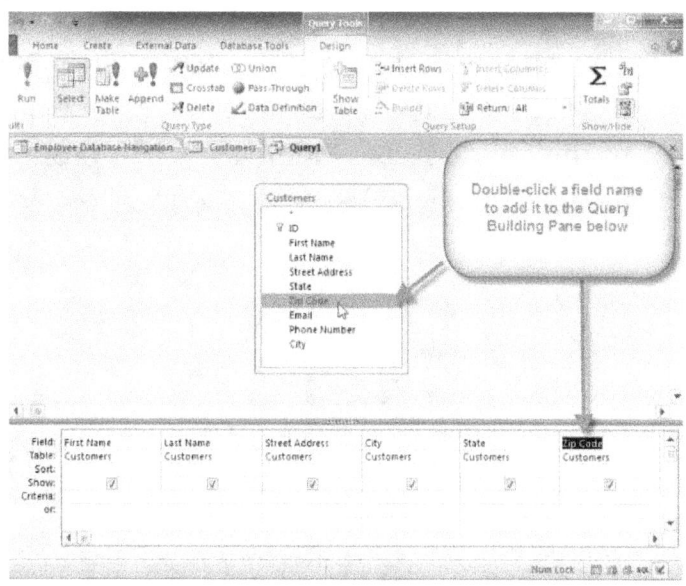

For this one-table query, we'll use very simple search criteria.

- We want to find our customers who live in a city called **Raleigh**, so in our **City** field, we'll type **"Raleigh"**. Typing "Raleigh" in **quotation marks** will retrieve all records with an **exact match** for "Raleigh" in the City field.

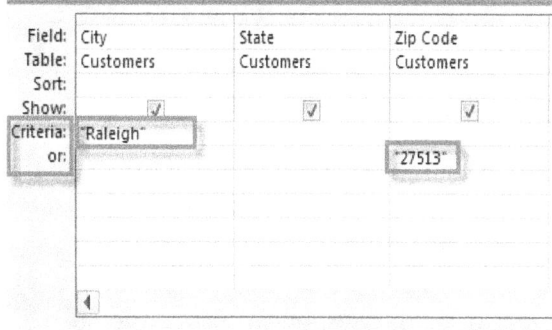

- Some customers who live in the suburbs live fairly close, and we'd like to invite them as well. We'll add their **zip code**, **27513**, as another criteria. Since we want to find customers who either live in

Raleigh **or** in the 27513 zip code, we'll type "27513" in the **or:** row of the **Zip Code** field.

7. After you have set your criteria, **run** the query by clicking the **Run** command on the **Query Tools Design** tab.

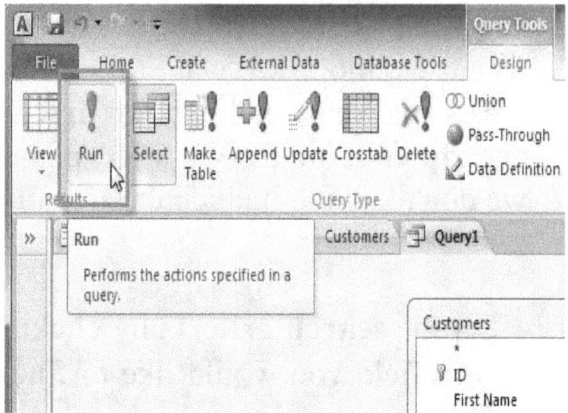

8. The query results will be displayed in the query's **Datasheet View**, which looks like a table. If desired, **save** your query by clicking the **Save** command in the Quick Access toolbar. When prompted to name it, type in the desired name, then click **OK**.

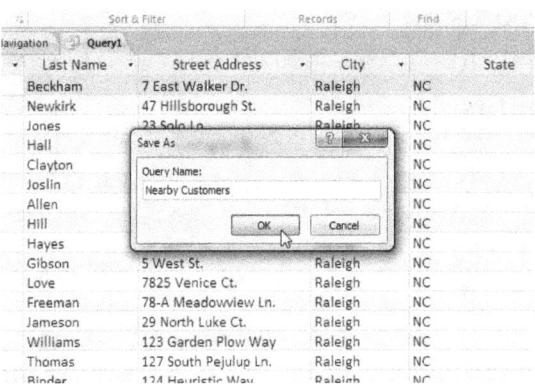

<u>Summary</u>

Access 2010 is a relational database application in the Microsoft 2010 Office suite that lets you enter, manage, and run reports on large amounts of data.

A **database** is a collection of data that is stored in a computer system. Databases allow their users to **enter**, **access**, and **analyse**their data quickly and easily.

A **relational database** is able to understand how lists and the objects within them **relate** to one another. They can populate database using no more than five fields and perform query using one or two fields.

 **L** esson5

Presentation Software

Objective

At the end of this chapter, the student should be able to:
 ➢ *create simple presentations using presentation software*

:

The students should be able to distinguish between Communication devices

---

How to Create a simple PowerPoint Presentation

No matter what the topic, a PowerPoint presentation can help you communicate an idea to an audience. Learn the basics before proceeding. These methods will teach you how to create a presentation from a PowerPoint template or create a fully customized presentation. Here are some steps to get you started.

Sample PowerPoint Presentations

Sample PowerPoint Presentation for School

Sample Photo Slideshow About Flowers

Method 1: Creating a Theme/Template Method For PC (Office 2010)

1. **Open PowerPoint.** You will see a blank screen with two boxes in the middle of the screen. One of the boxes says "Click to add title," the other says "Click to add subtitle."

2. **On the tab at the upper left side of your screen, hit the "File" tab.**

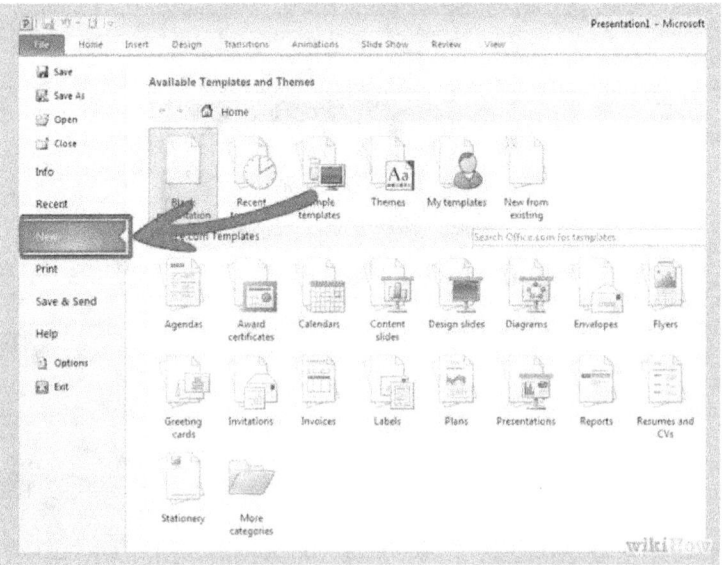

3. On the vertical toolbar to the left, hit the "New" tab.

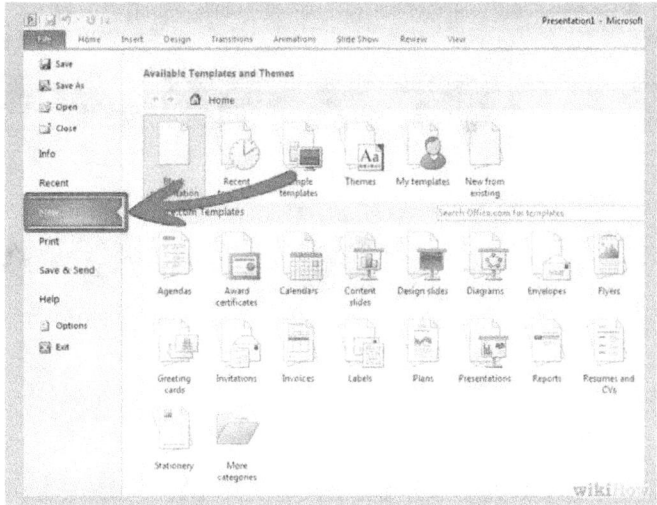

4. If you wish to use a template, click on the "Sample templates" box.

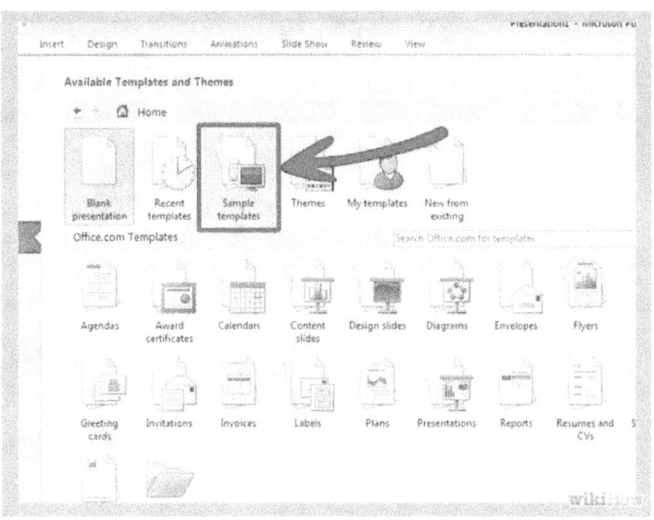

5. Click on the template you want to use, depending on the purpose of your presentation. *If you don't find the kind of template you need for your presentation, it's probably best to choose a theme.*

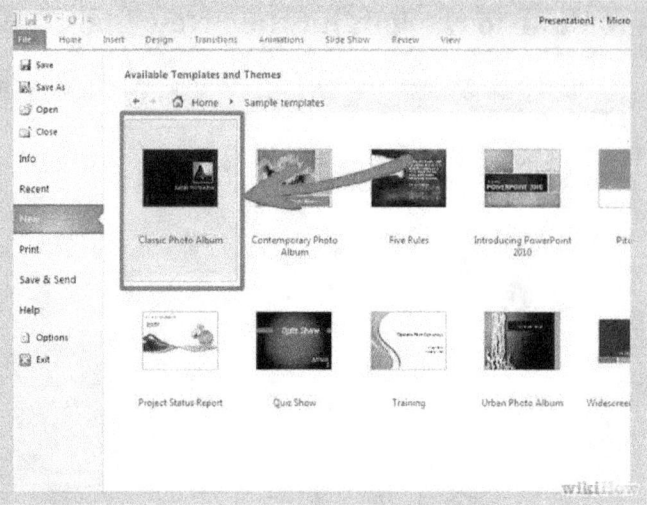

6. **If you wish to use a theme, click on the "Themes" box in the "New" tab.**

A theme is a slideshow with a preloaded background that can be used for general presentations.

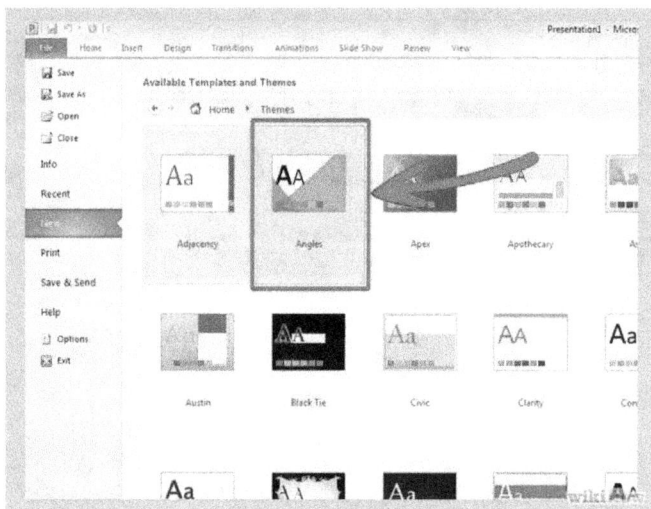

7. **Click on the specific template or theme you want to work with from the list of choices.**

8. Once your theme is loaded, click on the "Click to add title" and "Click to add subtitle" boxes and add the title and subtitle (if necessary) of your own presentation.

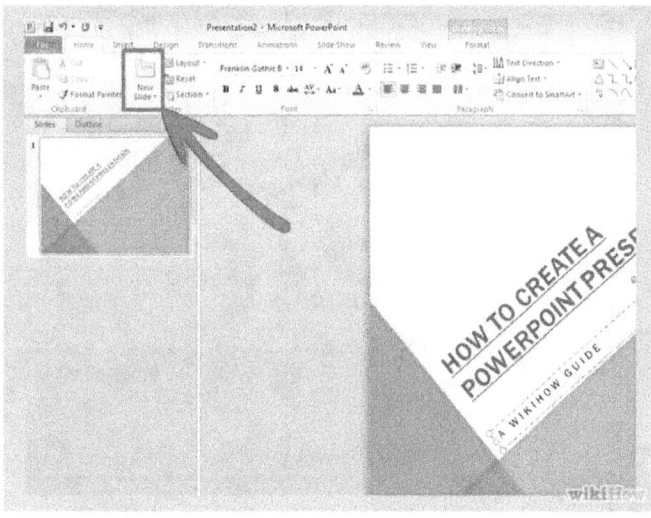

9. **After deciding on a title, click on the "New Slide" button in the "Slides" tab up top.** You can also create a new slide with the shortcut (Ctrl + M).

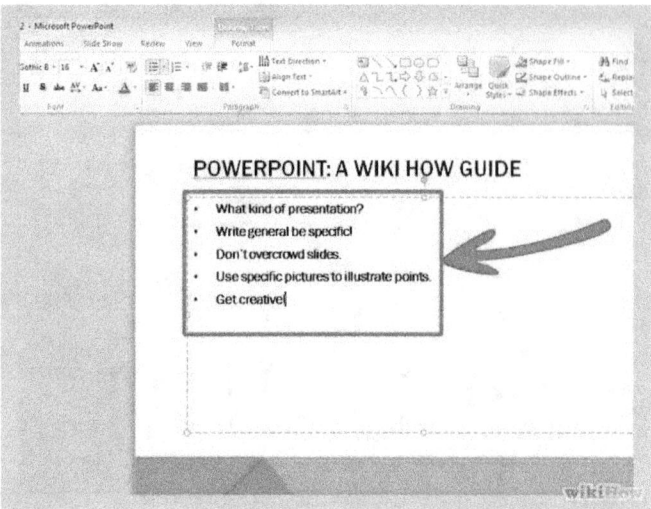

10. Continue adding information and pictures as you see fit. In PowerPoint, however, less is often more.

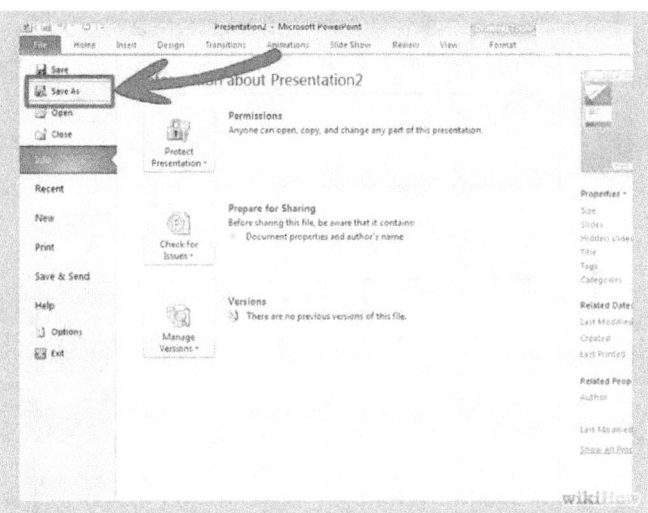

11. Once you are finished with your PowerPoint presentation, go to "File > Save As" and save your file so that you can retrieve it later

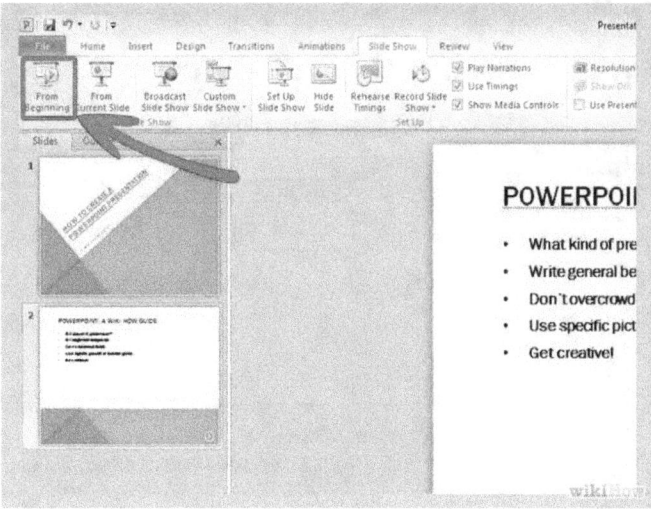

12. When you want to view your presentation as a series of slides, click on the "Slide Show" tab and then click on "From Beginning" top left.

Note: To filter through your slides, click the left and right arrows on your keypad to go back and forward, respectively

Method 2: Creating a Custom Presentation Method For Mac

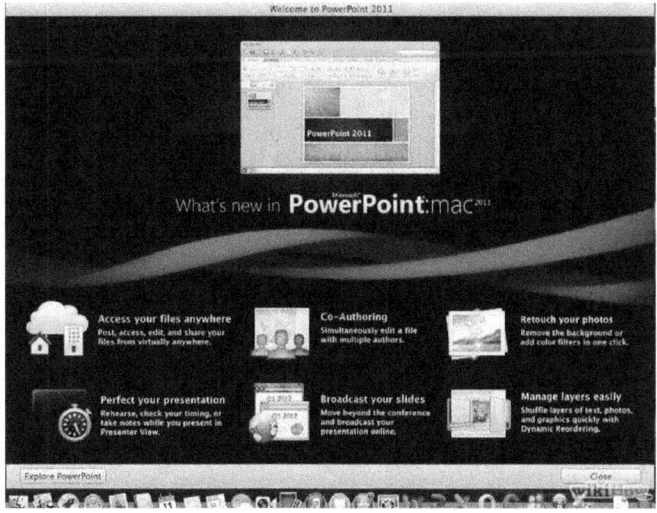

1. Open PowerPoint. Depending on your version, a blank presentation may open automatically, or you may need to select the option for a custom presentation.

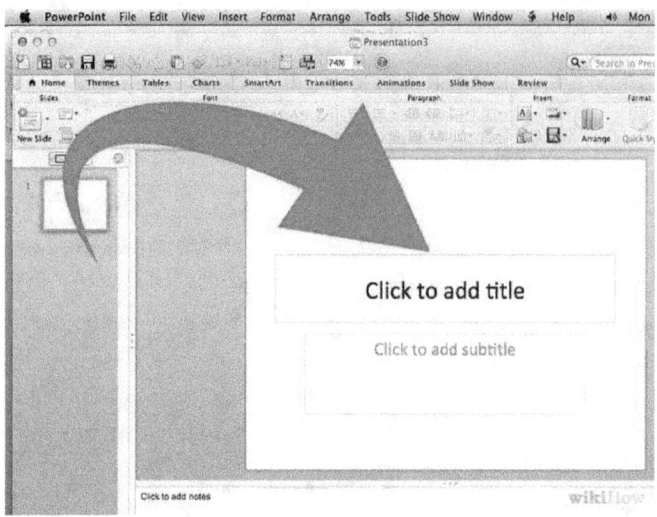

2. Create your first slide. If you want a title page for your presentation, you can use the default title page template provided by PowerPoint. If you want to change the format of the slide, you can pick from among the options in the "Slide Layout" toolbar. These options have different layouts of titles, text, pictures, charts, etc.

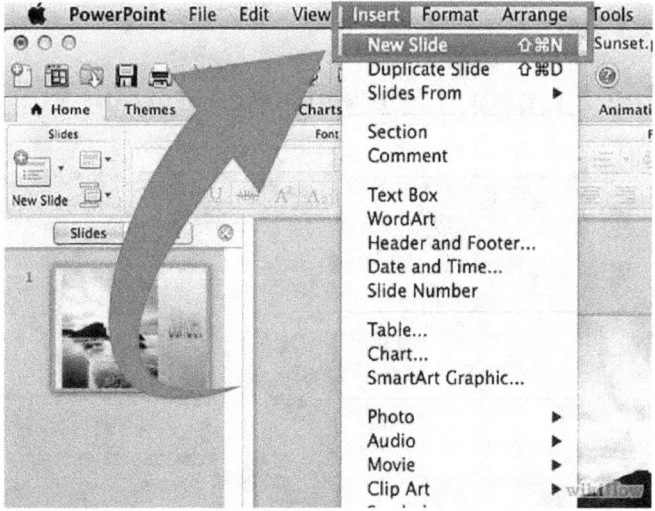

2. **Add a new slide.** You can do this either by clicking the "New Slide" button in the top toolbar, or by selecting "Insert > New Slide". Every time you create a newslide, you can manage its format using the "Slide Layout" toolbar.

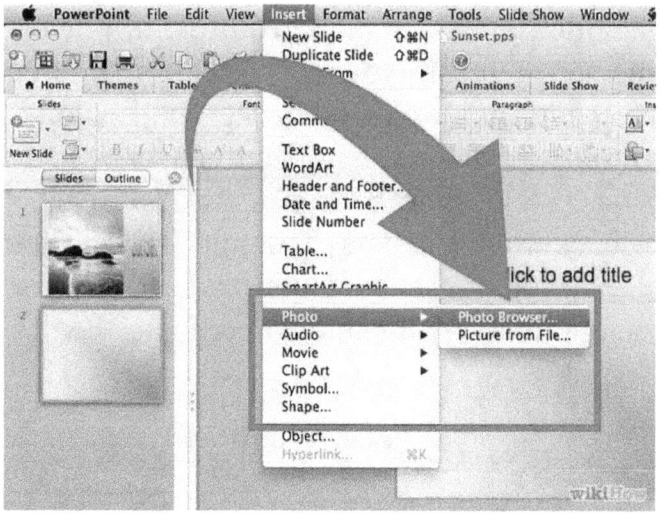

4. **Add content to your slides.** There are different ways to do this within each version of PowerPoint, and they may differ from version to version. The 2 main ways to add content (text boxes, pictures, charts, other multimedia files) to your slides are described here:

- You can add content using the "Insert" menu. To do this, click "Insert" and then choose the type of content that you want to add to that slide. You will be prompted to choose a file to insert. As you can see in the image below, there are a number of different options that you can choose, from Word Art to movies.

- You can add content directly from a slide. To do this, select a format from the "Slide Layout" toolbar that has content options built in. Then, click on the icon of the type of content that you wish to add, and navigate to find the appropriate file.

- **Change slide themes or backgrounds.** In PowerPoint, you can choose pre-made themes or create your own custom slide backgrounds. You can also combine themes with custom background colors. **Change slide themes or backgrounds.** In PowerPoint, you can choose pre-made themes or create your own custom slide backgrounds. You can also combine themes with custom background colors **Change slide themes or backgrounds.** In PowerPoint, you can choose pre-made themes or create your own custom slide backgrounds. You can also combine themes with custom background colors

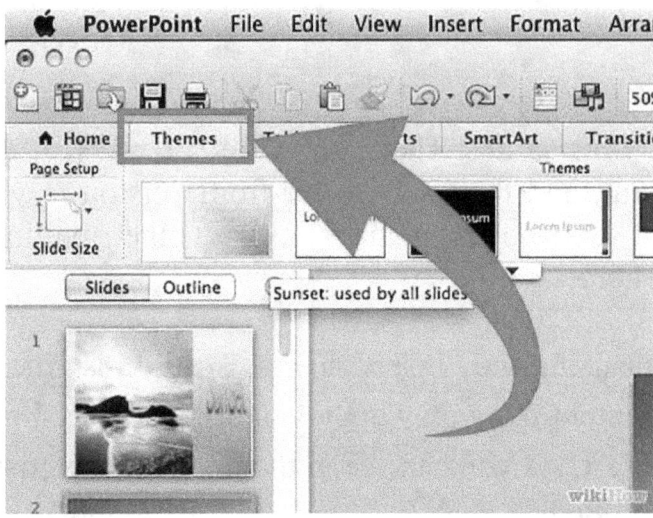

- To change background color, you can click "Format Background" in the Formatting Palette or select "Format > Slide Background..." from the main menu. There are tons of different colors and designs to choose from, so you will have to play around to find one that you like. When you are done, click "Apply" or "Apply To All" depending on whether you want that background on just the current slide or all slides.

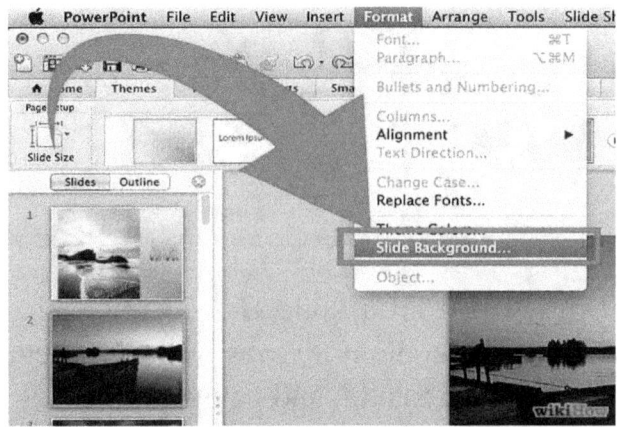

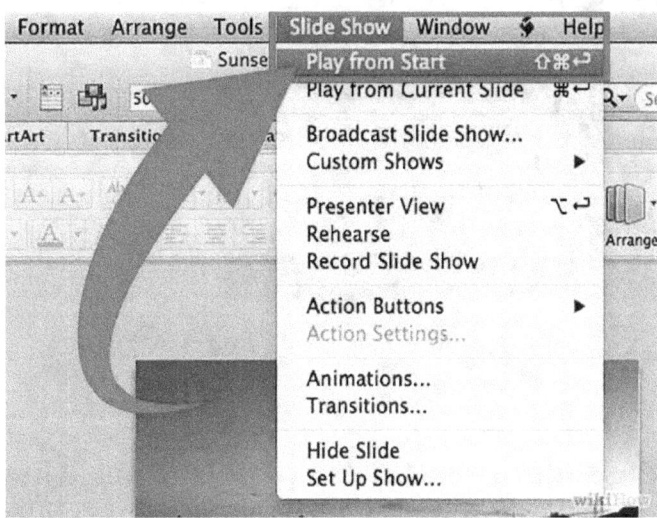

5. View your slideshow. To view your final product, you can either click "Slide Show" in the top toolbar or select "Slide Show > View Slide Show" in the main menu.

Method 3: Template/Theme Method For PC (Older)

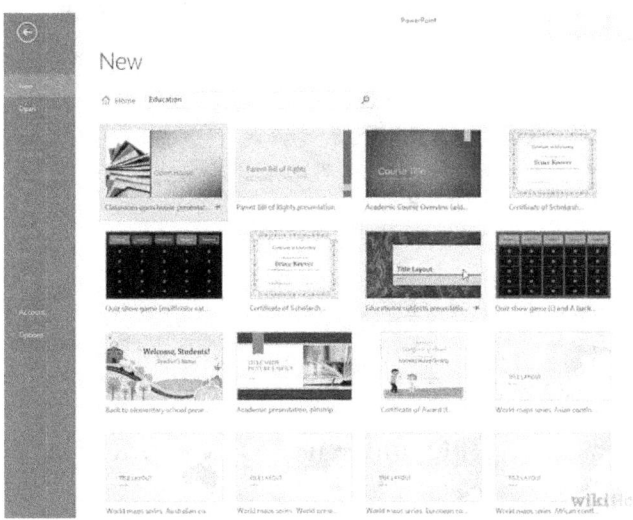

1. **Start with a template or theme.** A template or theme will dress up your presentation with pre-made layouts and color schemes. Choose one by clicking the Office orb in the upper-left corner, and selecting New. Then, on the left, select Installed Templates or Installed Themes.

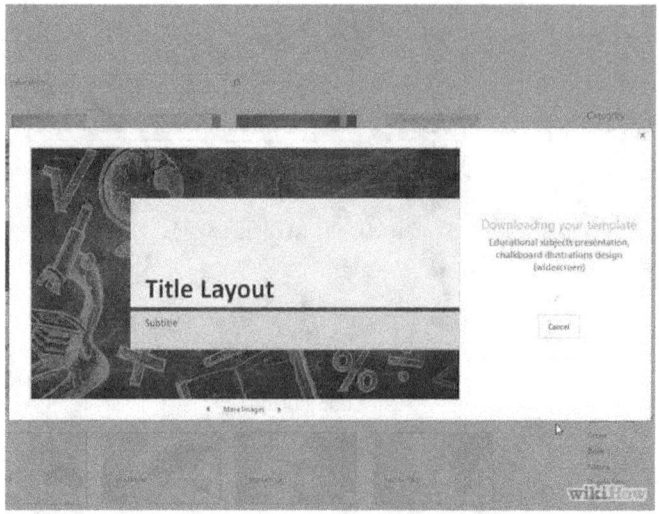

2. Browse through the slides from the template and see what you like. On the sidebar at left, you can click different template or theme slides to see what they look like. Here are a few things you can do with the different slides:

Duplicate slides. Right click on a slide, and select Duplicate Slide.

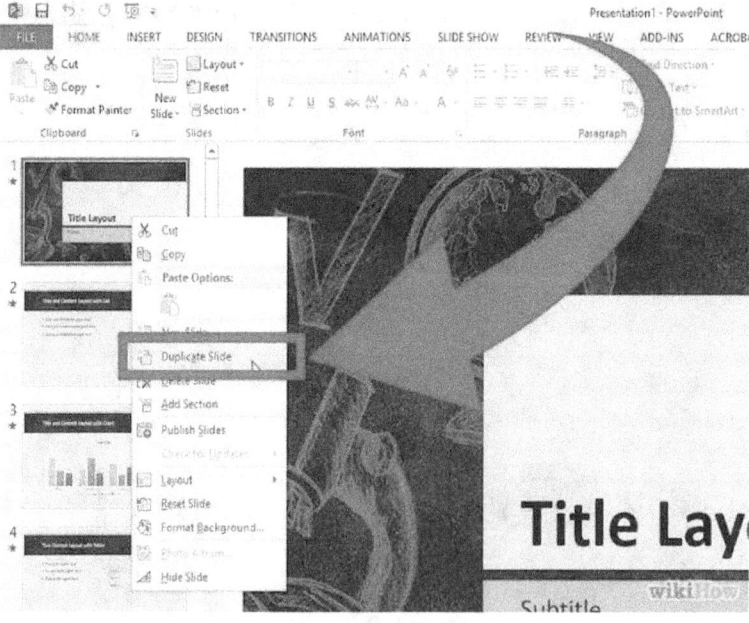

- Delete slides. Right click on a slide and select Delete Slide, or click Home on the top bar, then Delete Slide.

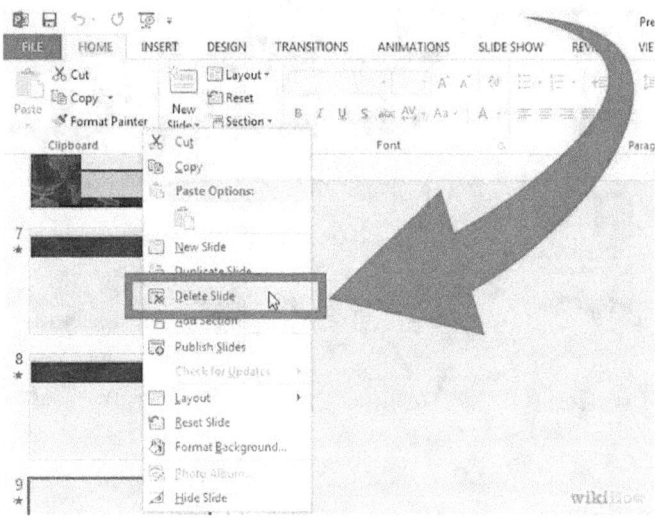

• Change the layout of your slides. You can select slides that have more or less text boxes, photo boxes, or any other template items you want. Select a slide, right click, and hover over Layout. Or, click Home on the top bar, and then the drop menu next to Layout.

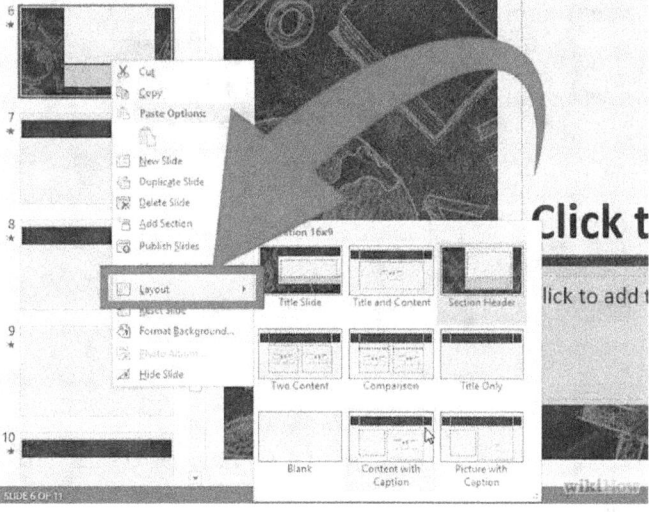

• Add slides. If you want your new slide to look exactly like the one before it, right click that slide and select New. Or, if you want a new slide with a completely different layout, click Home, then the drop menu under New Slide.

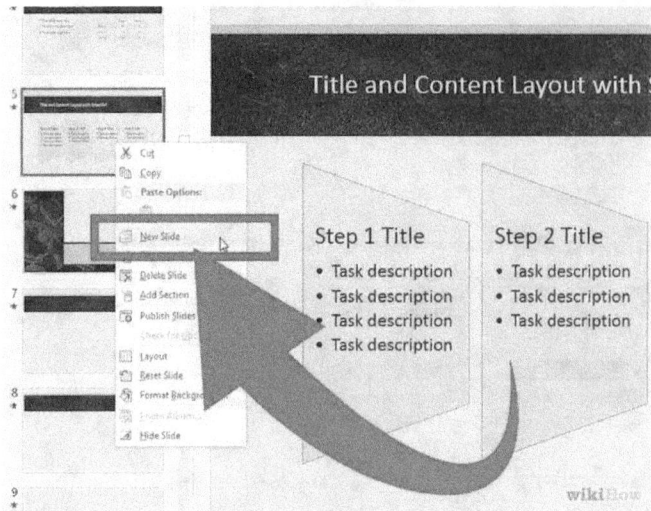

- Organize your slides. You can drag and drop slides in the sidebar to the left to reorder them.

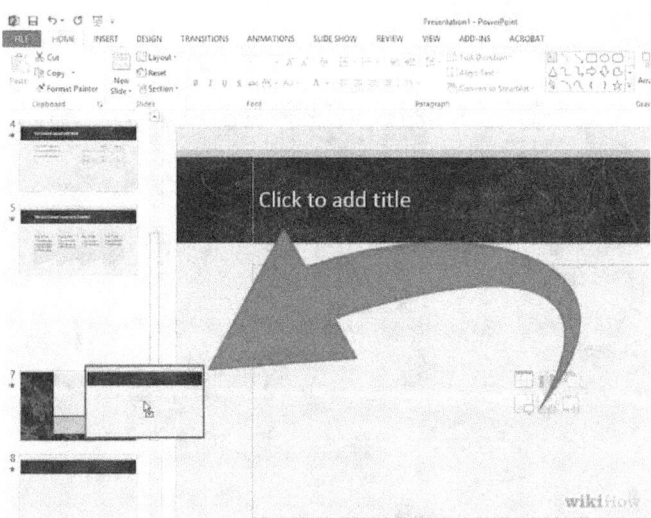

Start adding content. Here are some tips for putting information into your PowerPoint presentation:

- Use short, concise words to guide your audience, and let yourself do the detailed explaining. Keywords show that you know your subject when you go more in-depth during your powerpoint. For example, use "Fire Kiln" as a keyword in a PowerPoint, but explain the process during the actual presentation.

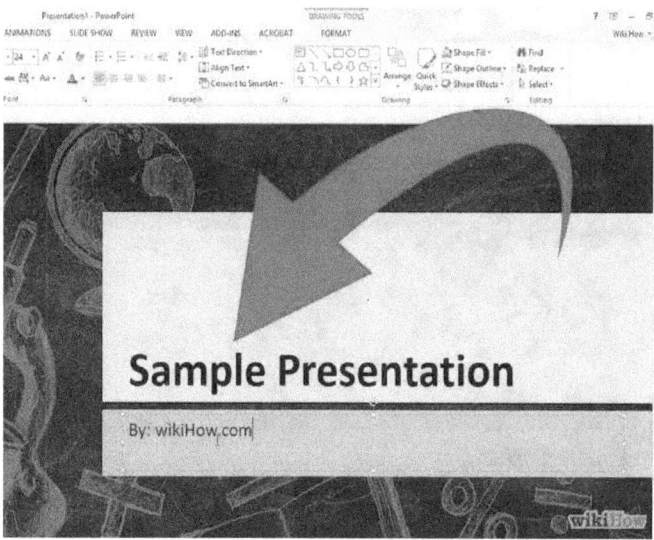

- Think bullet points. Don't use full sentences in your PowerPoint presentations unless it's absolutely necessary.

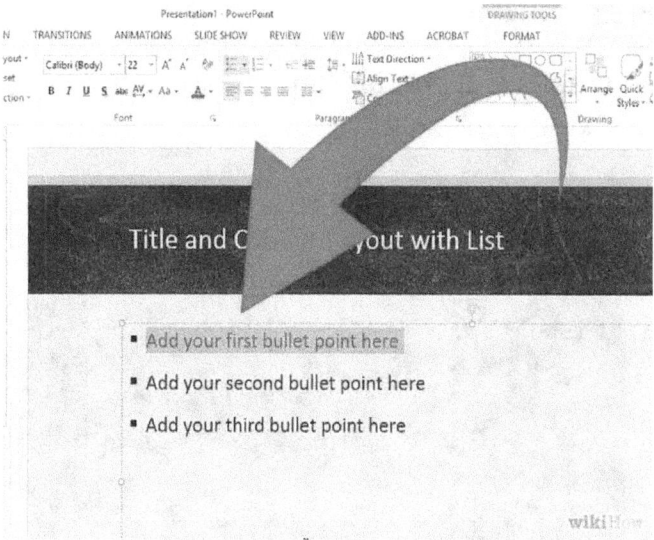

- Don't be afraid to spread information across multiple slides. It's better than overcrowding a PowerPoint!

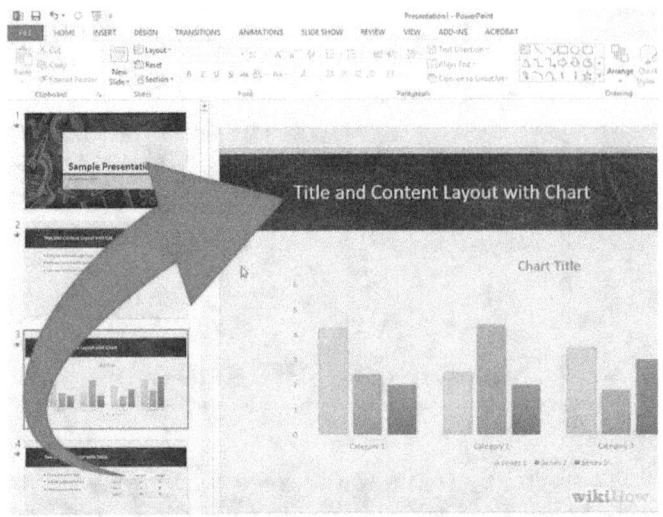

Add elements. To insert anything (text, charts, etc), simply click on the designated box to activate it and start inserting away.

Inserting pictures and graphs is a good idea to make your presentation more visually engaging. Break up your text!

- Inserting pictures and graphs is a good idea to make your presentation more visually engaging. Break up your text!

- Use color effectively in your PowerPoint. Have a theme of colors and be consistent when using them to highlight key points. This makes your presentation look more professional.

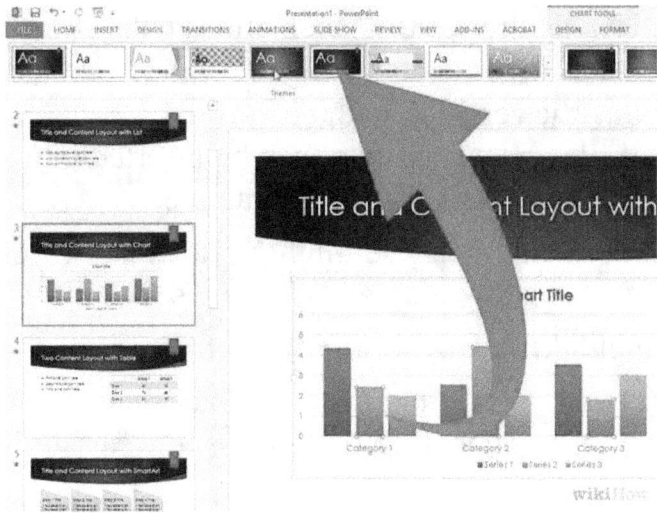

Test run your presentation. Click View, then Slide Show, or hit F5 to admire your handiwork

<u>Tips</u>

- Instead of saving the presentation with the extension *.ppt, go to FILE » SAVE AS and save it as *.pps (PowerPoint Show). This allows you to save the file on your desktop, so when you click on it, the presentation starts automatically. No opening up PowerPoint program first!

- Save your work constantly. This way, if you accidentally hit the exit button or your computer shuts down, you won't lose all your hard work!

- Make sure your PowerPoint presentation is compatible with the device you will be presenting it on. Your version of PowerPoint may be different than another computers version. To assure your presentation will always work with other people's computers, it may be a good idea to have a copy of Microsoft's <u>PowerPoint Viewer 2007</u> with you.

- Just about any type of file you can think of can be inserted into a presentation, even Macros to make PowerPoint presentations interactive.

- If you are proficient in Word, then you might notice that PowerPoint follows a lot of the same rules, such as highlighting and deleting slides like a Word paragraph.

- These instructions might differ slightly for different versions of PowerPoint.

- If you can't get the drift of it after making your second presentation (nothing fancy), it is good to get a guidebook from your local library or have someone show you how to make a simple presentation.

- Keep a backup copy with you. The corrupt flash drive, broken floppy disk, faulty Internet connection, and/or scratched CD could cause major problems if encountered.

- If you do not have PowerPoint, you can download the <u>OpenOffice.org Suite</u> and save files in PowerPoint format for free.

For a neat presentation, it is good to only have a few pictures or not too much writing. Seek to keep it simple and uncluttered

Warning!

- Don't use *too* many special effects as it can get distracting and annoying.
- Don't use too much text in one template. Otherwise it would look too crowded and strenuous to the eyes. Not to mention boring.

Remember the more objects embedded in a PowerPoint, the larger the file. So if you're planning on saving it on a disk, you have to keep the file small unless saving the file on a thumb drive (jump drive) or burning it on CD.

<u>Summary</u>

In creating powerpoint presentation, always include theuseofslides, transitions, timing, appropriate fonts, animations,layoutsandgraphics; effective communication.

Four Methods:

1. Creating a Theme/Template Method For PC (Office 2010)
2. Creating a Custom Presentation Method For Mac
3. Template/Theme Method For PC (Older)

Lesson 6

Dissemination of Documents

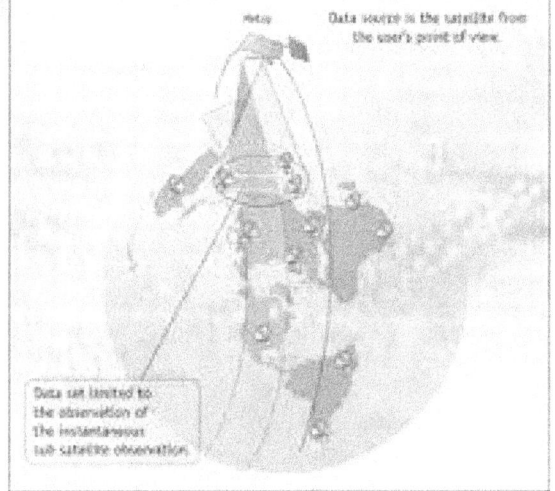

Objective

At the end of this chapter, the student should be able to:
- *integrate information to produce complete documentation*
- *disseminate complete documents using objects or data from different application software*
- *mail merge a certain document*

Once the objects or data are collated and created a complete documentation will be ready for dissemination to various placeholders. The dissemination process delivers the finished products so that it can be used to improve service delivery. There are times a document has the same kind of information, yet some of the content is unique.

For example, in letters to your customers, you can personalize each letter to address each customer by name. The unique information in each letter comes from entries in a data source. To minimize such time and effort, *you use mail merge to create a set of documents or letters that is sent to many customers.*

Mail merge is a software operation describing the production of multiple (and potentially large numbers of) documents from a single template form and a structured data source. The letter may be sent out to many "recipients" with small changes, such as a change of address or a change in the greeting line.

The mail merge process entails the following overall steps:

1. ***Set up the main document.*** The main document contains the text and graphics that are the same for each version of the merged document — for example, the return address in a form letter.
2. ***Connect the document to a data source.*** A data source is a file that contains the information to be merged into a document. For example, the names and addresses of the recipients of a letter.
3. ***Refine the list of recipients or items.*** Microsoft Word generates a copy of the main document for each recipient or item in your data file. If you want to generate copies for only certain items in your data file, you can choose which items (or records) to include.
4. ***Add placeholders, called mail merge fields, to the document.*** When you perform the mail merge, the mail merge fields are filled with information from your data file.
5. ***Preview and complete the merge.*** You can preview each copy of the document before you print the whole set.

You use commands on the **Mailings** tab to perform a mail merge.

IMPORTANT If you plan to use custom contact fields with the Contacts list in Microsoft Outlook or if you plan to use a Public Folders Contacts folder, you must <u>begin the mail merge process in Outlook</u>.

Set up the main document

1. Start and open the MS Word.

A blank document opens by default. Leave it open. If you close it, the commands in the next step are not available.

2. On   the **Mailings** tab,   in   the **Start   Mail Merge** group, click **Start Mail Merge**.

3. Click **Letters**.

You can also use mail merge to create:

• **A catalog or directory** The same kind of information, such as name and description, is shown for each item, but the name and description in each item is unique. Click **Directory** to create this type of document.
• **A set of envelopes**   The return address is the same on all the envelopes, but the destination address is unique on each one.
• **A set of mailing labels**   Each label shows a person's name and address, but the name and address on each label is unique.
• **A set of e-mail messages**   The basic content is the same in all the messages, but each message goes to the individual recipient and each message contains information that is specific to that recipient, such as the recipient's name or some other piece of information.

Resume a mail merge

If you need to stop working on a mail merge, you can save the main document and resume the merge later. Microsoft Office Word retains the data source and field information.

1.   When you're ready to resume the merge, open the document.

Word displays a message that asks you to confirm whether you want to open the document, which will run a SQL command.

2.   Because this document is connected to a data source and you want to retrieve the data, click **Yes**. If you were opening a document that you did not realize was connected to a data source, you could click **No** to prevent potentially malicious access to data.

The text of the document, along with any fields that you inserted, appears.

3.   Click the **Mailings** tab, and resume your work.

Connect the document to an external data source

To merge information into your main document, you must connect the document to an external data source, or a data file. If you don't already have a data file, you can create one during the mail merge process.

IMPORTANT If you use an existing list, make sure that it contains the information that you want to use, including all the columns and the rows. You can make some changes during the merge, but you can't open your data source separately during the merge. The merge process is easier if your data source is ready before you connect to it.

Choose a data file

1. On   the **Mailings** tab,   in   the **Start   Mail Merge** group, click **Select Recipients**.

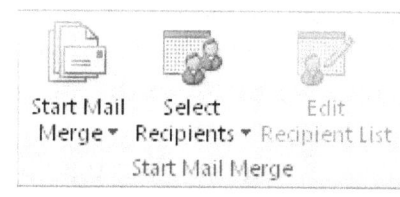

2. Do one of the following:
o **Use Outlook Contacts**   If you want to use your Contacts list in Microsoft Outlook, click **Select from Outlook Contacts**.

IMPORTANT For more information about using the Contacts list, see <u>Tips for working with Microsoft Outlook Contacts list</u>.

o **Use an existing data source file** If you have a Microsoft Excel worksheet, a Microsoft Access database, or another type of data file, click **Use Existing List**, and then locate the file in the **Select Data Source** dialog box.

For Excel, you can select data from any worksheet or named range within a
    workbook.

For Access, you can select data from any table or query that is defined in the
    database.

For another type of data file, select the file in the Select Data Source dialog box. If the file is not listed, select the appropriate file type or select All Files in the Files of type box. In a mail merge, you can use the following types of data files:

▪ Files from single-tier, file-based database programs for which you have installed an OLE DB provider or ODBC driver (a number of which are included with Microsoft Office 2010).
▪ An HTML file that has a single table. The first row of the table must contain column names, and the other rows must contain data.
▪ A Microsoft Word document. The document should contain a single table. The first row of the table must contain headings, and the other rows must contain the records that you want to merge.
▪ Any text file that has data fields separated (or delimited) by tab characters, or commas and data records separated by paragraph marks.

Create a new data file in Word

If you don't have a data file yet, click **Type New List**, and then use the form that opens to create your list. The list is saved as a database (.mdb) file that you can reuse.

NOTE If you installed Microsoft Office 2010 (instead of installing Word 2010 by itself*), you can also use Microsoft Query to construct a query and retrieve the data you want from an external data source.*

<u>Tips for working with Microsoft Office Outlook Contacts list</u>

Connecting to your Outlook Contacts folder is usually a straightforward process, but sometimes you may encounter a problem. Here are solutions to common problems that you may encounter:

I can't find my Outlook Contacts folder?

You may need to turn on the **Show this folder as an e-mail Address Book** property in Outlook, or you may need to change your Outlook user profile.

Turn on the Show this folder as an e-mail Address Book property

1. In Microsoft Outlook, click **Contacts**.
2. Right-click the **Contacts** folder that contains the information that you want to use for a mail merge, and then click **Properties** on the shortcut menu.
3. On the **Outlook Address Book** tab, make sure that the **Show this folder as an e-mail Address Book** check box is selected, and then click **OK**.

Change your Outlook user profile

An Outlook user profile is a group of e-mail accounts and address books. Usually, you need only one profile — but if you share your computer with other people or use different address books for different purposes, you can set up more than one profile. If, when you start your mail merge, you're using a profile that doesn't include the Contacts folder that you want to use, that folder won't be available.

To switch to a different user profile, restart Outlook. When you're prompted for a profile, choose the profile that includes the Contacts folder that you want to use in the mail merge.

If you aren't prompted for a profile and you know that you have more than one, you may want to set up Outlook so that it prompts you. To do this:

1.   Exit Outlook.
2.   In Control Panel, click **User Accounts**, and then click **Mail**.
3.   Click **Show Profiles**.
4.   To be prompted to select a profile each time you start Outlook, click **Prompt for a profile to be used**, and then click **OK**.

I get error messages about mail clients and tables?

If you try to connect to your Contacts folder during a mail merge in Word, and Outlook is not set up as your default e-mail program in Windows Internet Explorer, you will get an error message that says:

"Either there is no default mail client or the current mail client cannot fulfill the messaging request. Please run Microsoft Office Outlook, and set it as the default mail client."

To avoid getting this message during a mail merge, do the following:

1. Click the File tab.
2. Click **Options**.
3. Under **Start up Options**, select the **Make Outlook the default program for E-mail, Contacts, and Calendar**, and then click **OK**.

Start Word again, open your mail merge document, and connect to your Outlook Contacts folder.

I can't connect to an Outlook Contacts folder in Public Folders?

If you start a mail merge in Word and try to connect to an Outlook Contacts folder in **Public Folders**, you get an error message that says:

"The operation cannot be completed because of dialog or database engine failures. Please try again later."

If you try again later, you get the same error message.

To use a Public Folders Contacts folder as the data file for your mail merge, you have to start the mail merge from within Outlook.

Tips for formatting data in Excel

If your data file is an Excel worksheet that includes percentages, currency values, or postal codes, you can preserve the numeric formatting of the data by using Dynamic Data Exchange to connect to the Excel worksheet from Word. For example, you can make sure a five-digit postal code of 07865 from your data file is not displayed as the number 7865 (without the leading zero).

Before you connect to the worksheet, do the following in Word:

1. Click the File tab.
2. Click Options.
3. Click **Advanced**.
4. Scroll to the **General** section, and select the **Confirm file format conversion on open** check box.
5. Click **OK**.
6. With the mail merge main document open, in the **Start Mail Merge** group on the **Mailings** tab, click **Select Recipients**, and then click **Use Existing List**.
7. Locate the Excel worksheet in the **Select Data Source** dialog box, and double-click it.
8. In the **Confirm Data Source** dialog box, click **MS Excel Worksheets via DDE (*.xls)**, and then click **OK**. If you don't see **MS Excel Worksheets via DDE (*.xls)**, select the **Show all** check box.
9. In the **Microsoft Excel** dialog box, for **Named or cell range**, select the cell range or worksheet that contains the information that you want to merge, and then click **OK**.

NOTE   To prevent being prompted every time you open a data file, you can clear the **Confirm conversion at Open** check box after you connect to the worksheet.

Type a new list

1. In the **New Address List** dialog box, type the information for the first address, or record, that you want to include in your mail merge.

If you want to add or remove columns, click **Customize Columns**, and then make the changes that you want.

2. After you type all the information for your first record, click **New Entry**, and then type the information for the next record. Continue until you have typed information for all the records that you want to include.
3. When your new list is complete, click **OK**.
4. In the **Save Address** List dialog box, type a name for your new list, and then click **Save**.

Refine the list of recipients or items

When you connect to a certain data file, you might not want to merge information from all the records (or rows) in that data file into your main document.

To narrow the list of recipients or use a subset of the items in your data file, do the following:

1. On the **Mailings** tab, in the **Start Mail Merge** group, click **Edit Recipient List.**

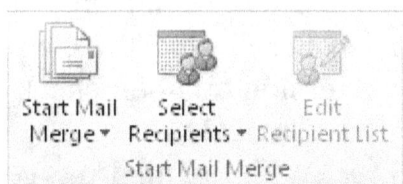

2. In the **Mail Merge Recipients** dialog box, do any of the following:

  ○ **Select individual records** This method is most useful if your list is short. Select the check boxes next to the recipients you want to include, and clear the check boxes next to the recipients you want to exclude.

If you know that you want to include only a few records in your merge, you can clear the check box in the header row and then select only those records that you want. Similarly, if you want to include most of the list, select the check box in the header row, and then clear the check boxes for the records that you don't want to include.

  ○ **Sort records** Click the column heading of the item that you want to sort by. The list sorts in ascending alphabetical order (from A to Z). Click the column heading again to sort the list in descending alphabetical order (Z to A).

If you want more complex sorting, click **Sort** under **Refine recipient list** and choose your sorting preferences on the **Sort Records** tab in the **Filter and Sort** dialog box. For example, you can use this type of sorting if you want recipient addresses to be alphabetized by last name within each postal code and the postal codes listed in numerical order.

  ○ **Filter records** This is useful if the list contains records that you know you don't want to see or include in the merge. After you filter the list, you can select or clear the check boxes to include or exclude records.

To filter records, do the following:

  i. Under **Refine recipient list**, click **Filter**.
  ii. On the **Filter Records** tab in the **Filter and Sort** dialog box, choose the criteria that you want to use for the filter.

For example, to generate letters only for addresses that list Australia as the country/region, you click **Country or Region** in the **Field** list, click **Equal to** in the **Comparison** list, and then type or select **Australia** in the **Compare to** list.

iii.   To refine the filter further, click **And** or **Or** and choose more criteria.

For example, to generate letters only for businesses in Munich, you filter on records whose **City** field contains **Munich** and whose **Company Name** field is not blank. If you use **Or** instead of **And** in this filter, your mail merge includes all Munich addresses as well as all addresses that include a company name, regardless of city.

To add recipients to the list, do the following:

iv.   Under **Data source**, click the name of your data file.
v.   Click **Edit**.
vi.   In the **Edit Data Source** dialog box, click **New Entry**, and then type the information for that recipient.

TIP   Depending on the type of data source that you use, some processes might not be available. If possible, make sure that your data file is complete before you connect it to your main document.

NOTE   If you have installed address validation software, you can click **Validate addresses** in the **Mail Merge Recipients** dialog box to validate your recipients' addresses.

Add placeholders, called mail merge fields, to the document

After you connect your main document to a data file, you are ready to type the text of the document and add placeholders that indicate where the unique information will appear in each copy of the document.

The placeholders, such as address and greeting, are called mail merge fields. Fields in Word correspond to the column headings in the data file that you select.

	A	B	C
1	Name	Last Name	Street Address
2	Nancy	Anderson	123 Main St.
3	Ann	Beebe	567 Country Rd.
4			
5			
6			
7			
8			
9			

1. **Columns** in a data file represent categories of information. Fields that you add to the main document are placeholders for these categories.

2. **Rows** in a data file represent records of information. Word generates a copy of the main document for each record when you perform a mail merge.

By putting a field in your main document, you indicate that you want a certain category of information, such as name or address, to appear in that location.

NOTE When you insert a mail merge field into the main document, the field name is always surrounded by chevrons (« »). These chevrons do not show up in the merged documents. They just help you distinguish the fields in the main document from the regular text.

What happens when you merge?

When you merge, information from the first row in the data file replaces the fields in your main document to create the first merged document. Information from the second row in the data file replaces the fields to create the second merged document, and so on.

Working with fields: Examples

You can add any column heading from your data file to the main document as a field. This gives you flexibility when you design form letters and other merged documents.

For example, suppose you are creating a letter to

notify local businesses that they have been selected for inclusion in your annual city guide. If your data file contains a Company column with the name of each business that you want to contact, you can insert the «Company» field instead of typing the name of each individual company.

You can combine fields and separate them by punctuation marks. For example, to create an address, you can set up the fields in your main document like this:

«First Name» «Last Name»
«Street Address»
«City», «State» «Postal code»

For things that you use frequently, like address blocks and greeting lines, Word provides composite fields that group a number of fields together. For example:

- The Address Block field is a combination of several fields, including first name, last name, street address, city, and postal code.
- The Greeting Line field can include one or more name fields, depending on your chosen salutation.

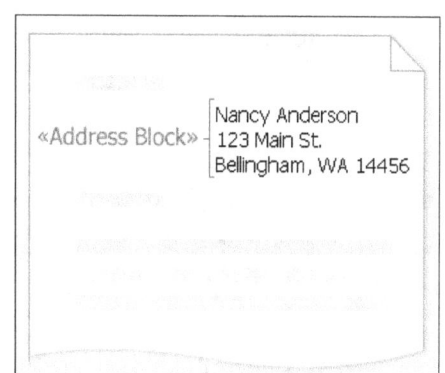

You can customize the content in each of these composite fields. For example, in the address, you may want to select a formal name format (Mr. Joshua Randall Jr.); in the greeting, you may want to use "To" instead of "Dear."

Map mail merge fields to your data file

To make sure that Word can find a column in your data file that corresponds to every address or greeting element, you may need to map the mail merge fields in Word to the columns in your data file.

To map the fields, click **Match Fields** in the **Write & Insert Fields** group of the **Mailings** tab.

The **Match Fields** dialog box opens.

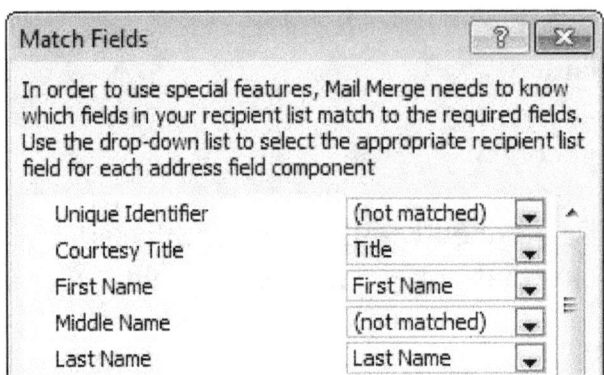

The elements of an address and greeting are listed on the left. Column headings from your data file are listed on the right.

Word searches for the column that matches each element. In the illustration, Word automatically matched the data file's **Title** column to **Courtesy Title**. But Word was unable to match other elements. From this data file, for example, Word can't match **Middle Name**.

In the list on the right, you can select the column from your data file that matches the element on the left. It is okay that **Unique Identifier** isn't matched. Your mail merge document doesn't need to use every field. If you add a field that does not contain data from your data file, it will appear in the merged document as an empty placeholder — usually a blank line or a hidden field.

Type the content and add the placeholders, or fields

1.   In the main document, type any content that you want to appear on every copy of the document.

To add a picture, such as a logo, click **Picture** in the **Illustrations** group on the **Insert** tab.

2.   Click where you want to insert the field.
3.   Use the **Write & Insert Fields** group on the **Mailings** tab.

Write & Insert Fields

4.   Add any of the following:

Address block with name, address, and other information

    a.   Click **Address block**.

    b.   In the **Insert Address Block** dialog box, select the address elements that you want to include and the formats that you want, and then click **OK**.

    c.   If the **Match Fields** dialog box appears, Word may have been unable to find some of the information that it needs for the address block. Click the arrow next to **(not matched)**, and then select the field from your data source that corresponds to the field that is required for the mail merge.

Greeting line

    d.   Click **Greeting line**.

    e.   Select the greeting line format, which includes the salutation, name format, and following punctuation.

    f.   Select the text that you want to appear in cases where Microsoft Word can't interpret the recipient's name, for example, when the data source contains no first or last name for a recipient, but only a company name.

    g.   Click **OK**.

    h.   If the **Match Fields** dialog box appears, Word may have been unable to find some of the information that it needs for the greeting line. Click the arrow next to **(not matched)**, and then select the field from your data source that corresponds to the field that is required for the mail merge.

Individual fields

You can insert information from individual fields, such as first name, telephone number, or the amount of a contribution from a list of donors. To quickly add a field from your data file to the main document, click the arrow next to **Insert Merge Field**, and then click the field name.

For more options with inserting individual fields in the document, do the following:

   i.   On the **Mailings** tab, in the **Write & Insert Fields** group, click **Insert Merge Field**.

   j.   In the **Insert Merge Field** dialog box, do one of the following:
   -   To select address fields that will automatically correspond to fields in your data source, even if the data source's fields don't have the same name as your fields, click **Address Fields**.
   -   To select fields that always take data directly from a column in your data file, click **Database Fields**.

   k.   In the **Fields** box, click the field you want.

   l.   Click **Insert**, and then click **Close**.

   m.   If the **Match Fields** dialog box appears, Microsoft Word may have been unable to find some of the information it needs to insert the field. Click the arrow next to **(not matched)**, and then select the field from your data source that corresponds to the field that is required for the mail merge.

NOTE   If you insert a field from the **Database Fields** list and then later switch to a data source that doesn't have a column with the same name, Word won't be able to insert that field information into the merged document.

Custom fields from Outlook contacts

The only way to include custom contact fields in your main document is to start the mail merge from within Outlook. First, set up a view of your contacts with the fields that you want to use in the merge. Then, start the mail merge. After you choose the settings that you want, Word will automatically open, and you can complete the merge.

Set up a view of your contacts that includes custom fields

1. In Outlook Contacts, on the **View** tab, click **Change View**, and then click **List**.
2. Right-click a column heading, and then click **Field Chooser** on the shortcut menu.

3. In the drop-down list at the top of the **Field Chooser** dialog box, select **User-defined fields in folder**.
4. Drag the field that you to add from the dialog box to the column headings. A little red arrow helps you place the field in the location that you want.

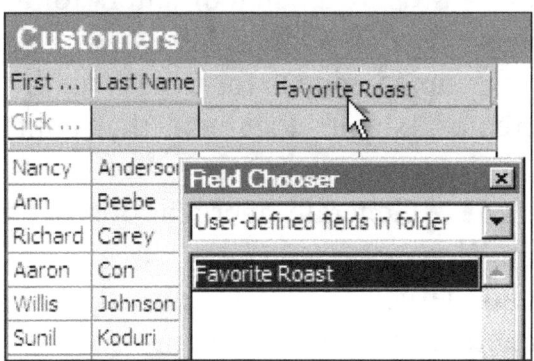

NOTE You can add a new field in the **Field Chooser** dialog box by clicking **New** at the bottom.

5. After you add all of your custom fields to the view, close the **Field Chooser** dialog box.
6. To remove a field that you do not want included in the mail merge, click the field name in the column heading in List view, and drag it off the column heading.

Run mail merge from Outlook

7. In Outlook Contacts, select individual contacts by pressing SHIFT and clicking to select a range or by pressing CTRL and clicking to select individuals. If you want to include all the contacts currently visible in the view, do not click on any contacts.
8. On the **Home** tab, click **Mail Merge**.
9. If you selected individual contacts to include in the mail merge, click **Only selected contacts**. If you want to include all the contacts that are currently visible in the view, click **All contacts in current view**.
10. If you configured the List view so that it displays exactly the fields that you want to use in the mail merge, click **Contact fields in current view**. Otherwise, click **All contact fields** to make all of the contact fields available in the mail merge.
11. If you want to generate a new main document for the merge, click **New document**. Otherwise, click **Existing document**, and click **Browse** to locate the document to use as the main document.

12. If you want to save the contacts and fields that you have selected, so that they can be reused, select the**Permanent file** check box, and then click **Browse** to save the file. The data is saved in a Word document as comma-delimited data.

13. Select any merge options you want:
   o **Form Letters**   Prepare a batch of letters for a mass mailing.
   o **Mailing Labels**   Set up address labels for a mass mailing.
   o **Envelopes**   Set up envelopes for a mass mailing.
   o **Catalog**   Create a single document that contains a catalog or address list.
   o **New Document**   Generate merged documents, which you can edit individually in Word.
   o **Printer**   Send merged documents directly to the default printer.
   o **E-mail**   Generate merged documents designed to be e-mail messages. When you are ready to complete the merge in Word, on the **Mailings** tab in the **Finish** group, click **Finish & Merge**, and then click **Send E-mail Messages**. The **Subject** line is filled with the text you typed in the **Mail Merge Contacts** dialog box in Outlook.

14. Click **OK**. When the document opens in Word, on the **Mailings** tab, in the **Write & Insert Fields** group, click the arrow next to **Insert Merge Field**, and then click the fields that you want to add the document.

NOTE

- You can't type merge field characters («« »») manually or use the **Symbol** command on the **Insert** menu. You must use mail merge.
- If the merge fields appear inside braces, such as { MERGEFIELD City }, then Microsoft Word is displaying field codes instead of field results. This doesn't affect the merge, but if you want to display the results instead, right-click the field code, and then click **Toggle Field Codes** on the shortcut menu.

Format the merged data

Database and spreadsheet programs, such as Microsoft Access and Microsoft Excel, store the information that you type in cells as raw data. Formatting that you apply in Access or Excel, such as fonts and colors, isn't stored with the raw data. When you merge information from a data file into a Word document, you are merging the raw data without the applied formatting.

When you add fields to your main document, you are ready to preview the merge results. You can make changes before you actually complete the merge. Sequentially, You can print the merged documents or modify them individually.

Summary

Mail merge is a software operation describing the production of multiple (and potentially large numbers of) documents from a single template form and a structured data source. The letter may be sent out to many "recipients" with small changes, such as a change of address or a change in the greeting line.

You can use mail merge to create:

- **A catalog or directory**   The same kind of information, such as name and description, is shown for each item, but the name and description in each item is unique. Click **Directory** to create this type of document.
- **A set of envelopes**   The return address is the same on all the envelopes, but the destination address is unique on each one.
- **A set of mailing labels**   Each label shows a person's name and address, but the name and address on each label is unique.
- **A set of e-mail messages**   The basic content is the same in all the messages, but each message goes to the individual recipient and each message contains information that is specific to that recipient, such as the recipient's name or some other piece of information

Chapter V

Business Document Preparation

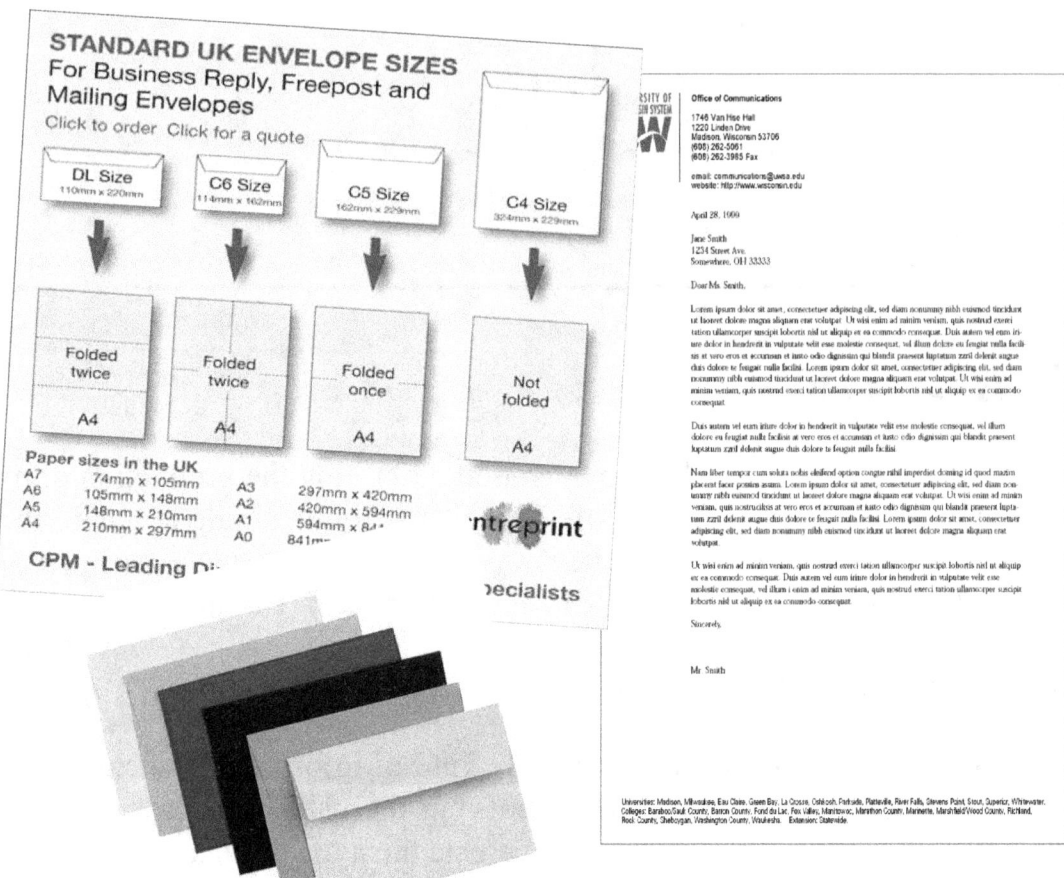

Highlights:

- *Paper size and Orientation*
- *Types of Stationery Document*
- *Stationery Document Preparation*
- *Styles of Letters*
- *Envelopes and Labels*
- *Correspondence and various media*
- *Various styles of Memoranda*
- *Meeting Documentation*
- *Manipulating Graphics*

L esson 1

Paper Size and Orientation

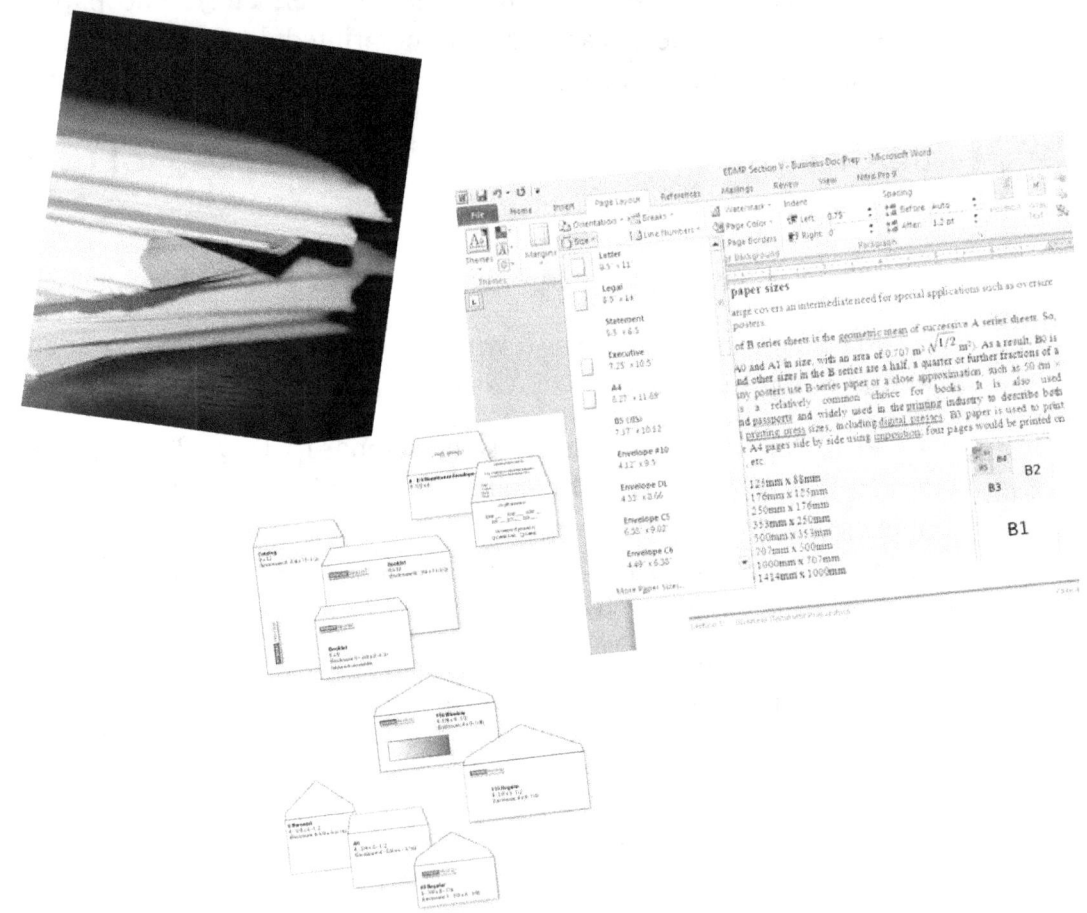

Objective

At the end of this chapter, the student should be able to:

- ➤ *identify sizes and orientation of paper appropriate for a certain business document*
- ➤ *identify the types of stationery documents*

Paper size

Many **paper size** standards conventions have existed at different times and in different countries. Today, there is one widespread international ISO standard (including A4, B3, C4, etc.) and a local standard used in North America (including letter, legal, ledger, etc.). The paper sizes affect writing paper, stationery, cards, and some printed documents. The standards also have related sizes for envelopes.

Full Range of the international standard size: ISO 216

'A' Range of paper sizes

The 'A' range is the main finished trimmed size of paper used in printing.

The series begins with A0 whose area is exactly 1 square metre and then the ratio of the sides of smaller A sizes are always 1:square root of 2.

The international paper size standard, ISO 216, is based on the German DIN 476 standard for paper sizes. ISO paper sizes are all based on a single aspect ratio of square root of 2, or approximately 1:1.4142. The base A0 size of paper is defined as having an area of 1 m^2. Rounded to the nearest millimetre, the A0 paper size is 841 by 1,189 millimetres (33.1 in × 46.8 in).

Successive paper sizes in the series A1, A2, A3, and so forth, are defined by halving the preceding paper size across the larger dimension. The most frequently used paper size is A4 measuring 210 by 297 millimetres (8.27 in × 11.7 in).

A8 74x52mm	A7
105mm x 74mm	A6
148mm x 105mm	A5
210mm x 148mm	**A4**
297mm x 210mm	A3
420mm x 297mm	A2
594mm x 420mm	
A1 841mm x 594mm	A0
1189mm x 841mm	

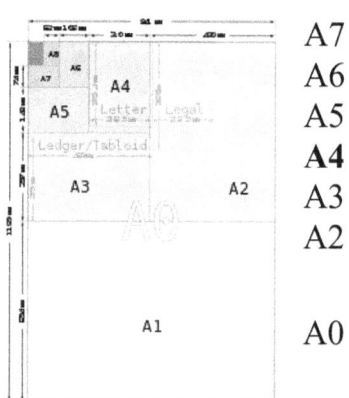

The significant advantage of this system is its scaling: if a sheet with an aspect ratio of $\sqrt{2}$ is divided into two equal halves parallel to its shortest sides, then the halves will again have an aspect ratio of $\sqrt{2}$. Folded brochures of any size can be made by using sheets of the next larger size, e.g. A4 sheets are folded to make A5 brochures. The system allows scaling without compromising the aspect ratio from one size to another—as provided by office photocopiers, e.g. enlarging A4 to A3 or reducing A3 to A4. Similarly, two sheets of A4 can be scaled down and fit exactly 1 sheet without any cutoff or margins.

The behavior of the aspect ratio is easily proven: on a sheet of paper, let a be the long side and b be the short side; thus, $a/b = \sqrt{2}$. When the sheet of paper is folded in half widthwise, let c be the length of the new short side: $c = a/2$. If we take the ratio of the newly folded paper we have:

$$\frac{b}{c} = \frac{b}{\frac{a}{2}} = \frac{2}{\frac{a}{b}} = \frac{2}{\sqrt{2}} = \sqrt{2}$$

Therefore, the aspect ratio is preserved for the new dimensions of the folded paper.

'B' Range of paper sizes

The 'B' range covers an intermediate need for special applications such as oversize documents and posters.

The area of B series sheets is the geometric mean of successive A series sheets. So, B1 is between A0 and A1 in size, with an area of 0.707 m² ($\sqrt{1/2}$ m²). As a result, B0 is 1 metre wide, and other sizes in the B series are a half, a quarter or further fractions of a metre wide. Many posters use B-series paper or a close approximation, such as 50 cm × 70 cm; B5 is a relatively common choice for books. It is also used for envelopes and passports and widely used in the printing industry to describe both paper sizes and printing press sizes, including digital presses. B3 paper is used to print two US letter or A4 pages side by side using imposition; four pages would be printed on B2, eight on B1, etc.

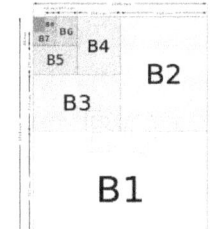

B7 125mm x 88mm	B6 176mm x 125mm
B5 250mm x 176mm	B4 353mm x 250mm
B3 500mm x 353mm	B2 707mm x 500mm
B1 1000mm x 707mm	B0 1414mm x 1000mm

'C' Range – Envelope Sizes

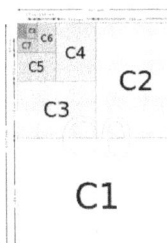

C8 81mm x 57mm
C7 114mm x 81mm
C6 162mm x 114mm
C5 229mm x 162mm
C4 324mm x 229mm

DL size 220mm x 110mm

The C series is used only for envelopes and is defined in ISO 269. The area of C series sheets is the geometric mean of the areas of the A and B series sheets of the same number; for instance, the area of a C4 sheet is the geometric mean of the areas of an A4 sheet and a B4 sheet. This means that C4 is slightly larger than A4, and B4 slightly larger than C4. The practical usage of this is that a letter written on A4 paper fits inside a C4 envelope, and C4 paper fits inside a B4 envelope.

ISO paper sizes (plus rounded inch values)

Format	A series[3]		B series[4]		C series[5]	
Size	mm × mm	in × in	mm × mm	in × in	mm × mm	in × in
0	841 × 1189	33.1 × 46.8	1000 × 1414	39.4 × 55.7	917 × 1297	36.1 × 51.1
1	594 × 841	23.4 × 33.1	707 × 1000	27.8 × 39.4	648 × 917	25.5 × 36.1
2	420 × 594	16.5 × 23.4	500 × 707	19.7 × 27.8	458 × 648	18.0 × 25.5
3	297 × 420	11.7 × 16.5	353 × 500	13.9 × 19.7	324 × 458	12.8 × 18.0
4	210 × 297	8.27 × 11.7	250 × 353	9.84 × 13.9	229 × 324	9.02 × 12.8
5	148 × 210	5.83 × 8.27	176 × 250	6.93 × 9.84	162 × 229	6.38 × 9.02
6	105 × 148	4.13 × 5.83	125 × 176	4.92 × 6.93	114 × 162	4.49 × 6.38
7	74 × 105	2.91 × 4.13	88 × 125	3.46 × 4.92	81 × 114	3.19 × 4.49
8	52 × 74	2.05 × 2.91	62 × 88	2.44 × 3.46	57 × 81	2.24 × 3.19
9	37 × 52	1.46 × 2.05	44 × 62	1.73 × 2.44	40 × 57	1.57 × 2.24
10	26 × 37	1.02 × 1.46	31 × 44	1.22 × 1.73	28 × 40	1.10 × 1.57

The tolerances specified in the standard are:

- ±1.5 mm (0.06 in) for dimensions up to 150 mm (5.9 in),
- ±2 mm (0.08 in) for lengths in the range 150 to 600 mm (5.9 to 23.6 in) and
- ±3 mm (0.12 in) for any dimension above 600 mm (23.6 in).

Paper sizes in North America

The U.S., Canada and Mexico use a different system of paper sizes compared to the rest of the world. The current standard sizes are unique to that continent, although due to the size of the North American market and proliferation of both software and printing hardware from the region, other parts of the world have become increasingly familiar with these sizes. The traditional North American inch-based sizes differ from those described below. "Letter", "legal", "ledger", and "tabloid" are by far the most commonly used of these for everyday activities. The origins of the exact dimensions of "letter" size paper (8 $\frac{1}{2}$ in × 11 in or 215.9 mm × 279.4 mm) are lost in tradition and not well documented.

North American paper sizes

Size	in × in	mm × mm	Similar Canadian P size
Letter	8.5 × 11	215.9 × 279.4	P4: 215 × 280
Government-Letter	8.0 × 10.5	203.2 × 266.7	
Legal	8.5 × 14	215.9 × 355.6	
Junior Legal	8.0 × 5.0	203.2 × 127	
Ledger	17 × 11	432 × 279	
Tabloid	11 × 17	279 × 432	

There is an additional paper size, to which the name "government-letter" was given by the IEEE Printer Working Group: the 8 in × 10 $\frac{1}{2}$ in (203.2 mm × 266.7 mm) paper that is used in the United States and Canada for children's writing. It was prescribed by Herbert Hoover when he was Secretary of Commerce to be used for U.S. government forms, apparently to enable discounts from the purchase of paper for schools, but more likely due to the standard use of trimming books (after binding) and paper from the standard letter size paper to produce consistency and allow "bleed" printing. In later years, as photocopy machines proliferated, citizens wanted to make photocopies of the forms, but the machines did not generally have this size paper in their bins.

U.S. paper sizes are currently standard in the United States, the Philippines and Chile. The latter two use U.S. "letter", but the Philippine and Chilean "legal" size is 8 $\frac{1}{2}$ in × 13 in (215.9 mm × 330.2 mm). ISO sizes are available, but not widely used, in both the U.S. and the Philippines.

In Canada, U.S. paper sizes are a de facto standard. The government, however, uses a combination of ISO paper sizes, and CAN 2-9.60M "Paper Sizes for Correspondence" specifies P1 through P6 paper sizes, which are the U.S. paper sizes rounded to the nearest 5 mm.

Mexico has adopted the ISO standard, but U.S. "letter" format is still the system in use throughout the country. It is virtually impossible to encounter ISO standard papers in day-to-day uses, with "Carta 216 mm × 279 mm" (letter), "Oficio 216 mm × 340 mm" (Government-Legal) and "Doble carta" (ledger/tabloid) being nearly universal. U.S. sizes are also widespread and in common use in Colombia.

Half letter

By extension of the American standards the half letter size meets the needs of many applications. It is also known as statement, stationery, Half A (from ANSI sizes) or simply half size. It is a piece of letter paper cut in half, 5.5" × 8.5" (140 × 216 mm). It is used for everything from personal letter writing to official aeronautical maps. Organizers, notepads, and diaries also often use this size paper thus 3 ring binders are also available in this size. Booklets of this size are created using word processing tools with landscape printing in two columns on letter paper which are then cut or folded into the final size.

ANSI paper sizes

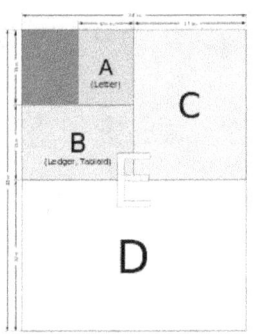

In 1996, the American National Standards Institute adopted ANSI/ASME Y14.1which defined a regular series of paper sizes based upon the *de facto* standard8 ½ in × 11 in (215.9 mm × 279.4 mm) "letter" size which it assigned "ANSI A". This series also includes "ledger"/"tabloid" as "ANSI B". This series is somewhat similar to the ISO standard in that cutting a sheet in half would produce two sheets of the next smaller size. Unlike the ISO standard, however, the arbitrary aspect ratio forces this series to have two alternating aspect ratios. To wit, "Letter" (8½" × 11", or ANSI A) is less elongated than A4, while "Ledger/Tabloid" (11" × 17", or ANSI B) is more elongated than A3. The ANSI series is shown below.

With care, documents can be prepared so that the text and images fit on either ANSI or their equivalent ISO sheets at 1:1 reproduction scale.

Name	in × in	mm × mm	Ratio	Alias	Similar ISO A size
ANSI A	8.5 × 11	216 × 279	1.2941	Letter	A4
ANSI B	11 × 17	279 × 432	1.5455	Ledger Tabloid	A3
ANSI C	17 × 22	432 × 559	1.2941		A2
ANSI D	22 × 34	559 × 864	1.5455		A1
ANSI E	34 × 44	864 × 1118		1.2941	A0

Architectural sizes

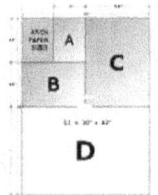

In addition to the ANSI system as listed above, there is a corresponding series of paper sizes used for architectural purposes. This series also shares the property that bisecting each size produces two of the size below, with alternating aspect ratios. It may be preferred by North American architects because the aspect ratios (4:3 and 3:2) are ratios of small integers, unlike their ANSI (or ISO) counterparts. Furthermore, the aspect ratio 4:3 matches the traditional aspect ratio for computer displays. The architectural series, usually abbreviated "Arch", is shown below:

Name	in × in	mm × mm	Ratio
Arch A	9 × 12	229 × 305	3:04
Arch B	12 × 18	305 × 457	2:03
Arch C	18 × 24	457 × 610	3:04
Arch D	24 × 36	610 × 915	2:03
Arch E	36 × 48	915 × 1220	3:04
Arch E1	30 × 42	762 × 1070	5:07
Arch E2	26 × 38	660 × 965	13:19
Arch E3	27 × 39	686 × 991	9:13

Other sizes

Name	in × in	mm × mm	Ratio	dot × dot
Organizer J	2.75 × 5	70 × 127	≈1.8142	
Compact	4.25 × 6.75	108 × 171	1.5833	
Marching Band Flip-Folder	6.75 x 5.25	171 × 133	≈0.77	
Organizer L, Statement, Half Letter, Memo, Jepps*	5.5 × 8.5	140 × 216	1.54	
Executive, Monarch	7.25 × 10.5	184 × 267	≈1.4483	
Choral Octavo	6.75 × 10.5	171 × 267	≈1.55	
Government-Letter	8 × 10.5	203 × 267	1.3125	
Foolscap, Folio[12]	8.27 × 13	210 × 330	≈1.5719	
Letter, Organizer M	8.5 × 11	216 × 279	≈1.2941	
Fanfold 12x8.5, German Std Fanfold	8.5 × 12	216 × 304	≈1.4118	612 × 864
Government-Legal, Folio	8.5 × 13	216 × 330	≈1.5294	
Legal	8.5 × 14	216 × 356	≈1.6471	
Quarto	9 × 11	229 × 279	1.2	
US Std Fanfold	11 × 14.875	279 × 377	≈1.3513	792 × 1071

Ledger, Tabloid, Organizer K, Bible	11 × 17	279 × 432		1.54
Super-B	13 × 19	330 × 483	≈1.4615	
Post	15.5 × 19.5	394 × 489	≈1.2581	
Crown	15 × 20	381 × 508		1.3
Large Post	16.5 × 21	419 × 533		1.27
Demy	17.5 × 22.5	445 × 572	≈1.2857	
Medium	18 × 23	457 × 584		1.27
Broadsheet	18 × 24	457 × 610		1.3
Royal	20 × 25	508 × 635		1.25
Elephant	23 × 28	584 × 711	≈1.2174	
Double Demy	22.5 × 35	572 × 889		1.5
Quad Demy	35 × 45	889 × 1143	≈1.2857	

Index and business cards

Name	in × in	mm × mm	Ratio
Index card	3 × 5	76 × 127	1.6
Index card	4 × 6	102 × 152	1.5
Index card	5 × 8	127 × 203	1.6
International business card *	$2\frac{1}{8}$ × 3.37	53.98 × 85.6	1.586
US business card	2 × 3.5	51 × 89	1.75
Japanese business card	≈2.165 × ≈3.583	55 × 91	≈1.65
Hungarian business card	≈1.969 × ≈3.543	50 × 90	1.8

Photographic paper sizes

Name	in × in	mm × mm	Ratio	
2R	2.5 × 3.5	64 × 89		1.4
-	3 × 5	76 × 127		1.6
LD, DSC	3.5 × 4.67	89 × 119	1.3 (4:3)	
3R, L	3.5 × 5	89 × 127	≈1.4286	
LW	3.5 × 5.25	89 × 133	1.5 (3:2)	
KGD	4 × 5.33	102 × 136	1.3 (4:3)	
4R, KG	4 × 6	102 × 152	1.5 (3:2)	

2LD, DSCW	5 × 6.67	127 × 169	1.3 (4:3)	
5R, 2L	5 × 7	127 × 178		1.4
2LW	5 × 7.5	127 × 190	1.5 (3:2)	
6R	6 × 8	152 × 203	1.3 (4:3)	
8R, 6P	8 × 10	203 × 254		1.25
S8R, 6PW	8 × 12	203 × 305	1.5 (3:2)	
11R	11 × 14	279 × 356		1.27
A3+, Super B	13 × 19	330 × 483	≈1.46154	

Postcard size limitations

Dimension	Minimum (inch)	Maximum (inch)
Height	3.5	4.25
Width	5	6
Thickness	0.007	0.016

This implies that all postcards have a width: height aspect ratio in the range 1.18 to 1.71.

The only ISO 216 size in the post card range is A6.

Traditional inch-based paper sizes

Traditionally, a number of different sizes were defined for large sheets of paper, and paper sizes were defined by the sheet name and the number of times it had been folded. Imperial sizes were used in the United Kingdom and its territories. Some of the base sizes were as follows:

Name	in × in	mm × mm	Ratio	
Emperor	48 × 72	1219 × 1829		1.5
Antiquarian	31 × 53	787 × 1346		1.7097
Grand eagle	28.75 × 42	730 × 1067		1.4609
Double elephant	26.75 × 40	678 × 1016		1.4984
Atlas*	26 × 34	660 × 864		1.3077
Colombier	23.5 × 34.5	597 × 876		1.4681
Double demy	22.5 × 35.5	572 × 902	1.5(7)	
Imperial*	22 × 30	559 × 762		1.3636
Double large post	21 × 33	533 × 838		1.5713
Elephant*	23 × 28	584 × 711		1.2174
Princess	21.5 × 28	546 × 711		1.3023
Cartridge	21 × 26	533 × 660		1.2381

Royal*	20 × 25	508 × 635	1.25
Sheet, half post	19.5 × 23.5	495 × 597	1.2051
Double post	19 × 30.5	483 × 762	1.6052
Super royal	19 × 27	483 × 686	1.4203
Medium*	17.5 × 23	470 × 584	1.2425
Demy*	17.5 × 22.5	445 × 572	1.2857
Large post	16.5 × 21	419 × 533	1.(27)
Copy draught	16 × 20	406 × 508	1.25
Large post	15.5 × 20	394 × 508	1.2903
Post*	15.5 × 19.25	394 × 489	1.2419
Crown*	15 × 20	381 × 508	1.(3)
Pinched post	14.75 × 18.5	375 × 470	1.2533
Foolscap*	13.5 × 17	343 × 432	1.2593
Small foolscap	13.25 × 16.5	337 × 419	1.2453
Brief	13.5 × 16	343 × 406	1.1852
Pott	12.5 × 15	318 × 381	1.2

* The sizes marked with an asterisk are still in use in the United States.

Paper Orientation

Paper orientation refers to how the paper is oriented with respect to the figure. The choices are *portrait* (the default), *landscape*, and *rotated*.

The figure below shows the same figure printed using the three different orientations.

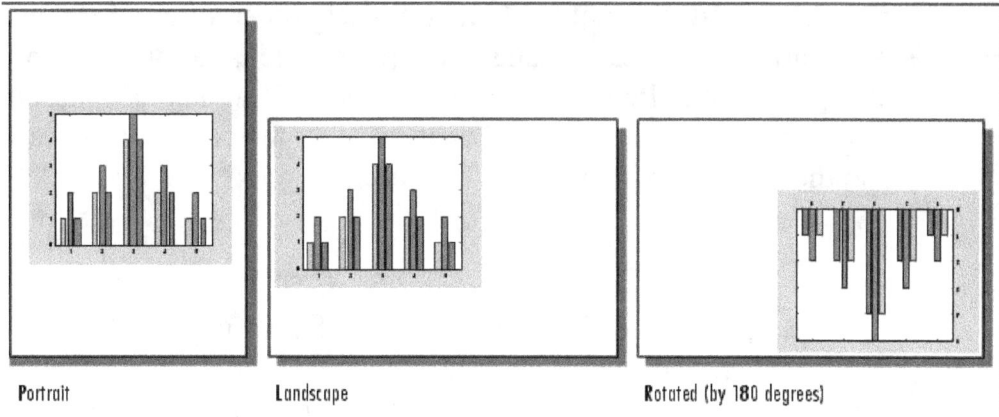

Portrait   Landscape   Rotated (by 180 degrees)

Figure 2-1: The Paper Orientation Settings

Note The rotated orientation is not supported by all printers. When the printer does not support it, landscape is used.

Changing Paper Orientation

To change the paper orientation, use any of the following:

- The **Paper** tab of the **Page Setup** dialog box
- MATLAB's Paper Orientation property or orient command

Changing the orientation can change the paper's size setting.

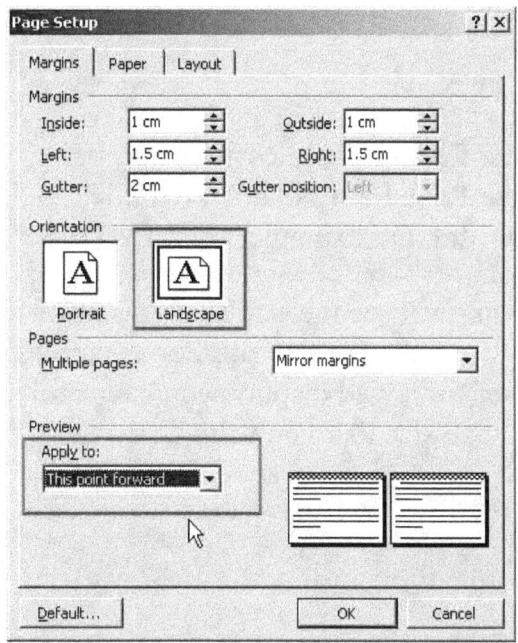

About page size, paper size, and orientation

Any publication layout that you select in Office Publisher 2007 includes the page size and orientation that are used most often for that particular type of publication. You can change the page size and orientation and preview your changes in the **Page Setup** dialog box. You can change the paper size and orientation and preview your changes and the relationship between the page size and the paper size in the **Print Setup** dialog box.

By setting the size or orientation of your page and paper separately, you can control where the page is located on the paper and avoid misaligned prints. You can also create a bleed off the edge of the page by printing on paper that is larger than your publication and trimming it down to the finished size, and you can print multiple pages on a single sheet.

Change the page size

This procedure sets the size of your publication. For example, you can use this method to select the size of the printed publication to print a poster that measures 22 inches by 34 inches when printed — regardless of whether your printer can handle a single large sheet of paper or whether you will print the poster as a number of overlapping sheets of paper (called tiles).

Note In Office Publisher 2007, you can create publications as large as 240 inches by 240 inches.

Choose a page size

1. In the **Format Publications** task pane, click **Change Page Size**.
2. In the **Page Setup** dialog box, click the icon that represents the page size that you want. For example, click **Letter 8.5 x 11"**.

   If you don't see the size that you want, you can scroll and choose a size from another publication type. For example, if you want to print your menu as a poster for a wall display, you can scroll to **Posters** and then click the icon for the page size that you want.

Create a custom page size

In the **Format Publications** task pane, click **Change Page Size**, and then do one of the following:

- In the **Page Setup** dialog box, under **Page**, enter the width and height that you want.
- In the **Page Setup** dialog box, select the publication type that you want, such as **Posters**, click **Create custom page size**, and then enter the width and height that you want under **Page**.

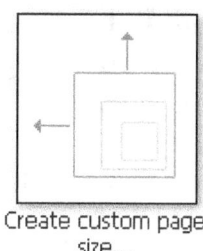

Create custom page size...

In the **Custom Page Size** dialog box, you can name your custom page size and specify the layout type and margins that you want.

After you create a custom page size, you can use it when you create new publications.

Notes   There is a limit to the area of a sheet of paper that your printer can print on. Different printers have different unprintable areas at the edges of the paper. These unprintable areas cannot be printed on, regardless of how you set your margins.

- If you change a publication's margins, you may want to move the objects in the publication to fit in the printable area. For example, if you decrease a publication's margins, you may want to take advantage of the new printable area by adding or moving text or pictures to the area.

Change the paper size

The printer that you use determines the paper sizes that you can print on. To check the range of paper sizes that your printer can print on, consult the manual for your printer, or view the paper sizes that are currently set for your printer in the **Print Setup** dialog box.

To print your publication on sheets of paper that match the publication page size, be sure that the page size and the paper size are the same. If you want to print your publication on a different size of paper — for example, to create a bleed or to print multiple pages on one sheet — change only the paper size.

1. On the **File** menu, click **Print Setup**.
2. In the **Print Setup** dialog box, under **Paper**, select the size of paper that you want from the **Size** list.

Note   The method for specifying a new paper size varies according to printer manufacturer and model. If your printer supports custom paper sizes, you can specify a custom paper size after you click **Properties**.

Change the page orientation

1. In the **Format Publications** task pane, click **Change Page Size**.
2. In the **Page Setup** dialog box, select the page size that has the orientation that you want.

Change the paper orientation

1. On the **File** menu, click **Print Setup**, and then click the **Publication and Paper Settings** tab.
2. Under **Orientation**, click **Portrait** for a vertical layout or **Landscape** for a horizontal layout.

Summary

The Sizes of paper are Letter, Legal and customized sizes ranges as follows:

    (a)   A3 - 29.7 em. x42 em.
    (b)   A4 - 21 em. x 29.7 em.
    (c)   A5 - 14.8 em. x 21 em.
    (d)   A6- 41.3 em. x 5.83 em.
    (e)   B5 - 17.6 em. x 25 em.
    (f)   C5 - 16.2 em. x 22.9 em.
    (g)   DL- 11 em. x 22 em.

The orientation of Paper refers to how the paper is oriented with respect to the figure. The choices are portrait (the default), landscape, and rotated.

Lesson 2

Types of Stationery Document

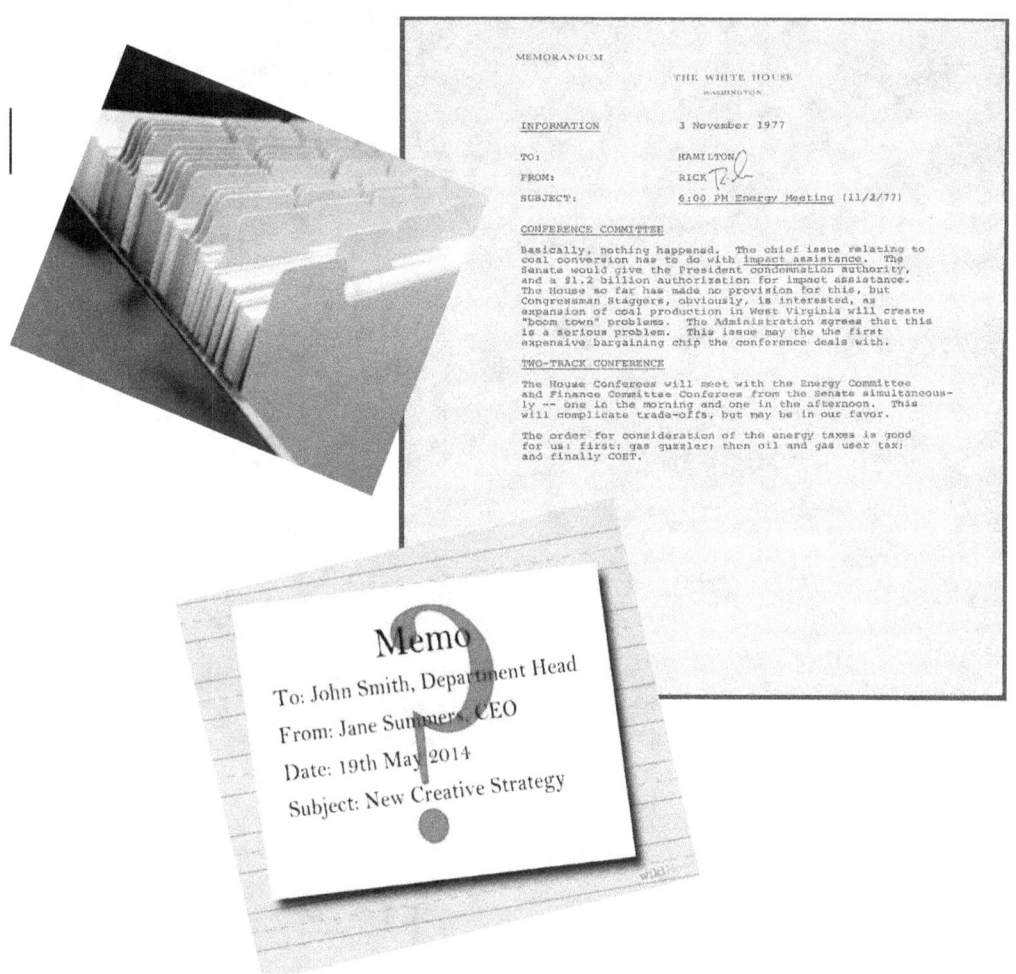

Objective

At the end of this chapter, the student should be able to:
- *select and use appropriate stationery for a given assignment*
- *create stationery according to the standard format applicable in a certain document*

- **letter head**

  Use this letterhead template to create personal stationery for a letter with a fresh look when an email won't do. Easily customize it for your preferences by using built in themes and color.

• MEMO

A **memorandum** was from the Latin verbal phrase *memorandum est.*, the gerundive form of the verb *memoro*, "to mention, call to mind, recount, relate", which means "It must be remembered (that)...". It is therefore a note, document or other communication that helps the memory by recording events or observations on a topic, such as may be used in a business office. The plurall form of the Latin noun *memorandum* so derived is properly *memoranda*, but if the word is deemed to have become a word of the English language, the plural *memorandums*, abbreviated to *memos*, may be used.

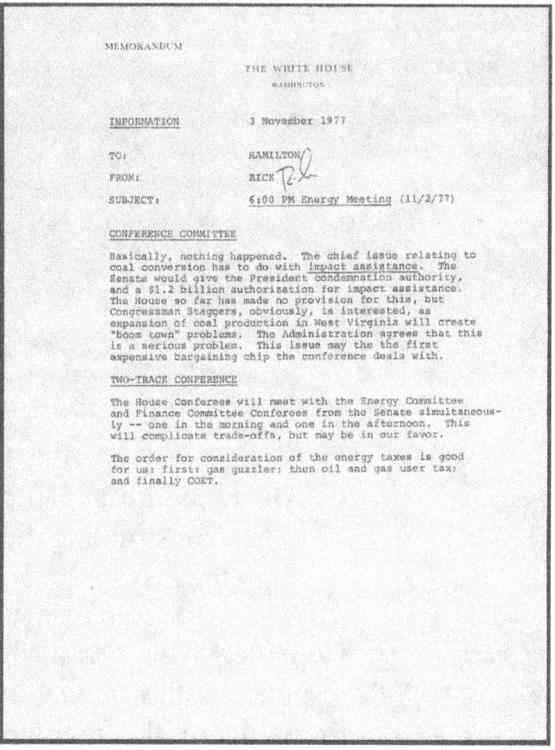

A **memorandum** can have only a certain number of formats; it may have a format specific to an office or institution. In law specifically, a memorandum is a record of the terms of a transaction or contract, such as a policy memo, memorandum of understanding, memorandum of agreement, or memorandum of association. Alternative formats include memos, briefing notes, reports, letters or binders. They could be one page long or many. They may be considered as grey literature. If the user is a cabinet minister or a senior executive, the format might be rigidly defined and limited to one or two pages. If the user is a colleague, the format is usually much more flexible. At its most basic level, a memorandum can be a handwritten note to one's supervisor. In business, a memo is typically used by firms for internal communication, as opposed to letters which are typically for external communication.

• WRITING A MEMO

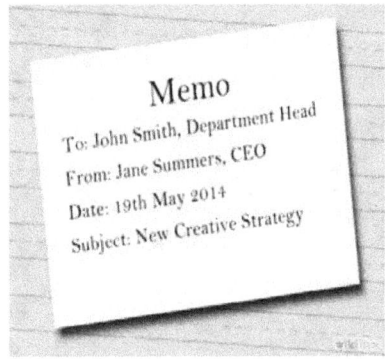

1. Write the heading segment. Specify who the memo is for and who sent it. The heading segment should also include the complete and exact date the memo was written, and the subject matter (what the memo is about). A sample heading would look like: To: Name and job title of the recipient From: Your name and job title Date: Complete date when the memo was written Subject: (or RE :) What the memo is about (highlighted in some way).

- Always address readers by their correct name; do not use nicknames.
- When constructing the heading, be sure to double space between sections and align the text.

2. **Consider who the audience should be.** In order to get people to read and respond to the memo, it's important to tailor the tone, length, and level of formality of the memo to the audience who will be reading it. Doing this effectively requires that you have a good idea of who the memo is intended for.

- Think about your audience's priorities and concerns are, and try to imagine why the information you are presenting would be important to them.
- Try to anticipate any questions your readers might have. Brainstorm some content for the memo, such as examples, evidence, or other information that will persuade them.
- Considering the audience also allows you to be sensitive to including any information or sentiments that are inappropriate for your readers

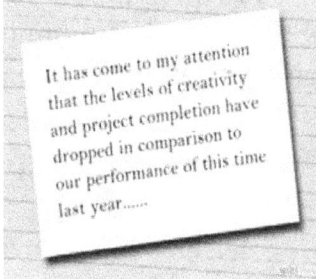

3. Introduce the problem or issue to your readers in the opening segment. Briefly give them the context behind the action you wish them to take. This is somewhat like a thesis statement, which introduces the topic and states why it matters.

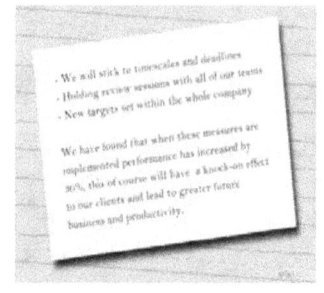

- Include only as much information as is needed, while still being convincing that a real problem exists.
- As a general guideline, the opening should take about ¼ of the total length of the memo.

up

4. **Suggest ways to address the issue in the summary segment.** What you are summarizing here are the key actions you would like your readers to take.

- This can also include some evidence to back up your recommendations.
- In a very short memo, it might not be necessary to include a separate summary segment. Instead, this can be integrated into the next segment, the "discussion segment".

5. **Support your course of action in the discussion segment.** Be persuasive. State how the readers will benefit from taking the action you recommend, or be disadvantaged through lack of action.

- Give evidence and logical reasons for the solutions you propose. Feel free to include graphics, lists, or charts, especially in longer memos. Just be sure they are truly relevant and persuasive⋅
- Start with the most important information, then move to specific or supporting facts.
- The general guideline for length is that the summary and discussion segments combined should comprise about ½ of the memo.

Close the memo with a friendly ending that restates what actions you want the reader to take. You might want to include a statement like, "I will be glad to discuss these recommendations with you later on and follow through on any decisions you make."

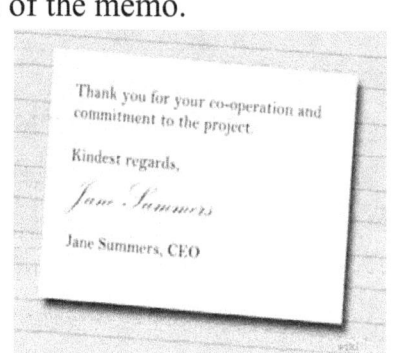

- Give the reader a sense of solidarity and optimism if possible.
- Emphasize a particular next step that they can take.
- This should generally take about ⅛ of the total length of the memo.

• COPY PAPER

Copy Paper – Usually a lightweight paper that is used in copy machines also known as reprographic paper, copier paper, dual-purpose, or xerographic paper. It's generally thin with a small amount of transparency. The grade of the paper is determined by brightness levels which Is how light is reflected from the paper. It is the largest category in the uncoated commodity printing paper grade and many governments use it for all of their laser printing, fax, and copier needs. U.S. copiers most frequently use 8-1/2″ x 11″ paper, but other sizes are available such as 8-1/2″ x 14″ and 11″ x 17″.

Recycled Copier Paper- About 9 percent of the copy paper used in the U.S. is made with recycled fibbers. Recycled copier paper is virtually indistinguishable from non-recycled, with similar performance, colour and cost.

Printer Paper- Can be any kind of paper that is used in computer printers. Some common examples include laser paper, inkjet paper, and photo paper. Printer paper is available in matte and glossy finishes.

Matte paper- has a bright white coating that dries quickly and is recommended for everyday printing.

Glossy paper- has a shiny coating that absorbs ink for spontaneous drying. Glossy paper is commonly used for printing photographs, posters, and other images

Inkjet Paper- Inkjet printers can print on a variety of paper types. It is best to choose a paper based on what you are printing. For example, plain copier paper is usually best for printing emails or other common documents. It provides good results and is relatively inexpensive. If you will be printing in color, a coater paper is usually recommended because it allows for sharper colors and a higher resolution image.

Specialty inkjet papers are available. Common examples include photo paper, glossy paper, business cards, and greeting cards.

Laser Paper- Although similar to inkjet paper, laser paper is specially designed for the toner used in laser printers. Specialty types of laser paper such as checks and labels are also available.

Photo Paper- Printing photos from a computer has become popular due to the increased use of digital cameras and the low cost of high-quality inkjet printers. Photo paper offers the best results for this type of printing and produces sharp, clear images.

Photo paper has a glossy finish that allows the ink to dry quickly and produces sharp images. Many companies sell photo paper in several sizes and weights, with the 4″ x 6″ size being one of the most common. This size is great for printing photos from your home printer.

• LABELS

A **label** is a piece of **paper**, **polymer**, cloth, metal, or other material affixed to a **container** or article, on which is **printed** a legend, information concerning the product, ownership, addresses, and many others. A label may also be printed directly on the container or article.

Labels have many uses: **product** identification, nametags, advertising, warnings, and other communication. Special types of labels called digital labels (printed through a digital printing) can also have special constructions such as RFID tags, **security printing**, and **sandwich** process labels.

Example:

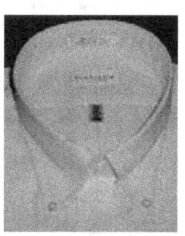

Bumper sticker in a car   *Label on a T-shirt*   Bottles of wine with label

• Index card

An **index card** (or **system card** in **Australian English**) consists of heavy **paper** stock cut to a standard size, used for recording and storing sm allamounts of discrete data.

It was invented by **Carl Linnaeus**, around 1760.

The most common **size** for index cards in **North America** and UK is 3 by 5 inches (76.2 by 127. 0mm), hence the common name **3by5 card**. Other sizes widely available include 4 by 6 inches (101.6 by152.4 mm), 5 by 8 inches (127.0 by 203.2 mm) and **ISO** sizeA7 (74 by 105 mm or 2.9 by 4.1 in). Cardsare available in blank, ruled and grid styles in avariety of colors. Special divider cards with protrudingtabs and a variety of cases and trays to hold thecards are also sold by stationers and office productcompanies. They are part of standard stationery andoffice supplies in the UnitedStates, but in othercountries, such as **China**, are not. They are virtually unknown in Russia and other former Soviet Union countries.

Index cards are used for a wide range of applicationsand environments: in the h ome to record and storerecipes, shopping lists, contact information and otherorg anizational data; in business to recordpresentation notes, project research and notes andcontact information; in schools as flash cards or othervisual aids; and in academic research to hold datasuch as bibliographical citations or notes. An often-suggested organization method is to use the smaller3-inch by 5-inch cards to record the title and citationinformation of works cited, while using larger cards forrecording quotes or other data. Index cards are usedfor many events and are very helpful for planning.

- Until the conversion of library catalogs beginning in the 1980s, the primary tool used to locate bookswas the card catalog in which every book was filed with three cards, filed alphabetically under itstitle, author and subject (if **non-fiction**). Similar catalogs were used by law firms and otherorganizations to organize large quantities of stored documents. However, the adoption of standardcataloging protocols throughout nations with international agreements, along with the rise of theInternet and the conversion of cataloging systems to digital storage and retrieval, have madewidespread use of index cards for cataloging purposes obsolete.

An index card in a **library card catalog**. In the computer age, this type of cataloging is now mostly obsolete.

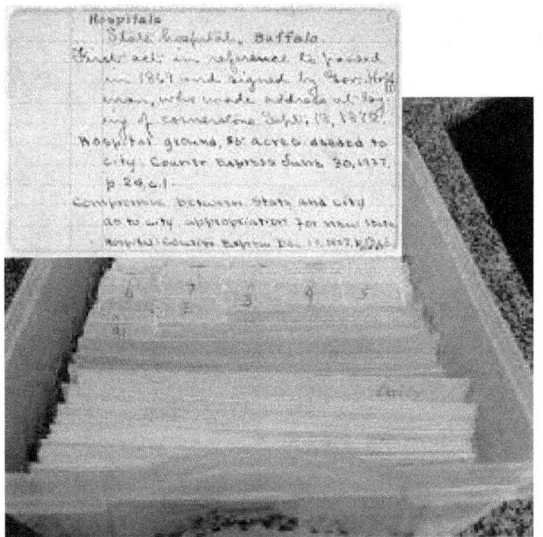

Example of a hand-written American indexcard.

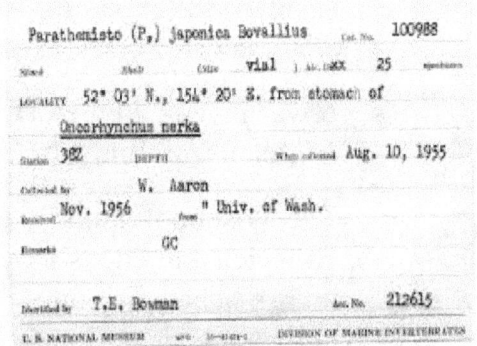

- **Cover Letter**

The **primary purpose of the cover letter** is to allow a potential employer to determine whether it is worth their time to examine your résumé. Fundamentally the cover letter provides you with an opportunity to stand out and show an employer a personal side of you and what you have to offer. Although the résumé serves a number of valuable functions, the cover letter can also give you a stronger chance of obtaining an interview, let you explain to the employer why they should hire you, and identify specifically why you are interested in the position. The following materials should provide you with the appropriate guidelines for developing an effective cover letter to accompany your résumé.

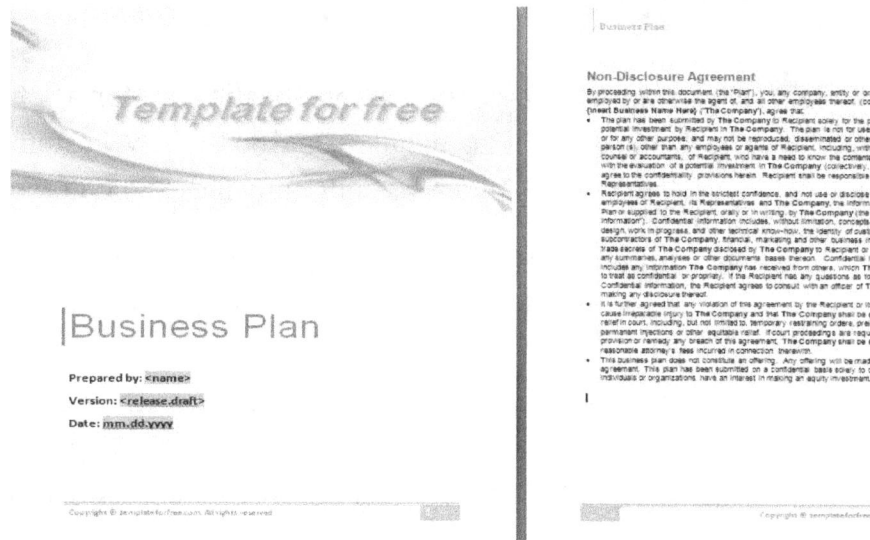

Summary

Letterhead are use to create personal stationery for a letter with a fresh look when an email won't do. Easily customize it for your preferences by using built in themes and color.

A **memorandum** was from the Latin verbal phrase *memorandum est.*, the gerundive form of the verb *memoro*, "to mention, call to mind, recount, relate", which means "It must be remembered (that)...". a memorandum is a record of the terms of a transaction or contract, such as a policy memo, memorandum of understanding, memorandum of agreement, or memorandum of association.

Copy Paper – Usually a lightweight paper that is used in copy machines also known as reprographic paper, copier paper, dual-purpose, or xerographic paper. It's generally thin with a small amount of transparency. The grade of the paper is determined by brightness.

The primary purpose of the cover letter is to allow a potential employer to determine whether it is worth their time to examine your résumé. Fundamentally the cover letter provides you with an opportunity to stand out and show an employer a personal side of you and what you have to offer.

L esson 3

Stationery Document Preparation

Dear Edward,

Maybe the reason you can't read Bella's mind is because there's nothing in her head.

Sincerely, Logic.

Objective

At the end of this chapter, the student should be able to:
➢ *produce letters using the most appropriate styles*
➢ *create a letter using the appropriate letterhead with tables*

Style Of Business Letter

Business letter can be written with different styles, such as:

• **Full Block**

Full block style is a letter format in which all text is justified to the left margin. In block letter style, standard punctuation is placed after salutations and in other headings. Open punctuation, however, refers to a modification of style where all nonessential punctuation is omitted. A few key factors will help you understand block style format and the difference that open punctuation makes.

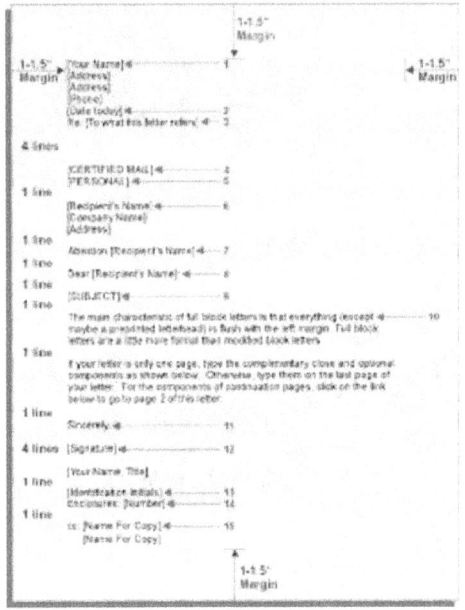

1. Return Address: If your stationery has a letterhead, skip this. Otherwise, type your name, address and optionally, phone number. These days, it's common to also include an email address.

2. Date: Type the date of your letter two to six lines below the letterhead. Three are standard. If there is no letterhead, type it where shown.

3. Reference Line: If the recipient specifically requests information, such as a job reference or invoice number, type it on one or two lines, immediately below the Date.

4. Special Mailing Notations: Type in all uppercase characters, if appropriate.

5. On-Arrival Notations: Type in all uppercase characters, if appropriate. You might want to include a notation on private correspondence.

6. Inside Address: Type the name and address of the person and/or company to whom you're sending the letter, three to eight lines below the last component you typed. Four lines are standard.

7. Attention Line: Type the name of the person to whom you're sending the letter.

8. Salutation: Type the recipient's name here. Type Mr. or Ms. [Last Name] to show respect, but don't guess spelling or gender.

9. Subject Line: Type the gist of your letter in all uppercase characters, either flush left or centered. Be concise on one line.

10. Body: Type two spaces between sentences. Keep it brief and to the point.

11. Complimentary Close: What you type here depends on the tone and degree of formality.

12. Signature Block: Leave four blank lines after the Complimentary Close to sign your name. Sign your name exactly as you type it below your signature. Title is optional depending on relevancy and degree of formality.

13. Identification Initials: If someone typed the letter for you, he or she would typically include three of your initials in all uppercase characters, then two of his or hers in all lowercase characters.

14. Enclosure Notation: This line tells the reader to look in the envelope for more. Type the singular for only one enclosure, plural for more.

15. cc: Stands for courtesy copies (formerly carbon copies). List the names of people to whom you distribute copies, in alphabetical order.

- **Block Format**

When writing business letters, you must pay special attention to the format and font used. The most common layout of a business letter is known as block format. Using this format, the entire letter is left justified and single spaced except for a double space between paragraphs.

1. Block Format Headings

In block letter format, all text is flush with the left margin. The sender's address is written at the top of the page, unless the letter is written on letterhead. After the sender's address or logo, a space is entered, followed by the date. After the date, another space is entered, and the recipient's full name and address are typed.

2. Salutation

In block letter style, the salutation should begin with "Dear" and should be followed with the proper prefix and last name of the recipient. Although many letter writers are used to following a salutation with a comma, the salutation is followed by a colon in block letter format.

3. Letter Body

The body of a block letter is written in single-spaced paragraphs aligned to the left margin. A single space is placed between paragraphs. Even in open punctuation, periods and commas are still necessary within paragraphs to separate sentences. However, if you include a list of bullet points in the letter, omit the punctuation.

4.Closing

In the closing of a block style letter, a formal salutation is again aligned against the left margin. In regular block format, a comma is placed after the closing.

• Semi-Block

The final, and least used, style is semi-block. It is much like the modified block style except that each paragraph is indented instead of left justified. Keep in mind that different organizations have different format requirements for their professional communication. While the examples provided by the OWL contain common elements for the basic business letter (genre expectations), the format of your business letter may need to be flexible to reflect variables like letterheads and templates. Our examples are merely guides.

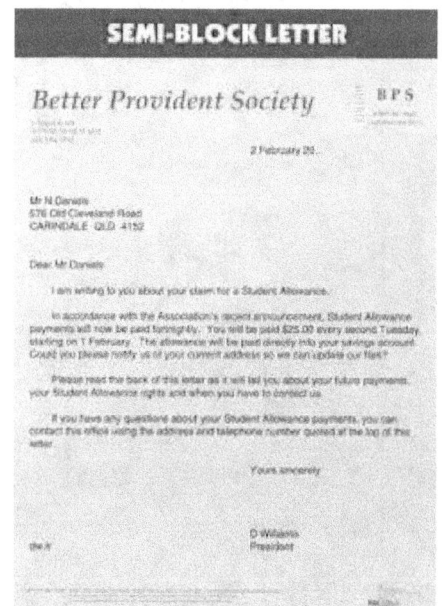

1. Font
Another important factor in the readability of a letter is the font. The generally accepted font is Times New Roman, size 12, although other fonts such as Arial may be used. When choosing a font, always consider your audience. If you are writing to a conservative company, you may want to use Times New Roman. However, if you are writing to a more liberal company, you have a little more freedom when choosing fonts.

2. Punctuation
Punctuation after the salutation and closing - use a colon (:) after the salutation (never a comma) and a comma (,) after the closing. In some circumstances, you may also use a less common format, known as open punctuation. For this style, punctuation is excluded after the salutation and the closing.

• Indented Format

The indented layout of business letters is what people are most used to because this is how letters were written before PCs which really has been a long time, come to think of it.

In a lot of countries indenting paragraphs in a business letter is still a must, and Dixie would like to remind you again that on this website she mostly focuses on the US ways. And in the US the indented letter does look a little outdated. On the other hand, a lot of companies still use it even in the US. Well, there are three layouts to choose from. And if you justify to yourself using this one, go for it.

Simplified-style

Simplified-style business letters contain all the same elements as the full-block and semi-block letters. Like the full-block format, the simplified format left-justifies every line except for the company logo or letterhead. The date line is either slightly right of center or flush with the center of the page. Letters written in the simplified format have fewer internal sections, such as the body, salutation and date line.

Using the simplified style is the most useful at times when you don't have a recipient's contact name. Because the simplified style does not require a salutation, you don't need the person's name. The simplified format does away with unneeded formality while maintaining a professional approach.

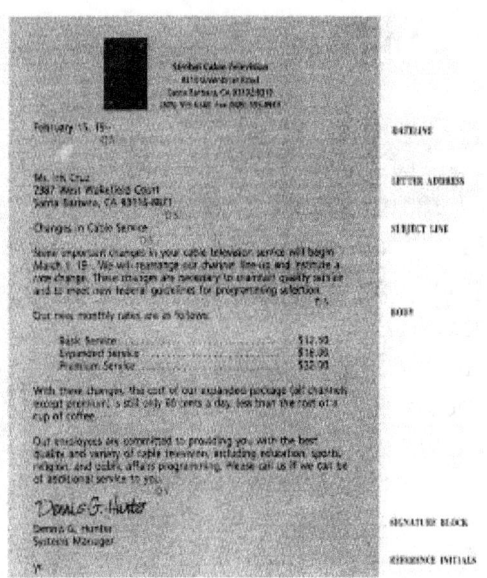

• Hanging-Indented Style

This very useful style places the first words of each paragraph prominently on the page. It is useful for letters that deal with a variety of different topics. However, for normal business communications, this style is very rarely used. The first line of the paragraph begins at the left-hand margin. And the other lines of the same paragraph are indented three to four spaces. This is the reversal of semi-indented style discussed in other page.

Skillswise

Writing a short letter

Hanna sent Maria flowers for her birthday. Maria wrote a note to say thank you.

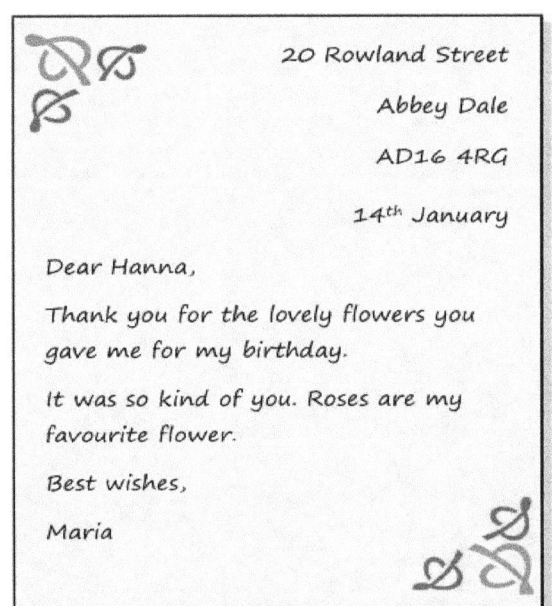

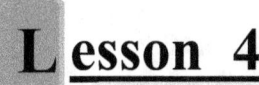

Lesson 4

Envelopes and Label

Mail merge with envelopes

Mail merge makes it easier to print envelopes for the people on your address list. It's a five-step process, and you can save time by starting with good data and paying extra attention to the details.

1. Set up your mailing list

The key to mail merge: Check your data before you start. Word pulls data from the list into each envelope. The better the data, the better your results.

If your mailing list is in an Excel spreadsheet, make sure the column for ZIP or postal codes is formatted as text so you don't lose any zeroes.

If you want to use your Outlook Contacts, make sure Outlook is your default email program.

If you don't have a list, you'll get a chance to make a list in Word during the mail merge. Get ready by pulling together all your address lists before you start. (After you type a list in Word, you can save it and use it the next time you run mail merge.)

2. Set up for envelopes

Setting up the envelope is a long process, but it doesn't take a long time.

Set up the envelope and check how it prints out

Before you run a batch of envelopes the wrong way through your printer, test the printer options and change them if you need to.

1. Click **File** > **New** > **Blank document**.
2. Click **Mailings** > **Envelopes**.

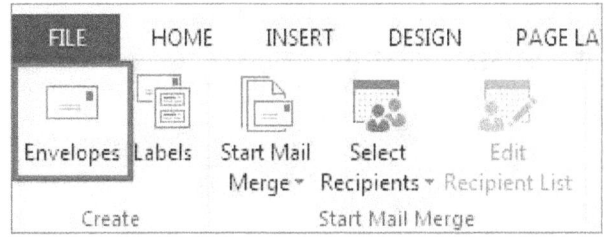

4. In the **Delivery address** box, type some text.

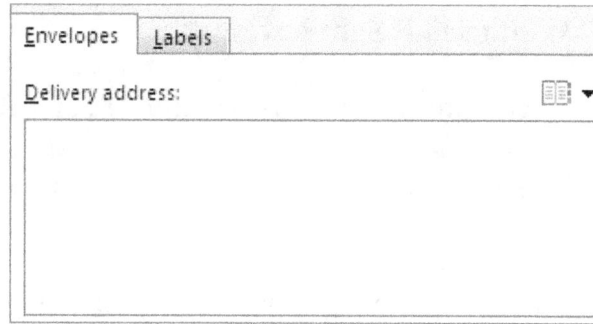

This is for testing the how the envelopes will look when you print them. It won't show up in your mail merge.

5. In the **Return address** box, type your return address.

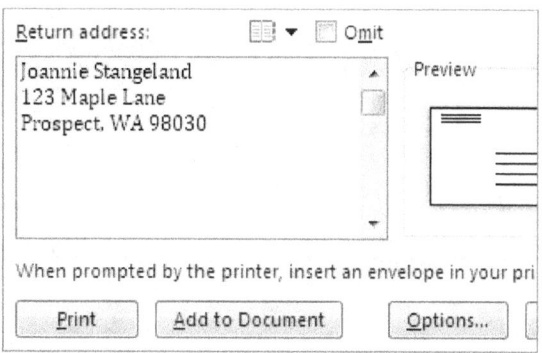

6. Click **Options** > **Envelope Options** tab.
7. In the **Envelope size** box, click the choice that matches the size of your envelopes.

If none of the choices matches your envelope size, scroll to the bottom of the list, click **Custom size**, and type your envelope's dimensions in the **Width** and **Height** boxes.

8. Click **Font** in the **Delivery address** and **Return address** sections to choose a font.
9. Make any position changes you want in the **From left** and **From top** boxes.

The **Preview** area shows you the envelope layout.

10. Click the **Printing Options** tab.

Your printer sends Word information about which way the envelope should be loaded into the printer. This information appears under **Feed method**.

11. Load the envelope the way it's shown under **Feed method**.

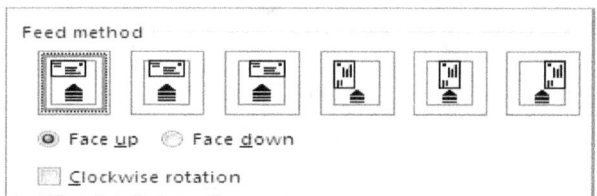

12. Click **OK**.
13. Click **Print** to print the envelope.
14. When Word prompts you to save the return address, click **Yes**.
15. Check that the envelope printed correctly.
16. If the envelope didn't print correctly, try adjusting the **Feed method** options.

When your test envelope prints the way you want, you're ready to begin the merge.

Start the mail merge

1. Click **Mailings** > **Start Mail Merge** > **Envelopes**.

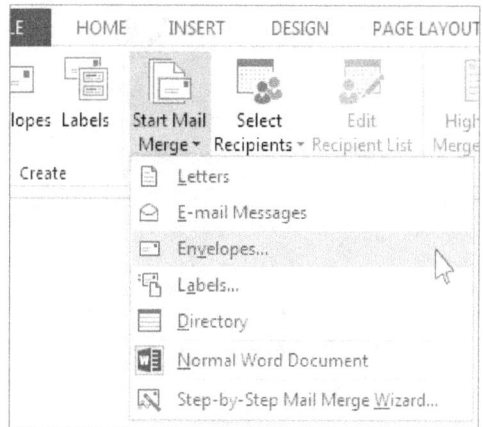

2. In the **Envelope Options** box, click **OK**.

   You already set this up when you were printing your test envelope.

Word creates a document that's sized to the envelope dimensions.

The return address appears in a frame on the page. To see the frame for the delivery address, click where you expect the address to appear.

3. Connect the envelopes to your address list

On the **Mailings** tab, click **Select Recipients** and click the option that matches your list.

If your mailing list is in an Excel spreadsheet, an Access database, or another type of data file, click **Use Existing List**. Then browse to your list and click **Open**.

If you're using your Outlook contacts, click **Choose from Outlook Contacts**.

If you don't have a list yet, choose **Type a New List**.

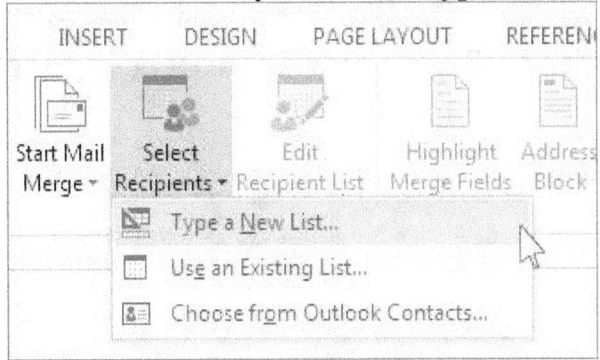

If you're printing envelopes for everyone on your list, skip ahead to step 4. If you're contacting only some of the people on your list—for example, people who live within 20 miles of your event—choose which people you want to include.

1. Click **Edit Recipient List**.

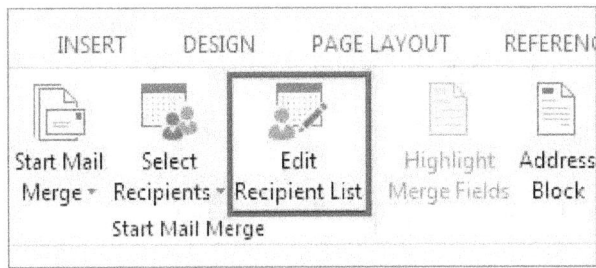

2. Check the names of the people you want to send your letter to.

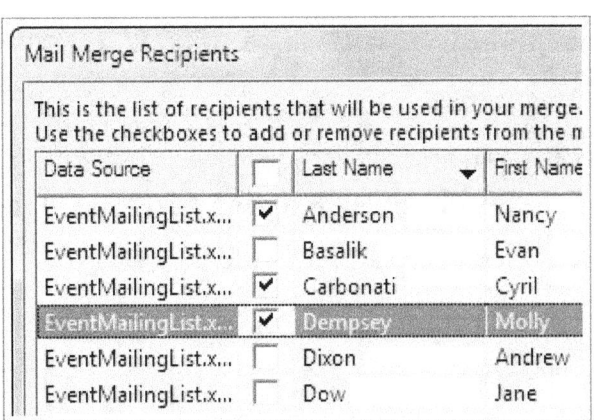

You can also sort or filter the list to make finding names and addresses easier.

4. Add the Address Block to the envelope

1. Click where you want the addresses to appear, and then click **Address Block**.

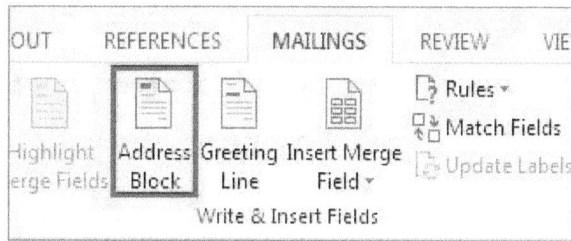

2. Choose how you want the name to appear.

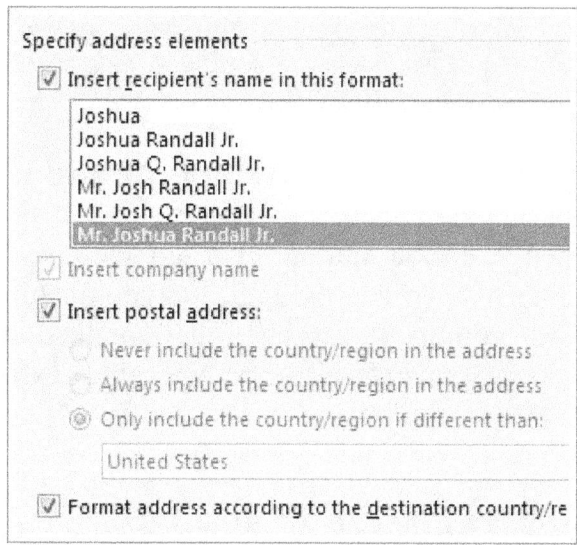

Tip   To be sure Word finds the names and addresses in your list, click **Match Fields**. Check that the fields you want appear in the list. If a field you want says **Not Matched**, click the drop-down list for that field and then click the column name that matches that column in your list.

5. Print the envelopes

1. Click **Preview Results**, and then click the arrows to make sure the names and addresses on the envelopes look right.

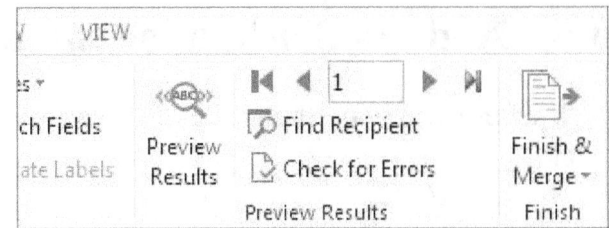

2. Click **Finish & Merge** > **Print Documents**.

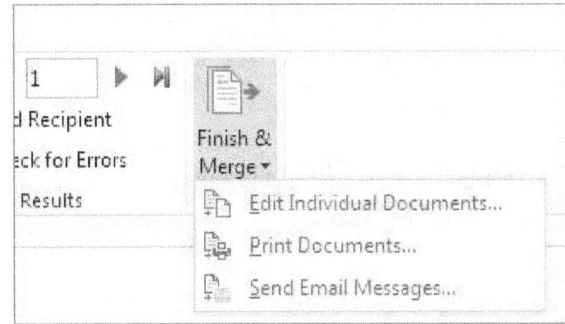

Save your mail merge envelope for next time

When you save the mail merge envelope document, it stays connected to your mailing list. To use the mail merge envelope again, open it and click **Yes** when Word prompts you to keep that connection. Then, if you want to change which addresses include in the merge, click **Edit Recipient List** to sort, filter, and select them.

Use Word mail merge for email

If you want to send a document to many people via email, but you want it to be personalized (such as ensuring each person is addressed individually), use Word for an email merge. In other words, each message you send out has the same information but certain parts of the message are unique.

An example of this might be a yearly yoga retreat that's coming up: You're responsible for sending out the invitation to each person who attended last year's event—all 170 of them. Word makes it fairly simple to send out this invitation to every one of your contortionist cohorts, each of them getting an email message addressed and personalized, just to—and for—them.

The basic steps to mail merge are the following:

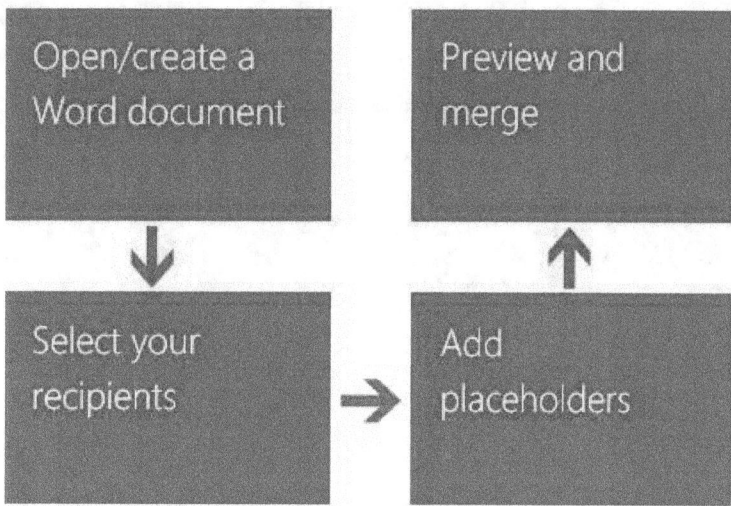

Important   Be sure you're using the same versions Outlook and Word: Microsoft Word 2013 and Microsoft Outlook 2013.

The mail merge process entails the following overall steps, and while this may seem complicated, it truly can be very straightforward with a little bit of setting up.

1. Set up the email message. In this step, you're going to open up Word to either a blank document or one you've already created and get started on the merging part of the process.
2. Connect the message to your address list. Your address list is the data source that Word will use in the mail merge. It's a file that contains the email addresses where the messages will be sent.
3. Add placeholders, called mail merge fields, to the email message document. When you perform the mail merge, the mail merge fields are filled with information from your address list.
4. Preview and complete the merge. You can preview each message before you send the whole set.

Set up the email message main document

1. Start Word and either create your message in the blank document or start Word and open up something you've already started.
2. Click **Mailings**> **Start Mail Merge**> **E-mail Messages**.

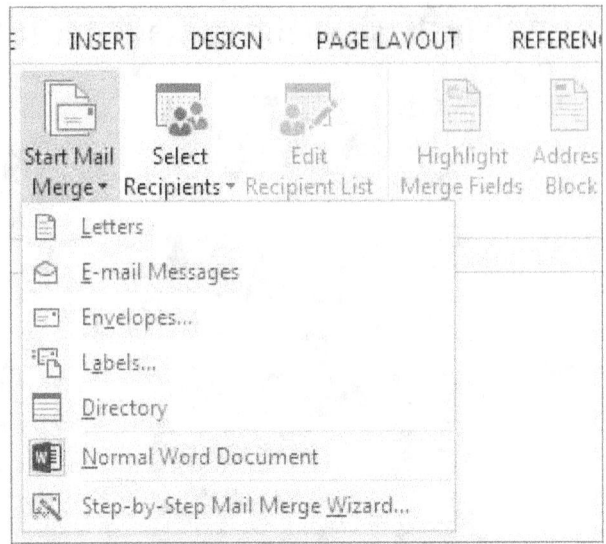

Connect the email message document to your list

Now it's time to choose your recipients from a data source (a fancy name for an address list). If you don't already have a data source, you can create one during the mail merge process. Be sure to check that your data source has a column for email addresses and that you have the email address of each person you're sending this to.

Click **Mailings** > **Select Recipients**, and choose the data source you want to use:

- To use the email addresses from your Outlook contacts, click **Choose from Outlook Contacts**. If Word prompts you to choose a contact list or and Outlook profile, click the list or profile you want to use in the merge.

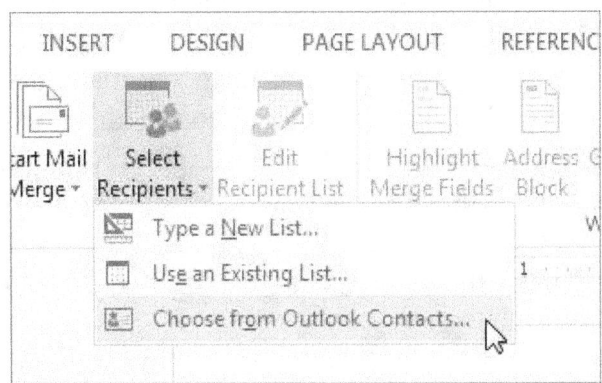

Important   Be sure to make any changes to your contact list in Outlook before you start the merge. You won't be able to change the list in Word.

- To use an address list that's in an Excel spreadsheet or an Access database, click **Use an Existing List** and then browse to your list.

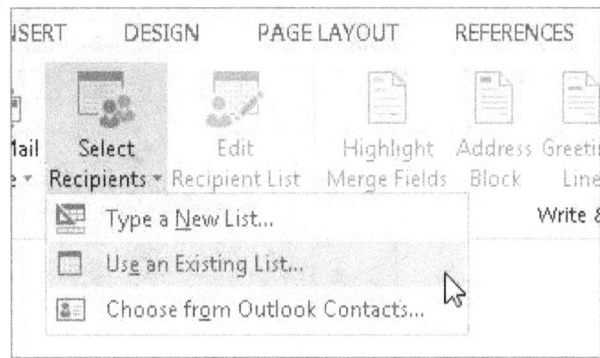

- If you don't have an address list yet, click **Type a New List** and fill in the form that Word opens. (The list you create is saved as a database file, or.mdb file, that you can reuse.

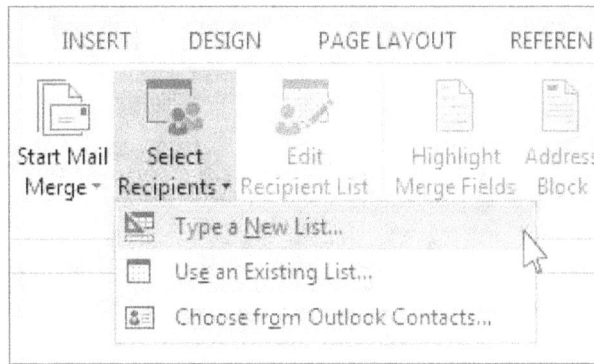

Note   The next time you want to use this list for a merge, click **Mailings** > **Select Recipients** > **Use an Existing List** and choose the list you made.

If you clicked **Use an Existing List**, Word automatically selects everyone on the list you chose. If you plan to use your entire list as is, you can skip to the next step.

To narrow the list of recipients, select the names you want in the **Mail Merge Recipients** box. (You can open the **Mail Merge Recipients** box by clicking **Mailings** > **Edit Recipient List**.)

Here are some ways to narrow your list:

- **Select individual records**   This is most useful if your list is short. Check the boxes next to the people you want to include, and uncheck the boxes next to the people you don't.

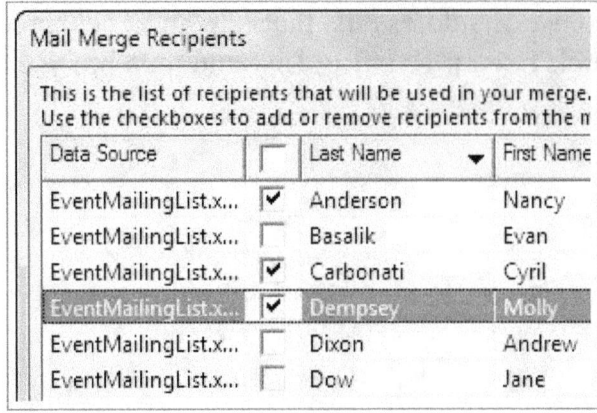

- **Sort records**   Click the column heading of the item that you want to sort by. The list sorts in ascending alphabetical order (from A to Z). Click the column heading again to sort the list in descending alphabetical order (Z to A).

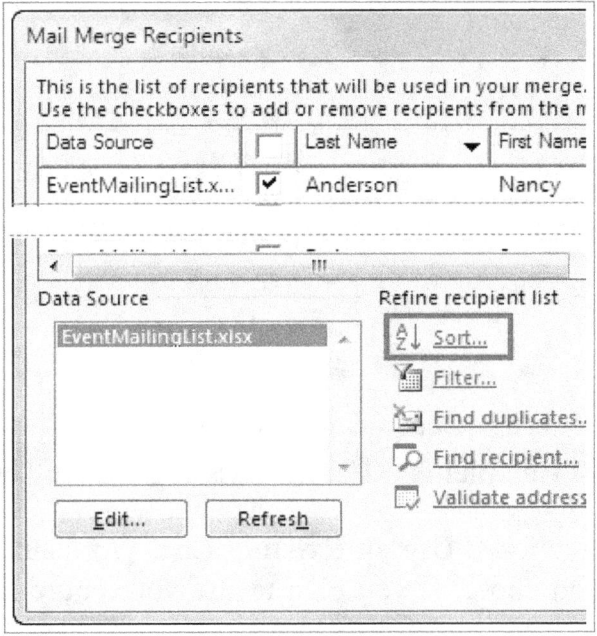

- **Filter records**   Under **Refine recipient list**, click **Filter**. This is handy when the list contains things that you know you don't want to see or include in the merge. After you filter the list, you can check or uncheck the boxes to include or exclude people.

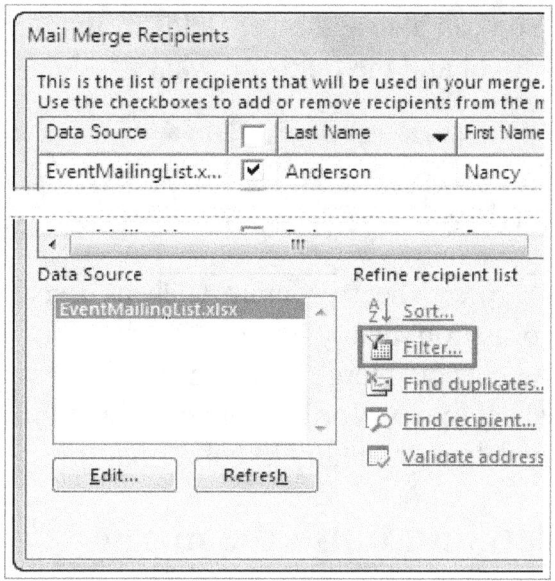

- **Add recipients**   To add people to the list, under **Data source**, click the name of your data file. Click **Edit** > **New Entry** and type the information for that recipient.

Add placeholders—or fields—to the email message document

After you connect your document to your address list, type the text of the message.

To personalize each message, add mail merge fields from your data source. For example, click **Mailings** > **Write & Insert Fields** > **Greeting Line** to add a line with the person's name.

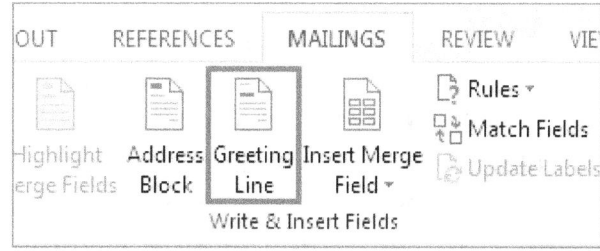

The **Insert Greeting Line** box opens, and you can choose whether you want to add "Dear" or "To" and how you want the person's name to appear. Word inserts a placeholder for the greeting line and then adds each name during the merge.

You can also add other fields from your data source by clicking **Insert Merge Field** and the field you want to add.

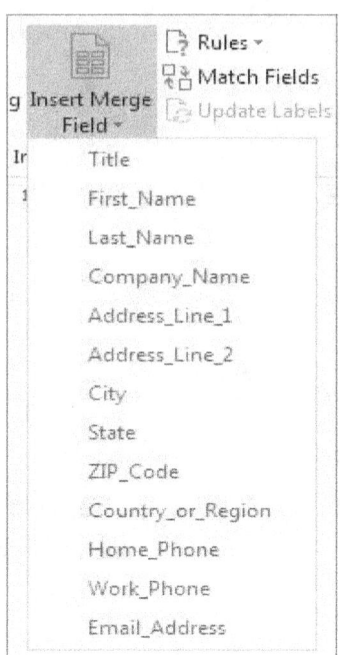

Formatting

A spreadsheet program such as Excel stores the information that you type inside cells as raw data. When you merge information from an Excel spreadsheet into a Word document, you are merging that raw data without any Excel formatting.

Preview and finish the merge

After you add fields to your email message's main document, you're ready to preview the merge results. When you're satisfied with the preview, you can complete the merge.

Preview the merge

Click **Mailings**, and a couple of groups to the right, you'll see **Preview Results**.

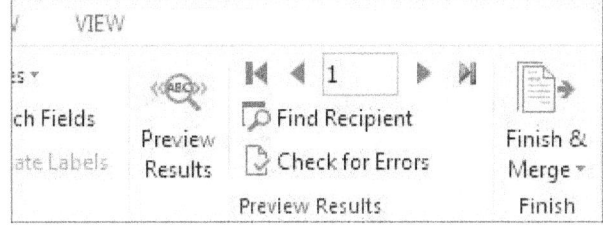

Now you can do any or all of the following:

1. Click **Preview Results**.(This option is available only if you chose one or more placeholder fields, such as greeting, name, address, etc.)
2. Page through each email message by clicking the blue arrows.
3. Preview a specific document by clicking **Find Recipient**.
4. Edit your recipient list—who's getting this message—by clicking **Mailings > Edit Recipient List**.

Complete the merge and send the messages

1. Click **Mailings> Finish & Merge> Send E-mail Messages**.
2. In the **To** box, select the name of the email address column in your list.

Note   Word sends an individual message to each email address. You can't Cc or Bcc other recipients. You also can't add attachments to the email merge message.

3. In the **Subject line** box, type a subject line for the message.
4. In the **Mail format** box, click **HTML** or **Plain text** to send the document as the body of the email message.

Important   If you send the document as a plain text email message, the email message won't include any text formatting or graphics.

Save the message

Save the message if you plan to use it for another mail merge.

When you save the email message's main document, you also save its connection to the data file you chose. The next time you open the email message main document, Word prompts you to choose whether to keep the connection to the data file.

5. If you click **Yes**, the document opens with information from the first record merged in.
6. If you click **No**, the connection between the email message main document and the data file is broken. The email message main document becomes a standard Word document.

<u>Summary</u>

Mail merge makes it easier to print envelopes for the people on your address list. It's a five-step process, and you can save time by starting with good data and paying extra attention to the details.

1. Set up your mailing list - *The key to mail merge: Check your data before you start. Word pulls data from the list into each envelope. The better the data, the better your results.*

2. Set up for envelopes- *Set up the envelope and check how it prints out then Start the mail merge*

3. Connect the envelopes to your address list - *On the Mailings **tab, click** Select Recipients **and click the option that matches your list.** If your mailing list is in an Excel spreadsheet, an Access database, or another type of data file, click; Use Existing List. Then browse to your list and click **Open.***

4. Add the Address Block to the envelope

5. Print the envelopes

L esson 5

Correspondence and Various Media

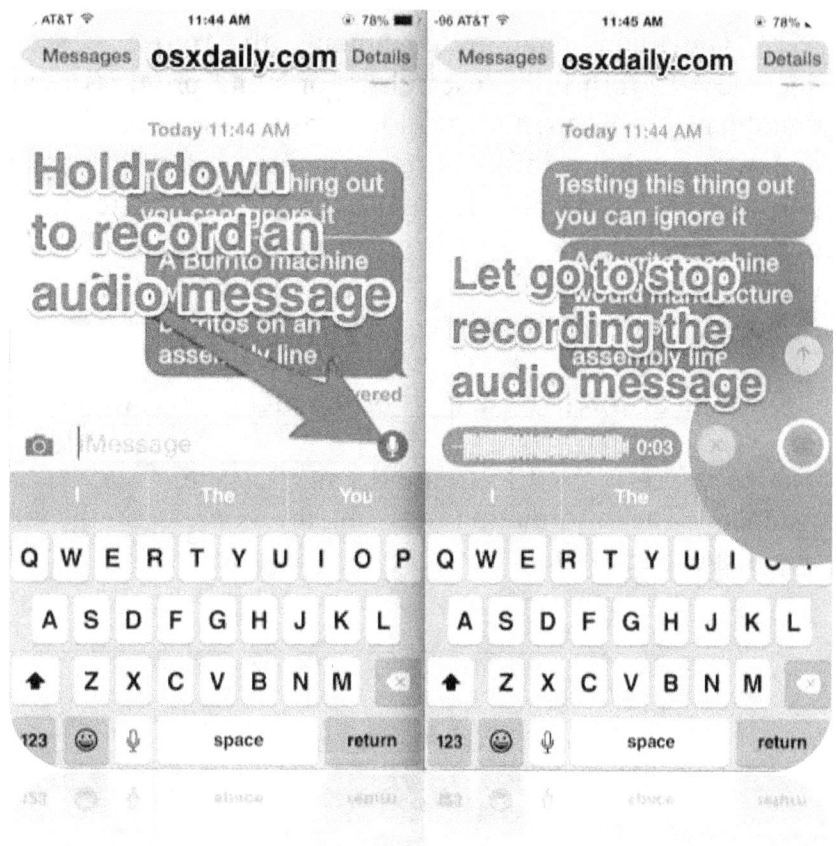

Objective

At the end of this chapter, the student should be able to:
- ➢ *prepare correspondence from skeleton notes and various media*
- ➢ *compose letters, memoranda, notes to include audio messages*

Memoranda

Memoranda are brief, informal reports used to establish a record. They generalize the communication process by transmitting the message from one or more authors to one or more recipients. E-mail messages typically take the form of memoranda.

The memorandum is among the most versatile of organizational documents. From brief research reports and progress reports to trip reports and thumbnail proposals, the memo form is widely used to communicate technical and administrative information. Memoranda are written for numerous internal purposes--for example, to request information, to make announcements, to outline policies, and to transmit meeting minutes. Thus, in most organizations, memos play a crucial role in establishing a record of decisions, requests, responsibilities, results, and concerns.

The distinctive element of the memorandum are:

The Heading is used to frame the message in a very accessible and transparent manner. The information sets out the context of the message and should be detailed enough to make the context very clear.

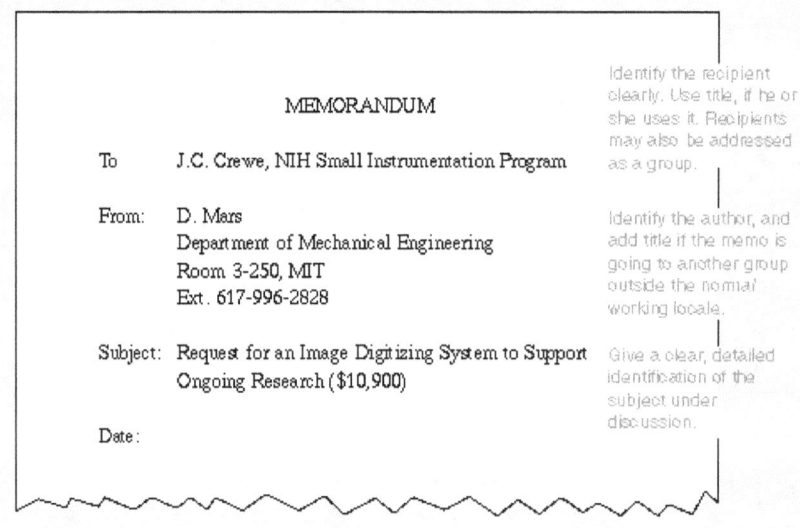

Body

Generally, organize the topics of the memorandum in order of importance, with the key statements first and the details further on. The memorandum should normally begin with a brief summary statement, in one or two sentences, identifying the key topic and the scope of the memorandum.

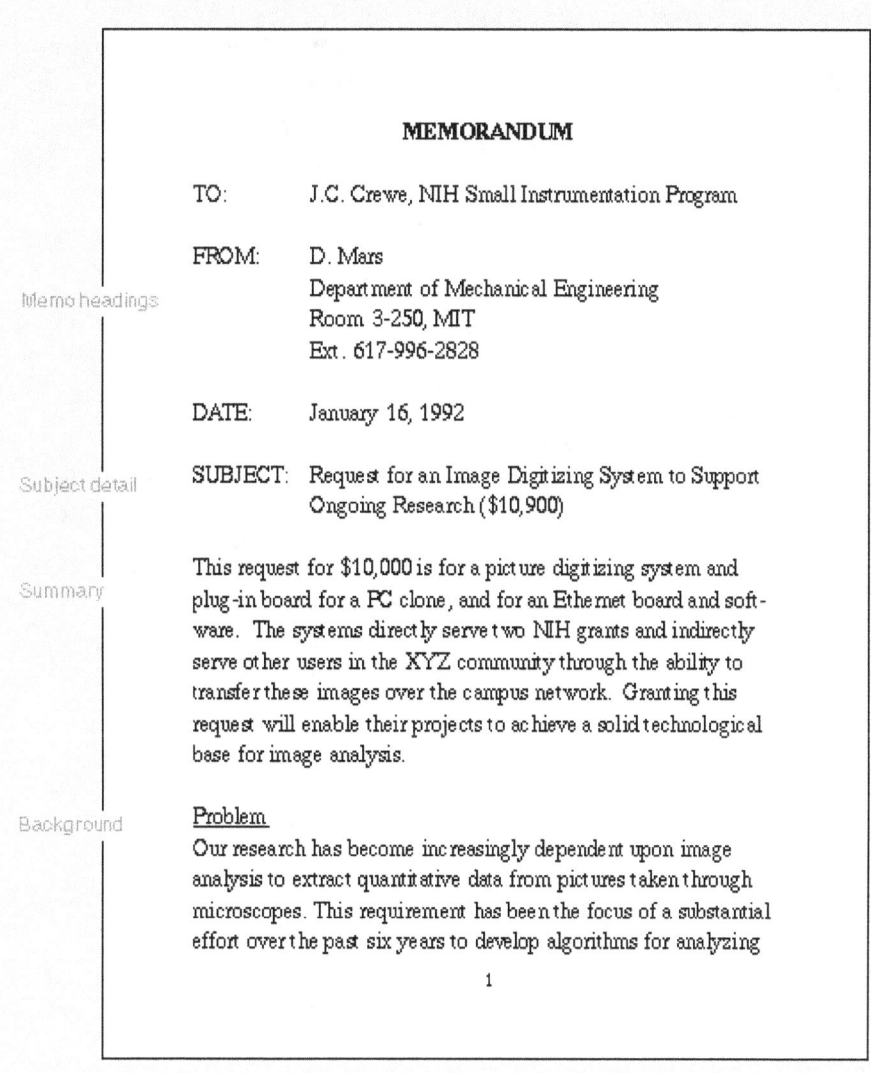

pictures with a computer. Unfortunately, the software has out-paced the picture digitizing systems that are available to us. We are in dire need of reliable commercial systems that will digitize pictures in color at better than 1000 x 1000 pixels per picture.

The Participating Grants

The two active NIH grants that will immediately benefit from the requested imaging system include:

- **HL 57OD. Mars**

  This grant investigates the influence of fluid shear stress on the structure and function of vascular endothelium. Imaging is used for cell shape analysis and detection of antibody stains.

- **HL 4500 R.F. Dodge**

  Research on aqueous outflow from eye and relation to glaucoma. Imaging used to extract quantitative data from electron micrographs of porous tissue.

Budget

The image system we have chosen is a Barneyscan Digitizer and plug-in board for a PC Clone ($8700), plus a PC clone and Ethernet board and software ($2200) to connect to the existing image analysis system on the MASSCOMP computer in the Fluid Mechanics Laboratory.

L esson 6

Meeting Documentation

Objective

At the end of this chapter, the student should be able to:
- ➢ *prepare documents for meeting*
- ➢ *create Notice of meeting, minutes, and Chairman's agenda*

Preparing is very important in having a successful meeting. Meetings are also a major part of most careers, so it can be a big deal! Follow these steps to help encourage success in your next meeting.

Preparing for a Meeting

1   Knowing how to prepare for a meeting is important for all employees and critical for any manager or leader.
Knowing when not to have a meeting is equally important.

2 **Decide the type of meeting you are going to have:**

3 Determine the roles and ask those participants to accept them.

The roles are the following:

Leader	
Facilitator	
Recorder	
Timer	
Participants	

4 Prepare a notice, this should include the date, time, agenda, and venue of the meeting. *Distribute the notice to the members in good time for the meeting.*

5 Attach the minutes of the previous meeting (if there has been one). *This gives members the chance to bring up anything they do not understand or disagree with.*

**6 Get basic items in place.** *Set out chairs and tables before the meeting begins. Provide pens and paper for everyone. Place a pitcher of water in the middle of the table and put glasses around the table.*

7 Call the meeting to order.

This means the chairperson asks everyone to stop talking as the meeting is about to begin. Determine the quarterly goals for the team. The agenda is a list of the topics you'll address to get to that objective, with a time limit to keep you on track.

For example:

> *1. Review the status of last quarter's goals (15 minutes),*

> *2. Round-table suggestions for goals (20 minutes), 3. Pick top 5 goals (10 minutes).*

8 Pass around the attendance book or sheet of paper and ask everyone attending to sign their names at the beginning of the meeting. *These names will be entered in the minutes.*

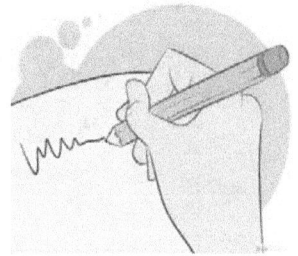

9 Ask the minutes secretary to write down the main points of the meeting for typing up later.

10 Ask if anyone has any other business, known as AOB, at the end of the formal meeting. *Set a date for the next meeting and formally close the meeting.*

Sample Board Meeting Minutes

Franze Co. Monthly Board Meeting
13 February 2013

Meeting called to order at 12:00 p.m. by CEO Taylor Cooper

Members present:
Taylor Cooper, CEO
Logan Shafter, CFO
Morgan Ely, *Senior Vice President, Marketing*
Elyse Chan, *Senior Vice President, Engineering*
Joyce Comer, *Senior Vice President, Consulting*
Lindsay Rogan, *Communication Strategist*
Mark Epstein, *Senior Vice President, Human Resources*
Shane Hale, *Engineering Specialist*
Nick Mitchell, *International Consulting Representative*
Ryan Marke, *Senior Vice President, Recruiting*

Members absent:
(none)

Approval of minutes:

- Motion: Approve minutes from 14 January 2013 board meeting
- Vote: Motion carried
- Resolved: Minutes from the meeting on 14 January 2013 approved without modification

Business:
Motion from Morgan Ely to submit the latest issue of company newsletter, *The Newswire*, for national award
Vote: 10 in favor, 0 opposed, 0 abstained
Resolved: Motion carried

Motion from Shane Hale to attain 10% more engineering materials for company
Vote: 4 in favor, 6 opposed
Resolved: Motion failed

Motion from Mark Epstein to hire 5 interviewed candidates to fill vacant positions at the company
Vote: 6 in favor, 4 opposed
Resolved: Motion carried

Meeting adjourned at 1:14 p.m. by CEO Taylor Cooper

How to Write an Agenda for a Meeting

An organized meeting needs a well-written agenda. Don't let your meeting become the overlong, inefficient slog that so many meetings seem to devolve into. By sticking to a detailed yet flexible agenda, you can keep your meeting streamlined and focused, ensuring that you meet all of your goals for your meeting in the shortest amount of time possible. Whether you're looking to write your own agenda, use a template, or make the most of an agenda you already have

Part 1 of 2: Writing an Agenda

Making an Agenda from Scratch

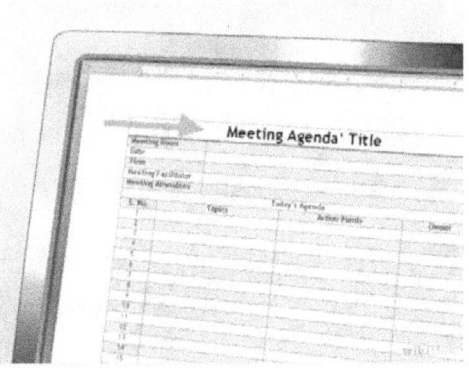

1 Start by giving your agenda a title. *From the most beautiful literature to the driest spreadsheet, almost every important document needs a title, and meeting agendas are no exception. Your title should tell the reader two things: First, that s/he is reading an agenda, and second, what topic the meeting is covering. When you've made a decision, place your title at the top of your blank document. The title doesn't have to flowery or complicated — in a business context, simple and direct titles are usually the best.*

Resist the urge to use fancy or large fonts for your title. In most situations, you'll want to use a plain, dignified font like Times New Roman or Calibri and to make your title the same size as the rest of the lettering on the document (or only slightly larger). Remember, the purpose of your title is to inform readers of what they are looking at, not necessarily to amuse or distract them.

Line Artists' Meeting
July 12, 2014
9:00 a.m to 3:00 pm
Pen Tower, Conference Room2

Meeting called by : Art Director
Attendees :

2 Include "*who?*", "*where?*", and "*when?*" information in the header. *Next, after the title, meeting agendas usually have a header which can vary in detail depending upon the level of formality your workplace encourages. This header is usually located about one line below the title. Generally, in the header, you'll want to include brief factual information about the meeting that doesn't have to do with the topic being discussed. This is so that people who aren't at the meeting can tell when and where it occurred and who was there. Below are some of the things you may want to include; regardless of the information you choose, be sure to clearly label each piece of information (bolding the label text works well here):*

1. **Date and time**. *These can be grouped together or in their own separate sections.*
2. **Location**. *If your business has multiple locations, you may want to write the address, whereas if it has just one location, you may want to name the room you're meeting in (e.g., Conference Room #3).*
3. **Attendees.** *Job titles are usually optional but not required.*
4. **Special individuals present**. *These may be special guests, speakers, or meeting leaders.*

Objective : To discuss long-term cost-cutting measures.

3 Write a brief objective statement. *Meetings that don't have a clearly-defined purpose risk wasting precious time as attendees decide what to talk about. Skip a line after your header and use bolded or underlined text to label your objective section with a title like "Objective" or "Purpose", followed by a colon or a line break. Then, in a few concise and to-the-point sentences, describe the items of discussion for the meeting. Aim to write about 1-4 sentences here.*

5. *For instance, if we're looking to write an objective statement for a budget meeting, we might use this one: "**Objective:** To outline key budget goals for the 2014-2015 fiscal year and discuss long-term cost-cutting measures. Additionally, R & D Director Marcus Feldman will present the results of a recent competitiveness study."*
6. *If you've ever written in a scientific context, think of the objective statement as the meeting's abstract or executive summary. You're essentially saying, in broad strokes, what you plan to be discussed at the meeting without going into any detail.*

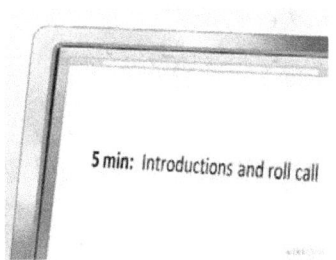

4 Write a schedule for the main points of the meeting. *Schedules help combat the common flaw that business meetings have for running far, far too long. Skip a line after your objective statement, give your schedule a bolded or underlined title, then begin making entries (which should correspond to the main topics of discussion) in your schedule. For ease of reading, give each entry its own line.*

7. *Label each entry with either the time you plan for it to begin and end or the amount of time you plan for each entry to take. Pick one system or the other and be consistent — mixing and matching looks unprofessional.*
8. *In other words, you'll want to label each schedule entry with either the start and end times for which you'd like that topic of conversation to take place during or simply specify how long you'd like it to take. For instance, one sample entry might look like either "**2:00 - 2:05**: Introductions and roll call" or "**5 min**: Introductions and roll call". You would, however, avoid switching between the two labeling systems.*

5 Allocate time in the schedule for any special guests. *If any guests are coming to your meeting to discuss topics of importance, you'll want to devote a chunk of the meeting's time to these people. Plan on assigning each guest a single schedule entry even if s/he has more than one topic of discussion. This way, each one will be able to organize his or her topics as s/he sees fit.*

To avoid embarrassing scheduling conflicts, contact the guests ahead of time to figure out how much time each one will need for their discussion topic.

6 Leave extra time at the end of the meeting for Q&A. *During this time, people can ask for clarification about confusing topics of discussion, offer their own follow-up opinions, suggest topics for future meetings, and make other comments. You can make this Q&A time explicit by including it as the final entry in your schedule or you can simply bring it up yourself after the final point of the meeting.*

If you reach the end of your meeting and no one has any additional questions to ask or comments to make, you can always end the meeting early. Many of your attendees will likely be thankful for this!

7   Optionally, provide an outline of the discussion topics. *Generally, the schedule is the "meat" of the meeting agenda — the part that people will look to to guide the discussion. However, while it isn't essential to go this extra mile, providing anadditional outline of key points can be a big help for confused meeting attendees. An outline allows attendees to have a reminder of the organisation of ideas presented at the meeting, helping people who have a hard time keeping track of every single topic mentioned. Below is a sample of the type of outline organization you will probably want to use (see How to Write an Outline for more information):*

9. I. High-priority Budget Items
     1.   A. Employee travel budget
B. Dealership fees

     1.   i. Negotiating a better deal?
C. Lobbying costs

10. II. Revenue-boosting Measures
     1.   A. Alternative service deals
     1.   i. Presenting options to customers
ii. Soliciting feedback

B. Re-investment in mobile technology
     11.   ...and so on.

8 **Check the agenda for errors before distributing it.** *Because some attendees may end up relying heavily on the meeting agenda, it's a very wise idea to proofread it for errors before giving it out. Doing so isn't just a courtesy to the attendees — it also reflects positively on your attention to detail and the value you have for your position.*

Additionally, ensuring there are no errors in your agenda can save you time and face, as spending time explaining an error-riddled agenda can get your meeting off track and be embarrassing for you, especially if important people are in attendance.

Using an Agenda Template

1 **Use a template included with a word processor.**

Many word processing programs, like Microsoft Office, Pages for Mac, and so on, have pre-made templates for a variety of personal and professional documents, which may include agendas for meetings. These templates make it remarkably quick and easy to produce a professional-looking document. Typically, these types of templates are pre-organized into logical sections with an aesthetically-pleasing arrangement — all you need to do is type the relevant information into the appropriate spaces and you're ready to go!

1. *Though every word processor is slightly different, most that have the ability to use templates will allow you to navigate to the templates by using the menu bar at the top of the program's window.*
2. *If your word processor can use templates, but doesn't have any templates suitable for meeting agendas, you may be able to download one from the program's creator's website. For instance, Microsoft Word templates are available from office.microsoft.com[1], while templates for Pages for Mac can be found on the Apple App store.*

2 Alternatively, download a template from a third-party source.

If your word processor doesn't come with any included agenda templates and you can't obtain any from its official site, don't worry — there are tons of free templates available online. A simple search on your preferred search engine for a query like "meeting agenda template" should yield dozens of relevant results. However, since not all of these results will be from official, reputable sources, it's important to be discriminating when it comes to choosing which templates to use. Below are a few third-party sites you may want to visit:

1. *Save Word Templates —This professional site offers many quality templates for Microsoft Word.*
2. *Word Templates Online[3] — Another good source for Word templates. However, this page offers only a few options.*
3. *iWorkCommunity[4] — a good Pages agenda template. However, this template is for older (pre-'09) versions of Pages.*

4. The App Store also has numerous templates for Pages. Unfortunately, not all of these are available for free.

3 Fill out the fields in your template. *Once you've located a suitable template in your word processor or downloaded one that you like, all you need to do is fill out the template with the necessary information. Most templates will have clearly-marked areas for you to type in names, times, topics for discussion, section titles, and so forth. Fill in all relevant fields to complete your agenda, then, when you're done, quickly check your work for errors. As convenient as agenda templates can be, they don't protect against spelling, grammar, and factual mistakes.*

Don't leave any fields blank. Nothing looks less professional than, for instance, having a schedule entry that reads only "Type here". If, for some reason, there are parts of the template you don't want to fill out, be sure to delete these rather than leave them unfilled.

4 **Make minor modifications to make your agenda fit your needs.**

Templates for meeting agendas can be incredibly convenient, but there's no reason why you might need to stick to the agenda's pre-prepared style and format exactly. Feel free to make changes to the template's content and style as you see fit to ensure that your agenda meets the standards that your business has set for you and that you have set for the meeting.

For instance, if you really like the look of a certain template, but its header section is so long that it's distracting, feel free to delete superfluous sections of the header as you see fit, as long as you do so in a way that doesn't ruin the formatting of the document or render the agenda ugly.

Part 2 of 2: Best Practices for Using an Agenda

1 Schedule the most important topics first.

When planning meetings, it's usually a good policy to front-load the schedule with the most important topics. This ensures two important things. First, it ensures that everyone will be able to discuss these important topics when they're at their sharpest and least-fatigued at the very beginning of the meeting. Second, it ensures that in the event that the meeting has to end early or certain attendees need to leave before it finishes, important topics have already been discussed.

Meetings don't always go the way you plan them to. If minor, unimportant topics get cut from the end of a meeting, it may be possible to resolve them on your own or to schedule another meeting for later. However, if you're unable to get to the biggest topics of discussion, your meeting has failed to achieve part of its purpose, which can be both frustrating and embarrassing for you. Keeping the most important topics at the top of your schedule *usually* avoids this problem.

2 Stick to your agenda's schedule, but be flexible.

When planning and conducting a meeting, one of the biggest dangers you'll want to look out for is the meeting going over its allotted time. Generally, employees hate overly-long meetings, and with good reason, as they can be tremendously boring and can prevent people from doing actual work instead. To ensure your meeting stays on schedule, you'll want to keep an eye on the clock and, when you get the opportunity, politely move the meeting forward by saying something like, "we should move to the next topic if we want to get out of here on time."

However, meetings often don't go as planned, so you'll need to be prepared to compensate if one part of your meeting runs longer than you would have liked. Be flexible while trying to cover as much ground as possible in the limited time you have for your meeting. For instance, if one part of your meeting runs long, you may need to shorten the discussion for other parts of your meeting or eliminate relatively unimportant parts of the meeting entirely to assure a timely conclusion.

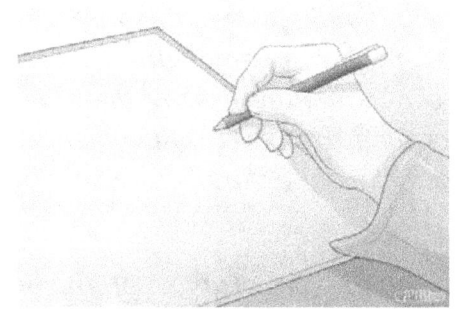

3 Start writing your agenda well in advance of the meeting.

Though agendas aren't necessarily as important as other types of business documents (like reports, data spreadsheets, presentation slides, etc.), you'll still want your agenda to be as professional and polished as possible, especially if you plan on sharing it with your coworkers at the meeting. To ensure you have enough time to produce a quality document, start writing your agenda as early as you reasonably can.

Starting early also gives you the benefit of being able to receive feedback on your agenda before the meeting. Sharing a draft of your agenda with coworkers or supervisors and asking for their input can help you fix flaws and add missing details that weren't present initially. If you wait until the last second to write your agenda, you may not have time to solicit this feedback.

While you may be able to get away with writing agendas for ordinary, everyday meetings the day before the meeting itself, Important meetings may require weeks of preparation.

4 Share the agenda with the attendees before the meeting.

To ensure that everyone arrives at the meeting with full knowledge of the topic to be discussed, you'll want to share the agenda with everyone beforehand. Depending on the company culture where you work, this may mean printing off numerous copies and delivering them in person, or simply emailing the agenda as an attachment. However you choose to distribute your agenda, be sure that it is free from technical errors before sending.

Depending on the importance of the meeting, you'll probably want to give attendees the agenda at least an hour or two before the meeting. For big, important meetings, sending the agenda a day or more in advance may be necessary.

Since people are often busy and forgetful, it's a smart idea to take several additional copies of the agenda with you to the meeting in case anyone forgets theirs.

Minutes

Keep accurate minutes of <u>meetings</u>, both formal and informal. Minutes are an essential part of organization life. They maintain an institutional memory of all actions taken or proposed and the key points of discussion. They also inform appropriate individuals who were not present at the meeting of the key action and discussion items.

Minutes can be formal or informal. Formal minutes are often required by federal, state, or local law, by-laws, charters, or regulations. They are usually distributed to the members of the group before the next meeting, and then approved (sometimes after being amended).

Some minutes are <u>legally</u> parts of the public record and available to anyone. Often, however, organizational minutes are private and confidential documents, which should be distributed only to appropriate individuals. If the minutes are confidential, each page should be stamped with a message such as "CONFIDENTIAL--DO NOT DISTRIBUTE."

The following information, adapted from *Robert's Rules of Order*, is usally included in formal minutes:

- The name of the group that is meeting and what kind of meeting it is (for example, a general meeting, an emergency meeting, or a meeting devoted to a single issue)
- Precisely where and when the meeting is being held
- Names of the group members in attendance and members absent; names of all other individuals present, except for public meetings with an audience
- The name of the person who called the meeting to order and at what time
- A report of whether or not the previous meeting's minutes were read and, if they were read, whether or not they were approved (or approved with modifications)
- Summaries of any reports presented to the group and any action taken on them (acceptance, approval, endorsement, referral)
- A summary of the discussion of each item on the <u>agenda</u> and any other important issues discussed at the meeting

- A record of all formal motions, including the name of the individual making the motion
- A record of the vote on all motions, including the number of votes for and against, and the number of abstentions
- The time that the meeting was formally concluded

Informal minutes also include the date of the meeting and the names of all members attending or absent, but they focus more on summarizing key points of discussion and listing all action items to be performed by individuals or the group.

MEMORANDUM

TO: Copyright Issues Group

FROM: Paula Stanley

DATE: July 9, 1996

SUBJECT: Copyright Committee, Greenhill College
                 Minutes of Regular Meeting, July 9, 1996

Members Present: Ms. Appelbaum, Dr. Blackburn, Dean Chan, Professor Garcia, Professor Greenberg, Professor Kozowski, Mr. Smith, Professor Snow, Ms. Stanley, Dr. Washington

Members Absent: Professor Keynes

Guest: Professor Arnold Alexander, Chair of the Faculty Senate

Dr. Blackburn called the meeting to order in the Library Conference Room at 1:15 p.m.

The minutes of the 14 June 1996 meeting were approved unanimously without comment or amendment.

Professor Greenberg and Ms. Stanley summarized the report of the legal review subcommittee (included with the meeting agenda) that Greenhill College owns any intellectual property developed by a faculty member in his or her major field except for textbooks, which are specifically excluded in the College's *Policies and Procedures*. The subcommittee report recommended that Greenhill College should also waive ownership interest in 1) artistic works that are not accomplished under a program of research and do not use Greenhill College facilities, and 2) intellectual property developed pursuant to a preexisting consulting agreement where there are no sponsored research obligations and there is little or no use of Greenhill College facilities.

Professor Snow moved to accept and endorse the subcommittee's report. With no discussion, the motion was passed with seven members voting yes, two members voting no, and one member abstaining.

The Committee then reviewed the "close-to-final" draft of the new Intellectual Policy Guidelines. Dean Chan moved to amend the Guidelines to add a statement that Greenhill College will retain a "shop right" in all intellectual property developed at Greenhill College, including journal articles and textbooks.

Dr. Washington expressed concern that such shop rights might encourage circulation of pirated copies of copyrighted works. There was then considerable discussion on possible protections that might be placed on journal articles and textbooks to ensure that copies made pursuant to Greenhill College's retained shop right do not proliferate outside Greenhill College.

Ms. Stanley suggested including notices or markers on both the electronic and printed forms of the articles and placing electronically distributed copies on a protected server. Dean Chan suggested that the acknowledgment that Greenhill College has a responsibility to make such efforts at protecting the material should be placed in a statement accompanying the Greenhill College reservation of shop rights.

With such protection built in, the Committee agreed that Greenhill College's shop rights should apply to the published version of a work. Julio Garcia felt that publishers might want to negotiate this. He volunteered to revise the motion to reflect the Committee's discussion and then to send it to the Copyright Committee of the AAP for their comments.

Professor Alexander felt that the "shop right" wouldn't be much of a problem for faculty but the change in the ownership policy might be, especially if it were perceived as a "give-back" by the faculty. He suggested we poll other colleges and universities to find out what their policies are. Alexander also suggested that the Faculty Policy Committee should also review the revised "shop right" provision before the Committee votes on the final guidelines at its next meeting on 5 August 1996.

The meeting adjourned at 3:30 p.m.

Next Meeting: August 5, 1996

Sample Club Meeting Agenda

Date/Time: Thursday, February 28, 2013 7 p.m. to 9 p.m.
Location: Sara Jane's house, 345 Sullivan Drive, Hamden, CT 06518
Attendees: Logan Smith, Megan Mark, Gaby Moore, Susan Johnson, Taylor O'Connor, Kendall Carroll

OBJECTIVE

Weekly discussion of club's book. This week, it's *The Wednesday Letters*. Assign leader to ask discussion questions and have lengthy discussion.

SCHEDULE

7:00 to 7:15: Welcome; appetizers and cocktails served – Sara Jane
7:15 to 7:30: Begin discussion and give overview of book – Gaby Moore
7:30 to 8:20: Discussion of book – Gaby Moore
8:20-8:30: Introduction of next book, *Final Appeal* – Kendall Carroll
8:30-9:00: Dessert and wrap-up – Sara Jane

ROLES/RESPONSIBILITIES

Food set-up: Taylor O'Connor
Discussion questions: Gaby Moore
Desserts: Megan Mark

Just Us Film
Production Meeting Agenda

Date/Time: January 15, 2016 11:00am - 1:30pm

Location: Conference Room B

Attendees:
Joshua Walker - Producer
Shara Jenkins - Writer / Director
Aren Vermont - Creative Director
Dalila Fialho - Director of Development

OBJECTIVES

- Review and finalize script

- Develop fundraising strategies for *JUST US* Film

- Finalize Pre-Production Timeline

SCHEDULE
11:00 to 11:15   Check-in, General Updates – Aren Vermont
11:15 to 11:45   Script Review, New Changes – Shara Jenkins
11:45 to 1:00   Fundraising Updates – Dalila Fialho
1:00 to 1:15   Pre- Production timeline – Joshua Walker
1:15 to 1:30   Announcements – All

ROLES/RESPONSIBILITIES
Note-taking: Joshua Walker
Mediation: Aren Vermont

<u>Summary</u>

Preparing a meeting is very important in having a successful meeting. Meetings are also a major part of most careers, so it can be a big deal!

The four major parts to prepare are the following:

Notice   of   meeting

Agenda

minutes,   and Chairman's agenda

Chapter VI

Specialized Document Preparation

Highlights:

- *Creative Displays*
- *Types of Documents*
- *Creating Template*

L esson 1

Creative Displays

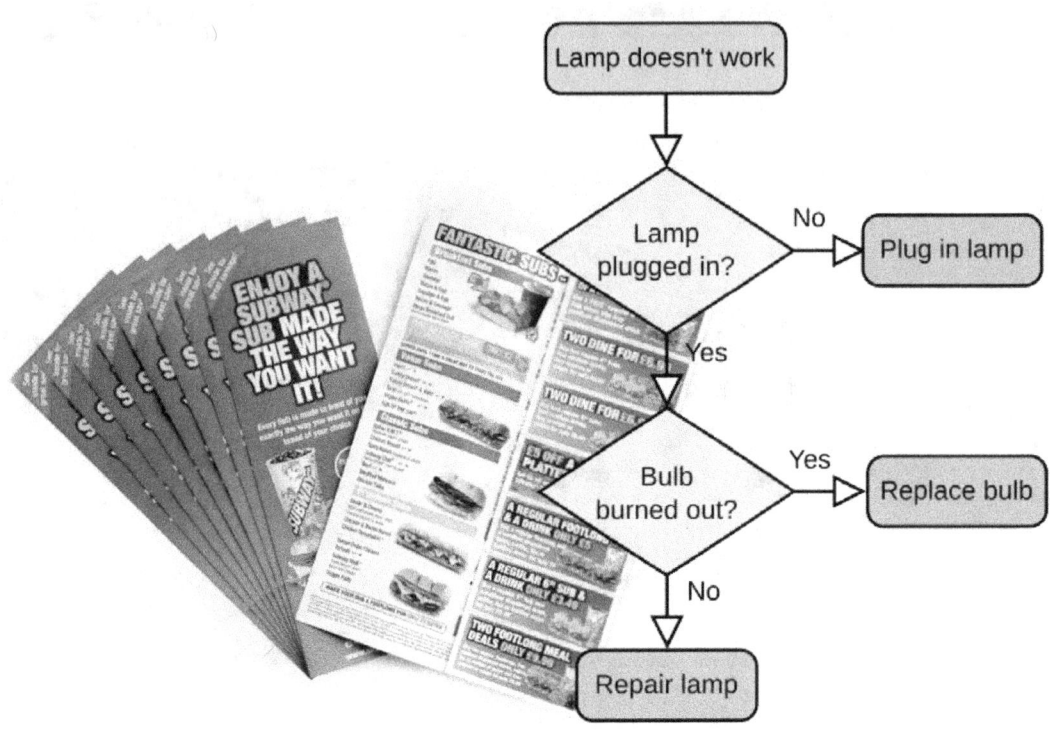

Objective

At the end of this chapter, the student should be able to:
➢ *produce effective and creative displays, given in a specific task*
➢ *create an advanced display presentation like flow charts, organization, charts and so on*

Section VI-Specialized Document Preparation

Sometimes it can be difficult to center and display a picture in a document just by dragging it around. Today we show you how to center pictures, images, and other objects perfectly in Word and PowerPoint.

- **Simple Displays**

Centering and displaying a Picture in MS Word 2010

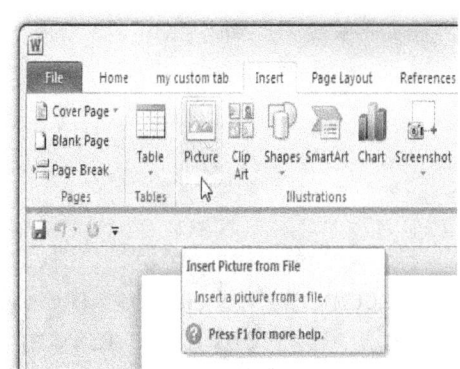

First let's insert a picture into our document. Click the Insert tab, and then click Picture

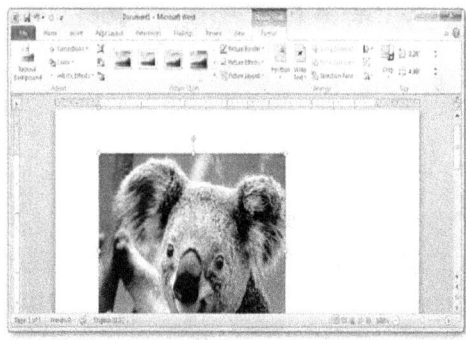

Once you select the picture you want, it will be added to your document. Usually, pictures are added wherever your curser was in the document, so in a blank document it will be added at the top left. Also notice Picture Tools show up in the Ribbon after inserting an image.

Note: The following menu items are available in Picture Tools Format tab which is displayed when you select the object or image you're working with.

How do we align the picture just like we want? Click Position to get some quick placement options, including centered in the middle of the document or on the top.

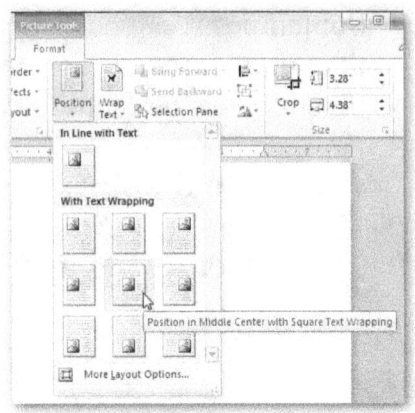

However, for more advanced placement, we can use the Align tool. If Word isn't maximized, you may only see the icon without the "Align" label.

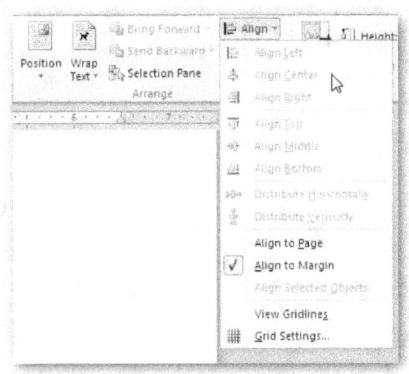

Notice the tools were grayed out in the menu by default. To be able to change the Alignment, we need to first change the text wrap settings. Click the Wrap Text button, and any option **other** than "In Line with Text". Your choice will depend on the document you're writing, just choose the option that works best in the document.

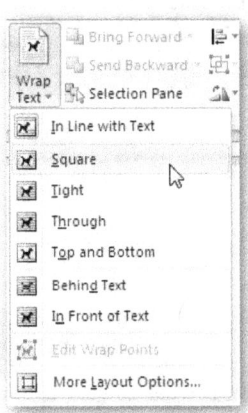

Now, select the Align tools again. You can now position your image precisely with these options.

Align Center will position your picture in the center of the page widthwise.

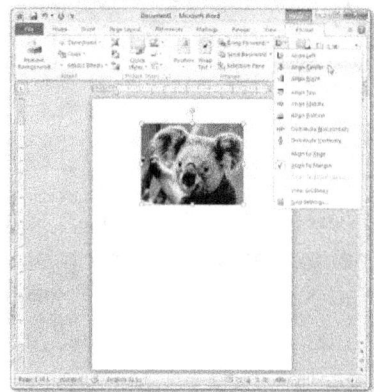

Align Middle will put the picture in the middle of the page height-wise.

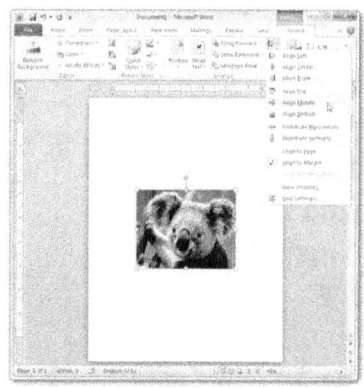

This works the same with textboxes. Simply click the Align button in the Format tab, and you can center it in the page.

And if you'd like to align several objects together, simply select them all, click Group, and then select Group from the menu.

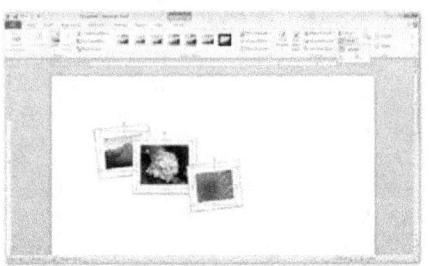

Now, in the align tools, you can center the whole group on your page for a heading, or whatever you want to use the pictures for.

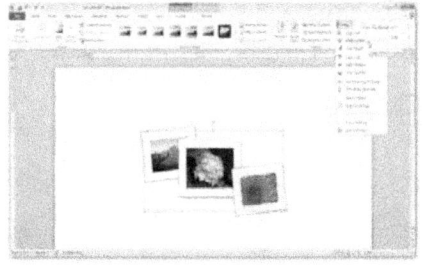

These steps also work the same with Office 2007.

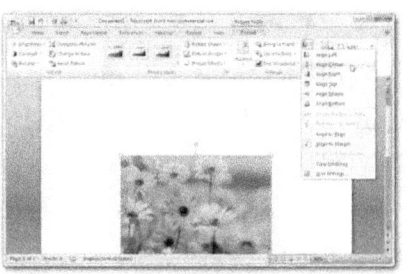

Center objects in PowerPoint

This works similar in PowerPoint, except that pictures are automatically set for square wrapping automatically, so you don't have to change anything. Simply insert the picture or other object of your choice, click Align, and choose the option you want.

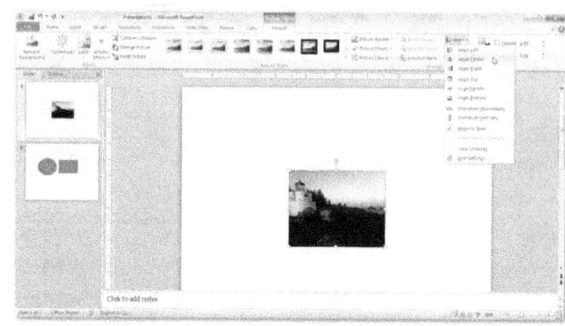

Additionally, if one object is already aligned like you want, drag another object near it and you will see a Smart Guide to help you align or center the second object with the first. This only works with shapes in PowerPoint 2010 beta, but will work with pictures, textboxes, and media in the final release this summer.

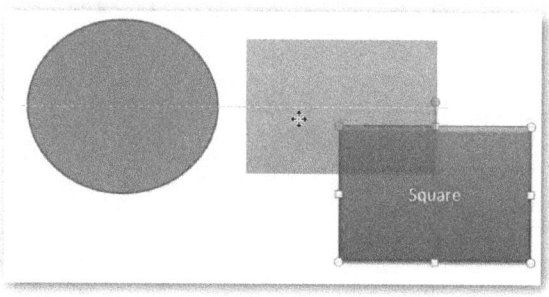

*These are good methods for centering images and displaying objects in Word and PowerPoint. From creating **simple displays** to emphasizing your message in a PowerPoint presentation like producing invitations, cards, notices and menus. This is also suitable in creating columnar work, one and two page programmes flyer too.*

Examples of simple displays:

Columnar work

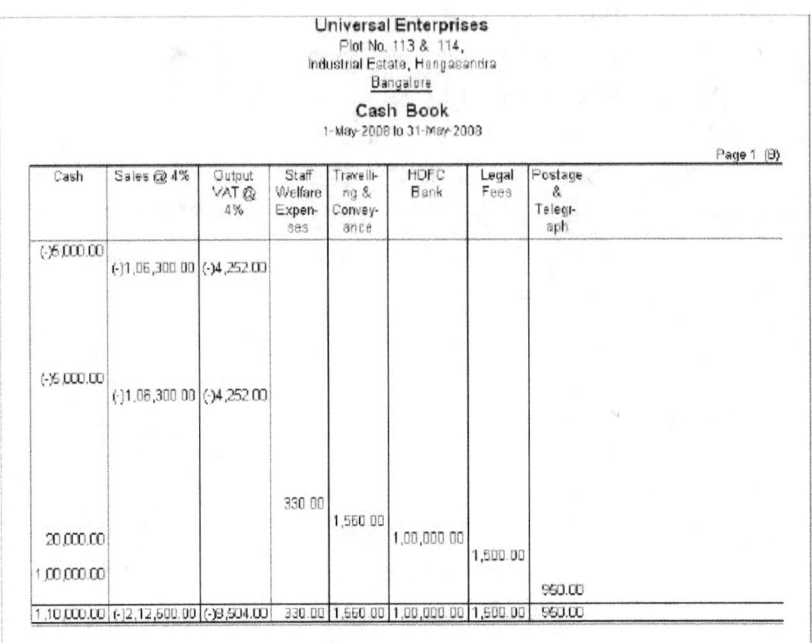

Figure 6.5 Columnar Cash Book

Advanced Displays

Examples of Advanced displays:

A flowchart is traditionally defined as a detailed diagram of the operations or equipment through which material passes. But a flowchart can be any kind of schematic diagram which shows pictorially or by means of symbolic representations a sequence of operations for any process. A common form of flowchart depicts the sequence of subroutines and flow of information within computer programs.

Example:

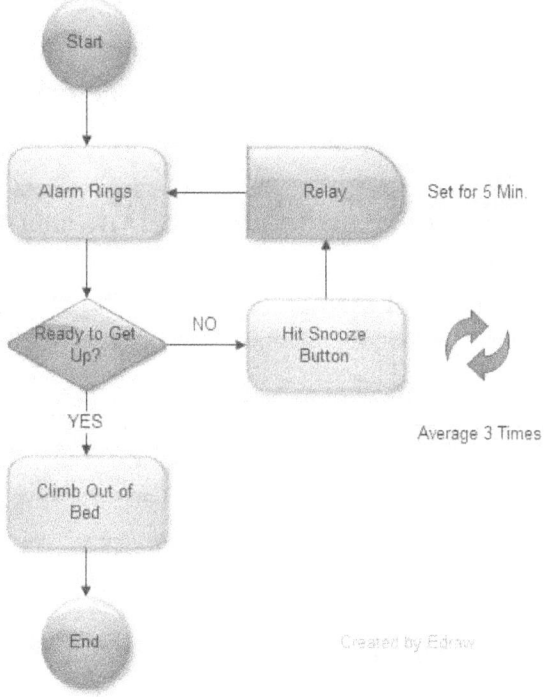

How to create a flow chart

Keywords   flowchart; animate flow chart; customize flow chart; style flow chart

A flow chart shows sequential steps in a task or process. There are many different SmartArt layouts that you can use to illustrate the steps in a process, including layouts that can contain pictures.

A Picture Accent Process layout, one of many process layouts, which you could use to show pictures related to the sequential steps in a task or process. For example, you could use a Picture Accent Process layout to show the process of how kitchen scraps can become compost for a garden.

This article discusses how to create a flow chart that contains pictures. You can use the methods described in this article to create or change almost any SmartArt graphic. Try different layouts to achieve the results you want.

By using a SmartArt graphic in Microsoft Office Excel 2007, Microsoft Office Outlook 2007, Microsoft Office PowerPoint 2007, or Microsoft Office Word 2007, you can create a flow chart and include it in your worksheet, e-mail message, presentation, or document.

Create a flow chart with pictures

1. On the **Insert** tab, in the **Illustrations** group, click **SmartArt**.

2. In the **Choose a SmartArt Graphic** gallery, click **Process**, and then double-click **Picture Accent Process**.
3. To add a picture, in the box you want to add it to, click the picture icon select the picture you want to display in the chart, and then click **Insert**.
4. To enter text, do one of the following:
o Click **[Text]** in the Text pane, and then type your text.
o Copy text from another location or program, click **[Text]** in the Text pane, and then paste your text.

NOTE   If the Text pane is not visible, click the control.

o Click in a box in the SmartArt graphic, and then type your text.

NOTE   For best results, use this option after you add all of the boxes that you want.

Add or delete boxes in your flow chart

Add a box

1. Click the SmartArt graphic that you want to add a box to.
2. Click the existing box that is located closest to where you want to add the new box.
3. Under **SmartArt Tools**, on the **Design** tab, in the **Create Graphic** group, click the arrow under **Add Shape**.

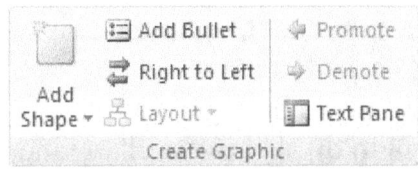

If you don't see the **SmartArt Tools** or **Design** tabs, make sure that you've selected the SmartArt graphic.

4. Do one of the following:
   o To insert a box at the same level as the selected box but following it, click **Add Shape After**.
   o To insert a box at the same level as the selected box but before it, click **Add Shape Before**.

To Delete a box

To delete a box, click the border of the box you want to delete, and then press DELETE.

NOTE When you need to add a box to your flow chart, experiment with adding the box before or after the selected box to get the placement you want for the new box. It's simple to fix common SmartArt mistakes.

To add a box from the Text pane:

a. Place your cursor at the beginning of the text where you want to add a box.
b. Type the text that you want in your new box, press ENTER, and then to indent the new box, press TAB, or to negative indent, press SHIFT+TAB.

To Move a box in your flow chart

- To move a box, click the box, and then drag it to its new location.
- To move a box in very small increments, hold down CTRL while you press the arrow keys on your keyboard.

To Change the colors of your flow chart

To quickly add a designer-quality look and polish to your SmartArt graphic, you can change the colors or apply a SmartArt Style to your flow chart. You can also add effects, such as glows, soft edges, or 3-D effects. In Office PowerPoint 2007 presentations, you can animate your flowchart.

You can apply color combinations that are derived from the theme colors to the boxes in your SmartArt graphic.

1. Click the SmartArt graphic whose color you want to change.
2. Under **SmartArt Tools**, on the **Design** tab, in the **SmartArt Styles** group, click **Change Colors**.

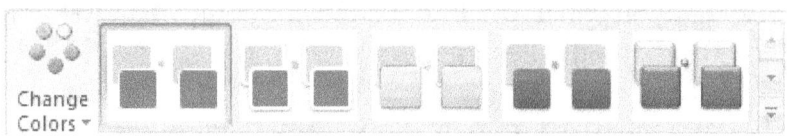

If you don't see the **SmartArt Tools** or **Design** tabs, make sure that you've selected a SmartArt graphic.

3. Click the color combination that you want.

TIP   When you place your pointer over a thumbnail, you can see how the colors affect your SmartArt graphic**Change the line color or style of a box's border**

1. In the SmartArt graphic, right-click the border of the box you want to change, and then click **Format Shape**.
2. To change the color of the box's border, click **Line Color**, click **Color**, and then click the color that you want.
3. To change the style of the box's border, click **Line Style**, and then choose the line styles you want.

To Change the background color of a box in your flow chart

1. Right-click the border of a box, and then click **Format Shape**.
2. Click the **Fill** pane, and then click **Solid fill**.
3. Click **Color** 🪣▾, and then click the color that you want.
4. To specify how much you can see through the background color, move the **Transparency** slider, or enter a number in the box next to the slider. You can vary the percentage of transparency from 0% (fully opaque, the default setting) to 100% (fully transparent).

To Apply a SmartArt Style to your flow chart

A SmartArt Style is a combination of various effects, such as line style, bevel, or 3-D, that you can apply to the boxes in your SmartArt graphic to create a unique and professionally designed look.

1. Click the SmartArt graphic whose SmartArt Style you want to change.
2. Under **SmartArt Tools**, on the **Design** tab, in the **SmartArt Styles** group, click the SmartArt Style that you want.

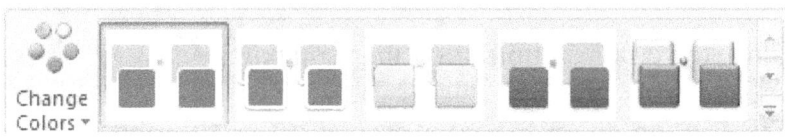

To see more SmartArt Styles, click the More button ⬇.

If you don't see the **SmartArt Tools** or **Design** tabs, make sure that you've selected a SmartArt graphic.

NOTE

- When you place your pointer over a thumbnail, you can see how the SmartArt Style affects your SmartArt graphic.
- You can also customize your SmartArt graphic by moving boxes, resizing boxes, adding a fill or effect, and adding a picture.

To Animate your flow chart

If you're using Office PowerPoint 2007, you can animate your flow chart to

1. Click the SmartArt graphic that you want to animate.
2. On the **Animations** tab, in the **Animations** group, click **Animate**, and then click **One by one**.

Emphasize each box.

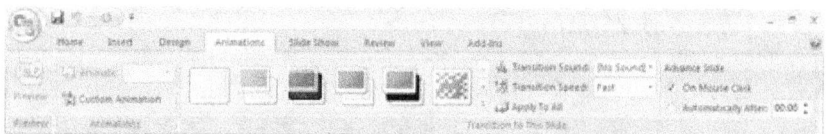

NOTE   If you copy a flow chart that has an animation applied to it to another slide, the animation is also copied.

Summary

Kinds of effective and creative displays:

Simple Displays

- Centering and displaying work - columnar work, ruled and unruled, notices, menus, invitations, cards, one and two page programmes, flyers.

Advanced Displays

- Flow Charts, organization charts, graphs (linked and embedded), newsletters, 4/6/8 page leaflets.

Exercise VI.1

Name: _____   **Score:** ___ /50

Level/Section: _____   **Date:** _____

Direction: *Type the following organisational chart on letter-sized paper using landscape orientation and following all instructions. Use the following margins: 1.5" (3.81 cm) left and 1" (2.54 cm) right, 1" (2.54 cm) top and bottom.(50marks).*

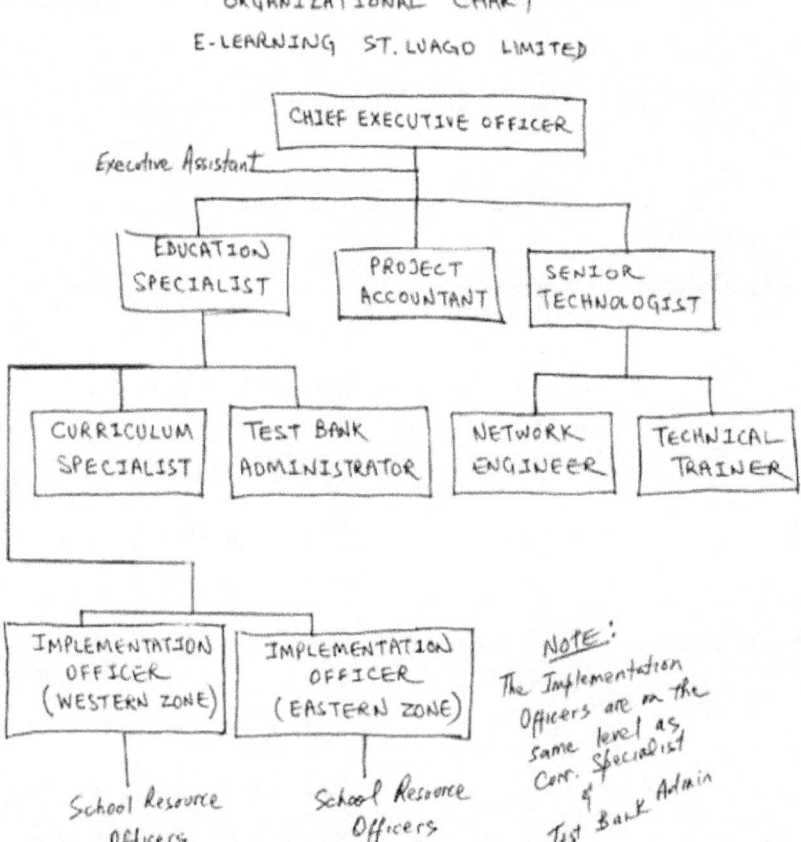

L esson 2

Types of Documents

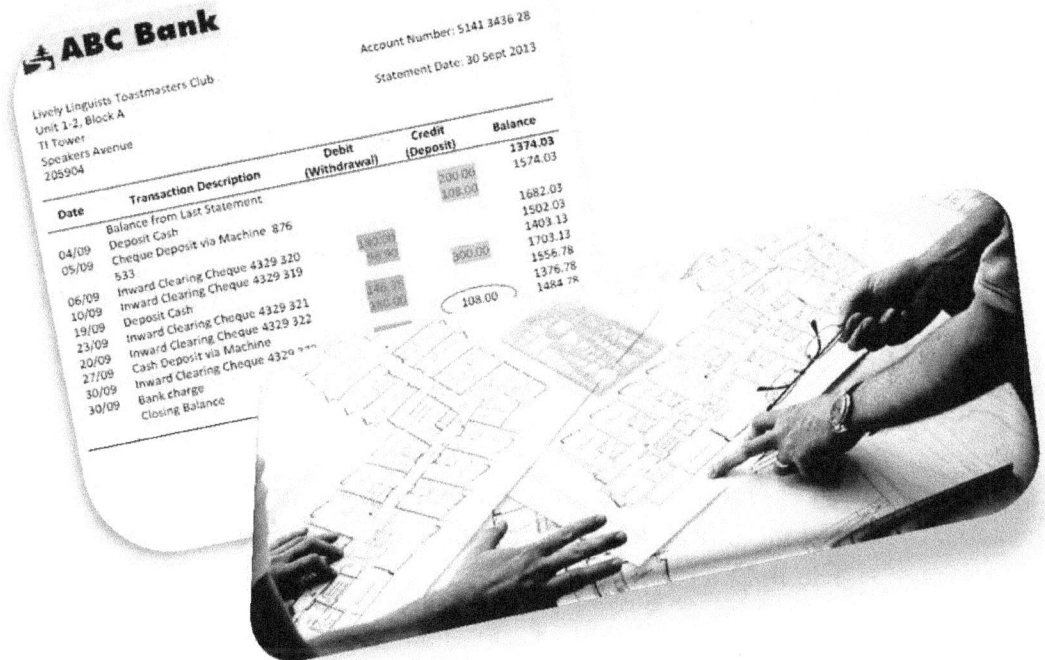

Objectives

At the end of this chapter, the student should be able to:
- *prepare different types of documents using appropriate formatting*
- *create a newsletter for four or more pages of leaflets, reports, proposals and so on*
- *create any format on legal documents, technical, literary documents and any financial statement*

Different Types of Documents

I. Newsletters

A **newsletter** is a regularly distributed publication that is generally about one main topic of interest to its subscribers. Newspapers and leaflets are types of newsletters.

How to create a six (6) pages leaflet:

The tri-fold (or standard) leaflets uses both sides of the paper with three panels on each side.

If you can afford to engage the services of a professional brochure designer and a commercial printer then go for it. If not, consider doing everything in-house.

It is fairly easy to create a tri-fold leaflets, back and forth to make it six pages using Microsoft Word.

1. **Create a new, blank document**
   On the Standard toolbar, click New Blank Document ▯.

2. **Page Setup**
   a. Change page margins

   - On the "File" menu, click "Page Setup", and then click the "Margins" tab.
   - Under Margins, set margins to 0.5"

   b. Change page orientation

   Under Orientation, click "Landscape".

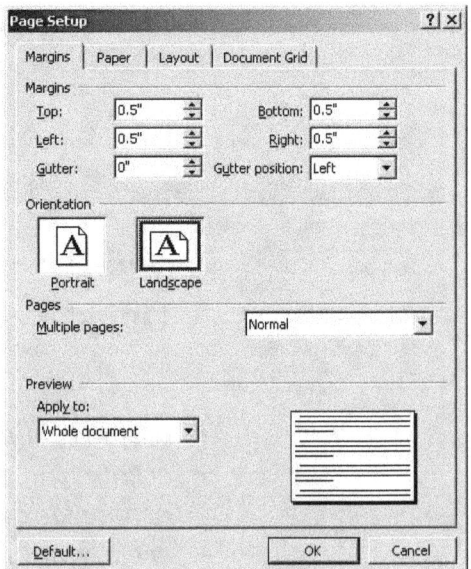

3. **Set up Columns**

Click on "Format" on the Toolbar, choose "Columns"
   a. Under Presets, click "Three"
   b. Under Width and spacing, change the spacing (i.e., gutter between the columns) to **twice** that of margins set in 2(a) above.

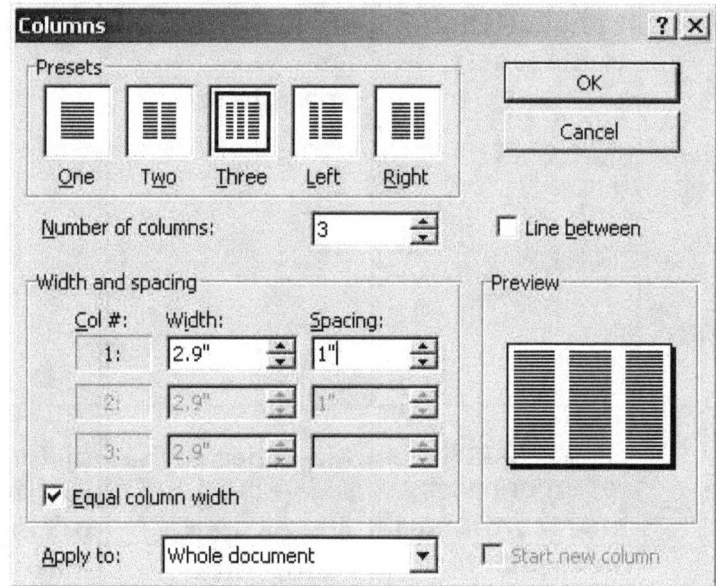

   c. Select "Line between" to visualise the columns, then click "OK"

   You can remove the lines after the design is completed but before printing.

Now you can begin designing your brochure. Keep a mockup of the folded brochure by your side and always refer to it so as not to be confused as to the contents for each panel.

For example, newsletters are distributed at schools to inform parents about things that happen in that school.

4/6/8   page   leaflets sample:

map, directions, nearby airport, other transportation to the resort **4**	full address and contact infor like phone, email, and web site. small picture **back**	Resort Name Logo Picture or graphic slogan **front**
Activities at the resort or nearby the resort. some small pictures are nice. **1**	Amenities of the resort like pool, arcade, golf, eating, etc. Include small pictures **2**	picture of the rooms, perhaps pricing, list amenities of the rooms and services offered to the rooms. **3**

Reports sample:

Proposals sample:

Section VI-Specialized Document Preparation

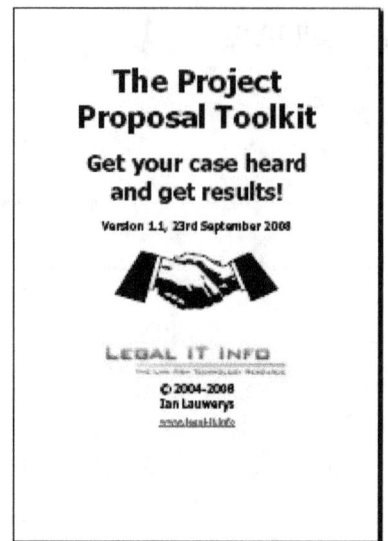

**The Project
Proposal Toolkit**

**Get your case heard
and get results!**

Version 1.1, 23rd September 2008

LEGAL IT INFO
THE LAW FIRM TECHNOLOGY RESOURCE

© 2004-2008
Ian Lauwerys
www.legal-it.info

II. Legal documents

legal document - (law) *is a legal term of art that is used for any formally executed written document that can be formally attributed to its author,[1] records and formally expresses a legally enforceable act, process,[2] or contractual duty, obligation, or right, and therefore evidences that act, process, or agreement.*

Examples of legal documents:

Wills - *a legal document declaring a person's wishes regarding the disposal of their property when they die.*

This is the last Will and testament of me Michael Wilmers of 1 Any Street Any Town ANY 1AN married to Anne Wilmers.

1. REVOCATION

I hereby revoke all former Wills and testamentary dispositions made by me and declare this to be my last Will.

2. APPOINTMENT OF TRUSTEES

I appoint my wife Anne Wilmers and CAPITA TRUST COMPANY LIMITED of Phoenix House 18 King William Street London EC4N 7HE (hereinafter called "the Company") to be the Executors and Trustees of this my Will ("my Trustees") and I declare that the Company is appointed in accordance with its terms and conditions as last published before the date hereof and shall be entitled to remuneration for its services (free from all taxes and without abatement) according to its scale of fees in force at the date of my death with power to charge remuneration in accordance with any later scale of fees of the Company for the time being in force.

3. BURIAL

I wish my body to be buried.

4. MONETARY LEGACIES

I give the following monetary legacies:

> 4.1. The sum, free of tax, of £10,000.00 (ten thousand pounds) to my brother Clifford Wilmers of 3 Some Road Some Town 8UU 9OP.

5. SPECIFIC LEGACIES

I give the following specific legacies:

> 5.1. My Ford Escort Registration X123 ABC, subject to tax, to my brother Clifford Wilmers of 3 Some Road Some Town 8UU 9OP.

6. MINOR LEGATEE

I direct that if any specific or monetary legatee has not reached 18 years at the time when the legacy is payable my Executors may pay the legacy to the parent or guardian so that their respective receipts shall be a full discharge to my Executors.

7. RESIDUARY ESTATE

7.1. If my wife Anne Wilmers survives me for 28 days I give my residuary estate (subject to the payment of my debts, funeral, and testamentary expense and legacies) to her.

7.2. If my wife does not survive me as aforesaid, I give my residuary estate to my trustees on trust to pay my debts, funeral and testamentary expenses, and legacies to ...

THIS SECTION OF TEXT HAS BEEN REMOVED - THIS WILL IS A SAMPLE ONLY AND MUST NOT BE USED

... the child or children shall take by substitution and, if more than one, in equal shares, the share of my estate which his, her or their parent would have taken had he or she survived me.

7.3. If there are no surviving beneficiaries (or children of beneficiaries) as aforesaid then the residue of my estate shall be given to such UK charities as my Trustees, at their absolute discretion, shall nominate.

8. ADMINISTRATIVE PROVISIONS

In addition to all other powers that are given by law I grant the following powers to my Trustees:

8.1. to appropriate all or any part of my Residuary Estate as they think fit in or towards the satisfaction of the interest of any beneficiary and may place a value on that part appropriated as they think fit without requiring the consent of the beneficiary or the parent or guardian if the beneficiary is a minor.

8.2. Section 31 of the Trustee Act 1925 shall apply to the income ...

THIS SECTION OF TEXT HAS BEEN REMOVED - THIS WILL IS A SAMPLE ONLY AND MUST NOT BE USED

... subsection (1) had been omitted.

8.3. the provisions of Section 19 of the Trusts of Land and Appointment of Trustees Act 1996 shall not apply to any trust created by my Will so that no beneficiaries shall have the right to require the appointment or the retirement of any Trustee or Trustees.

8.4. if any of my trustees are solicitors or other persons engaged in any profession or business (which for the avoidance of doubt shall include a Trust Corporation) they may charge and be paid their usual professional charges for work done by themselves or the firm in the administration of my estate and the trusts arising under my Will including acts which a trustee not engaged in any profession or business could have done personally.

9. POWERS TO INVEST

In addition to all other powers that are given by law I grant the following powers to my Trustees:

9.1. to invest in the security of such stocks, funds, securities or ...

THIS SECTION OF TEXT HAS BEEN REMOVED - THIS WILL IS A SAMPLE ONLY AND MUST NOT BE USED

... powers on investing and transposing investments in all respects as if they were absolutely entitled beneficially to the money liable to be invested.

9.2. to purchase within the United Kingdom freeholds and leaseholds with more than 70 years unexpired for the purpose of providing a place of residence for ...

THIS SECTION OF TEXT HAS BEEN REMOVED - THIS WILL IS A SAMPLE ONLY AND MUST NOT BE USED

... presumptive and all such property shall be vested in them upon trust to sell the same.

9.3. to engage the services of an investment adviser or advisers as they may from time to time think fit upon such terms and conditions as to remuneration as they shall in their absolute discretion think fit.

9.4. to provide whether by way of retention or of purchase such chattels as they shall in their absolute discretion think fit for the use or enjoyment of any such beneficiary whose interest in the trusts declared by my Will has become vested or is contingent, expectant or presumptive and they shall not be bound to see to the repair, maintenance or insurance of such chattels and shall not be liable in any respect for any failure to repair, maintain or insure such chattels.

9.5. the same full and unrestricted power to sell, lease, mortgage, charge, purchase or in any way deal with any land, buildings or other property wheresoever situated which or the proceeds of sale of which are comprised in my estate as if they were absolute and beneficial owners of them.

9.6. the full and unrestricted power to sell, lease, hire, deposit or store or in any way deal with any chattels wheresoever situated which or the proceeds of which are comprised in my estate as if they were the absolute and beneficial owners of them.

9.7. to borrow money with or without giving security and on such terms ...

THIS SECTION OF TEXT HAS BEEN REMOVED - THIS WILL IS A SAMPLE ONLY AND MUST NOT BE USED

... the purchase of assets or subscription to assets to be held as part of my estate and no lender from whom they may borrow money in exercise of this power need enquire as to the propriety, amount or purpose of such borrowing.

9.8. in relation to any insurance policy or polices forming part of my estate to borrow on the security of such insurance policy or policies or to convert surrender or sell such insurance policy or policies as they shall in their absolute discretion think fit to the intent that they shall have the full and unrestricted powers of dealing with such insurance policy or policies in all respects as if they were absolutely entitled to them beneficially.

9.9. to dispose of any of my personal chattels which are of trivial value or which they may consider impractical to sell or hold on the trusts of this my Will.

10. PROTECTION OF TRUSTEES

No executor or trustee shall be liable for any loss to my estate however arising except as a result of their fraud or dishonesty.

11. MINOR'S RECEIPT

Where a person is a minor (that is to say under 18 years of age or over 18 years of age but not of an age where the minor was entitled to capital outright) my Trustees may pay money to which the minor becomes entitled whether income or capital to any of the following and in each case their receipt shall be a complete discharge:

11.1. the minor, if he or she has attained 16 or over;

11.2. the minor's parent or guardian, in which case my Trustees are under no further obligation to enquire into the use of the money; or

11.3. a third party for the benefit of the minor;

or my Trustees may resolve to hold the money on trust for the minor absolutely (in which case the administrative provisions and powers to invest of my Will will continue to apply to the money).

Any vested and absolute gift made by this Will or any codicil to it to someone ...

THIS SECTION OF TEXT HAS BEEN REMOVED - THIS WILL IS A SAMPLE ONLY AND MUST NOT BE USED

... the age of 16 and that person's receipt shall be a good discharge to them for the gift.

12. CLAUSE HEADINGS

The headings to clauses are inserted for convenience only and do not affect the construction or interpretation of this Will.

13. CHARITY AS BENEFICIARY

The receipt of any authorised officer of any charity shall be a sufficient discharge to my Trustees.

If any charity benefiting by my Will is not in existence at the time of my death, my Trustees shall exercise their absolute discretion and pay the legacy given by my Will to any other charity or charities (and if more than one, in shares as they shall in their absolute discretion determine) having similar objectives to the charity that was to benefit by my Will.

Dated _____

_____
Signed by the above named Michael Wilmers

In our joint presence and then by us in his.

Name of first witness   _____

Address of first witness   _____

                                   _____

Occupation of first witness　＿＿＿＿＿＿＿＿＿＿

Signature of first witness　＿＿＿＿＿＿＿＿＿＿

Name of second witness　＿＿＿＿＿＿＿＿＿＿

Address of second witness　＿＿＿＿＿＿＿＿＿＿

＿＿＿＿＿＿＿＿＿＿

Occupation of second witness ＿＿＿＿＿＿＿＿＿＿

Signature of second witness　＿＿＿＿＿＿＿＿＿

Lease example:

LEASE

BASIC RENTAL AGREEMENT OR RESIDENTIAL LEASE

This Rental Agreement or Residential Lease shall evidence the complete terms and conditions under which the parties whose signatures appear below have agreed. Landlord/Lessor/Agent, _____, shall be referred to as "OWNER" and Tenant(s)/Lessee, _____, shall be referred to as "RESIDENT." As consideration for this agreement, OWNER agrees to rent/lease to RESIDENT and RESIDENT agrees to rent/lease from OWNER for use solely as a private residence, the premises located at _____in the city of _____.

1. **TERMS:** RESIDENT agrees to pay in advance $_____ per month on the ____ day of each month. This agreement shall commence on ____,___ and continue; (check one) A.__ until _____, ___ as a leasehold. Thereafter it shall become a month-to-month tenancy. If RESIDENT should move from the premises prior to the expiration of this time period, he shall be liable for

all rent due until such time that the Residence is occupied by an OWNER approved paying RESIDENT and/or expiration of said time period, whichever is shorter. B.__ until _____, _____ on a month-to-month tenancy until either party shall terminate this agreement by giving a written notice of intention to terminate at least 30 days prior to the date of termination.

2. **PAYMENTS:** Rent and/or other charges are to be paid at such place or method designated by the owner as follows _____. All payments are to be made by check or money order and cash shall be acceptable. OWNER acknowledges receipt of the First Month's rent of $_____, and a Security Deposit of $_____, and additional charges/fees for _____, for a total payment of $_____. All payments are to be made payable to _____.

3. **SECURITY DEPOSITS:** The total of the above deposits shall secure compliance with the terms and conditions of this agreement and shall be refunded to RESIDENT within _____ days after the premises have been completely vacated less any amount necessary to pay OWNER; a) any unpaid rent, b) cleaning costs, c) key replacement costs, d) cost for repair of damages to premises and/or common areas above ordinary wear and tear, and e) any other amount legally allowable under the terms of this agreement. A written accounting of said charges shall be presented to RESIDENT within _____ days of move-out. If deposits no not cover such costs and damages, the RESIDENT shall immediately pay said additional costs for damages to OWNER.

4. **LATE CHARGE:** A late fee of $_____, (not to exceed ___% of the monthly rent), shall be added and due for any payment of rent made after the _____ of the month. Any dishonored check shall be treated as unpaid rent, and subject to an additional fee of $_____.

5. **UTILITIES:** RESIDENT agrees to pay all utilities and/or services based upon occupancy of the premises except _____.

6. **OCCUPANTS:** Guest(s) staying over 15 days without the written consent of OWNER shall be considered a breach of this agreement. ONLY the following individuals and/or animals, AND NO OTHERS shall occupy the subject residence for more than 15 days unless the expressed written consent of OWNER obtained in advance _____.

7. **PETS:** No animal, fowl, fish, reptile, and/or pet of any kind shall be kept on or about the premises, for any amount of time, without obtaining the prior written consent and meeting the requirements of the OWNER. Such consent if granted, shall be revocable at OWNER'S option upon giving a 30 day written notice. In the event laws are passed or permission is granted to have a pet and/or animal of any kind, an additional deposit in the amount of $_____ shall be required along with additional monthly rent of $_____ along with the signing of OWNER'S Pet Agreement. RESIDENT also agrees to carry

insurance deemed appropriate by OWNER to cover possible liability and damages that may be caused by such animals.

8. **LIQUID FILLED FURNISHINGS:** No liquid filled furniture, receptacle containing more than ten gallons of liquid is permitted without prior written consent and meeting the requirements of the OWNER. RESIDENT also agrees to carry insurance deemed appropriate by OWNER to cover possible losses that may be caused by such items.

9. **PARKING:** When and if RESIDENT is assigned a parking area/space on OWNER'S property, the parking area/space shall be used exclusively for parking of passenger automobiles and/or those approved vehicles listed on RESIDENT'S Application attached hereto. RESIDENT is hereby assigned or permitted to park only in the following area or space _____. The parking fee for this space (if applicable is $_____ monthly. Said space shall not be used for the washing, painting, or repair of vehicles. No other parking space shall be used by RESIDENT or RESIDENT'S guest(s). RESIDENT is responsible for oil leaks and other vehicle discharges for which RESIDENT shall be charged for cleaning if deemed necessary by OWNER.

10. **NOISE:** RESIDENT agrees not to cause or allow any noise or activity on the premises which might disturb the peace and quiet of another RESIDENT and/or neighbor. Said noise and/or activity shall be a breach of this agreement.

11. **DESTRUCTION OF PREMISES:** If the premises become totally or partially destroyed during the term of this Agreement so that RESIDENT'S use is seriously impaired, OWNER or RESIDENT may terminate this Agreement immediately upon three day written notice to the other.

12. **CONDITION OF PREMISES:** RESIDENT acknowledges that he has examined the premises and that said premises, all furnishings, fixtures, furniture, plumbing, heating, electrical facilities, all items listed on the attached property condition checklist, if any, and/or all other items provided by OWNER are all clean, and in good satisfactory condition except as may be indicated elsewhere in this Agreement. RESIDENT agrees to keep the premises and all items in good order and good condition and to immediately pay for costs to repair and/or replace any portion of the above damaged by RESIDENT, his guests and/or invitees, except as provided by law. At the termination of this Agreement, all of above items in this provision shall be returned to OWNER in clean and good condition except for reasonable wear and tear and the premises shall be free of all personal property and trash not belonging to OWNER. It is agreed that all dirt, holes, tears, burns, and stains of any size or amount in the carpets, drapes, walls, fixtures, and/or any other part of the premises, do not constitute reasonable wear and tear.

13. **ALTERATIONS:** RESIDENT shall not paint, wallpaper, alter or redecorate, change or install locks, install antenna or other equipment, screws, fastening devices, large nails, or adhesive materials,

place signs, displays, or other exhibits, on or in any portion of the premises without the written consent of the OWNER except as may be provided by law.

14: **PROPERTY MAINTENANCE:** RESIDENT shall deposit all garbage and waste in a clean and sanitary manner into the proper receptacles and shall cooperate in keeping the garbage area neat and clean. RESIDENT shall be responsible for disposing of items of such size and nature as are not normally acceptable by the garbage hauler. RESIDENT shall be responsible for keeping the kitchen and bathroom drains free of things that may tend to cause clogging of the drains. RESIDENT shall pay for the cleaning out of any plumbing fixture that may need to be cleared of stoppage and for the expense or damage caused by stopping of waste pipes or overflow from bathtubs, wash basins, or sinks.

15. **HOUSE RULES:** RESIDENT shall comply with all house rules as stated on separate addendum, but which are deemed part of this rental agreement, and a violation of any of the house rules is considered a breach of this agreement.

16. **CHANGE OF TERMS:** The terms and conditions of this agreement are subject to future change by OWNER after the expiration of the agreed lease period upon 30-day written notice setting forth such change and delivered to RESIDENT. Any changes are subject to laws in existence at the time of the Notice of Change Of Terms.

17. **TERMINATION:** After expiration of the leasing period, this agreement is automatically renewed from month to month, but may be terminated by either party giving to the other a 30-day written notice of intention to terminate. Where laws require "just cause", such just cause shall be so stated on said notice. The premises shall be considered vacated only after all areas including storage areas are clear of all RESIDENT'S belongings, and keys and other property furnished for RESIDENT'S use are returned to OWNER. Should the RESIDENT hold over beyond the termination date or fail to vacate all possessions on or before the termination date, RESIDENT shall be liable for additional rent and damages which may include damages due to OWNER'S loss of prospective new renters.

18. **POSSESSION:** If OWNER is unable to deliver possession of the residence to RESIDENTS on the agreed date, because of the loss or destruction of the residence or because of the failure of the prior residents to vacate or for any other reason, the RESIDENT and/or OWNER may immediately cancel and terminate this agreement upon written notice to the other party at their last known address, whereupon neither party shall have liability to the other, and any sums paid under this Agreement shall be refunded in full. If neither party cancels, this Agreement shall be prorated and begin on the date of actual possession.

19. **INSURANCE:** RESIDENT acknowledges that OWNERS insurance does not cover personal property damage caused by fire, theft, rain, war, acts of God, acts of others, and/or any other causes, nor

shall OWNER be held liable for such losses. RESIDENT is hereby advised to obtain his own insurance policy to cover any personal losses.

20. **RIGHT OF ENTRY AND INSPECTION:** OWNER may enter, inspect, and/or repair the premises at any time in case of emergency or suspected abandonment. OWNER shall give 24 hours advance notice and may enter for the purpose of showing the premises during normal business hours to prospective renters, buyers, lenders, for smoke alarm inspections, and/or for normal inspections and repairs. OWNER is permitted to make all alterations, repairs and maintenance that in OWNER'S judgment is necessary to perform.

21. **ASSIGNMENT:** RESIDENT agrees not to transfer, assign or sublet the premises or any part thereof.

22. **PARTIAL INVALIDITY:** Nothing contained in this Agreement shall be construed as waiving any of the OWNER'S or RESIDENT'S rights under the law. If any part of this Agreement shall be in conflict with the law, that part shall be void to the extent that it is in conflict, but shall not invalidate this Agreement nor shall it affect the validity or enforceability of any other provision of this Agreement.

22. **NO WAIVER:** OWNER'S acceptance of rent with knowledge of any default by RESIDENT or waiver by OWNER of any breach of any term of this Agreement shall not constitute a waiver of subsequent breaches. Failure to require compliance or to exercise any right shall not be constituted as a waiver by OWNER of said term, condition, and/or right, and shall not affect the validity or enforceability of any provision of this Agreement.

23. **ATTORNEY FEES:** If any legal action or proceedings be brought by either party of this Agreement, the prevailing party shall be reimbursed for all reasonable attorney's fees and costs in addition to other damages awarded.

24. **JOINTLY AND SEVERALLY:** The undersigned RESIDENTS are jointly and severally responsible and liable for all obligations under this agreement.

25. **REPORT TO CREDIT/TENANT AGENCIES:** You are hereby notified that a nonpayment, late payment or breach of any of the terms of this rental agreement may be submitted/reported to a credit and/or tenant reporting agency, and may create a negative credit record on your credit report.

26. **LEAD NOTIFICATION REQUIREMENT:** For rental dwellings built before 1978, RESIDENT acknowledges receipt of the following: (Please check)
    ___ Lead Based Paint Disclosure Form
    ___ EPA Pamphlet

27. ADDITIONS AND/OR EXCEPTIONS

_____.

28. NOTICES: All notices to RESIDENT shall be served at RESIDENT'S premises and all notices to OWNER shall be served at

_____.

29. INVENTORY: The premises contains the following items, that the RESIDENT may use.

_____.

30. KEYS AND ADDDENDUMS: RESIDENT acknowledges receipt of the following which shall be deemed part of this Agreement: (Please check)
___ Keys #of keys and purposes _____
___ House Rules ___ Pet Agreement ___ Other _____

31. ENTIRE AGREEMENT: This Agreement constitutes the entire Agreement between OWNER and RESIDENT. No oral agreements have been entered into, and all modifications or notices shall be in writing to be valid.

32. RECEIPT OF AGREEMENT: The undersigned RESIDENTS have read and understand this Agreement and hereby acknowledge receipt of a copy of this Rental Agreement.

RESIDENT'S Signature _____

Date_____

RESIDENT'S Signature _____

Date_____

OWNER'S or Agent's Signature _____

Date_____

Conveyance documents – *is a document by which a property transfer of title from one party to another is effected.*

DEED OF CONVEYANCE BY MORTGAGEE

THIS DEED is made at .... on this .... day of ...., 20.....

BY AND BETWEEN:

(1) ...., a partnership/company [choose] having its registered offices at .... hereinafter referred to as 'the Vendor' of the ONE PART

(2) Sh./Smt............................... aged about......................years, son/daughter/wife of Shri ...., residing at...hereinafter referred to as 'the Purchaser' of the SECOND PART.

(3) .... a company/partnership firm, having its registered offices at .... hereinafter referred to as 'the Mortgagee' of the THIRD PART

WHEREAS the Vendor herein was absolutely seized and possessed of the land and premises situated at .... hereinafter referred to as the "Property" and is more particularly described in the Schedule annexed to this Deed;

AND WHEREAS by a Deed of Mortgage dated the .... day of ...., 20....... (the 'Mortgage Deed') made between the said Mortgagee and the Vendor herein (therein referred to as the 'Mortgagor'), the Vendor in consideration of the sum of Rs .... lent and advanced by the Mortgagee, granted and conveyed whole of the Property to the Mortgagee with rights TO HOLD and to use the same, subject to redemption and on the terms and provisions as contained in the said Mortgage Deed;

AND WHEREAS the said Mortgage Deed is registered at the office of the Sub Registrar at .... under Serial No ...... of Book No. .... on...........................;

AND WHEREAS the said Mortgage Deed provided that in the event of any default on part of the Mortgagor including any failure to make timely payments of the principal sum on the due date or payment of the interest on the said principal sum, as and when they are due or if the Mortgagor commits breach of any term or condition or provision of the Lease Deed, the Mortgagee is entitled to call back the principal amount and the interest due to the Mortgagee, as if the due date had expired and in that event to sell the said Property by public auction and without the intervention of the Court;

AND WHEREAS the Vendor is in default under the said Mortgage Deed and the Mortgagee has given all requisite notices to the Mortgagor as provided by law;

AND WHEREAS the Mortgagee in exercise of its power contained in the said Mortgage Deed had put up the property for sale by public auction through M/s.................. auctioneers

Deed of Conveyance by Mortgagee   1

Agreements - A negotiated and usually legally enforceable understanding between two or more legally competent parties.

Although a binding contract can (and often does) result from an agreement, - an agreement typically documents the give-and-take of a negotiated settlement and a contract specifies the minimum - acceptable standard of performance.

Agreement of Sale
Resale Terms

This agreement of sale is made on date 2008 between HomEx Medical (a.k.a. Seller) and YOUR SCHOOL (a.k.a. Buyer).

ITEM:	Complete 3-CD Set with/without PDF Transcripts.
LABEL(S):	Private label, per Buyer specifications.
WHOLESALE PRICE:	$129.00 USD/Set.
SHIPPING:	Insured carrier. (Approx: $15.00)
TERMS OF USE:	Owners and agents of YOUR SCHOOL understand and agree that each Complete 3-CD Set is a single-user item which cannot be duplicated, in whole or in part, audio or text, digitally or otherwise, without written consent of Seller.
BULK WHOLESALE PRICING:	Wholesale price of $129 per Complete 3-CD Set will be granted for quantities of 10 Complete 3-CD sets. Further discounts may apply based on higher quantities requested by Buyer. Buyer's wholesale price guaranteed for future re-orders placed at least every 60 days.
PRIVACY:	Buyer and Seller agree to keep private the identity of the other party. Buyer may NOT market their private label CD sets using the Absolute Experience brand, trademark or logo. Seller may NOT market the Absolute Experience brand using Buyer's brand, trademark or logo.
PAYMENT OPTIONS:	Credit card via phone or online via Paypal. Net-30 invoicing available for re-orders with established account.
RESALE:	Buyer reserves the right to resell their private label 3-CD Sets of Absolute Experience to single users for an amount determined by Buyer. Buyer has the right to resell private label CD sets via YOUR SCHOOL and all affiliate sites.

Your Representative	Date	Agent	Date
Company		HomEx Medical	
Street		7 Lawrence Place	
City, State Zip		New Oxford, PA 17350	

Endorsements and contracts - *is an agreement having a lawful object entered into voluntarily by two or more parties, each of whom intends to create one or more legal obligations between them.*

ATHLETE ENDORSEMENT AGREEMENT
(Beverage)

THIS ENDORSEMENT AGREEMENT ("Agreement") is entered into as of _____ _____ (the "Effective Date") by and among _____ _____("Company"), and _____("Athlete"), in connection with the endorsement of, and the advertising and promotion for, Company's product _____ _____("Product").

RECITALS

A.   The Company is in the business of manufacturing certain beverages, including the Product;

B.   Athlete is a nationally recognized professional athlete;

Now, Therefore, in consideration of the mutual covenants contained herein, the parties agree as follows:

Section 1.   **TERM:** The term ("Term") of this Agreement shall commence on the date hereof and shall continue for _____ years.

Section 2.   **SERVICES:** Athlete shall participate in _____still photo sessions and/or video shoot day ("Service Day") per year on a date to be mutually agreed during each year of the Term. On such agreed dates, Athlete's services may be up to _____ _____consecutive hours. Athlete shall also make himself available over the Term for _____ _____radio, television and press interviews per year to promote the Product.

Athlete shall also participate in_____ personal appearances ("Personal Appearances") each year during the Term on dates and times to be mutually agreed upon. The Personal Appearances shall not involve a public and/or private autograph signing session. One (1) Personal Appearance each year must be a meet and greet located at_____. One (1) Personal Appearance each year must occur during the _____ season, and must take place at a location within a thirty (30) mile radius of _____ _____. Any Personal Appearances outside of a thirty (30) mile radius from _____shall require the approval of the Athlete and, to the extent so approved, Company shall be responsible for all first class travel, local limousine and lodging costs associated therewith. A Personal Appearance shall be up to 2 consecutive hours. Any additional Personal Appearances shall be on dates and times and for compensation to be mutually agreed upon.

During the Term of this Agreement, Athlete agrees to personally autograph _____ _____items, as requested by Company (and which shall be provided by Company). Such items may be used by Company for internal corporate or local market publicity

III. **Technical documents** – *is a documents that informs and instructs readers about science and technology. It can include detailed information about scientific theories, as well as instructions for using software and hardware.*

Example of Technical documentation

Builder or Architect Specifications sample

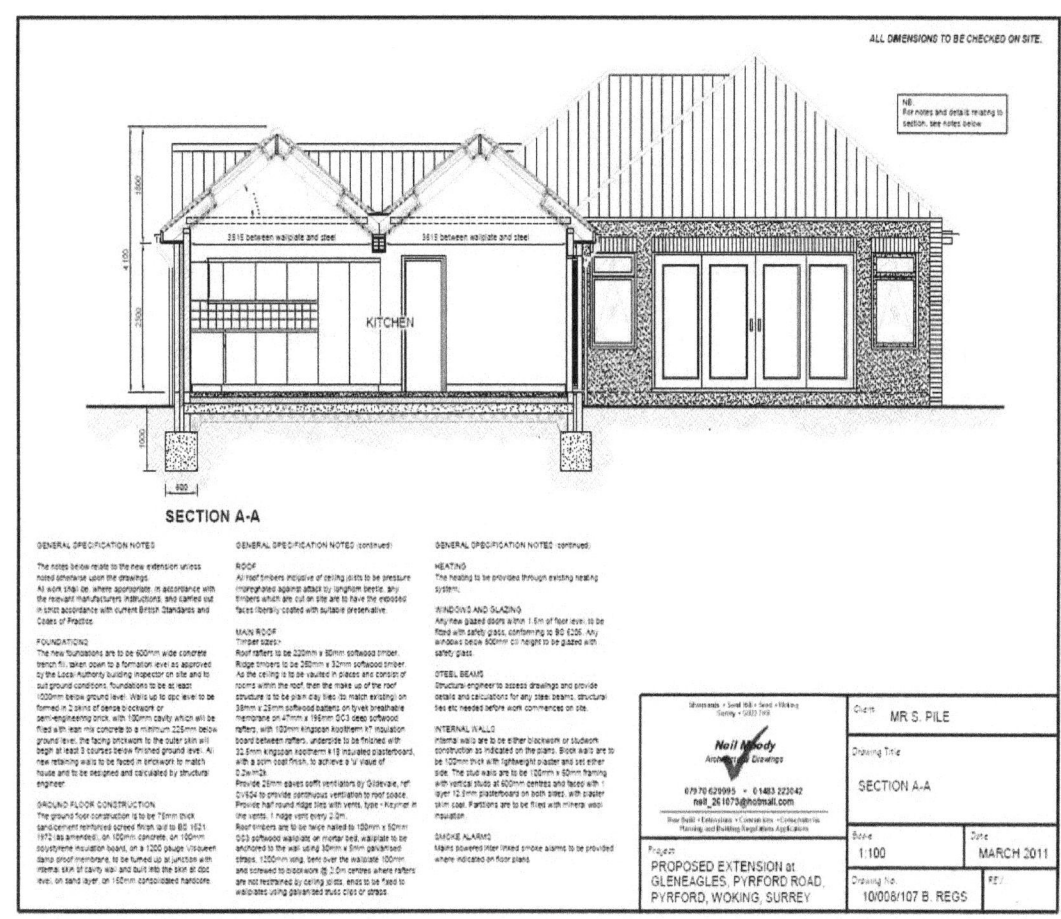

		Qty	Unit	Rate	£	p
	D GROUNDWORK					
	D20 Excavating and filling					
	Excavating by machine					
	Topsoil to be preserved, average depth					
a	0.150 m	60.6	m2	1.55	93	93
	To reduce levels, maximum depth not exceeding					
b	0.25 m	15.15	m3	3.36	50	90
	Trenches, width over 0.30 m, maximum depth not exceeding					
c	1.00 m	19.13	m3	10.26	196	27
	Breaking out					
	Existing materials					
d	concrete floor area for new drain pipe to disable cubicle including making good where disturbed after installation.		item		63	48
	Disposal					
	Off site by machine to tip average 15 km from site					
e	loaded by machine from spoil heaps	31.23	m3	12.39	386	94
	Filling to excavations					
	Material arising from the excavations					
f	exceeding 0.25 m	3.05	m3	13.26	40	44
	Filling to make up levels					
	Imported hardcore					
g	not exceeding 0.25 m	6.81	m3	25.17	171	41
h	exceeding 0.25 m	7.94	m3	43.12	342	37
	Surface treatments					
	Compacting					
i	surface of hardcore, with sand	44.46	m2	1.92	85	36
j	bottom of excavation	44.46	m2	0.67	29	79
	E IN SITU CONCRETE/LARGE PRECAST CONCRETE					
	E10 Mixing/casting/curing in-situ concrete					
	Ready mixed concrete					
	Plain in situ concrete 1:2:4 - 20 mm aggregate					
k	foundations	4.3	m3	80.34	345	46
l	beds, thickness not exceeding 150 mm	4.39	m3	88.26	387	46
m	filling to hollow walls	0.99	m3	139.04	137	65

Section VI-Specialized Document Preparation

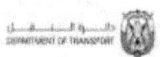

3 PREPARATION OF THE BILL OF QUANTITIES

"Quantity" or "Quantities"?

3.1 The Standard Bill of Quantity

The Standard Bill of Quantities is prepared in accordance with the Civil Engineering Standard Method of Measurements (CESMM4), (4th Edition-2012), by the Institute of Civil Engineers, United Kingdom.

Refer Section 3 of CESMM4 for the details of preparation of the Bill of Quantities.

3.2 How to prepare the project Specific Bill of Quantity

The Standard Bill of Quantities has been developed to provide all possible items that could be required in a project. However, project specific BOQ shall consist of items necessary for the execution of the particular project. The Consultants must customize SBOQM to be project specific by deleting the unused items (including only the items required for the project) and adding new items relevant to the particular project.

Preamble shall be modified to include any new items which are non-standard to CESMM4 and deleting the unused items.

Check font size - these two seems to be the same size for different levels of headings

3.2.1 Numbering and Referring System

Each item has an item number as well as specific CESMM4 coding and numbering and that CESMM4 coding and numbering can be used in various parts of the proposed BOQ structure.

While modifying the BOQ for any specific projects, the BOQ item reference remains constant. That is, the item numbering shall not be changed even if there is discontinuity of the items due to omission of the some items from SBOQM and addition of new items relevant to the particular project.

In order to have control on items, a serial number for the items used must be provided by the Consultant while preparing project specific BOQ. A column has been provided in the SBOQM for serial number so that continuity of the items in any BOQ section can be assured.

3.2.2 Addition of New Items

New items are inserted in relevant part of SBOQM in the place in a sequential order as per the CESMM4 coding number.

Space

Measurement/coverage rules for standard items shall be as per CESMM4, but measurement/coverage rules of non-standard items shall be as per the Preamble to the Bill of Quantities.

Page 6

IV. **Literacy documents** - *the knowledge and skills required to locate and use information contained in various formats, including job applications, payroll forms, transportation schedules, maps, tables and charts.*

Example of literacy documents:

Plays for radio sample

```
1                                                                    2.

    CHICO:          I'm a feel sorry, boss. But I joosta can't
                    sleep at home.
    GROUCHO:        Why not?
    CHICO:          I ain't gotta no desk.
    GROUCHO:        Well, I'm not sure that you've got a job either...
                    I waited in court all morning for you to bring me
                    those Carrington divorce papers. Why didn't you
                    show up?
    CHICO:          Well, I no tink doze papers was a very important.
    GROUCHO:        My legal papers and you didn't think they were
                    important? Well, they were very important.
                    (SHORT PAUSE - THEN QUICKLY) I had my lunch
                    wrapped in those papers!
    CHICO:          Awright, I bring you another lunch. I bring you
                    nice a tomayto sandwich.
    GROUCHO:        Tomato? Ravelli, in my social circle we call
                    it tomahto.
    CHICO:          Oh, you want it tomahto. I thought you wanted it
                    today. Aw right, I bring you a tomato sandwich
                    tomahto.....
    GROUCHO:        Ravelli, I think I've been overestimating your
                    intelligence. Why, I've been telling everybody
                    you're a halfwit.
    CHICO:          Halfwit? Dat's duh kinda sandwich I gonna
                    bring you. Half wit butter and half witout.
    GROUCHO:        I see... You know, you're in a position to do me
                    a great favor.
```

Theatre and   television sample

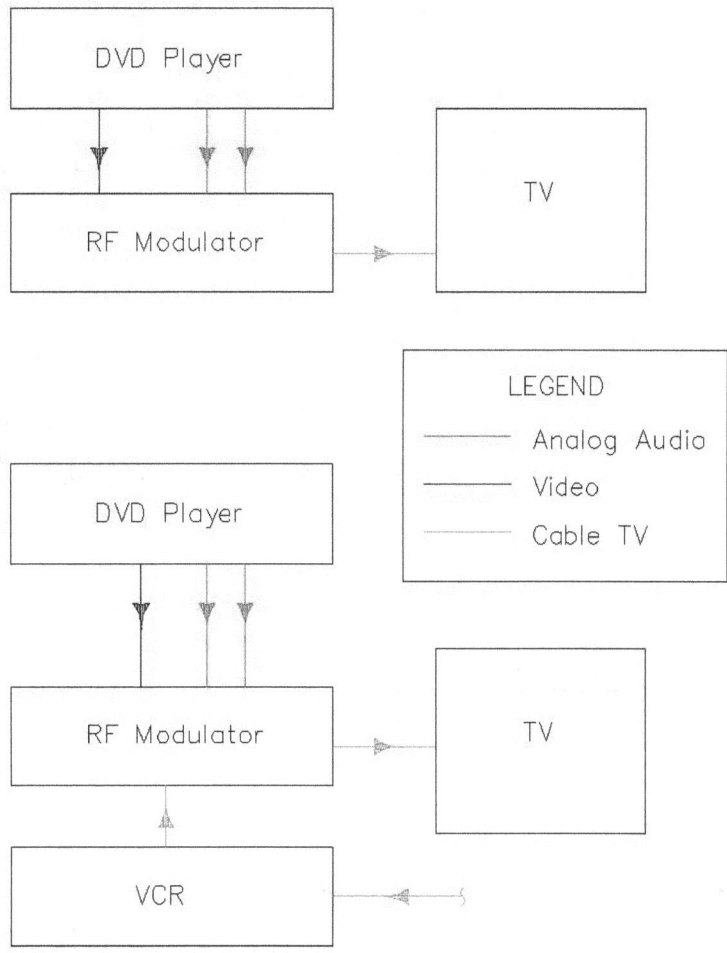

Actors' scripts sample

How to read a podcast script and not sound like you're reading

If you've listened to my Trafcom News Podcast, you've probably heard me say that I'm not a big fan of reading in a podcast, unless you're deliberately sharing the passage of a book or article. However, in the real world, we know that podcast scripting is not uncommon. Just recently, I've had to coach a few people on how to record audio that didn't sound stilted or silly. This is more difficult than it sounds.

Here are the tips I shared, based on my experience in scriptwriting, voiceover and podcasting.

slow down here

- Prepare. Do not read the script cold.
- Let's assume that the script is well written but still needs to be tweaked for the ear. Look for too-long passages, complex sentences, or phrases that can only be understood by the eye, not the ear. Revise them.
- Next, mark up the script. If you can, print it out double-spaced and grab a red or blue pen. Using whatever kind of marks you're comfortable with, add the following accents to your script: pauses, emphasized words, slower pace, faster pace. See the image for a brief example.
- Look up the pronunciation of any words you're not sure of (for example, Ih-ROCK, not EYE-rock for Iraq) and write them out phonetically if you need to.
- Read your script – aloud. Don't just mumble it. Say it. How do you feel when you read it?

Index cards sample

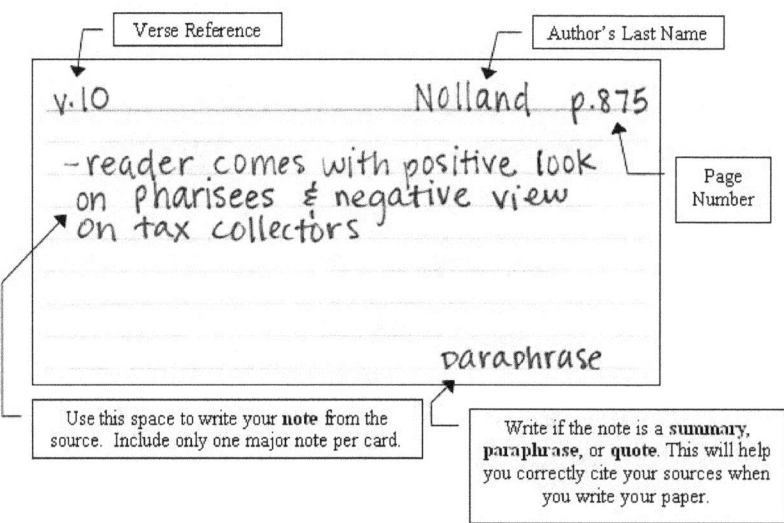

IV. **Financial statement** *(or **financial** report) is a formal record of the **financial** activities of a business, person, or other entity. Relevant **financial** information is presented in a structured manner and in a form easy to understand.*

Example of financial statement:

Trial Balance sample

Trial Balance
December 31, 2005

Account Title	Debit	Credit
Cash	$7,000	
Accounts Receivable	3,000	
Office Supplies	3,000	
Office Equipment	5,000	
Bank Loan		$5,000
Accounts Payable		1,000
Common Stock		10,000
Consulting Revenue		7,000
Rent Expense	600	
Salaries Expense	2,500	
Supplies Used	1,200	
Utilities Expense	700	
Total	$23,000	$23,000

Balance Sheet sample

Example Company
Balance Sheet
December 31, 2012

ASSETS			LIABILITIES		
Current assets			**Current liabilities**		
Cash	$	2,100	Notes payable	$	5,000
Petty cash		100	Accounts payable		35,900
Temporary investments		10,000	Wages payable		8,500
Accounts receivable - net		40,500	Interest payable		2,900
Inventory		31,000	Taxes payable		6,100
Supplies		3,800	Warranty liability		1,100
Prepaid insurance		1,500	Unearned revenues		1,500
Total current assets		89,000	Total current liabilities		61,000
Investments		36,000	**Long-term liabilities**		
			Notes payable		20,000
Property, plant & equipment			Bonds payable		400,000
Land		5,500	Total long-term liabilities		420,000
Land improvements		6,500			
Buildings		180,000			
Equipment		201,000	Total liabilities		481,000
Less: accum depreciation		(56,000)			
Prop, plant & equip - net		337,000			
Intangible assets			**STOCKHOLDERS' EQUITY**		
Goodwill		105,000	Common stock		110,000
Trade names		200,000	Retained earnings		229,000
Total intangible assets		305,000	Less: Treasury stock		(50,000)
			Total stockholders' equity		289,000
Other assets		3,000			
Total assets		$ 770,000	Total liabilities & stockholders' equity		$ 770,000

The notes to the sample balance sheet have been omitted.

Profit and Loss Statement

Business Name

Business Address
Suburb

Profit & Loss Statement
for the period 1 January 2009 to 31 December 2009

Income

Sales	$120,200.00	
Services	$55,000.00	
Other Income	$2,520.00	
Total Income		$177,720.00

Expenses

Accounting	$2,500.00	
Advertising	$7,500.00	
Assets - Small	$100.00	
Bank Charges	$962.40	
Cost of Good Sold	$22,500.00	
Depreciation	$2,385.00	
Electricity	$2,994.90	
Hire of Equipment	$4,200.00	
Insurance	$1,221.00	
Interest	$2,401.66	
Motor Vehicle	$1,203.50	
Office Supplies	$962.11	
Postage & Printing	$725.00	
Rent	$15,610.00	
Repairs & Maintenance	$1,082.00	
Stationery	$660.00	
Subscriptions	$3,690.00	
Telephone	$2,165.00	
Training / Seminars	$2,200.00	
Wages & Oncosts	$65,000.00	
Total Expenses		$140,062.57

Profit / (Loss) $37,657.43

Income and Expenditure

EXAMPLE: SERVICE ACCOUNT   APPENDIX D

SERVICE USER OR LOCATION: <u>MAITLAND</u>   MONTH: <u>February</u> YEAR ' <u>00</u>   BANK ACCOUNT NUMBER: <u>217400 465-786</u>

BANK ACCOUNT				INCOME AND EXPENDITURE		CASH FLOAT			
Credits Money In Pensions, salaries, deposits and interest	Debits Money Out Including, fees, transfers etc.	Bank Account balance Must match the bank Book	Date Date in bankbook/day cash is in/out of house	Description Reasons for transaction 'Bank fees' 'to household account' 'Money programme', 'movies' Include cheque number in description	Receipt Number	Cash tin in Money from bank/Money returned from Wallet	Cash tin Out Purchases made/cash to resident's wallet	Cash float balance Cash held by staff on premises in purse or cash tin	Signature Sign every entry
Opening Balance =		$1487.33	01/2/00	BALANCES CARRIED FORWARD		Opening Cash on hand =		$89.45	Alfred Brown
-	-	-	02/2/00	MILK	1	-	$2.70	$86.75	Alfred Brown
-	$4.70	$1482.63	03/2/00	Account Keeping Fee	-	-	-	-	Alfred Brown
-	$804.89	$677.74	03/2/00	B-Pay Energy Australia	2	-	-	-	Alfred Brown
-	$210.00	$467.74	03/2/00	To purse for house groceries	-	$210.00	-	$296.75	Alfred Brown
-	$72.40	$395.34	03/2/00	Telstra Bill Chq#145008	3	-	-	-	Alfred Brown
-	-	$395.34	03/2/00	Checked and Correct	-	-	-	$296.75	Alfred Brown
-	-	-	04/2/00	House Groceries- Woolworths	4	-	$146.45	$150.30	Alfred Brown
-	-	-	04/2/00	Milk and biscuits	5	-	$9.80	$140.50	Anita Taylor
-	-	-	05/2/00	Fruit and Bread	6	-	$3.40	$137.10	David Watchman
$180.00	-	$575.34	07/2/00	EPay transfer resident contribution	-	-	-	-	David Watchman
$180.00	-	$755.34	07/2/00	EPay transfer resident contribution	-	-	-	-	Marie Shearer
$180.00	-	$935.34	07/2/00	EPay transfer resident contribution	-	-	-	-	Marie Shearer
-	$210.00	$725.34	07/2/00	To purse for house groceries	-	$210.00	-	$347.10	Anita Taylor
-	$65.50	$659.84	09/02/00	Butchers	7	-	$56.00	$291.10	David Watchman
-	-	-	09/2/00	House Groceries - Woolworths	8	-	$211.25	$79.85	Anita Taylor
-	$25.00	$634.84	11/2/00	Bobs Lawn care chq#155651	9	-	-	-	Anita Taylor
-	-	-	12/2/00	Milk and Bread	10	-	$13.55	$66.30	David Watchman
-	-	$634.84	12/2/00	Balance Checked and correct	-	-	-	$66.30	Anita Taylor
$540.00	$1392.49	$634.84	12/2/00	END OF PAGE TOTALS	-	420.00	443.15	$66.30	Anita Taylor
TOTAL	TOTAL	CARRY OVER	DATE	PAGE _1_ OF ___ FOR THIS MONTH		TOTAL	TOTAL	CARRY OVER	Initial confirmation of transfers from bank Account to float

---

Section VI-Specialized Document Preparation

AN INVOICE sample

Princess Beauty Salon
Where beauty is excellence
●●●●●●●●●●●●●●●●●●●●●●●●●●●●●●●●●●●●
●●●●●●●●●●●●●●●●●●●●●●●●●●●●●●●●●●●●

Invoice

Date: May 27, 2009

Invoice# [3638]

To	*Donna Stanley*
	Niche Hair Salon
	West Bay the Strand #4
	Cayman Islands KY1-1432
	1345-945-6785
	Customer Id: 54542464

Salesperson	Job	Payment Terms	Due Date
Denise Langley	Deliver	Due on receipt	June 1st 2009

Qty	Description	Unit Price	Total
100	Hair Pins	23.00	150.00
75	Hair Nets	20.00	100.00
3	Bottles of conditioner	50.00	190.00

Section VI-Specialized Document Preparation

		Subtotal	440.00
		Sales Tax	55.00
		Total	495.00

Make all checks payable to Princess Beauty Salon

Thank you for your business!

Princess Beauty Salon West Bay the Plaza Cayman Islands

KY1-1432 (tel) 936-7587 (fax) 769-0987 princess@gmail.com

Bank Statement sample

FIRST BANK OF WIKI
1425 JAMES ST, PO BOX 4000
VICTORIA BC V8X 3X4   1-800-555-5555

CHEQUING ACCOUNT STATEMENT
Page : 1 of 1

JOHN JONES
1643 DUNDAS ST W APT 27
TORONTO ON M6K 1V2

Statement period	Account No.
2003-10-09 to 2003-11-08	00005-123-456-7

Date	Description	Ref.	Withdrawals	Deposits	Balance
2003-10-08	Previous balance				0.55
2003-10-14	Payroll Deposit - HOTEL			694.81	695.36
2003-10-14	Web Bill Payment - MASTERCARD	9685	200.00		495.36
2003-10-16	ATM Withdrawal - INTERAC	3990	21.25		474.11
2003-10-16	Fees - Interac		1.50		472.61
2003-10-20	Interac Purchase - ELECTRONICS	1975	2.99		469.62
2003-10-21	Web Bill Payment - AMEX	3314	300.00		169.62
2003-10-22	ATM Withdrawal - FIRST BANK	0064	100.00		69.62
2003-10-23	Interac Purchase - SUPERMARKET	1559	29.08		40.54
2003-10-24	Interac Refund - ELECTRONICS	1975		2.99	43.53
2003-10-27	Telephone Bill Payment - VISA	2475	6.77		36.76
2003-10-28	Payroll Deposit - HOTEL			694.81	731.57
2003-10-30	Web Funds Transfer - From SAVINGS	2620		50.00	781.57
2003-11-03	Pre-Auth. Payment - INSURANCE		33.55		748.02
2003-11-03	Cheque No. - 409		100.00		648.02
2003-11-06	Mortgage Payment		710.49		-62.47
2003-11-07	Fees - Overdraft		5.00		-67.47
2003-11-08	Fees - Monthly		5.00		-72.47
	*** Totals ***		1,515.63	1,442.61	

Receipts.*sample*

Company Name Here

Address Line Here
Phone: 555-555-555555
Fax: 123-123-123456
Email: abc@example.com
Website: www.websiteaddress.com

Cash Receipt

Cash Receipt #: 123456788   **Date:** DD/MM/YYYY

Cash Received From _____ of $ _____

For _____

Total Amount Due	
Amount Received	
Balance Due	

Payment Received in:

Cash	
Cheque	
Other	

Cash Receipt Template

_____
Signed By

<u>Summary</u>

Different Types of Documents

A **newsletter** *is a regularly distributed <u>publication</u> that is generally about one main topic of <u>interest</u> to its <u>subscribers</u>. <u>Newspapers</u> and <u>leaflets</u> are types of newsletters*

Legal document - (law) *is a <u>legal</u> <u>term of art</u> that is used for any formally executed written <u>document</u> that can be formally attributed to its author,[1] records and formally expresses a legally enforceable act, process,[2] or contractual duty, obligation, or right, and therefore evidences that act, process, or agreement.*

Technical documents – *is a documents that informs and instructs readers about science and technology. It can include detailed information about scientific theories, as well as instructions for using software and hardware.*

Literary documents -*the knowledge and skills required to locate and use information contained in various formats, including job applications, payroll forms, transportation schedules, maps, tables and charts.*

Financial statement *(or **financial** report) is a formal record of the **financial** activities of a business, person, or other entity. Relevant **financial** information is presented in a structured manner and in a form easy to understand.*

L esson 3

Creating Templates

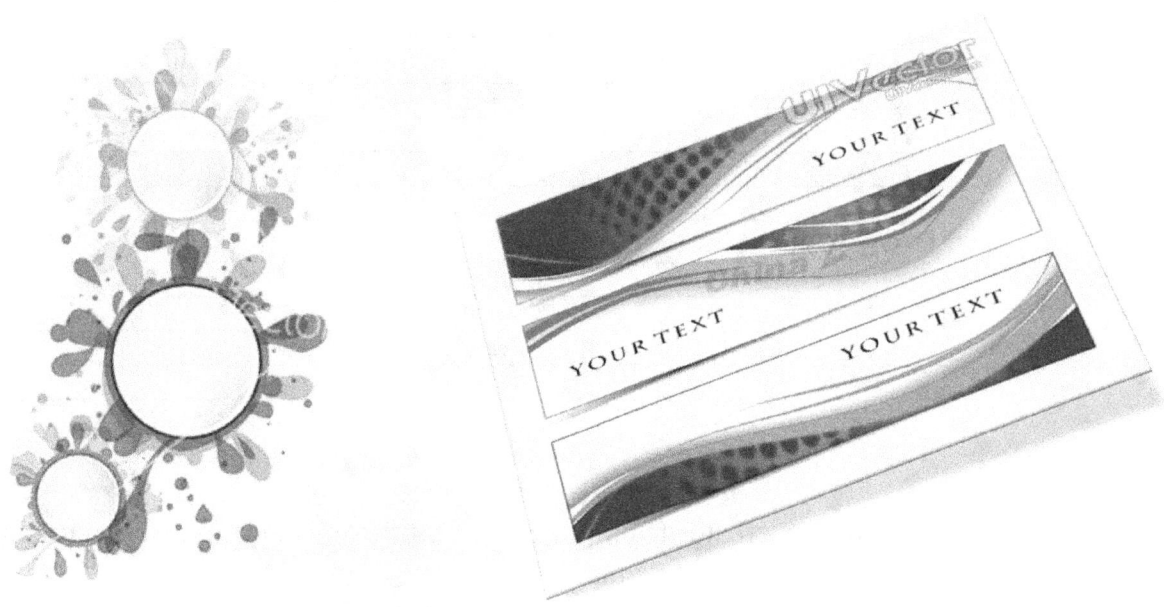

Objective

At the end of this chapter, the student should be able to:
➤ *create a template with or without the use of wizard*
➤ *create a template by using the help options in MS word*

Templates are files that help you design interesting, compelling, and professional-looking documents or workbooks. They contain content and design elements that you can use as a starting point when creating a document. All the formatting is complete; you add what you want to them.

Example:

Cash Receipt			
Date:		Receipt Number:	
Received From:			
For Payment Of:			
Payment Amount: $			$.
Payment Method		Previous Balance:	
Check	☐	Amount Paid:	
Cash	☐	New Balance:	
Money Order	☐	Received By:	
Credit Card	☐	Memo:	

You can create a template or modify any specialized document on any Office program you are using.

For Word - You can create a document or existing template and then save it as your very own custom template. Examples are the newsletters for 4/6/8 page leaflets, reports, proposals, continuation pages, news and other forms of press release or Legal documents like Wills, leases, conveyance documents, agreements, endorsements and contracts.

For PowerPoint - You can modify a presentation or an existing template and then save it as your own custom template. Templates can contain layouts, theme colors, theme fonts, theme effects, background styles, and even content.

For Excel - You can modify a sheet, workbook, or existing template, and then save it as your very own custom template. Examples are financial statement like balance sheet, trial balance, profit and lost statement, budgets, bank statement, invoices, and reports.

Steps in creating templates <u>without</u> the use of wizard and help option,

1. Open the document.
2. Add, delete, or change any text, graphics, or formatting, and make any other changes that you want to appear in all new documents that you base on the template.
3. On the **File** menu, click **Save As**.
4. On the **Format** pop-up menu, For **Word** - click **Word Template (.dotx)** or for **Powerpoint** -click **PowerPoint Template (.potx)** or for **Excel** - click **Excel Template (.xltx)**.
5. In the **Save As** box, type the name that you want to use for the new template, and then click **Save**.

   Unless you select a different location, the template is saved in /Users/ *username*/Library/Application Support/Microsoft/Office/User Templates/My Templates.

   If you are using Mac OS X 7 (Lion), the Library folder is hidden by default. To show the Library folder, in the Finder, click the **Go** menu, and then hold down OPTION .

6. On the **File** menu, click **Close.**

Tip   To organize templates, use the Finder to create a new folder in /Users/ *username*/Library/Application   Support/Microsoft/Office/User Templates/My Templates, and then save your template in the new folder. If you are using Mac OS X 7 (Lion), the Library folder is hidden by default. To show the Library folder, in the Finder, click the **Go** menu, and then hold down OPTION .

In creating templates <u>with</u> the use of wizard and help options, You can customize an existing template to make it even more useful. Add static information to the existing template, and then save the file again (as a template).

1. On the **Standard** toolbar, click **New from template** .
2. In the left navigation pane, under **TEMPLATES**, click **All**.

    Note If you can't find a template, you can search for a template based on keywords in the **Search** box.

3. Click a template that is similar to the one that you want to create, and then click **Choose**.
4. Add, delete, or change any text, graphics, or formatting, and make any other changes that you want to appear in all new documents that you base on the template.
5. On the **File** menu, click **Save As**.
6. On the **Format** pop-up menu, , For **Word** - click **Word Template (.dotx)** or for **Powerpoint** -click **PowerPoint Template (.potx)** or for **Excel -** click **Excel Template (.xltx)**.
7. In the **Save As** box, type the name that you want to use for the new template, and then click **Save**.

    Unless you select a different location, the template is saved in */Users/ username/Library/Application Support/Microsoft/Office/User Templates /My Templates.*

    If you are using Mac OS X 7 (Lion), the Library folder is hidden by default. To show the Library folder, in the Finder, click the **Go** menu, and then hold down OPTION.

Tip To organize templates, use the Finder to create a new folder in /Users/ *username*/ Library/ Application Support/ Microsoft/ Office/ User Templates/My Templates, and then save your template in the new folder. If you are using Mac OS X 7 (Lion), the Library folder is hidden by default. To show the Library folder, in the Finder, click the **Go** menu, and then holddown OPTION .If you are using Mac OS X 7 (Lion), the Library folder is hidden by default. To show the Library folder, in the Finder, click the **Go** menu, and then hold down OPTION.

<u>Summary</u>

Templates are files that help you design interesting, compelling, and professional-looking workbooks.

Creating templates with or without the use of wizard and help options for any specialized document can be made through MS Office program.

Exercise VI.3

Name: _____   **Score:** ___ **/50**

Level/Section: _____   **Date:** _____

Direction: Create a template as shown below:

SAMPLE CONTRACT

Student _____ . Date_____

Teacher _____

Target Behavior *participating in P.E.*_____

Acceleration Agreement

For *participating in gym class*_____

you will receive *1 token*_____

When you have earned *5* , they can be exchanged for

*a coke*_____

As soon as you earn *25* tokens, you will earn ~~~_____

Deceleration Agreement

If you are *not participating*_____

1. *will take away 1 token*_____

If you question or argue, *you will be sent to timeout*

If you refuse to go to time-out, *you will recieve a detention*

_____

Expiration Date: _____   Signed _____
                                              (student)

_____
(teacher)

Chapter VII

Electronic Communication

Highlights:

- *Types of Electronic Communication*
- *Features of e-mail*
- *Electronic Communication Media*
- *Communication technologies*
- *File Organization Methods*
- *Selection of Communication Media*

L esson 1

Types of Electronic Communication

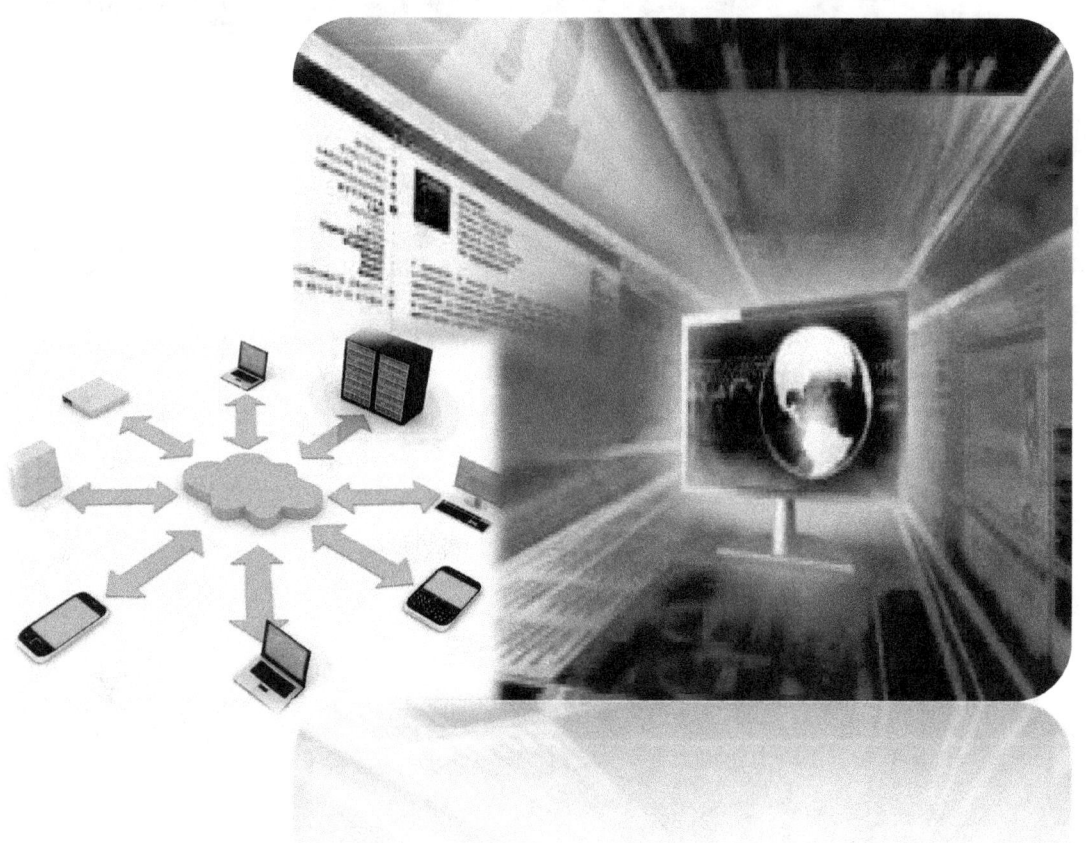

Objective

At the end of this chapter, the student should be able to:
- ➤ *discuss various types of electronic communication*
- ➤ *interact by the use of telecommuting, e-mail, social media or any other current electronic communication*

The internet has provided new ways to communicate using various tools electronic communication. Today, organization interact differently with the various stakeholders – board members, employees, customers and suppliers depending on the nature of message, the goals, and the strength of available tools, such as telephone, e-mail, fax, voice mail and text message. One of the major advantages of electronic communication is that it lets combine numerous types of media such as text, graphic, sounds and video – in a single message by the use of various <u>electronic communication.</u>

.

Types of Electronic Communication

- **Internet: World wide web tools**

  The Internet- also known as the Net- is the world's largest network.

  In fact, the Internet is a network of networks. A network is a set of computers that are connected to each other to freely share resources. The network providers the infrastructure that supports a wide range of services.

Internet services may be accessed through both wired and wireless connections. Many schools and offices have an always-on Internet connection provided by an Internet service provider (ISP).   Many office workers and receptionists use the Internet on a day-do-day basis to transmit information electronically.

The electronic communication services facilitated by the Internet are:

Services	Examples
Electronic mail	*Gmail. Hotmail*
Instant messaging	*MSN. Google Talk*
VoIP telephone	*Skype, MSN Video Call*
World Wide Web	*Facebook, Twitter, YouTube*

The World Wide Web, abbreviated to **WWW** and commonly known as the Web, is a system of interlinked hypertext documents called web pages. These web pages are stored on web servers scattered all over the Internet. A web browser is software used to view web pages. You may have used Internet Explorer, Firefox, Safari or Chrome- all examples of web browsers.

The terms **Internet** and **World Wide Web** are often used in everyday speech without much distinction. However, the Internet and the World Wide Web are not one and the same. The Internet is a global system of interconnected computer networks. In contrast, the Web is one of the services that runs on the Internet. It is a collection of interconnected documents and other resources.

Web communication is different from hard-copy publication because hypertext and the Web support non sequential navigation through online documents that are in essence "authored" by readers as they follow one of a potentially unlimited number of pathways through a "document."

Guidelines for Composing Web Documents and Web Sites

- Provide a graphical map of your Web site to help your audience conceptualize the organization, extent, and usefulness of information available there.
- Limit presentation of information to one screenful whenever possible (unless you are maintaining an online archive of reports originally published in hard copy).
- Limit the size of video and audio files to be downloaded (downloading video clips even a few minutes long can be a time-consuming process, turning the World Wide Web into the World Wide Wait).
- Follow the general guidelines for graphical representation when creating figures and other static illustrations.
- Show the context or reason for a link to another file or part of a file (or to another Web site) so that your audience can decide beforehand if they want to go there.

Hypertext

Hypertext is a compositional tool as well as a conceptual approach to communication. As a compositional tool, hypertext markup languages allow the author of a hypertext to establish links among the parts of a document, or between any number of complete documents, for ease of reference or for amplification of an idea. Since the reader of a hypertext can choose to follow these links or not (and in some contexts, such as a Web site, establish new links), hypertext tools also permit the reader to become an "author" as well. The "final" hypertext document, therefore, may take any number of forms, depending upon the needs of the audience.

Hypertext technical documents are very useful for training and for communicating instructions and procedures.

Guidelines for Creating Hypertext Links

- Consider the audience for your document, their limitations and demands.
- Let subject matter determine the kind and number of links between documents (or Web sites). Unexplained and arbitrary links will make your audience feel "lost in hyperspace."
- Structure the pathway of links in a coherent, useful way. Move your reader from general principles or important first steps down into subsidiary elements of your topic.
- Establish a context for a link when that link is to related but not crucial supporting material. That way, readers can decide if they want to access that information at that time.

Facsimile (fax)

A **facsimile (shortened to fax)** is a document sent over a telephone line. Fax services are available using:

- ✓ Standalone fax machine
- ✓ Multifunction devices
- ✓ Fax servers
- ✓ Internet fax service

A standalone fax machine requires either a dedicated or a shared telephone line for its operation. It may be set up automatically receive an incoming transmission (after a pre-set numbers of rings) or the transmission may be received manually (the receptionist must answer the call as a voice call, then press the start button). A benefit of using a fax is that employees within an office can be audibly alerted to an incoming fax or they may see the printed fax on the machine.

Only hard copy documents may be sent using standalone fax machine. To overcome this limitation, multifunction devices are used. Multifunction device usually integrates scanning, printing and faxing capabilities into one device. It allows a hard copy document to be scanned to a file and faxed.

In many corporate environments, standalone fax machine. To have been replaced by fax servers and other computerized systems capable of receiving and storing incoming faxes electronically, and then routing them to users on paper or via email. Such systems have the advantage of reducing costs by eliminating unnecessary printouts and reducing the number of inbound phone lines needed by an office.

One of the key **advantages of using facsimile** as a means of communicating electronically is the higher level of confidentiality it offers when compared with unencrypted material sent over the Internet. In some countries, electronic signatures on contracts are not recognized by law while faxed contracts with copies of signatures are, so fax machines enjoy continuing support in business.

Short message service (SMS)

Short message service (SMS) is the text communication server component of phone, web or mobile communication systems, using standardized communications protocols that allow the exchange of short text messages between fixed line or mobile phone devices. SMS text messaging is now is the most widely used data application in the world. More SMS messages are sent daily than e-mails.

Across the Caribbean, businesses use SMS for billing notification and appointment scheduling as well as time-sensitive tasks. Government agencies use SMS to send our health, weather and security alerts to their citizens.

With the popularity of Blackberry devices for business use, the Blackberry Messenger application (BBM) is used daily by millions of business people to communicate.

Teleconferencing

A teleconference is a call between people in two or more locations linked by telephone. It uses special telephony equipment to provide the sound quality needed for productive, natural meetings. In an increasingly global business environment, teleconferencing is an ideal way to improve communications among individuals and groups, enhance collaboration and decision-making, while saving time and reducing travel costs.

Videoconferencing

A videoconference is a meeting facilitated by interactive telecommunication technologies, which allows two or more locations to simultaneously interact via two-way video and audio transmissions. Participants are able to see and hear each other as if all persons were in the same room. Additionally, they may share soft copy documents.

Videoconferencing can enable individuals in distant locations to participate in meetings at short notice, with time and money savings. Technology such as VoIP can be used in conjunction with desktop videoconferencing to enable low-cost face-to-face business meetings without leaving the desk. Especially for businesses with widespread offices, the technology is also used for telecommuting, in which employees work from home. Web-based tool such as Skype and Illuminate may be used for group videoconferencing.

- **Telecommuting**

Telecommuting is a work arrangement in which employees enjoy flexibility in working location and hours. A telecommuter- a person who telecommuters- "travels" or commuters to work via telecommunications technology to work from home, while others use mobile telecommunications technology to work from coffee shops or other locations. Using special software and a computer system equipped with a modern (or an Internet connection).

Telecommuters are able to access and work on documents stored on the company's network.

- **Electronic mail**,

Electronic mail (e-mail) allows for the almost instantaneous transmission of a message from one computer through a network to one or more other computers and is rapidly becoming one of the main forms of both professional and personal communication.

Social media are computer-mediated tools that allow people to create, share or exchange information, ideas, and pictures/videos in virtual communities and networks. *Social media* is defined as "a group of Internet-based applications that build on the ideological and technological foundations of Web 2.0, and that allow the creation and exchange of user-generated content." Furthermore, social media depend on mobile and web-based technologies to create highly interactive platforms through which individuals and communities share, co-create, discuss, and modify user-generated content. They introduce substantial and pervasive changes to communication between businesses, organizations, communities, and individuals. These changes are the focus of the emerging field of techno self studies.

Social media are different from traditional or industrial media in many ways, including quality, reach, frequency, usability, immediacy, and permanence. There are many effects that stem from internet usage. According to Nielsen, internet users continue to spend more time with social media sites than any other type of site. At the same time, the total time spent on social media in the U.S. across PC and mobile devices increased by 99 percent to 121 billion minutes in July 2012 compared to 66 billion minutes in July 2011. For content contributors, the benefits of participating in social media have gone beyond simply social sharing to building reputation and bringing in career opportunities and monetary income, as discussed in Tang, Gu, and Whinston (2012).

Examples of Social Media are Facebook, Twitter, Internet forums, weblogs, podcasts and so on.

Social networking Services

Facsimile, multifunctional devices. Scan to man Scan to file;

Summary

Types   of   Electronic Communication are:

- *Internet: World Wide Web*
- *Social Media (e.g. internet forums, weblogs, podcasts)*
- *Social Networking Services (e.g. Facebook, Twitter)*
- *facsimile (fax)*
- *short message services (SMS)*
- *Telecommuting*
- *Teleconferencing or videoconferencing*
- *Electronic Mail*
- And any other current electronic communication

Activity 1

Research the services offered by at least three Internet Service Providers in your country and complete the following table:

Name of ISP	Type of Service (ADSL or cable)	Bandwidth	Price per month in US$

Activity 2

1. Which browser was first? Was it Firefox, Safari, Netscape, Internet Explorer, Opera or Chrome?

2. Use Web to conduct research to determine the following:

Browser	Firefox	Chrome	Safari	Netscape	Internet Explorer	Opera	others
a. The year each browser was released							
b. Which browsers are proprietary and which are open source (Use the Web to research these terms)							
c. Which browser is the most popular internationally							

Lesson 2

Features of e-mail

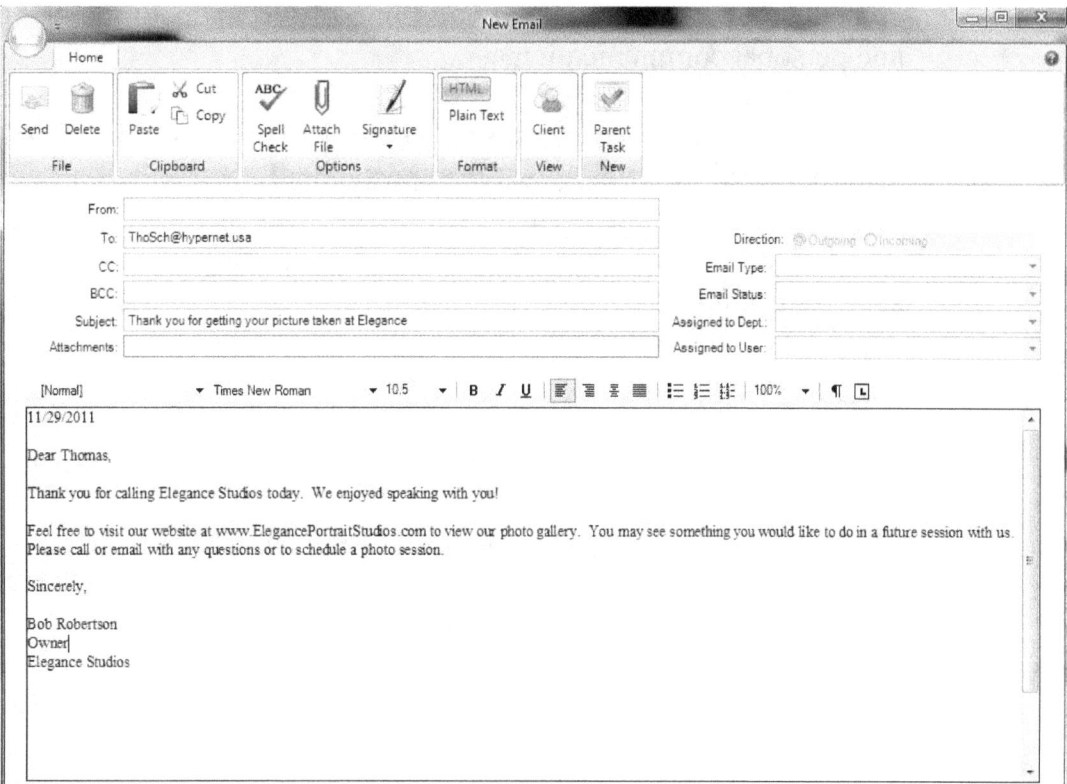

Objective

At the end of this chapter, the student should be able to:
- *explain various features of e-mail*
- *compose and send a well-organized email messages to any individual or group.*

Short for **electronic mail**, **e-mail** or **email** is a message that may contain text, files, images, or other attachments sent through a network to a specified individual or group of individuals.

Electronic mail (e-mail) allows for the almost instantaneous transmission of a message from one computer through a network to one or more other computers and is rapidly becoming one of the main forms of both professional and personal communication.

The first e-mail was sent by Ray Tomlinson in 1971. By1996, more electronic mail was being sent than postal mail.

The following is an Internet e-mail address example.

support@computerhope.com

Arnaiz@gmail.com

The first portion all e-mail addresses, the part before the @ symbol, contains the alias, user, group, or department of a company. In our above example **support** is the Technical Support department at Computer Hope.
Next, the @ (at sign) is used as a divider in the e-mail address; required for all SMTP e-mail addresses since the first message was sent by Ray Tomlinson.

How to send and receive e-mail

E-mail Program

To send and receive e-mail messages you can use an **e-mail program**, also known as an **e-mail client**, such as Microsoft Outlook or Mozilla Thunderbird. When using an e-mail client, you must have a server that stores and delivers your messages; provided by your ISP or in some cases, another company. An e-mail client needs to connect to the server to download new e-mail, whereas email stored online (see next section) updates automatically when you visit the site.

E-mail Online

An alternative way of sending and receiving e-mail (and the more popular solution for most people) is an online e-mail service or webmail. Examples include Hotmail, Gmail, and Yahoo Mail. Many of the online e-mail services, including the aforementioned ones, are free or have a free account option.

Features of an E-Mail

Like a telephone conversation, e-mail is immediate and informal. Like a <u>memorandum</u>, it is more precise than an oral conversation, it provides a record of the communication, and it can send a single message to a large number of people.

Unlike telephone conversations or memoranda, e-mail should not be considered private. E-mail is sent through public networks where messages are often copied multiple times during transmission.

When writing a new e-mail message, it should look something like the example window below.

Basics of an e-mail message

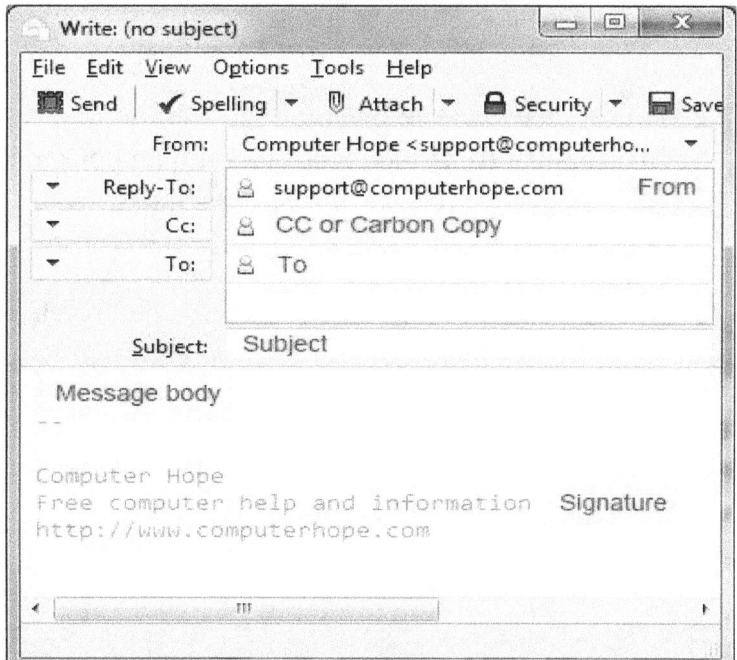

As can be seen, several fields are required when sending an e-mail.

1) The **To** field is where you type the e-mail address of the person who you are sending the message to,

2) **From** should contain your e-mail address, If you are replying to a message, the To and From fields are automatically filled out; if it's a New Message, you'll need to enter them manually.

3) Next, the CC or Carbon Copy field allows you to send a copy of the message to another e-mail address, but is not mandatory.

4) Short for **Blind Carbon Copy**, **BCC** sends copies of e-mail without displaying any of the names or e-mails in the e-mail. Keep in mind that most programs do not display the BCC field; however, anyone familiar with their e-mail program can enable this field to see all e-mail addresses and names.

   Tip: *To help protect privacy and e-mail contacts, we suggest sending the e-mail individually to each address or using a third-party mailing program to distribute your e-mail.*

5) The **Subject Line**, although not required, should consist of a few words describing what the e-mail is about.

6) Finally, the **Message Body** is the location you type your main message. It often contains your signature at the bottom; similar to a hand-written letter.

7) A **signature** or **signature block** is data used for identification purposes most often found in e-mail messages. A signature may be as simple as the individual's name or alias, contain additional information such as a job description, company, e-mail address, position, phone number, URL, quote, funny saying or joke.

   Below is an example of the Computer Hope signature sent with all of our e-mails.

Computer				Hope
Free	computer	help	and	information
http://www.computerhope.com				

Signatures are also often found on online communities and forums as a way for a user to identify themselves, something they enjoy, etc. When referring to a virus, a **signature** is short for virus signature.

E-mail signature etiquette

- ✓ Keep the signature as small and simple as possible. We suggest no more than four lines.
- ✓ Your signature doesn't need to be a complete bio of yourself. If you have five different phone numbers, you shouldn't post all five of them in your signature. Often a cell phone number is enough.
- ✓ Have a divider or empty lines between the signature and main message.
- ✓ Don't advertise more than your web page. Everyone gets bombarded enough by e-mail solicitation.

8) When referring to e-mail, an **attachment** is a file sent with the an e-mail message. An attachment can be a picture, a word document, a movie, a sound file, an excel document, or any other file that requires another program to open it.

Tip: *In addition to the files mentioned above, attachments may also include computer viruses, Trojans, worms, or other malware. Unless you were expecting an attachment from the user sending you the e-mail, we suggest not open the attachment, even if it is from someone you know. Viruses and worms can use address books to help spread the virus and make it appear to be a valid e-mail.*

The basic unit of a memorandum is the single 8½-by-11-inch page, the basic unit of an e-mail is the 22-line screen. Consequently, e-mails should be kept short and concise. Finally, because e-mails are generated so easily, many individuals receive scores of messages every day.

Guidelines for Writing Effective E-Mail

- As in other forms of communication, start with *you*--a statement acknowledging the recipient.
- Keep your message short.
- Make <u>heading</u> clear and exact.
- If something is urgent, mark it "Urgent."
- Include a short introduction indicating exactly to what you are responding, even if the original message is included.
- If the e-mail is important, print it out and <u>proofread</u> it carefully before you send it.
- Take time to cool off.
- Remember that a message can end up anywhere.
- Remember that electronic privacy doesn't exist.
- E-mail etiquette is still evolving:
    1. *Avoid using all capital letters.*
    2. *Do not forward an e-mail without permission.*
    3. *Keep e-mail addresses confidential.*

Summary

Short for **electronic mail**, **e-mail** or **email** is a message that may contain <u>text</u>, <u>files</u>, <u>images</u>, or other <u>attachments</u> sent through a network to a specified individual or group of individuals.

Electronic mail (e-mail) allows for the almost instantaneous transmission of a message from one computer through a network to one or more other computers and is rapidly becoming one of the main forms of both professional and personal communication.

Lesson 3

Electronic Communication Media

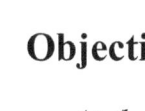

Objective

At the end of this chapter, the student should be able to:
➢ *define electronic communication media*
➢ *discuss the advantages and disadvantaqes of electronic communication media*

Electronic mail has many advantages when compared with traditional postal mail (snail mail) and also which compared with other forms of electronic communication such as fax.

But there are also advantages and disadvantages of electronic communication media:

Advantages:

a.) Speed of delivery

E-mail is received almost immediately after it is sent, usually within minutes. An added advantage is that within minutes the sender is able to receive a delivery receipt that confirms whether the message was delivered to a recipient's mailbox. Similarly, if the delivery failed, notification of the failure is almost instantaneous. With postal mail, undelivered mail take days or weeks to be returned to the sender, if at all.

b.) Low cost

There is no direct cost associated with sending an e-mail. Whilst there is a cost for the electricity, computer time and internet access, there is no direct cost for an envelope, paper and postage. Hundreds of e-mail may be sent worldwide for the cost of one item of local postal mail.

c.) Sending to multiple recipients simultaneously

A single e-mail may be sent to multiple recipients, whereas an item of postal mail would have to be sent as separate physical items to each recipient. The e-mail is likely to reach each recipient's mailbox at the same time. This is particularly important when distributing time-sensitive documents such as news release. Some corporate e-mail servers will allow one message to be sent to up to 5,000 recipients at once.

d.) Ability to send multiple types of attachments

Various the types may be attached to e-mail messages. This allows attachments containing text-based documents, graphics, sound and video to be included. Compression features built into e-mail software allow relatively large files to be sent in a short time. This is particularly advantageous in situations where multiple copies of a multi-page document may be sent as an attachment, which is then downloaded, printed, bound and distributed at the receiving end.

e.) Anytime, anywhere access

A big advantages of an e-mail message over conventional fax and postal mail is the ability to access e-mail anywhere at any time. Because e-mail is usually stored on a server, recipients may choose to configure their mail account such that a copy is retained on the server. In this way e-mail may be accessed from any devise with an Internet connection at any time.

f.) Ease or reference

The text of a previous e-mail message can easily be included as part of a reply to that message. Thus, e-mail correspondents are able to keep the replies in context for each message. Including this context is not only polite, but also makes an e-mail message more accurate and understandable.

Disadvantages:

a.) Receipt of unsolicited bulk e-mail

Unsolicited bulk e-mail (spam), frequently with commercial content, is sent in large quantities to an indiscriminate set of recipients. These unsolicited messages have a tendency to clog up mailboxes and also serve to carry malware (viruses and other programs that infect computer systems). Businesses are disadvantaged because.

- It costs the recipient time and resources to download these messages.
- Important and urgent messages cannot be accused on a timely basis because unsolicited bulk mail has to be downloaded first.

b.) Spreading of and infection by malware

An e-mail may carry and deliver malware to an unsuspecting recipient. The business may be disadvantaged as result of:

- The message (and possibly future messages) being blocked by the recipient's computer system as unsafe, thereby causing the message(s) to go undelivered, sometime without the knowledge of the sender.
- The computer (and possibly the entire network) being infected if an e-mail containing a virus, Trojan horse, or spyware is mistakenly opened.

c.) **Ease of violation of privacy**

Electronic documents may be copied or forwarded without the sender's knowledge with relative ease. All that is needed is for the recipient to hit the 'Forward' button or download and otherwise share the contents of the e-mail message. E-mail can compromise the security of an organisation because sensitive information can be easily distributed accidentally or deliberately.

d.) Volume of data The volume of telecommunication information is increasing in such a fast rate that business people are unable to absorb it within relevant time limit.1

e.) Cost of development Electronic communication requires huge investment for infrastructural development. Frequent change in technology also demands for further investment.

g.) Undelivered data Data may not be retrieved due to system error or fault with the technology . Hence required service will be delayed

h) Legal status Data or information, if faxed, may be distorted and will cause zero value in the eye of law.

Summary

Advantages and Disadvantaqes of electronic communication media:

Advantages	Disadvantages
Speed of delivery	Receipt of unsolicited bulk e-mail
Low cost	Spreading of and infection by malware
Sending to multiple recipients simultaneously	Ease of violation of privacy
Ability to send multiple types of attachments	Volume of data
Anytime, anywhere access.	Cost of development
Ease of reference	Undelivered data
Electronic copy of message may be stored for later use	Legal status

Lesson 4

Communication Technologies

Objective

At the end of this chapter, the student should be able to:
➢ *discuss other new and emerging communication technologies*
➢ *use a simple cell phone or a feature phone as a smart phone for communication*

An **emerging technology** (as distinguished from a conventional technology) is a field of technology that broaches new territory in some significant way, with new technological developments.

Examples of currently emerging technologies include educational technology, information technology, nanotechnology, biotechnology, cognitive science, robotics, and artificial intelligence.

New technological fields may result from the technological convergence of different systems evolving towards similar goals. Convergence brings previously separate technologies such as voice (and telephony features), data (and productivity applications) and video together so that they share resources and interact with each other, creating new efficiencies.

Emerging technologies are those technical innovations which represent progressive developments within a field for competitive advantage; converging technologies represent previously distinct fields which are in some way moving towards stronger inter-connection and similar goals. However, the opinion on the degree of impact, status and economic viability of several emerging and converging technologies vary.

For instance, Young people's engagement with emerging communication technologies (such as social networking and mobile phone technology) is an essential method of socialization. Given the constant accessibility offered by these technologies, and the blurring between online and offline social spheres, emerging communication technologies afford for business, career, job opportunities, social networking but sometimes diverse opportunities for the perpetration of sexual violence.

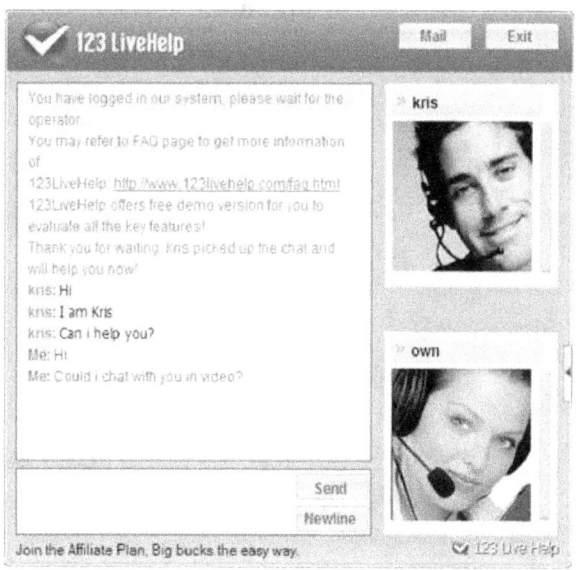

- The study found that emerging communication technologies help facilitate sexually violent acts, before, during and after an offence. Specifically, technologies help to increase the accessibility of potential victims:
  - **Before** a sexually violent act. Social networking in particular can provide a false sense of connection between offender and victim. For example, the act of 'friending' enhances the feeling of 'trust'.
  - **During** the act of sexual violence, technologies can be used to record non-consensual sexual activity. Threats to distribute this material can be used to further coerce and victimise.
  - **After** an act of either consensual or non-consensual sexual activity, offenders can distribute images to cause further harm to victims. Technologies are also used post-assault to contact, threaten or abuse victims.
- A lack of clarity on how a range of online behaviours should be conceptualized has hampered the development of appropriate and effective responses to the issue. While the law has a role to play in addressing such issues, appropriate conduct for using technologies is better addressed through a primary prevention approach to the promotion of personal ethics and respect. A study by: **Dr Antonia Quadara** Coordinator, Australian Centre for the Study of Sexual Assault

The examples of communication technologies that help us all talk to each other are:

1. Phones

2. Mobile phones

3. Television

4. Internet

5. Radio

The usage and features of emerging communication technologies are the following:

A *smart phone* is a pocket-sized handheld networked device that is a phone, a portable media players, a digital camera, a video camera, and a handheld computer. It can browse web sites, send and receive email, download and read certain files and documents, and often, be used for GPS navigation as well.

And though it may be hard for those of you have smart phones to believe, not everyone has a smart phone. Millions of people simply cannot afford a smart phone. Some of them use a simple cell phone, with very limited capabilities: the ability to make and receive phone calls and text messages. Some people have something that's more than a cell phone but less than a smart phone: they have a *feature phone*, which has some web browsing capabilities.

A simple cell phone as a smart phone has the ability to make and receive phone calls and text messages. That's pretty much it. It might come with some additional stand-alone features: stop watch, alarm clock, calculator, reminders, a few games, even a flashlight. There's no ability to browse the web. And, yet, it can still be used with some cloud-based tools. You won't be browsing the web with such a phone, but you can use a number of web-based tools on your computer to set up your cell phone so that it can send information to the web via text message, and so that you can receive important updates via text message.

But be careful! How many text messages each hour - or just in a day - do you *really* want to receive? Try one app or tool, see how you like it, and adjust it as needed before you try another:

Google Calendar
You can set up a Google Calendar so that you will receive text message updates before certain meetings - or every meeting, as you like. You can receive more than one update at any interval you choose - 10 minutes before, 30 minutes before, a certain number of hours before, days before, whatever. To do this, you have to register your phone to Google Calendar SMS.

In addition, once you have registered your phone with your Google Calendar account, you can text GVENT (48368) to request your next scheduled event, or all of your events within the next two days.

Recommendations from Google

When you need an address, or perhaps restaurant suggestions in the area, text GOOGL (46645) with whatever information you have, for example "sushi" (without the quotes), and then the Zip code or city and state. Within minutes, you should receive a listing of places. But be careful - this needs to be a very specific request, not something that will result in a massive text dump onto your phone.

Social media can be used for many things: staying in touch with friends and family, promoting your cause, and keeping up with trending topics and news. Knowing how to use social media is an essential 21st century skill.

Example:

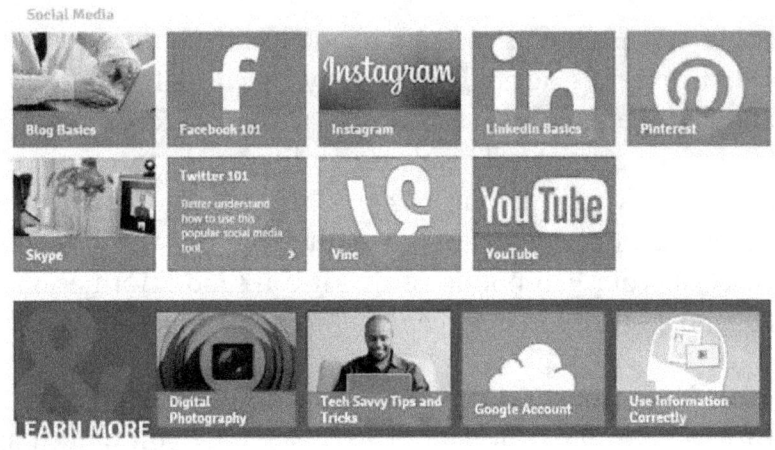

smsmyrss.com
Create a free account with just your email address and mobile phone number. Then, enter RSS feeds for weather web sites, police web sites, blogs, a Yahoo group, or any other web site that will have breaking news you want - as long as the site has an RSS feed, you can get updates via text message. Super easy to disable and re-enable feeds (that's great for traveling).

Twitter
Updating your Twitter via SMS is as easy as sending a text. Create a Twitter account via the web and configure the settings with your cell phone number, per this Twitter support page. Once you have configured your phone and settings, you can upload messages to Twitter, and you can decide what kinds of messages you want to receive. For instance, you can receive select updates from followers of your choice; on each profile, next to the follow button, there is a small button with a cellphone on it - clicking that will automatically send their status updates to you via SMS. There's also a lot you can do with Twitter just via text message.

Facebook

Uploading to Facebook is similar to Twitter: you need to register your phone and then activate it for text messaging. If you don't want your friends to see your phone number, make sure you uncheck the box on the right side of the page. You will receive a personalized email to post status updates or send photos to your profile, which you text the email address and it will automatically update for you.

You can also receive status updates, messages and wall posts from friends via SMS - however, if you have anything more than just a handfull of friends on Facebook, your phone will be consumed with receiving text messages - more than you could ever read.

Your Blog

Some blog sites, like Blogger / BlogSpot and posterous.com, allow you to configure your settings such that you can post updates via text message.

Paypal

After linking your mobile number to your account, you can check your PayPal balance by texting *bal* or *balance* to PAYPAL (729725), and you will receive a text back with the information. You can send money by texting PAYPAL (729725) with the specific amount and the recipient's phone number or email address. You can also request money by texting the same number with *Get* plus the specific amount *from* the person you're requesting from's number. Once you are SMS-savvy with these PayPal basic features on PayPal, there are a few more advanced options you can try - see the Paypal web site for more information.

A feature phone as a smart phone

Some people have something that's more than a cell phone but less than a smart phone: they have a *feature phone*, which has some web browsing capabilities. With such a phone, you can do everything that's listed under the previous section regarding simple cell phones. AND, you can do even more.

First, check your web browsing functions - try going to, say, Twitter. Some phones have web browsing functions, but they aren't very good. I highly recommend you download Opera for feature phones, even if you already have a web browser function on your feature phone - it will often perform better, or be able to access sites when the browser tool that came with your feature phone won't.

In addition:

> biNu is a free mobile phone application that provides simple access to many Internet based applications such as Facebook, Twitter, Wikipedia, news, sports, weather etc. The web site says "biNu is designed and optimized for mobile wireless devices and provides instant response times, even on slower networks." Data transferred to a phone using biNu is heavily compressed, which should reduce your phone use times (and carrier charges). biNu is capable of running on most mobile phones made after 2001 - Java-enabled phones that "support a minimum level of CLDC 1.1 and MIDP 2.0."

Traffic.com will send you traffic alerts via email or SMS updates regarding roads you frequent (dangerous conditions, accidents, construction, etc.). It can also be configured to provide an alternate way home.

Summary

An **emerging technology** (as distinguished from a conventional technology) is a field of technology that broaches new territory in some significant way, with new technological developments.

Social media can be used for many things: staying in touch with friends and family, promoting your cause, and keeping up with trending topics and news *(Twitter, Facebook, smart-phones, blogs).*

L esson 5

File Organization Methods

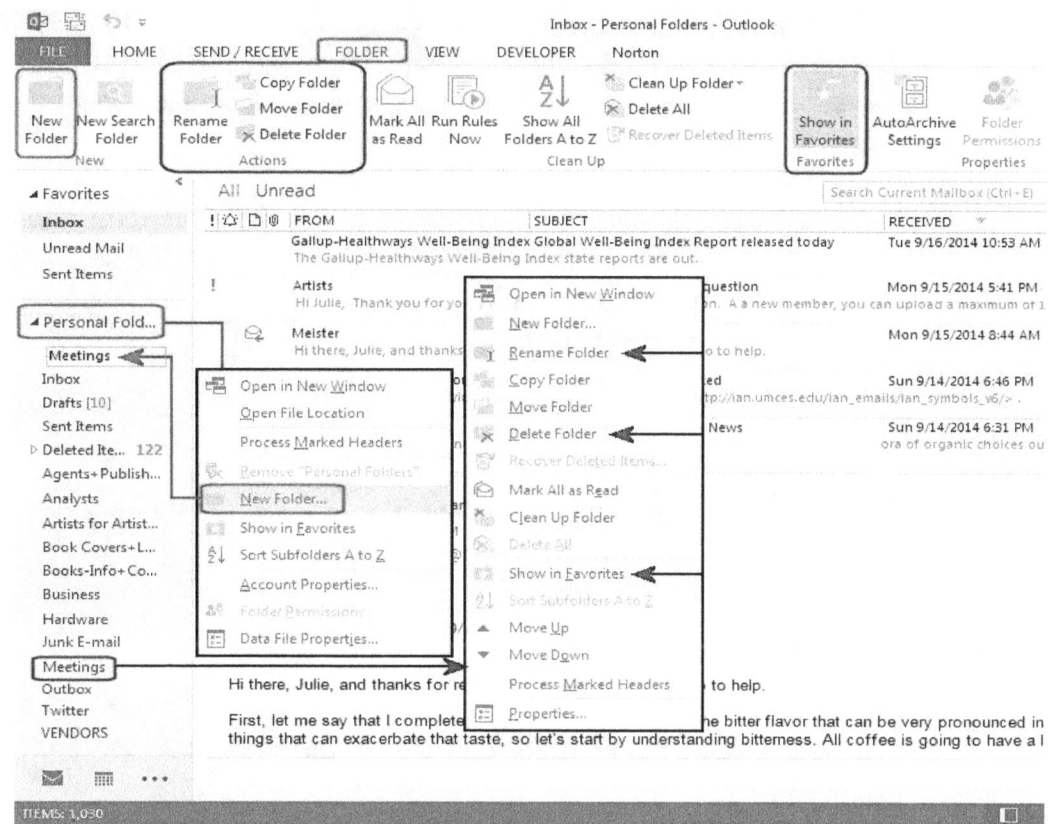

Objective

At the end of this chapter, the student should be able to:
- ➤ *discuss file organization methods using e-mail*
- ➤ *store and sort mail by date , sender and subject.*
- ➤ *make a contact list of organization*

How to Organize files in Email

a) Use a Classic Inbox

First, these inboxes never get the categories and prioritization perfectly right. They force you to go through all your email to ensure you don't miss anything and encourage you to keep getting spammy useless emails by sweeping them under the rug.

To use a more classic inbox in Gmail, click the gear icon and select Settings. Click over to the Inbox tab, click the Inbox type box, and select Unread first. All the tabs and priority options will vanish.

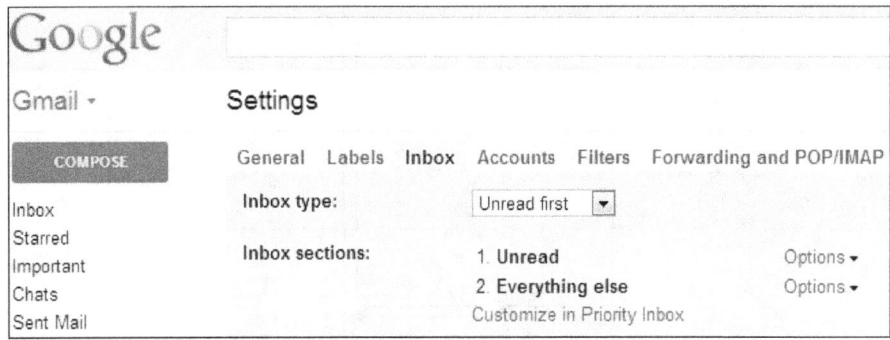

b) Unsubscribe From Email You Don't Care About

With tabbed categories and priorities disabled, all your email will be sorted into one big pile. All of those useless social-network notification emails and newsletters you don't care about will be in your inbox along with your actual important emails.

This is good — rather than just sweeping emails you don't want to see under the rug, you should stop them from arriving completely.

Consider the type of emails you don't want to see. Common types of *useless emails* include *Facebook and Google+ notifications, promotional emails,* and *newsletters* you may have inadvertently signed up for. Whenever an email you don't want to see arrives, open it and use the Unsubscribe link — you'll generally find these at the very bottom of the email — to unsubscribe from the email and prevent it from arriving in the future.

Note: you shouldn't use the Unsubscribe link if an email is actually spam, as the spammer will take this as a sign someone is reading the email and send even more spam your way. Click the Spam button if it's a real spam email and click Unsubscribe if it's a legitimate organization.

c) Send Useless Emails You Can't Unsubscribe From to the Trash

Some companies either haven't gotten the memo or don't care. Rather than pursue legal action to get off their email lists, you can simply create a filter that sends all future emails from them to your trash, where you don't have to see them.

When dealing with such an email in Gmail, open it, click the More link, and select Filter messages like these. Tune your filter to block the emails — for example, if you never care about receiving other emails from that sender, you can filter based on their email address. Use your filter to send all such emails to the trash.

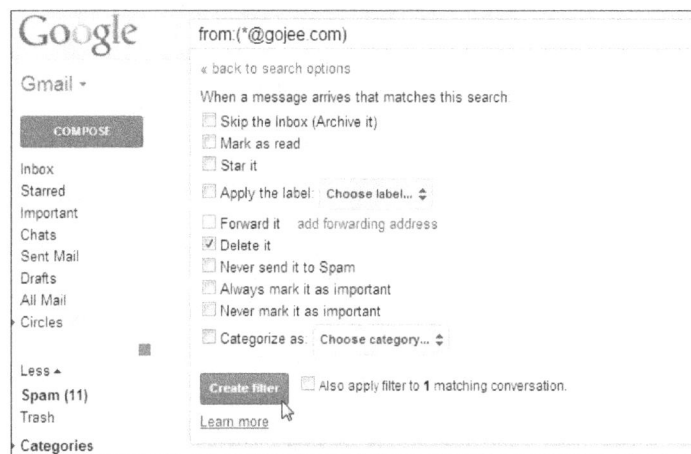

d) Automatically Archive Emails You Don't Want to See

Some emails are important to have, but you may not want to see them anyway.

For example, online stores may send you a confirmation receipt every time you purchase something from them. It's good to have such receipts just in case you need them, but if you frequently purchase products and never want to see such emails, you may want to prevent them from reaching your inbox in the first place.

This applies to many different types of email — for example, PayPal sends you a "We're transferring money to your bank" email each time you withdraw money. You may want this email for your records, but you may not want to see it in your inbox.

If you automatically archive such emails as they come in, you can put this process on autopilot. Just open such an email, click the More button in Gmail, and select Filter messages like these. Tune your filter to encompass the emails you want to catch — probably based on the Subject, if it's always the same. Tell Gmail to automatically archive the emails and mark them as read so they won't bother you.

You can also have Gmail automatically apply a label to them, such as "Automatically Archived" or a more specific label. This will allow you to quickly find the emails in the future if you actually need them.

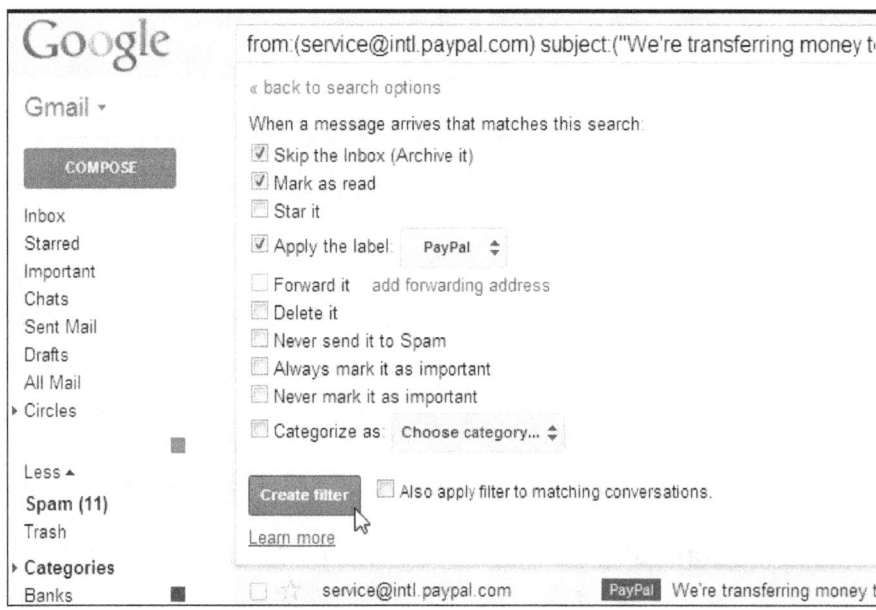

e) Set Up Automatic Labels

If you've followed this process, you should have been able to cut down on the volume of incoming emails. Now we'll help you sort the emails you do care about.

This part is optional, but it can help if you receive a lot of email — particularly for different purposes. For example, you may have <u>combined several Gmail accounts into one inbox</u> and get all your personal and work emails in the same place.

Try creating filters that automatically sort your incoming email into specific labels. For example, you can have emails from your Bank automatically get a "Bank" label. You could have personal emails get a "Personal" label and work emails get a "Work" label. Receipts for purchased products could get a "Receipts" label. There's no need to do this part manually — just set up Gmail so it will automatically sort your email into categories for you.

Color-code all these labels and you can have your email client automatically categorize your emails and show you at a glance where they're from. To color-code a label in Gmail, click its color box in the left pane and select a new color.

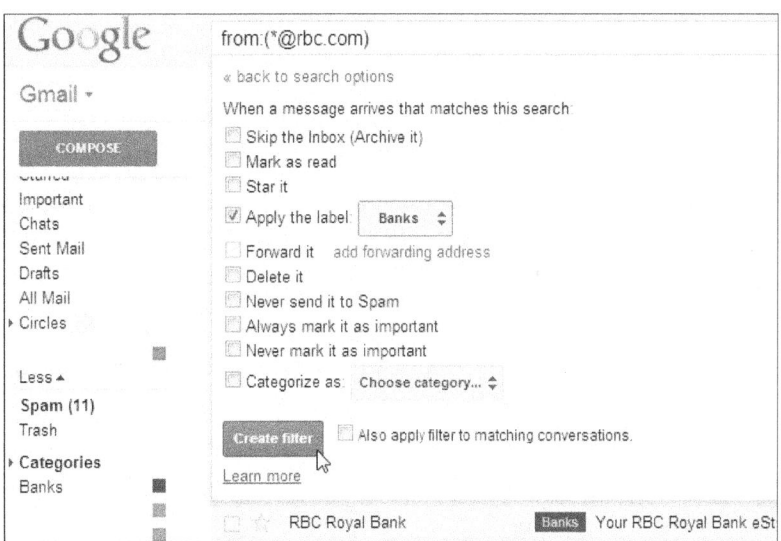

With such a label system, you can even have the Gmail app on Android and email notifiers on other platforms notify <u>you only when new messages arrive in important labels</u>, preventing notification overload.

If there are certain emails that you want to be highlighted — perhaps emails from your boss or spouse — you could set up a filter to automatically star messages from that sender when they arrive. You can select a "Starred first" inbox type in your Gmail inbox settings, so such important emails would automatically rise to the top of your inbox. This would happen exactly according to how you configure Gmail — you wouldn't have to fight with the inbox priority system and try to teach Gmail what's actually important.

Summary

How to Organize files in Email:
➤ *Use a Classic Inbox*
➤ *Unsubscribe From Email You Don't Care About*
➤ *Send Useless Emails You Can't Unsubscribe From to the Trash*
➤ *Automatically Archive Emails You Don't Want to See*
➤ *Set Up Automatic Labels*

Lesson 6

Selection of Communication Media

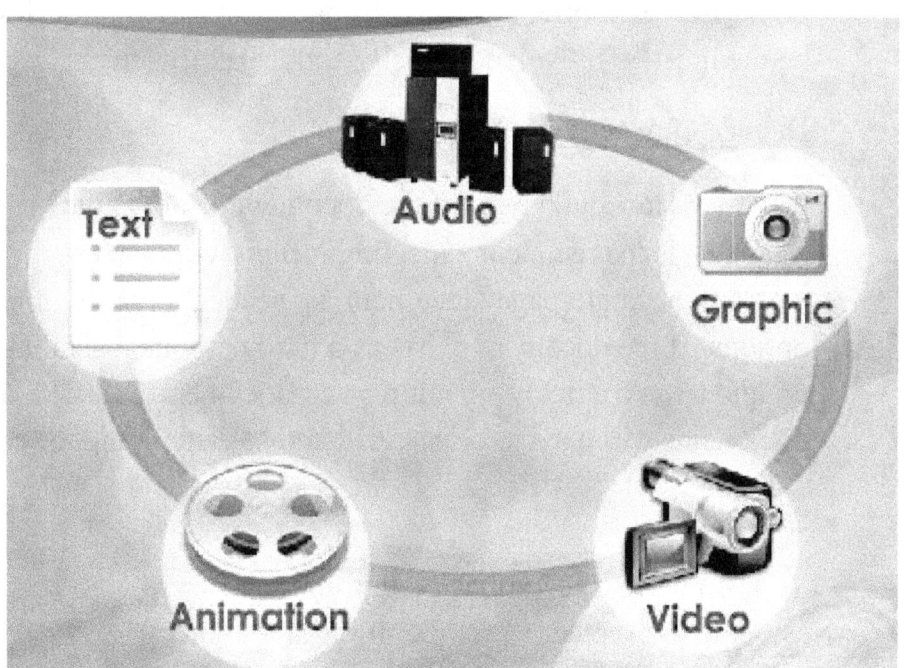

Objective

At the end of this chapter, the student should be able to:
➢ *identify factors to be considered in the selection of communication media.*
➢ *to distinguish between Communication devices and communication media*

Selection of Communication Media

In selecting which communication media to use to deliver a message following **factors** would be considered. Note that some factors will be conflict with others.

For example, the method that offers the highest level confidentially may be the most effective, most costly and least efficient.

Degree of urgency

- How quickly must the document be delivered?
- Is the recipient expecting it right way?

If a single-page document is needed urgently then fax and e-mail are options. If the document exists as a hard copy then sending it by fax will it to the recipient very quickly. A multi-page document will take a lot time to fax as the documents will need to be scanned and so e-mail might better option.

Genre

- What is the format of the material to be presented, i.e. is the information an oral format, in an audible format such as a recording, in a written for or in a visual format including graphics?

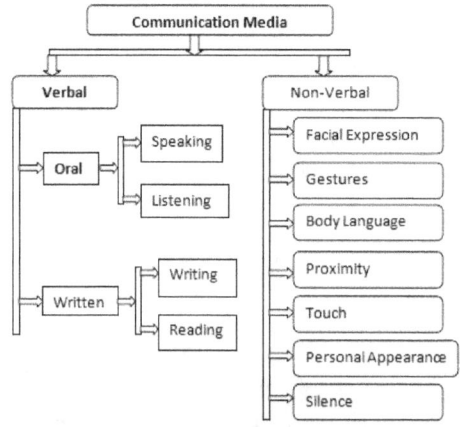

Information in an oral format has to be transmitted over the telephone during a teleconference or videoconference or recorded and attached outbound e-mail. If written, the document may be faxed or e-mailed. And in a static format

(Such as PowerPoint presentation), then the documents may be e-mailed. For audio and audiovisual materials, if in a dynamic for (Such as a live presentation) a videoconference is required.

Level of confidentiality

- How sensitive is the information being transmitted?
- Has the recipient requested that the information be kept confidential?
- Will the disclosure of all or part of the information diminish the value of information being transmitted?

The risk of unauthorized interception and disclosure exist in every medium of communication, including e-mail, especially if the information is sent unencrypted. Facsimile can also present problems for confidentially. Faxes are often of hands of one or more intermediaries before reaching their intended recipient. Including for example, Administrative assistants and mailroom employees. Also, misdirection may result by entering just one of the phone number digits incorrectly.

It is not, however, reasonable to require that a mode of communicating information must be avoided simply because interception or dissemination of the information is a violation of law.

Local/time zone

- What is the local time of the location of sender?
- What is the local time at the destination of the recipient?
- Is the recipient likely to still be in the office even awake?

In some cases senders and recipients are in the geographically remote locations in different time zones. For example, when it is 8 am in the Caribbean it is between 7pm and 9pm in Australia. For this reason, it may not matter whether a fax or e-mail sent as it is not likely to be received for a few hours. Time differences do, however, affect communication via voice calls or teleconferencing.

Cost

- What will each of the options cost?
- Which is the least expensive?
- Which is the most expensive?

E-mail is likely to be the least expensive in all cases, regardless of the size of the attachment or the destination of the message. Depending on the destination and the number of pages (hence the duration of a call), a fax transmission may work out more expensive that a brief teleconference between local participants, similarly, a relatively long teleconference among a number of international participants will be more costly than a local fax.

Organizations usually try to minimize the cost of their operations. This means that the lowest cost method should be chosen where possible.

Efficiency

How much effort required to:

- Get a documentation in the format required by a particular medium:
- Initiate the connection required:
- Transmit the document?

Efficiency is a ratio that measures output in relation to input. If a method takes more effort that it is really worth then it may make sense to select another medium.

Effectiveness

- Will the selected method allow for the transmission to be done within the time (urgency) and time zone while maintaining the required level of confidentiality?
- Will it use the lowest cost method that it also the most efficient of the options available?

Summary

Factors to be considered in the selection of communication media:

Degree of urgency.

Genre (oral, written, Visual).

Level of confidentiality.

Location/time zone.

Cost, efficiency, effectiveness

Activity 1

Use the meeting planner at http://www.worldtimerserver.com/meeting-panner.aspx to set up a meeting on the first Tuesday next month. The meeting will be at 8 am Kingston, Jamaica time and the other participants will be in Australia, St., Vincent and California, USA.

Record the meeting times in your notebook.

Chapter VIII

Document Management

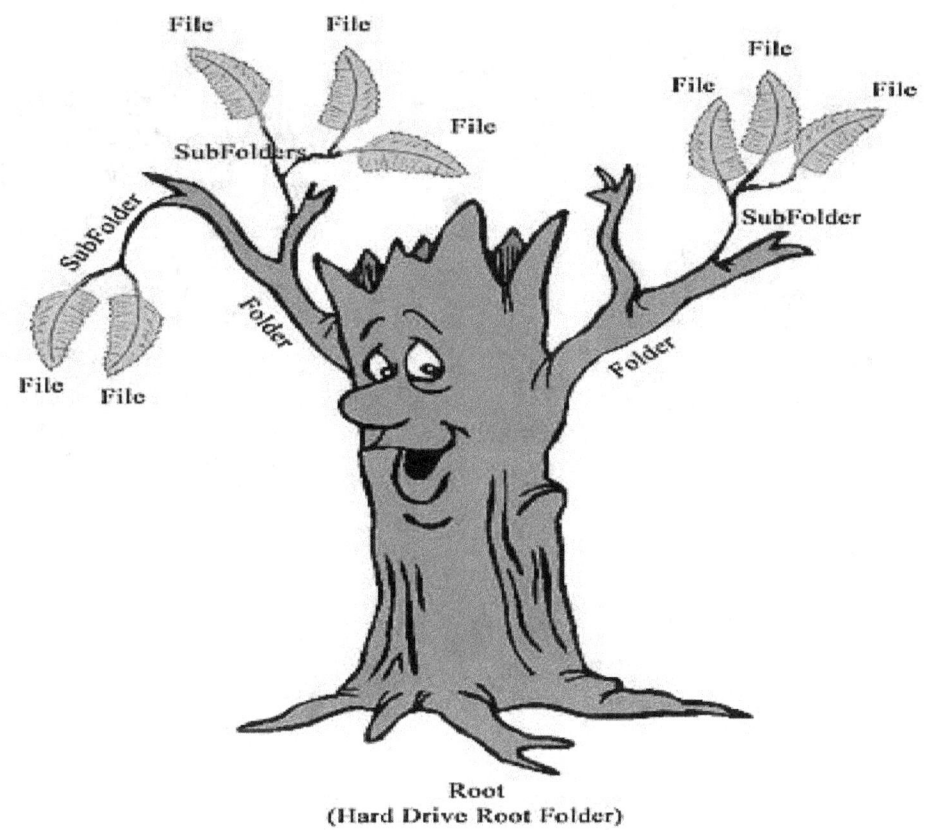

Root
(Hard Drive Root Folder)

Highlights:

- *Manual and electronic filing system*
- *Types of document*
- *Electronic Filing system*
- *Integrity of Files*
- *Security of Files*
- *Retention of Files*
- *Tracing of Documents*

L esson 1

Manual and electronic filing system

Objective

At the end of this chapter, the student should be able to:

➢ *define the manual and electronic filing system*
➢ *distinguish between a manual and electronic filing system*
➢ *compare between a manual and electronic filing system in relation to their advantages and disadvantages*

Manual filing systems

A manual filing system is one where the documents are arranged by hand into folders and stored in filing cabinets.

Advantages

Manual systems have a number of advantages over their electronic counterparts.

> ➢ They are still accessible in the vent of a power outage.
> ➢ They are more secure from the point of view that physical access is required i.e. they cannot be hacked remotely.
> ➢ They do not require the users to know how to use the computer.

Disadvantages

If someone has taken out a particular file, then other people have to wait for him/her to be finished before they can view it.

> ➢ Finding a particular document can be time consuming, particularly if it is not in the correct location.
> ➢ Manual filing systems take up a lot of space.

Electronic filing systems

An electronic filing system is a system of organizing files that utilizes hard drive space or network space. The system may either be computer software, an Internet-based program, or a simple file and folder system on the desktop of a computer. Electronic filing systems are used on multiple devices, ranging from our cell phones to our video game consoles to our digital video recorders.

Function

An electronic filing system utilizes an electronic device, such as a computer, to store and organize files for easy access. Simply placing school assignments in a folder on the desktop of your computer creates an elementary electronic filing system. Electronic filing systems offer the ability to organize various types of files on one operating system, or one type of file on a specific operating system. Electronic filing systems are used by gaming consoles, MP3 players, and throughout various applications on a computer.

Features

A computer alone is a vast electronic filing system offering various features. It begins with a large filing system, the hard drive, and splits into smaller and smaller electronic filing systems within the programs and applications on the computer. The "My Documents" folder on a computer is an electronic filing system arranging your documents in order of time created, alphabetically, or most often used, depending on your preferences. Most electronic filing systems offer the ability to search or browse through the files, allowing you to pinpoint the needed file out of the lot.

Benefits

Electronic filing systems allow us to easily find the information and files we need at the time we need them. Libraries and bookstores use electronic filing systems to keep track of the location of books. Thanks to these filing systems we can visit a kiosk, type in the book we are looking for, and be directed to it in a fraction of the time it would take us to fumble through the room trying to figure it out on our own.

Warning

While electronic filing systems relieve us of a lot of stress when they are working, they can cause chaos when they are out of order. Doctor's offices that run on electronic systems are at a loss when the power is out, or when a server tears up and must be replaced. It is always best to have a backup system when the primary system is out of commission.

Potential

Gaming consoles, computers and various handheld devices are becoming more and more advanced and the Internet is being utilized even more as a large, infinite capacity electronic filing system. Inventors and technicians believe that in a few short years we'll be able to access files from various locations all over the world, from wherever we are, at the touch of a button. In some instances, this belief is already coming to life

Advantages

➤ Since electronic filing systems utilize computers, information can be retrieved much quicker than with manual systems.

➤ Electronic filing systems also require much less space.

➤ Information that would normally fill up entire rooms if it were stored on paper, can now easily fit onto tiny disks.

➤ Electronic filing systems also make it much easier to share and access information. If information is stored electronically, several people from all over the world can access it simultaneously. A manual system, on the other hand, would require each person to physically go to the location where the information is stored in order to access it.

Disadvantages

➤ It uses computers, so when the power goes out you cannot access the information.

➤ Information that is stored electronically is vulnerable hackers.

Summary

A manual filing system is one where the documents are arranged by hand into folders and stored in filing cabinets.

An electronic filing system is one where documents are stored in computer files and organized hierarchically into folders on electronic media. The term hierarchically simple means that folders can be placed inside folders.

L esson 2

Types of Document

Objective

At the end of this chapter, the student should be able to:
- ➤ *identify types of documents used in data processing*
- ➤ *distinguish the differences between source, turnaround and machine readable documents*

Data processing refers to a class of programs that organize and manipulate data, usually large amounts of numeric data. Accounting programs are the prototypical examples of data processing applications. In contrast, word processors, which manipulate text rather than numbers, are not usually referred to as data processing applications.

The Analysis, Visualization and Data Documentation enable others to verify the quality of a given data product, and ideally, to reproduce it. It is critical that the steps followed to create that product be properly documented. For instance visualizations, plots, statistical outputs, a new dataset created by integrating multiple datasets, and so on. Whenever possible, document your workflow (the process used to clean, analyze and visualize data) noting what data products are created at each step. However, the different types of documents to be used in the course of data processing includes the source document, turnaround document and machine readable document.

A *source document* is a document whose content is needed to provide the basis, justification and/or validation of information created by a project.

Most projects have source information that forms the basis for the project's work.

Example:

o Customer specifications
o Internal business requirements
o Governmental or international authority standards to be referenced by the project
o Governmental or international authority regulations or codes of practice to be referenced by the project
o Marketing plans
o Competitors' product analyses

Such information is typically used as the source of, and/or justification for, and/or validation of, the information created in the project's database.

A **turnaround document** is a computer-created form that will be used to enter data as extra information added to it, and then returned to become an input document to be printed.

Example:

o meter cards are produced for collecting readings from gas meters, photocopiers, water meters and so on.

o some invoices or subscription renewal promotions are created by

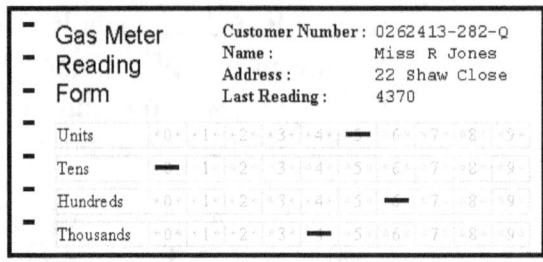

first selecting names and addresses from a computerized customer file along with any relevant information, such as amount due and/or customer matchcode

These are filled in by the customer and then printed onto a turnaround document, which is sent to the customer.

Machine readable documents

Machine-readable data is data (or metadata) which is in a format that can be understood by a computer. **In a** form that a computer can accept. Machine-readable data includes files stored on disk or tape, or data that comes from a device connected to a computer. Even typewritten pages can be considered machine-readable if you have an optical character recognition (OCR) system.

Example:

A **machine-readable passport (MRP)** is a machine-readable travel document (MRTD) where the data on the identity page is encoded in optical character recognition format.

Two types of Machine-readable data:

1. **Human-readable data** that is marked up so that it can also be read by machines.

Traditional word processing documents, hypertext markup language (HTML) and portable document format (PDF) files are easily read by humans but typically are difficult for machines to interpret. . (examples; micro formats, RDFa)

2. **Data file formats** intended principally for machines.

Format in a standard computer language (not English text) that can be read automatically by a web browser or computer system. (Example: RDF,XML - extensible markup language, JSON and CSV- comma separated values).

Summary

Data processing refers to a class of programs that organize and manipulate data, usually large amounts of numeric data.

Types of documents used in data processing

A source document is a document whose content is needed to provide the basis, justification and/or validation of information·created by a project.

A **turnaround document** is a computer-created form that will be used to enter data as extra information added to it, and then returned to become an input document to be printed.

Machine-readable data is data (or metadata) which is in a format that can be understood by a computer. In a form that a computer can accept. Machine-readable data includes files stored on disk or tape, or data that comes from a device connected to a computer.

L esson 3

Electronic Filing System

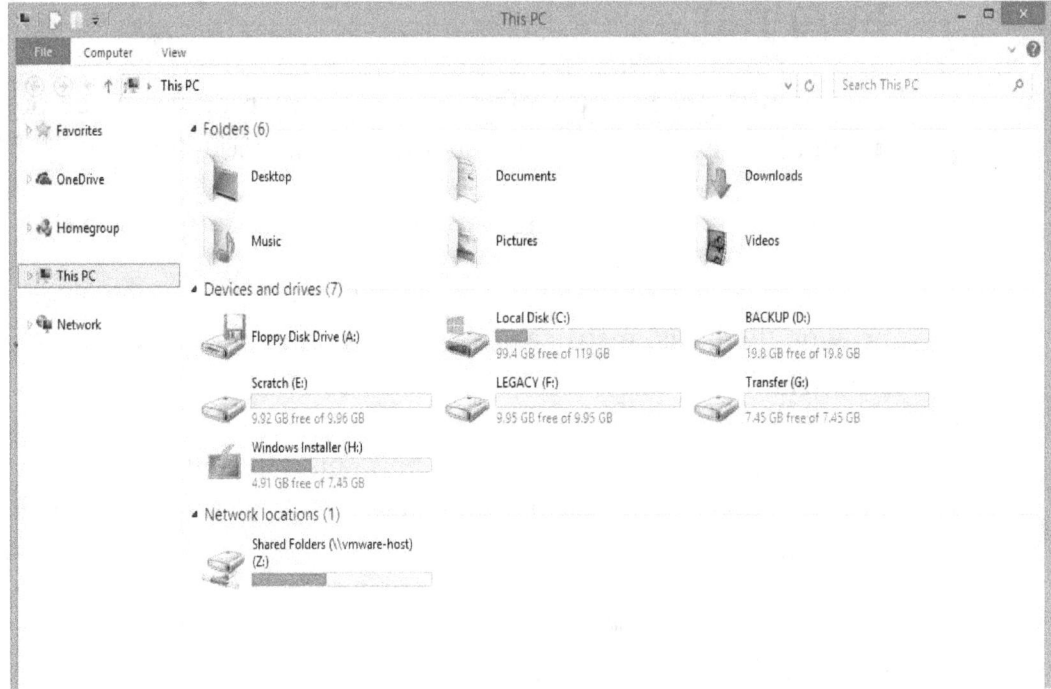

Objective

At the end of this chapter, the student should be able to:
➤ *manipulate an electronic filing system from creating to saving of files and folders*
➤ *organize files into folder, subfolders and drive*
➤ *identify the file extension containing executable and other categories*

An electronic filing system is one where documents are stored in computer files and organized hierarchically into folders on electronic media. The term hierarchically simple means that folders can be placed inside folders.

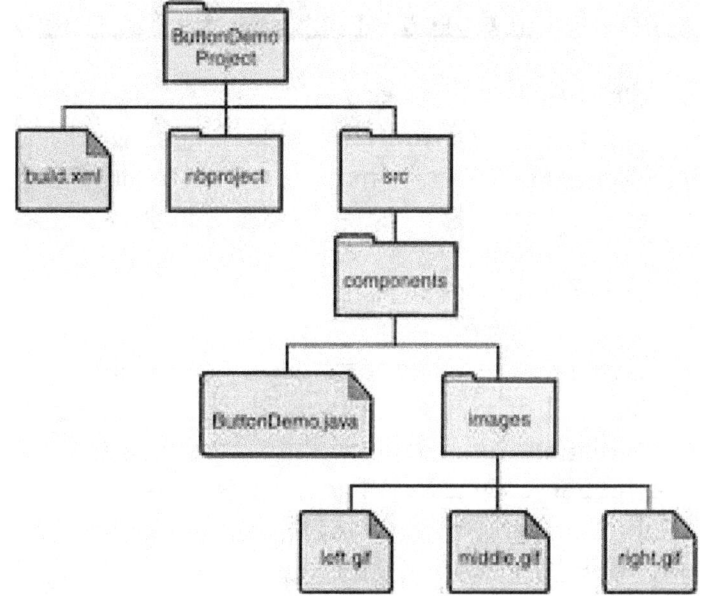

A hierarchical folder layout

There are several parallels between electronic filing systems and manual ones. For instance, virtual folders play the same role as physical ones and disks can be thought of as electronic filing cabinets.

A hierarchical structure display method adapted to an electronic filing system which manages files in a hierarchical management system, comprising:

> *storing one or more image data files in a first storage means for a page unit;*
> storing a page management table and retrieval text data in a second storage means separate from the first storage means, said page management table including at least a cabinet name, a folder name, a document name, a page name, a retrieval keyword, and a storage position in said first storage means to manage said one or more image data files according to said hierarchical management system;
> *retrieving at least one of said retrieval keyword and said retrieval text data stored in said second storage means based on a specified retrieval condition, and displaying one or more file names of said one or more image data files which match said retrieval condition;*
> *selecting and inputting a file name from said one or more file names; and*

> displaying a cabinet name, a folder name, a document name, and a page name of an image data file based on said selected and input file name, referring to said page management table in a tree form.

Organization of drives, folders and files in a hierarchical structure

One obvious way is to arrange them the same way they are displayed above – have a **drives** and **folder** for the Excel filed, one for Word and another for PowerPoint. However, it may be better to have a folder for your 2014 files and one for your 2015 files.

What are drives?

Drives are used to store data. Almost all computers come with at least two drives: a hard drive (which is used to store large volumes of data) and a floppy drive (which stores smaller volumes of data that can be easily transported from one computer to another). The hard drive is typically designated the C:\ drive and the floppy drive is typically designated the A:\ drive. If you have an additional floppy drive, it is typically designated the B:\ drive. If your hard drive is partitioned or if you have additional drives, the letters D:\, E:\, F:\, and so on are assigned.

What are folders?

Folders are used to organize the data stored on your drives. The files that make up a program are stored together in their own set of folders. You will want to organize the files you create in folders. You will want to store files of a like kind in a single folder.

What are files?

A file is an object on a computer that stores data, information, settings, or commands that are used with a computer program.

A computer usually used Windows as operating the entire system. To open Windows Explorer, locate Windows Explorer on your Start menu and then click on it. Alternatively, hold down the Windows key and type e (Windows-e).

How does Windows organize files from drives and folders organized?

Windows organizes folders and files in a hierarchical system. The drive is the highest level of the hierarchy. You can put all of your files on the drive without creating any folders. But, that is like putting all of your papers in a file cabinet without organizing them into folders. It works fine if you have only a few files, but as the number of files increases, there comes a point at which things become very difficult to find. So you create folders and put related material together in folders.

A diagram of a typical drive and how it is organized is shown here.

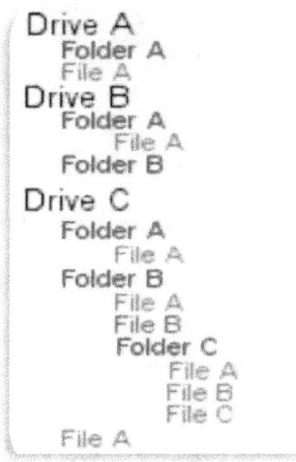

At the highest level, you have some folders and perhaps some files. You can open any of the folders and put additional files and folders into them. A hierarchy develops.

From Windows Explorer window, when you open Windows Explorer, the screen shown here will appear.

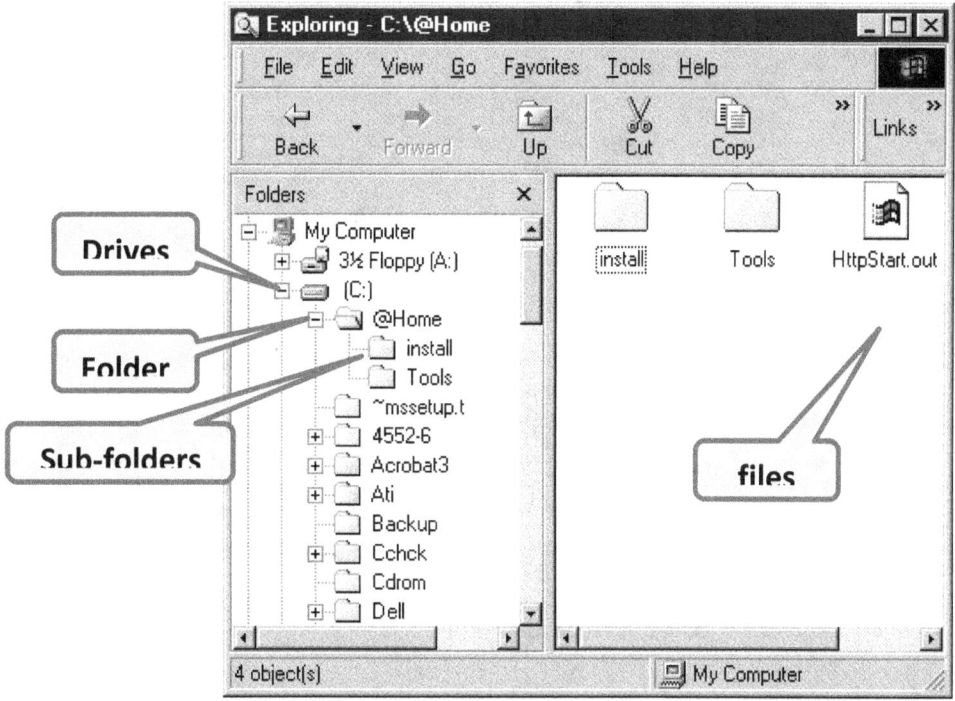

Windows explorer separates the window into two panes. If you click on an object in the left pane, the contents of the object displays in the right pane. Click on Desktop and the contents of the Desktop folder display on the right. Click on My Computer and your computer resources display on the right. To see the contents of a drive, click on the drive. To see the contents of a folder, click on the icon for the folder in the left pane.

To create a new folder when in Windows Explorer:

1. In the left pane, click on the drive or folder in which you want to create the new folder.
2. Click on any free area in the right pane. A context menu will appear.
3. Highlight New.
4. Click on Folder.
5. Type in a name for the folder.

In **Windows Explorer Views** control how Windows Explorer displays information in the right pane. Windows Explorer provides you with the following choices: Large Icons, Small Icons, List, and Details. Large Icons and Small Icons, as their names imply, determine the size of the icon. List displays all of the files and folders without supplying the size, type, or date modified. Details displays the size, type, and date modified. To change the view:

1.   Right-click on any free area in the right pane. A context menu will appear.
2.   Highlight View.
3.   Select the view you want from the drop-down menu.

To delete a file or folder:

Deleting is getting rid of a file/folder in their current storage location. Deleted files/folders never disappear completely but are temporarily placed in the recycle bin to avoid permanent disappearance of a file/folder if it was deleted by mistake.

1.   Right-click on the file or folder you want to delete. A context menu will appear.
2.   Click on Delete. Window Explorer will ask, "Are sure you want to send this object to the recycle bin?"
3.   Click on "Yes."

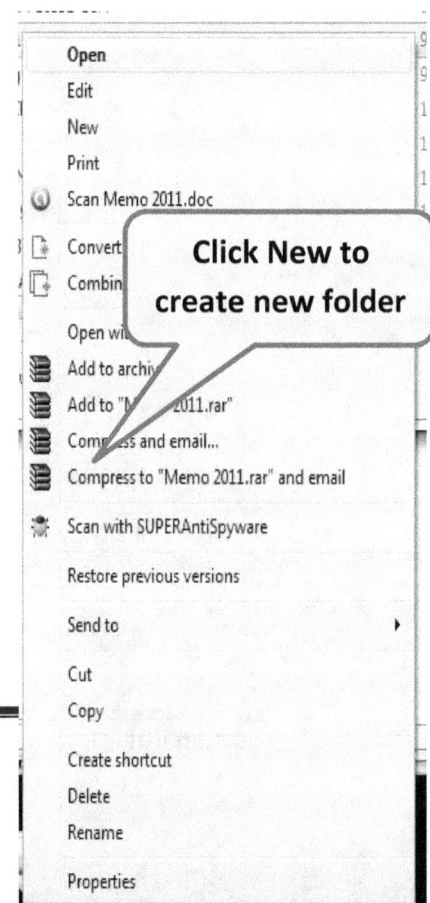

To copy a file or folder:

When you copy a file or folder, you are making a duplicate of the original item that you can then modify, delete, or store independently of the original.

     1.   Right-click on the file or folder you want to copy. A context menu will appear.

     2.   Click on Copy. The file or folder should now be on the Clipboard.

     3. To cut a file or folder:

To move a file or folder:

You can move your files and folders in Windows. Moving a file or an entire folder (including its contents) allows you to organize your files better or create a more logical structure of files to navigate through. Windows XP makes it a simple process to move files or folders to a different location.

     First, cut the file or folder through the following steps

     1.   Right-click on the file or folder you want to cut. A context menu will appear.

     2.   Click on Cut. The file or folder should now be on the Clipboard.

     Note: Cutting differs from deleting. When you cut a file, the file is placed on the Clipboard. When you delete a file, the file is sent to the Recycle Bin.

     Then, paste the file or folder to a certain location through the following steps

     1.   After cutting or copying the file, right-click on the object or in the right pane of the folder to which you want to paste. A context menu will appear.

     2.   Click on Paste.

To rename a file or folder:

This means giving a folder a new name from the previous.

     1.   Right-click on the file or folder. A context menu will appear.

     2.   Highlight Rename.

     3.   Type the new name then click Enter key.

To sort files or folders:
Sorting is arranging files/folders in a particular order i.e. alphabetically, by date, modification date, type and size.

Windows provides several new ways for you to arrange and identify your files when viewing them in folders, such as My Documents. When a folder is open, you can access each of the following view options on the **View** menu.

Show in Groups

Show in Groups allows you to group your files by any detail of the file, such as name, size, type, or date modified. For example, if you group by file type, image files appear in one group, Microsoft Word files appear in another group, and Excel files in another. Show in Groups is available in the Thumbnails, Tiles, Icons, and Details views. To show your files in groups, on the **View** menu, point to **Arrange Icons by**, and then click **Show in Groups**.

Thumbnails

Thumbnails view displays the images a folder contains on a folder icon so you can quickly identify the contents of the folder. For example, if you store pictures in several different folders, in Thumbnails view, you can tell at a glance which folder contains the pictures you want. Windows displays up to four images on a folder background, by default. Or, you can choose one picture to identify a folder in Thumbnails view. The complete folder name is displayed under the thumbnail.

Tiles

Tiles view displays your files and folders as icons. The icons are larger than those in Icon view, and the sort information you select is displayed under the file or folder name. For example, if you sort your files by type, "Microsoft Word document" appears under the file name for a Microsoft Word document.

Filmstrip

Filmstrip view is available in picture folders. Your pictures appear in a single row of thumbnail images. You can scroll through your pictures using the left and right arrow buttons. If you click a picture, it is displayed as a larger image above the other pictures. To edit, print, or save the image to another folder, double-click the picture.

Icons

Icons view displays your files and folders as icons. The file name is displayed under the icon; however, sort information is not displayed. In this view you can display your files and folders in groups.

List

List view displays the contents of a folder as a list of file or folder names preceded by small icons. This view is useful if your folder contains many files and you want to scan the list for a file name. You can sort your files and folders in this view; however, you cannot display your files in groups.

Details

In Details view, Windows lists the contents of the open folder and provides detailed information about your files, including name, type, size, and date modified. In Details view you can also show your files in groups.

To choose the details you want to display, on the **View** menu, click **Choose Details**.

Selecting files/folders
Selecting is highlighting files/folders for manipulation.

o *To select consecutive files or folders, click the first item, press and hold down SHIFT, and then click the last item.*

o *To select nonconsecutive files or folders, press and hold down CTRL, and then click each item.*

o *To select all the files and folders in the window, on the **Edit** menu, click **Select All.***

-If you have selected all files or folders and then want to clear the selection, click in a blank area in the folder window.

Refresh command
To refresh means to reload a window for better performance or to update displayed information with current data.

To refresh:

1. ***right click*** *on a blank area in a folder or desktop window*
2. *on the dropdown menu that appears click **refresh command***

Recycle Bin
This is the place in which Windows stores deleted files. You can retrieve files you deleted in error, or you can empty the Recycle Bin to create more disk space.

Organization is key for business as well as personal use. Having a good organizational skills is very important, especially when dealing with documents - which all of us do at some point.

In today's world, organization is made simple for us through the use of computers and electronic filing systems. Although this tool is available to us, we may still need a little help using it to the greatest benefit. If this describes your relationship with electronic filing, the following **guidelines** might prove beneficial:

1. Decide what information you want to organize electronically.

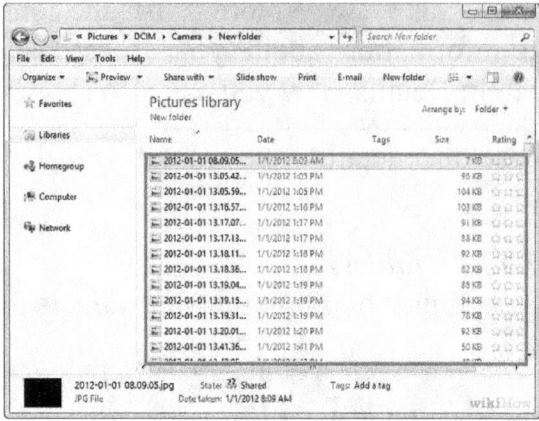

2. Create one main electronic folder that will hold all others related to the set of information you wish to organize. You may choose to label this folder whatever you like, however, most computers will have a basic default setup of folders including My Documents, My Pictures, My Music, etc. that may be useful for this purpose. Hint - when labeling folders, try to be as concise as possible, using the least amount of words that will clearly convey what the folder contains.

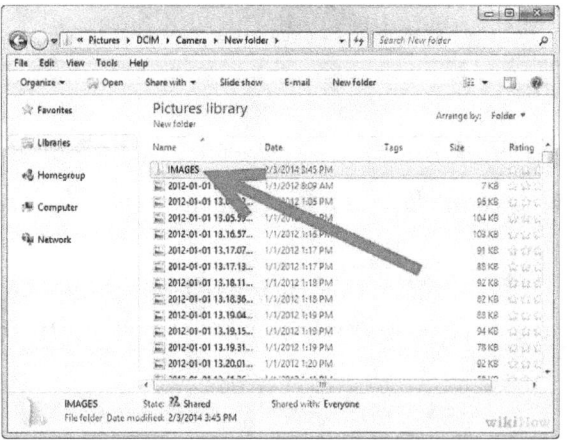

3. Depending on the amount of information that you wish to organize, you may also need to create subfolders within the main folder. For example, if you were trying to organize your taxes electronically, you might label the main folder "Taxes" and each subfolder by year. This type of folder-subfolder organization will keep your files in quick and easy access.

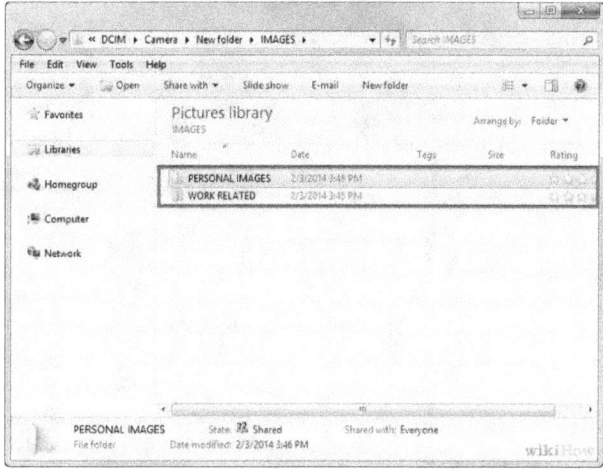

4.   Within the folders, it is best to include dates on all documents, and arrange them chronologically by such. You may want to include the date of the document in its file name as well.

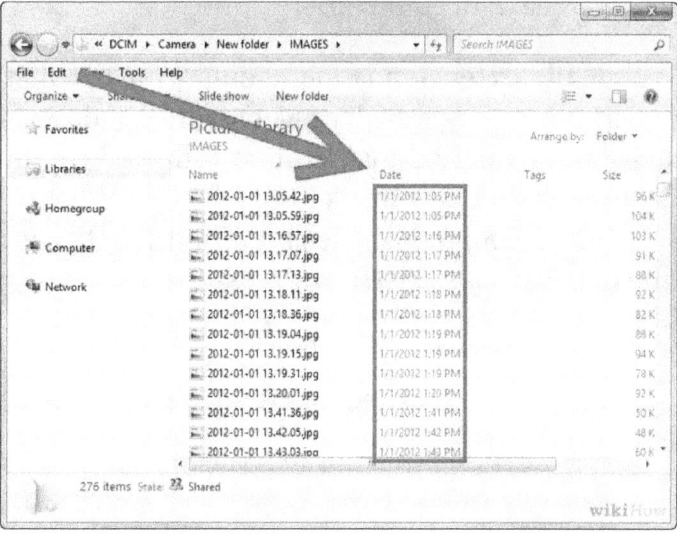

5.   Be sure to continue backing up your files to a disk, preferably every three to four weeks.

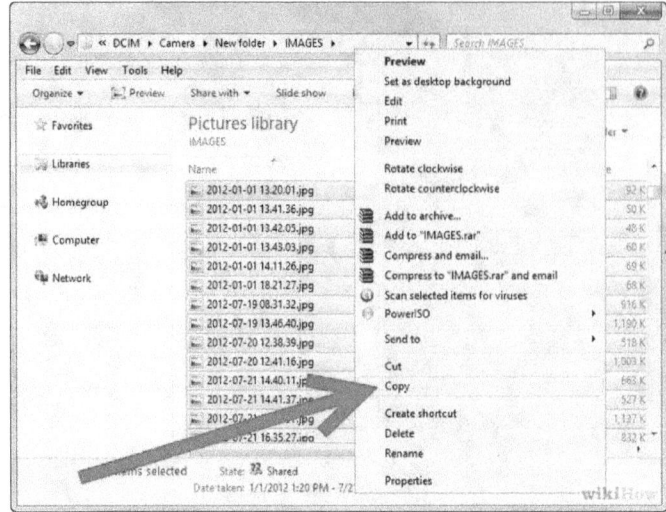

Just like with manual systems, determining how best to organize your files requires some thought. You have to consider what groups of files and files extensions have in common.

A **file extension** is the ending of a file that helps identify the type of file in operating systems such as Microsoft Windows. In Microsoft Windows, the file extension is a period that is often followed by three characters, but may also be one, two, or four characters long.

For example: the filename "myfile.txt" has an extension of ".txt", which is a file extension associated with text files.

Computer Files with File Extensions

File name is "regedit" the extension is ".exe"

regedit.exe	7/25/2012 9:08 PM	Application	156 KB
RtlExUpd.dll	6/7/2010 3:27 PM	Application extens...	1,223 KB
setupact.log	2/7/2013 5:18 PM	Text Document	182 KB
setuperr.log	11/14/2012 8:02 AM	Text Document	0 KB

http://www.computerhope.com

In the above example, the first file shown in Explorer is "regedit.exe", "regedit" is the name of the file, and ".exe" is the file extension that identifies this file as an executable file. The next file "RtlExUpd.dll", which is a DLL file and another example of a file, and finally the last two files are log files. As can be seen in this example, by having file extensions you can quickly identify the type of file and have a better idea of how that file may be opened and organized.

An **executable file** is a file that is used to perform various functions or operations on a computer. Unlike a data file, an executable file cannot be read because it has been compiled.

On an IBM compatible computer, common executable files are .BAT, .COM, .EXE, and .BIN. Depending on the operating system and its setup, there can also be other executable files.

In a graphical user interface (GUI) such as Microsoft Windows, files are shown as unique icons that relate to the program that opens the file. For example, the picture is an example of the icon associated with Adobe Acrobat PDF files. If this file was on your computer, double-clicking the icon in Windows would open that file in Adobe Acrobat or the PDF reader installed on the computer.

The different file extensions commonly used for documentation are the following:
- Microsoft Excel Files – .xls, xlm, .xlsx, .xlr, .xml and so on
- Microsoft Word Files –.doc, docx, .dot and so on
- Microsoft Powerpoint Files –.ppt, pptx, .ppi, .pot, .pps, .ppz and so on
- Graphics or pictures Files- .gif, .jpg, .jpeg, .png, .bmp, .img, .pdf and so on
- Database files- .dbf, .dbk, .dbo, .dbx, db2, .adp, .mdn and so on

However, for you to be familiar about file extensions, review Table 1 on INDEX part of this book or check the website **Computer Hope**

Summary

An electronic filing system is one where documents are stored in computer files and organized hierarchically into folders on electronic media.

Guidelines on Organising files electronically

Decide what information you want to organize electronically.

Create one main electronic folder that will hold all others related to the set of information you wish to organize.

Depending on the amount of information that you wish to organize, you may also need to create subfolders within the main folder.

Within the folders, it is best to include dates on all documents, and arrange them chronologically by such.

Be sure to continue backing up your files to a disk, preferably every

Activity VI II.3

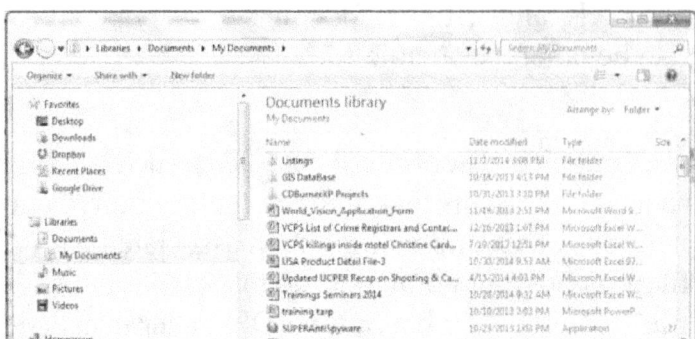

A. From the **Start** menu of your Windows, click on **Computer** tab then double click **Documents** tab under **Libraries** tab to show folder **My Documents** as shown on the figure above. Perform the following carefully:

1. Create a new folder under folder "My documents" and name it into "My1stCreation" .
2. Under the newly created folder, create a subfolder and name it into "My2ndCreation".
3. Copy the folder "My1stCreation" into your Desktop.
4. Go to your desktop folder then Rename the newly transferred folder into "MyBakup".
5. From your Desktop, move the new folder (MyBakup) to the previous folder My Documents.
6. Delete the subfolder "My2ndCreation" under folder "MyBakup".

B. Open any existing document or spreadsheet you want to duplicate or create a new Microsoft Word or Excel, then perform the following:

1. Under **File** menu, click **Save as** to create a new document or spreadsheet and name the file into "Document-1" under folder "My Documents".
2. Open the folder "My documents", then copy the newly created document into Desktop.
3. Go to your desktop folder then Rename the newly transferred file into "Document-2".
4. From your Desktop, move the new file (Document-2) to the previous folder My Documents.
5. Close the existing open document, then delete the file first file Document-1.

Exercise VIII.3

Name: _____   Score: _____/_____

Level/Section: _____   Date: _____

A. Describe the following terms: (2 mark each)

      1. files
      2. file extension
      3. Executable file
      4. electronic filing system
      5. Hierarchical structure

B. Give at least two example of file extensions containing the following: (1 mark each)

      1. executable codes
      2. word documents
      3. spreadsheets
      4. presentations
      5. graphics or pictures

C. How would you organize the files and folders in a hierarchical structure?

Lesson 4

Integrity of Files

Objective

At the end of this chapter, the student should be able to:
- ➤ *explain issues related to the integrity of files in relation to overwrite protection*

File integrity is the state of a computer (electronic) file in which no alteration, addition, or deletion has been made, and which is exactly the way it was stored by its originator.

Some issues related to the integrity of files in relation to overwrite protection, restricted access and encryption of read only access in a file.

OVERWRITE PROTECTION PERIOD

Overwrite protection period
- Is the amount of time (since the last backup) in which data is protected from being overwritten
- Is specified in hours, days, weeks, or years
- Resets to maximum whenever data is written to the media

The Overwrite protection period is the amount of time that the media is protected from being overwritten. The default Overwrite protection period for a media set is Infinite - Don't Allow Overwrite, this can however be customized by the user within the properties of the media set. If the Overwrite protection period is set to four weeks for example, the media will be protected from being overwritten for four weeks. After the four weeks are over, the media becomes "recyclable" and can be overwritten. The Overwrite protection period starts at the end of the job run, not the beginning and is extended each time a media is modified "to be explained in more detail later". Additionally any media that has an overwrite protection of "none" is immediately available to be overwritten.

APPEND PERIOD

Append period
- Is the amount of time that data may be added (appended) to the media since the media were first written to, erased, or overwritten
- Is specified in hours, days, weeks, or years
- Starts when a piece of media is allocated; resets only when the piece of media is overwritten

The Append period is the amount of time that data may be added (appended) to media. While the default Append period for a media set is Infinite - Allow Append this too can be customized by the user within the properties of the media set. If the Append period is set to four weeks for example, the media can be appended to for the next four weeks. After the four weeks are over, the media can no longer be appended to. The Append period starts at the time that a media is first allocated to a media set, this does not extend as data is written to the media as the overwrite protection period does.

How do they work together?

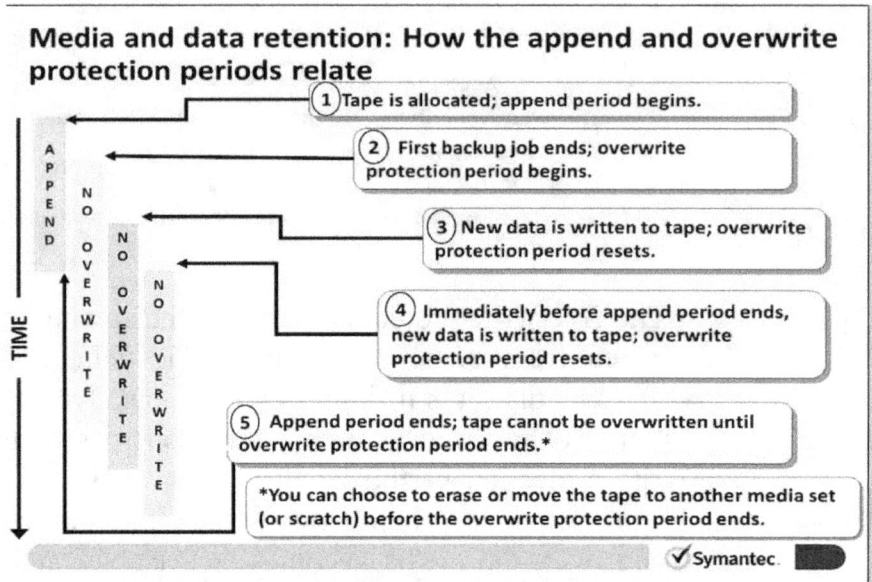

Media and data retention: How the append and overwrite protection periods relate

1. Tape is allocated; append period begins.
2. First backup job ends; overwrite protection period begins.
3. New data is written to tape; overwrite protection period resets.
4. Immediately before append period ends, new data is written to tape; overwrite protection period resets.
5. Append period ends; tape cannot be overwritten until overwrite protection period ends.*

*You can choose to erase or move the tape to another media set (or scratch) before the overwrite protection period ends.

So we now know what the overwrite protection and append periods are and how they work but how exactly do they work together and affect one another. Recall my mentioning above when the periods begin, the overwrite protection period begins each time the media is modified and the append period begins when the media is first allocated to the media set. With this in mind we can see that the overwrite protection period doesn't have a bearing on the append period while the append period has a direct impact on the overwrite protection period. The append period dictates how long the media is allowed to be modified. View the screen shot to the right for a visual representation of this process.

Overwrite protection/Retention Period Disk Storage

When writing data to a disk location the overwrite protection period provides the same type of protection as it does when writing to tape media. The protection period does not allow the backup set to be overwritten until it has reached the end of its protection. Backup Exec versions 2010 and prior will allow the media to be overwritten within the backup folder. With Backup Exec 2012 once the overwrite protection period "Retention period" has expired Backup Exec will actually reclaim the space that is being occupied by the expired media deleting the backup set all together provided it is not the last backup of a resource.

A **read-only** file is any file with the read-only attribute turned on. Some common files that are read-only by default in Windows include boot.ini, io.sys, msdos.sys and others.

A file with the read-only attribute turned on can be opened and accessed normally by your computer, but you will not be able to make changes to it. In other words, "writing" to the file is disabled.

Read-only files can be deleted and moved, but Windows will prompt you with a special dialog box asking you to confirm that you want to move or delete the read-only file.

Examples: *"I have an important spreadsheet document that I share with other users at work. If any of the formulas were to be accidentally changed, the entire spreadsheet would be useless. To help protect the spreadsheet, I set the read-only attribute on the file. Now if anyone makes changes and then tries to save them, they won't be able to."*

Summary

File integrity is the state of a computer (electronic) file in which no alteration, addition, or deletion has been made, and which is exactly the way it was stored by its originator.

The **Overwrite protection** period is the amount of time that the media is protected from being overwritten. The default Overwrite protection period for a media set is Infinite.

The **Append** period is the amount of time that data may be added (appended) to media. While the default Append period for a media set is Infinite.

A **read-only** file is any file with the read-only attribute turned on. Some common files that are read-only by default in Windows include boot.ini, io.sys, msdos.sys and others.

Lesson 5

Security of Files

Objective

At the end of this chapter, the student should be able to:
- *discuss issues related to the security of files*
- *secure files from drivers and folders*

Security of Files is imperative to recognize that automated systems, which provide essential services, are vulnerable to natural disasters or to someone who has the resources to compromise a computer system. Appropriate security measures should be taken to ensure protection from accidental and deliberate threats to confidentiality and integrity of data. Whilst it is accepted that absolute security is unrealistic, steps should be taken to optimize your computer system at a cost that is relative to the reduction in the risk.

Some issues on the security of files on computers is paramount and *the use of password* access, *firewall* and *disaster recovery mechanisms* are strongly recommended for users.

How do we used password to protect files and folders in Windows?

Before password protecting any document, you may want to create a backup of the non-password protected files and folder in case you forget the password in the future.

The majority of Microsoft Windows operating systems do not come with a method of password protecting your sensitive files and folders. If you're using Microsoft Windows 3.x, Windows 95, or Windows 98, you need to download or purchase a third-party program to password protect your files and folders in Windows; skip down to the other security solutions section if you're using one of these operating systems.

Things to remember when encrypting or password protecting files and folders:

<u>Microsoft Windows XP professional users</u>

The steps below for encrypting the files on Windows XP Professional applies to users who are using a computer that has different accounts. If you are using a single account, see the other security solutions section.

1. Select the file or folder you want to encrypt.
2. Right-click the file or folder and click **Properties**.
3. Click the **Advanced** button.
4. Check "**Encrypt contents to secure data**" option.
5. Click **Apply** and then **Ok**.

Encrypt contents to secure data is grayed out

This will be grayed out if you're using the home edition of Microsoft Windows XP. See the steps below for securing the contents of your folders in Windows XP home.

Show "Encrypt" on the context menu

The newest version of TweakUI also enables you to show the Encrypt option in the context menu. To do this, follow the steps below.

1. **Open TweakUI**.
2. In the TweakUI window, select **Explorer**
3. In the right side of the window under Settings, locate **Show 'Encrypt' on context menu** and check the box. This option should be below **Prefix 'shortcut to' on new shortcuts** and above **Show 'View workgroup computers' in NetPlaces**.

- I'm missing Show "Encrypt" on the context menu in TweakUI.

Microsoft Windows XP home users

1. Select the file or folder you want to encrypt.
2. Right-click the file or folder and click **Properties**.
3. Click the **Sharing tab**.
4. Check the box **Make this folder private**
5. Click **Apply** and then **Ok**.

Make this folder private is grayed out

In order for this option to work in Microsoft Windows XP Home edition, you must meet the below requirements.

1. The hard drive must be formatted in NTFS and not FAT32 File System.
2. T7ziphe folder you're attempting to encrypt must be in your own personal folder. For example, if your name is bob, you must be encrypting a folder that is or that is contained within the below folder: C:\Documents and Settings\Bob\

Microsoft Windows Vista/7/8 users

Unfortunately, Windows Vista, Windows 7, and Windows 8 do not provide any features for password protecting files or folders. You need to use a third-party software program to accomplish this.

If you want to encrypt a file or folder, this can be done by following these steps:

1. Select the file or folder you want to encrypt.
2. Right-click the file or folder and click **Properties**.
3. Click the **Advanced** button.
4. Check **"Encrypt contents to secure data"** option.
5. Click **Apply** and then **Ok**.

Note:7 If you are not able to select the "Encrypt contents to secure data" option (it is greyed out) or do not see the option in general, you likely have a version of Windows that does not support this feature, like Home edition. It is also possible that the hard drive where the files are located is not formatted as NTFS, as this is a requirement for the encryption feature.

There are other security solutions for protecting your files and folders in Windows

➢ *For file and folders not frequently used*

If you need to password protect files or folders that you do not frequently use, one of the simplest ways is to compress the folder and files with a compression utility and password protect the compressed file. However, each time you want to work with or modify the files, you need to uncompress the files using the password.

Windows ME and Windows XP users - Windows ME and Windows XP come with their own compression utility. This utility can also be used to compress and password protect files.

Windows Vista and Windows 7 users - Windows Vista and Windows 7 also include a compression utility. However, password protection for the compressed files is not possible without the use of a third-party software program.

Tip: When a file is compressed, users can still view a listing of the files in the compressed file. If you want both your file names and the contents to be hidden, move all the files into a single folder and password protect that folder.

➢ *For file and folders frequently used or accessed*

If you need to password protect or encrypt data you frequently use, you need to install a third-party program that allows you to protect your files and folders. Below are some free and commercial solutions.

- **7-Zip** - A free file and folder zipping utility, which also includes the ability to password protect zipped files and folders.
- **AxCrypt** - An excellent free encryption utility that enables users to encrypt all files within a folder and not allow those files to be viewed unless a passphrase (password) is known.
- **Folder Guard** - A commercial version of a password protection software that enables you to password protect files, folders, and other Windows resources.
- Protected Folder- For a small fee, it's an excellent software program that enables you to password protect folders.

Things to remember when encrypting or password protecting files and folders

1. There is no such thing as a 100% protected file. There are numerous tools, utilities, and instructions for how to break encryption and passwords on files. However, the protection methods listed above will protect your files from the majority of users who may encounter them. If you are working with really sensitive data, we suggest a commercial product for protecting your files and data.

2. Even though a file or folder may be password protected, it still can be deleted (unless the program supports the ability to protect files from being deleted). Always remember to backup all your files, even those protected by passwords.
3. If you forget the password, unless you're willing to spend the time attempting to break it or pay someone else to break the password, all the data in the file or folder will be lost. Thus, it is important to backup a copy of the non-password protected files or folders, just in case.

Password

Password is sometimes abbreviated as **PWD** (not to be confused with the Linux pwd command), a **password** is a set of secret characters or words utilized to gain access to a computer, web page, network resource, or data. Passwords help ensure that computers or data can only be accessed by those who have been granted the right to view or access them.

Strong password - Term used to describe a password that is an effective password that would be difficult to break. Often a strong password has between six and ten characters (the more the better), numbers, other characters, and both upper and lowercase characters. Below is an example of a strong password.

1SecreT!2

Weak password - A password that is not an effective password because it's easy to remember. Names, birth dates, phone numbers, and easily guessable words are considered weak passwords. Below is an example of a weak password.

secret

Encrypt

The process of making data unreadable by other humans or computers for the purpose of preventing others from gaining access to its contents. **Encrypted** data is generated using an encryption program such as PGP, encryption machine, or a simple encryption key and appears as garbage until it is decrypted. In order to read or

!

Section 7.11 - Document Management

use the data, it must be decrypted, and only those who have the correct password or decryption key are able to make the data readable again.

A very basic encryption technique known as **simple substitution**, **substitution cipher**, or**Caesar cipher** (named after Julius Caesar) that shifts the letters of the alphabet over a few characters. For example, as shown below the alphabet has been shifted over four characters.

What is a safe way to remember my passwords?

Keeping track of all your passwords can be a daunting task. However, there are dozens of different programs known as password managers designed to keep track of all your passwords for you securely. We highly recommend **Keepass** a free, open source, and small password manager that is easy to use. This program can be found and downloaded from**http://keepass.info/**

If you want an online tool that you can sync between multiple devices including your phone, tablet, and different computers as well as Autofill your form fields we highly recommend **Dashlane**. Dashlane makes it extremely easy to manage your passwords and warns about unsecure passwords and shared passwords. Dashlane can be found on the Android and Apple stores and downloaded from **http://www.dashlane.com/**

Keeping your passwords in a program such as Keepass or Dashlane will encrypt your password data and is a much better solution than saving your passwords in a unencrypted text document or even worse on a Post-it note stuck to your monitor.

For password protecting Microsoft Word and Excel documents

The following steps give users of Microsoft Word and Excel instructions on password protecting their documents. One should be note that it's generally a good idea to create a backup copy of your file without a password in the event that you forget it. Should you choose to do so, it is best not to store the unprotected file locally, but rather on a USB stick.

1. Open Microsoft Word or Excel and the document or spreadsheet you want to put a password on.
2. In the top left-hand corner of the screen, Click the **Microsoft Office Button**.
3. In the dropdown menu that appears, move your mouse cursor over **Prepare** and click **Encrypt Document**.
4. Once you have selected a password, type it in the **Password box**, then click **OK**.
5. Type your password one more time in the **Reenter Password** field and click **OK.**
6. **Save** the file to save your new password.

Password to open - Entering a password for this option makes the file only readable by users who know the password.

Password to modify - Similar to read-only, this option allows the file to be viewed, but only users with the password may edit and save the file. Keep in mind, however, that a user could open the file then copy its contents to their own document.

Removing a password - To remove the password from a protected document, follow the steps in the previous section, but delete the characters entered in the Password fields.

Firewall

A **firewall** is a software utility or hardware device that limits outside network access to a computer or local network by blocking or restricting network ports. Firewalls are a great step for helping prevent un-authorized access to a company or home network.

Windows Firewall
http://www.computerhope.com

Example: a hardware firewall, the ZyXEL ZyWALL a Unified Security Gateway with a Firewall and other security features.

In addition to hardware firewalls like that shown above, basic hardware firewalls are also commonly found in most network routers and can be configured and setup through the router setup.

ZyXEL ZyWALL with Firewall

Software firewalls are designed to protect the computer they are installed onto by blocking any unrestricted programs from sending and receiving information from the network or Internet.

A good example of a software Firewall is the *Windows Firewall* that is included with Microsoft Windows.

1.1 Things you should know about this tool before you start

A firewall acts like a doorman or guard for your computer. It has a set of rules about what information should be let in and out of your computer. A firewall is the first program that receives and analyses incoming information from the Internet and the last program that scans outgoing information to the Internet.

It prevents hackers or other intruders from accessing personal information stored on your computer, and prevents malware programs from sending information to the Internet without your authorization. **COMODO Firewall** is a well-known and respected firewall software. It is free software, which means you can use it without purchasing a license.

Running a custom firewall program may initially require considerable time and effort to ensure that all the settings are correct and suited to the way you use your computer. After an initial learning period, the firewall will work seamlessly, requiring minimal intervention on your part.

Warning!: Never access the Internet without a firewall installed and running on your computer! Even if your Internet modem or router has its own firewall, it is strongly recommended that you have one installed on your computer as well.

Disaster Recovery Mechanism

What You Can Recover?

Computer Crashed? Important Files deleted? We got them all recovered!

Supported Files

DocumentDOC/DOCX, XLS/XLSX, PPT/PPTX, PDF, CWK, HTML/HTM, INDD, EPS, etc.

PhotoJPG, TIFF/TIF, PNG, BMP, GIF, PSD, CRW, CR2, NEF, ORF, RAF, SR2, MRW, DCR , WMF, DNG, ERF, RAW, etc.

VideoAVI, MOV, MP4, M4V, 3GP, 3G2, WMV, ASF, FLV, SWF, MPG, RM/RMVB, etc.

AudioAIF/AIFF, M4A, MP3, WAV, WMA, MID/MIDI, OGG, AAC, etc.

Message & EmailsPST, DBX, EMLX, etc.

ArchiveZIP, RAR, SIT, etc.

Supported Devices	 **Recycle Bin:**PC/Mac/Laptop/Handy...	**Memory Cards:**SD, SDHC, microSD, miniSD, CF, SmartMedia, MMC, XD...
	Hard Drives: Dell, IBM, HP, Toshiba, Sony...	 **Removable Drives**Seagate, WD, Apple, Samsung, Toshiba...
	Flash DrivesUSB Drives, Jump Drives, Pen Drives, Thumb Drives...	**Digital Camera/Camcorder:**Canon, Kodak, Nikon, Sony, JVC...

Data loss scenarios	**Accidental deletion**	• "Shift + Del" without backup • Deleting files by right- clicking menu or just pressing 'Delete' button • Emptying Recycle Bin without backup
	Formatting	• "Media/Drive is not formatted, would you like to format it now?" • Disk initialization when digital camera memory card is just connected • Unexpectedly formatted hard drive
	Improper operation	• Factory setting of device without backup • Turning off the camera during the writting process • Using the same memory card in

different cameras
- Pulling out SD card while the camera is on
- Improper partition or partition error

- Computer virus
- Unexpected power off
- Reinstalled windows system or hard disk crash
- The partition structure on a hard disk was fragmented or partition table is invalid.

Also cases like

Summary

Security of Files is imperative to recognize that automated systems, which provide essential services, are vulnerable to natural disasters or to someone who has the resources to compromise a computer system.

Password is sometimes abbreviated as **PWD** (not to be confused with the Linux pwd command), a **password** is a set of secret characters or words utilized to gain access to a computer, web page, network resource, or data.

A **firewall** is a software utility or hardware device that limits outside network access to a computer or local network by blocking or restricting network ports. Firewalls are a great step for helping prevent un-authorized access to a company or home network.

Lesson 6

Retension of Files

The **retention period** of a document is an aspect of records management represents the period of time a document should be kept or "retained" both electronically and in paper format. At the termination of the retention period, the document is usually destroyed.

The term is generally used by accountants and tax professionals whose occupation involves dealing with legal documents that only need to remain in existence for a certain amount of time.

The retention period varies for different types of records.

For example, *business incorporation documents have a permanent retention period (meaning that they should be retained and never be destroyed), but receipts for tax-deductible purchases by an individual taxpayer usually have a three-year retention period (and can often be safely discarded after that point.)*

The length of the retention period vary by industry and are based on the likelihood that the document will be needed at some point in the future for litigation reasons. Records that will serve no further purpose (as determined by the length of their retention period) are destroyed for space issues, usually by paper shredders. Document retention periods also differ by country as well as by document type.

Lesson 7

Tracing of Document

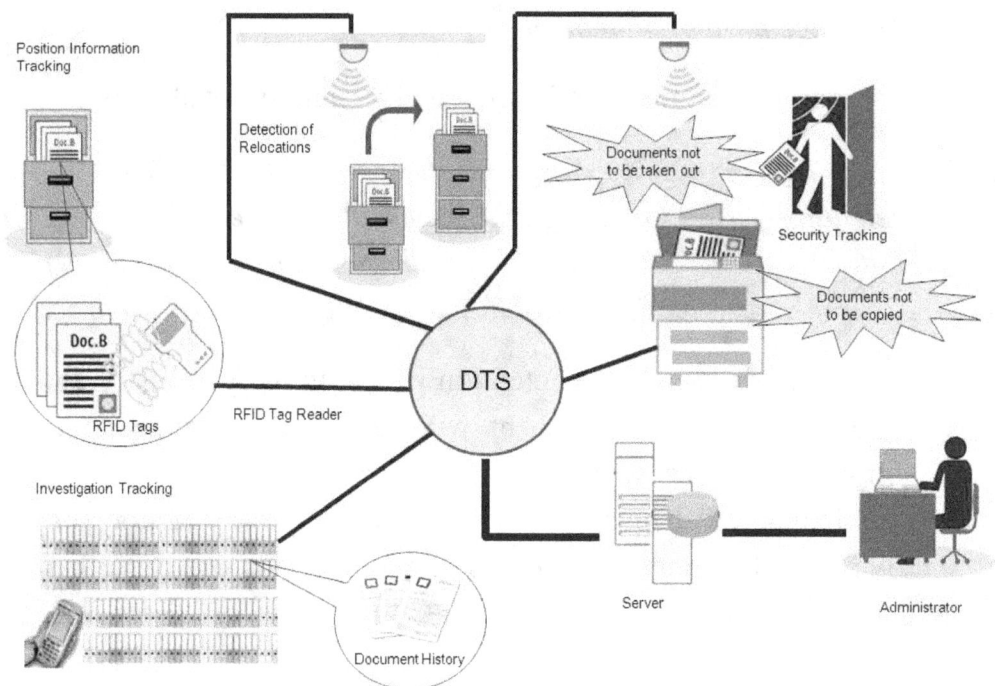

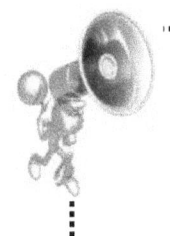

Objective

At the end of this chapter, the student should be able to:
➢ *explain methods for tracing document versions*

Method for tracing documents version:

1. **Versioning** successive versions of documents that change over time.

2. **Metadata** is data that describes other data. Meta is a prefix that in most information technology usages means "an underlying definition or description." Metadata summarizes basic information about data *stored on document, including date created, date modified, date accessed, owner, access privileges*, which can make finding and working with particular instances of data easier.

There are two *metadata* types:

1. Structural *metadata*, about the design and specification of data structures or "data about the containers of data"; and
2. Descriptive *metadata* about individual instances of application data or the data content. *Metadata* was traditionally in the card catalogs of libraries.

Chapter IX

Ethics

Highlights:

- *Concepts of Intellectual Property*
- *Intellectual Property Laws*
- *Ethical standard with respect to Intellectual Property*
- *Concept of plagiarism*
- *Guidelines to avoid plagiarism*
- *Acceptable standard of work*
- *Desirable habits and work attitudes*

L esson 1

Concepts of Intellectual Property

Objective

At the end of this chapter, the student should be able to:
- ➤ *define intellectual property*
- ➤ *explain the concept of intellectual property*

What is Intellectual Property?

Intellectual property (IP) conceptualized as the protection of the rights of persons who produce, gather or disseminate ideas and information, including authors, singers and journalists. It relates to items of information or knowledge that can be incorporated into tangible objects at the same time in an unlimited number of copies at different locations anywhere in the world. The property is not in those copies but in the information or knowledge reflected in them.

Therefore, the most important aspect of intellectual property is the created work to be protected. IP is usually divided into two categories:

For example:

- **Industrial property** -business owners are granted exclusive rights on the use of Inventions (patents), Trade marks (words, phrases, symbols), Industrial designs, and geographical indications which were established by them.

- **Copyright** - creative artistes are granted copyrights on Novels, Poems, Plays, Films, Musical works, and Artistic works for their creations like drawings, Paintings, Photographs, Sculptures and Architectural design.

Copyright

Copyright is a legal term used to describe the rights that creators have over their literary and artistic works. Works covered by copyright range from books, music, paintings, sculpture and films, to computer programs, databases, advertisements, maps and technical drawings.

What is protected by copyright?

Copyright protects the expression of ideas (e.g. words and illustrations). Ideas alone are not protected.

The following may be protected under copyright law:

- Literary works (e.g., written works, source codes of computer programs)
- Dramatic works (e.g.,. scripts for films and dramas)
- Musical works (e.g., melodies)
- Artistic works (e.g., paintings, photographs)
- Published editions of the above works
- Sound recordings
- Films
- Television and radio broadcasts
- Cable programmes
- Performances

What is not protected by copyright?

Subject matter not protected by copyright include:

- Ideas or concepts
- Discoveries
- Procedures
- Methods
- Works or other subject matter that have not be made in a tangible form in a recording or writing
- Subject matter that is not of original authorship

Copyright and registered designs

When an artistic work, such as a drawing or a sculpture, is applied to a product and industrially produced (i.e. more than 50 copies of the products are produced), the copyright protection will no longer cover that artistic work. It may be protected as a registered design under the Registered Designs Act (Cap. 266), if the registration criteria are met.

Rights of a copyright owner

Literary, dramatic and musical works	Authors enjoy the exclusive rights to: - reproduce the work;

	- publish the work; - perform the work in public; - communicate the work to the public; and - make an adaptation of the work.
Artistic works	Artists enjoy the exclusive right to: - reproduce the work; - publish the work; and - communicate the work to the public.
Published editions of literary, dramatic, musical or artistic works	The publisher has the exclusive right to make a reproduction of the edition.
Sound recordings	The producer of a sound recording enjoys the exclusive rights to: - make a copy of the sound recording; - rent out the sound recording; - publish the sound recording if it is unpublished; and - make available to the public a sound recording by means or as part of a digital audio transmission.* * Where the sound recording is made available to the public through a non-interactive digital audio transmission, the producer of the recording shall be entitled to equitable remuneration. This remuneration can be agreed between the parties or determined by the Copyright Tribunal.

Films	The producer of a film enjoys the exclusive rights to: • make a copy of the film; • cause the film to be seen in public; and • communicate the film to the public.
Television and radio broadcasts	The broadcaster enjoys the exclusive rights to: • make a recording of the broadcast; • rebroadcast; • communicate the broadcast to the public; and • cause the broadcast to be seen or heard by a paying audience.
Cable programmes	The producer of the cable programme enjoys the exclusive rights to: • make a recording of the cable programme; • communicate the cable programme to the public; and • cause the cable programme to be seen or heard by a paying audience.
Performances	The performer has the right to authorise the following uses: • allow the performance to be seen and heard, or seen or heard, live in public; • make a direct or indirect sound recording of his live performance; • make available a recording of the

| | performance to the public in such a way that the recording may be accessed by any person from a place and at a time chosen by him; |
| | <ul><li>sell, rent, offer for sale, distribute or import such recordings for these purposes;</li><li>publish a recording of a performance (if not previously published); and</li><li>communication of the live performance to the public (including broadcasting, internet dissemination and inclusion of the performance in a cable programme).</li></ul> |

"Communicate" means to transmit by electronic means a work or other subject matter, whether or not it is sent in response to a request, and includes:

1.   broadcasting;
2.   inclusion in a cable programme; and
3.   the making available of the work or other subject matter in such a way that the work or subject matter may be accessed by any person from a place and at a time chosen by him (e.g. access over the internet).

Term of protection
The duration varies according to the type of copyright work concerned.

| Literary, dramatic, musical and artistic works | 70 years from the end of the year in which the author died.

Specifically for photographs, or if the work is published after the death of the author, it lasts for 70 years, from the end of the year in which the work was first published. |
| Published editions of | 25 years from the end of the year in which the |

literary, dramatic, musical or artistic works (layout)	edition was first published.
Sound recordings and films	70 years from the end of the year in which the sound recording or film was first published.
Broadcasts and cable programmes	50 years from the end of the year of making the broadcast or cable programme.
Performances	70 years from the end of the year of the performance.

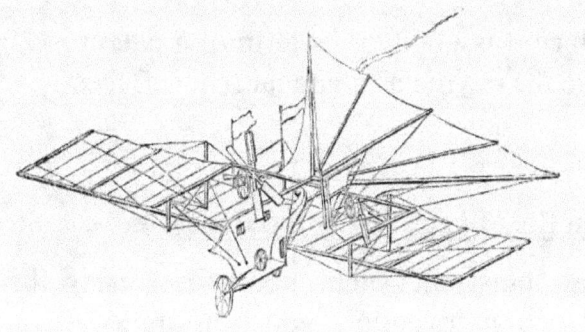

(IMAGE: CLIPART.COM)

Patents

A patent is an exclusive right granted for an invention. Generally speaking, a patent provides the patent owner with the right to decide how - or whether - the invention can be used by others. In exchange for this right, the patent owner makes technical information about the invention publicly available in the published patent document.

(IMAGE: WIPO/GEN A)

A patentable invention can be a product or a process that gives a new technical solution to a problem. It can also be a new method of doing things, the composition of a new product, or a technical improvement on how certain objects work.

Once it is granted, its term of a patent is 20 years from the Date of Filing, subject to the payment of annual renewal fees.

The benefits of registering a patent

Once you register a patent, apart from using the patent to prevent others from exploiting your invention, you can employ it to raise funds for your business, license it to third parties for commercial returns or sell the patented invention.

For an invention to be patentable, it must, in general, satisfy three key criteria:

<u>**1. New**</u> – The invention should not be publicly known in any way, anywhere in the world.

Owners of inventions should be careful to keep the invention secret until a patent application has been successfully made. If the idea has already been talked about, commercially exploited, advertised or demonstrated, then the novelty of the invention may be compromised.

If the invention needs to be disclosed to a third party before a patent application has been made, a non-disclosure agreement should be drawn up.

Once a Date of Filing has been obtained for the patent application, the invention can claim a "Patent Pending" status and the applicant can proceed to disclose the invention as indicated in the patent application to interested parties. As part of the application process, the patent application will be published after 18 months and if the statutory requirements are met. Once published, details of the invention will be made available for public inspection.

2. Inventive step – The invention must be something that represents an improvement over any existing product or process that is already available.

The improvement must not be obvious to someone with technical skills or knowledge in the invention's particular field. If an invention is new yet obvious to a person skilled in the art, the invention would not fulfil the inventive step requirement.

3. Industrial application – The invention must be useful and have some form of practical application. It should be capable of being made or used in some form of industry.

The following is not a patentable invention:

- An invention of a method for the treatment of the human or animal body by surgery or therapy, or of a diagnosis practised on the human or animal body.
- An invention that could encourage offensive, immoral or anti-social behaviour, even if it satisfies the key criteria for patents.

Trademarks

A trademark is a sign capable of distinguishing the goods or services of one enterprise from those of other enterprises. Trademarks date back to ancient times when craftsmen used to put their signature or "mark" on their products.

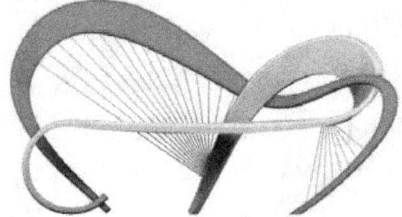

(IMAGE: COURTESY OF MIHAIL STAMATI)

A trade mark can be represented graphically in the form of your company's logo or a signature.

Through a registered trade mark, you can protect your brand (or "mark") by restricting other people from using its name or logo.

Once acquired, a trade mark can last indefinitely as long as you renew it every 10 years. Because a registered trade mark is a form of IP, you can license or assign it to others.

The benefits of registering a trade mark

It is not compulsory to register a trade mark in Singapore.

For a mark that is not registered, you may rely on your rights under the common law action of "passing off" to protect your mark against imitation or infringement.

However, if you register a trade mark in relation to your goods and/or services, you are effectively gaining a statutory monopoly of your mark. A trade mark can add value to your business because it can be used to protect your market share, you can license it to third parties such as a franchisee, or you can sell it outright for a specified value. You can also use a trade mark to help you to raise equity for the development of your business.

Trade Mark Classification

Singapore uses the International Classification of Goods and Services, under the Nice Agreement, to classify trade mark registrations. This classification sets out 34 different classes of goods and 11 classes of services that a trader can register in relation to a mark. The full list of classes can be found here.

Letters, words, names, signatures, labels, devices, tickets, shapes, colours or any combination of these elements can be registered as a trade mark but a mark must be distinctive and capable of distinguishing your goods or services from similar ones of other traders.

The following are some common examples of marks that cannot be registered as a trade mark:

- Marks that are descriptive (e.g. super, best, cheap, one dozen)
- Marks that are common to your trade (ones that have become well accepted in relation to your trade and do not distinguish the goods or service you are offering)
- Marks that could offend or promote immoral behaviour
- Deceptive marks (ones that could misrepresent the nature, quality or geographical origin of the goods or services)
- Marks that are identical to earlier marks
- Marks that could cause confusion (similar or identical to an earlier mark and in relation to similar or identical goods or services provided by the owners of the earlier mark)
- Marks that are identical or similar to Well Known Marks

You can check whether the mark you wish to register is similar or identical to an earlier mark via eFiling.

Trade mark symbols

If you successfully register a trade mark, you are permitted to use the ® symbol next to your mark. Another common symbol associated with trade mark is ™ – this denotes that the mark is being used by the company as their trade mark but it does not mean that the mark is registered or protected under the trade mark law.

Other marks

There are a number of other types of marks that you might find are appropriate for your business.

- **Certification mark**

  This mark is granted to people who wish to certify the characteristics of a particular goods or service. The certification can relate to the origin, material or mode of manufacture of the goods, or the performance, quality or accuracy of a service. By applying for a certification mark, goods and services are easily distinguishable from other non-certified goods or services on the market. For example, if your product is organic, you may be in a position to use a certified organic mark on your packaging.

- **Collective marks**

  This is a sign that is used to distinguish the goods and services offered by an association or group of traders from those being offered by non-members of the association. Once registered, all members of the group can use the collective mark; it is an effective way to indicate that your business is a member of a wider group of traders.

Government agency marks (Rule 13)

IPOS has a separate database for all logos or devices that are used by government agencies. These may not be registered marks if the agency isn't providing goods or services. However, if you are looking to register a logo that might be similar to one being used by a government agency, you will need to seek permission from that particular organization before you utilize it.

Industrial designs

An industrial design constitutes the ornamental or aesthetic aspect of an article. A design may consist of three-dimensional features, such as the shape or surface of an article, or of two-dimensional features, such as patterns, lines or color.

A design refers to the features of a shape, configuration, pattern or ornament applied to an article by any industrial process. If you register a design, you will be protecting the external appearance of the article. Registered Designs are used primarily to protect designs for industrial use.

The benefits of registering a design

By registering a design, you obtain a right to ownership and the right to prevent others from using the design without your permission. You can exploit your design in many ways. You may use it to better protect your market share by barring copying by others, license it to third parties for commercial returns or sell the design for a sum of money.

To qualify for registration, a design must, in general, satisfy two key criteria:

1. The Design must be new – The registered design must not have been registered in Singapore or elsewhere, or published anywhere in the world before the date of application of the first filing. Thus the owner of a design should be careful not to disclose the design to anyone until a design application is filed.

Generally, a design is not new if it:

- has been registered;

- has been published anywhere in the world, in respect of the same or any other article; or
- differs only in immaterial details, or features, from other designs that are commonly found in trade.

2. The Design must be industrially applied onto an article – The registered design has to be applied to an article by an industrial process. This means that more than 50 copies of the article must have been or are intended to be produced for sale or hire.

Designs that cannot be registered

Under the Registered Designs Act and Rules, the following cannot be registered:

- Designs that are contrary to public order or morality.
- Computer programmes or layout designs of integrated circuits.
- Designs applied to certain articles; such as wall plaques, medals and medallions, and printed matter primarily of a literary or artistic character (e.g. calendars, certificates, coupons, greeting cards, leaflets, maps, playing cards, postcards, stamps, and similar articles).
- Methods or principles of construction.
- Designs that are solely functional.

Designs that are dependent upon the appearance of another article, of which it is intended by the designer to form an integral part of another article, so that either article may perform its function.

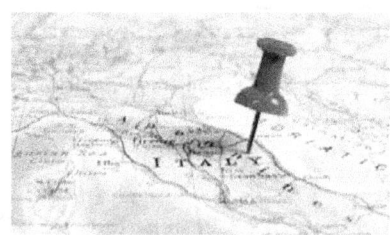

(PHOTO: ISTOCKPHOTO.COM/MATTJEACOCK)

Geographical indications

Geographical indications and appellations of origin are signs used on goods that have a specific geographical origin and possess qualities, a reputation or characteristics that are essentially attributable to that place of origin. Most commonly, a geographical indication includes the name of the place of origin of the goods.

A geographical indication (GI) is a sign that identifies a product as originating from a particular location which gives that product a special quality or reputation or other characteristic. Well-known examples of GIs include Bordeaux (wine), Darjeeling (tea) and Tuscany (olive oil).

Protection for a GI

Under the Geographical Indications Act, it is not necessary to file an application to protect the GI.

In Singapore, a GI can be protected under the Geographical Indications Act (Cap. 117B). It may also be eligible for registration as a trade mark under the Trade Marks Act (Cap. 332).
A GI is distinct from a trade mark. A GI informs consumers that a product comes from a certain place and has special qualities due to that place of origin, while a trade mark is used to distinguish a business' goods or services from those of its competitors. A GI may be used by all producers or traders whose products originate from that place and which share typical characteristics, while a trade mark gives its owners the right to prevent others from using the trade mark.

In Singapore, the law protects only the GIs of a country which is a member of the World Trade Organization, a party to the Paris Convention for the Protection of Industrial Property, or a country designated by the Singapore Government as a qualifying country from which GIs of that country can be protected. In addition, the GI must be protected in its country of origin. The producer, trader or association of such producers or traders of any such GI enjoy automatic protection.

GIs that are not protected

It is important to note the following instances where a GI will not be protected:

- It is immoral or against public order;
- It is no longer in use or no longer protected in the country of origin;
- It has become the common name in Singapore for the goods or services which it identifies;
- [for wines and spirits] it has been used continuously for at least 10 years preceding 15 April 1994 or in good faith preceding that date;
- It is confusingly similar to a trade mark for which rights had been acquired before the GI is protected in its country of origin; or
- It is the name of a person or a predecessor in a particular business.

Rights and remedies

In Singapore, a producer, trader or an association of producers or traders can sue for false use of a GI by an unauthorized party when the GI is used in a situation where it is misleading, unfair or dishonest, or where the GI used identifies a wine or spirit that does not originate from the place as indicated by the GI.

A producer, trader or an association can exercise his rights under the Geographical Indications Act by taking legal action against the infringing party.

Summary

Intellectual property conceptualized as the protection of the rights of persons who produce, gather or disseminate ideas and information, including authors, singers and journalists

<u>**Types of intellectual property**</u>

- Copyright
- A patent
- A trademark
- An industrial design
- Geographical indications

Lesson 2
Intellectual Property Laws

Intellectual property (IP) is protected in law by, for example, patents, copyright and trademarks, which enable people to earn recognition or financial benefit from what they invent or create. By striking the right balance between the interests of innovators and the wider public interest, the IP system aims to foster an environment in which creativity and innovation can flourish.

Rights that are protected by intellectual property laws are:

    a) **Economic rights:** *involves the payment for use of the product by third parties.*

    b) **Moral rights:** *violating the integrity and reputation of the author through misrepresentation or misquoting of the work.*

Intellectual property rights include: Copyright, Patents, Trade marks, Law of confidence and Design rights.

Copyright Law

Copyright protects works from being copied without permission.

Copyright goes beyond mere copying, however, and extends to other activities such as making an adaptation of the work in question, performing or showing the work in public, broadcasting the work and dealing with infringing copies of the work.

The types of works protected by copyright are literary works which includes:

> ➢ *computer programs,*
> ➢ *preparatory design material for computer programs and databases,*
> ➢ *dramatic,*
> ➢ *musical and artistic works,*
> ➢ *sound recordings,*
> ➢ *films,*
> ➢ *broadcasts,*
> ➢ *cable programmes and typographical arrangements of published editions.*

Copyright protection has a long duration and general yardstick being the life of the author (creator) plus 70 years or depending on the type of work, 50 or 70 years from the end of the year during which the work was created or published.

The major attractions of copyright as a form of protection are that it is free and that no formalities are required, it is automatic upon the creation of the work in question.

Copyright law is of vital importance to the Computer software industry and to people who prepare, record or transmit all sorts of works (for example, literary works such as books, reports, letters or musical works) using computer technology.

Copyright law is governed by the *Copyright, Designs and Patterns Act 1988*, the main provisions of which came into force on 1st August 1989, and subsequent amendments, together with a wealth of case law.

Databases were protected as compilations (being a form of literary work) until the *Copyright and Rights in database Regulations 1997* which came into force on 1st January.

Copyright in Tanzania -*Copyright and Neighbouring Rights Act No. 7 of December 1999*. Copyright and Neighbouring Rights Regulations G.N. No. 214 A, June 2000.

The Copyright Society of Tanzania (COSOTA), under Ministry of Industry, Trade and Marketing, is vested with power to administer the Copyright Act. Intellectual Property

Patent Law

Patent Law is mainly concerned with new inventions such as a new type of computer hardware, or a new process for use in manufacture of Integrated circuits (ICs).v For an invention to be protected by a patent, an application must be made to the Patent Office which is an expensive and lengthy process but if granted, the patent can be renewed for a total period of up to 20 years.

The relevant statute dealing with the patent law is the Patent Act 1977.

To be patentable, an invention must be novel (new), involve an inventive step, be capable of industrial application and not be excluded. Intellectual Property May 10, 2011

Patents in Tanzania-*The Patents Act No. 1 of 1987* as amended by Acts Nos. 13 and 18 of 1991 *The Patents Regulations G.N. 190 of 1994*

Business Registrations and Licensing Agency (BRELA), under the Ministry of Industry, Trade and Marketing, is vested with power to administer the patents Act

Trademark Law

Trade marks are often in the form of a name or a symbol and registration is provided for by the *trade Marks Act 1994*. Marks may be registered in respect of goods or services.

To be registrable, the mark must be *distinctive* and capable of being represented *graphically*. Trade marks are very important as they become associated with successful products and purchasers normally buy or order goods or services by reference to the mark.

The main purpose of trade mark law is to serve as an indicator of trade origin. Thus business goodwill and reputation is protected but this has a secondary effect of also protecting the buying public from deceptive practices.

In computer technology, the trade mark law also deals with domain name disputes, and infringement or dilution of trademarks on Internet.

Trade mark Law in Tanzania- *Trade and Service Marks Act No. 12 of 1986.*

Trade and Service Marks Regulations G.N. 40 of March 2000

The Law of confidence

The law of confidence protects information.

The difference with Copyright and patent law, is that the law of confidence is not defined by statute and derives almost entirely from case law.

The scope of this branch of intellectual property is considerable and protects trade secrets, business know how, and information such as list of clients and contracts, information of a personal nature and even ideas which have not been yet been expressed in a tangible form *(e.g., an idea for a new computer program)*.

The contents of many databases are protected by the law of confidence. However the major limitation is that the information concerned must be of a confidential nature and the effective nature of the law of confidence is largely or completely destroyed if the information concerned fall into the public

The law of confidence can be a useful supplement to copyright and patent law as it can protect ideas before they are sufficiently developed to attract copyright protection or to enable an application for a patent to be made.

Law of confidence is very flexible and has proved capable of taking new technological development in its stride.

The Industrial design law

In this case there are two types of right: registered design and design right which is not registrable.

- ➤ **Registered** is available for features of articles which appeal to the eye while
- While **design right** is intended to protect any aspect of the shape or configuration of articles without any requirement for visual attractiveness.
- **The durations of the rights** are different, being 25 years for registered designs and a maximum of 15 years for design right (but limited to 10 years of commercial exploitation). The appropriate statutes are the Registered Design Act 1949 (as amended) and Part III of the Copyright, Design and Patents Act 1988

Industrial Designs in Tanzania- *(Protection) Ordinance of 1936, cap. 219, Ord. 1936 No. 2 (F) PI 1938, 46.* In the process of drafting new Industrial Designs Legislation for 2002.v Also administered by BRELA

Summary

Rights that are protected by Intellectual property

Economic rights: the level of payment for use of the product by third parties.

Moral rights: violating the integrity and reputation of the author through misrepresentation or misquoting of the work.

Intellectual property rights include: Copyright, Patents, Trade marks, Law of confidence and Design rights.

Lesson 3

Ethical standard with respect to intellectual property

The copyright concept

Publishers or distributors as those who enter into agreements with producers to record, film or print the material and distribute it in ways that would secure the financial interests of producers and prevent the unethical use of the material

Consumers or users as those who have access to all types of information but must acknowledge the source or seek permission of the producer through the publisher, who may charge a fee under certain circumstances.

Producers or owners as those who maintain ownership and control over their material and receive financial' reward from the user, through the publisher

<u>Summary</u>

The copyright concept

Publishers or distributors as those who enter into agreements with producers to record, film or print the material and distribute it in ways that would secure the financial interests of producers and prevent the unethical use of the material

Consumers or users as those who have access to all types of information but must acknowledge the source or seek permission of the producer through the publisher, who may charge a fee under certain circumstances.

Producers or owners as those who maintain ownership and control over their material and receive financial' reward from the user, through the publisher

L esson 4

Concept of Plagiarism

Objective

At the end of this chapter, the student should be able to:
- ➢ *explain the concept of plagiarism be*
- ➢ *avoid the commission of plagiarism*

Plagiarism conceptualized as the use of someone's intellectual property without giving appropriate credit.

Many people now use computers, the Internet and the World Wide Web for research. Since articles appear as electronic text and include images, the physical act of copying the work of others is much easier.

The common activities for students and business people committed and considered acts of plagiarism are the following:

- Turn in someone else's work as their own;
- Fail to put a quote in quotation marks;
- Give incorrect information about the source of a quotation;
- Copy words or ideas from someone else without giving credit;
- Change words but copy the sentence structure of a source without giving credit;
- Copy so many words or ideas from a source that it makes up the majority of their work, whether giving credit or not.

According to the Merriam-Webster Online Dictionary, to 'plagiarize' means:

1. To commit literary theft
2. To use (another's production) without crediting the source.
3. To steal and pass off (the ideas or words of another) as one's own.
4. To present as new and original an idea or product derived from an existing source.

In other words, **plagiarism** is an act of fraud. It involves both stealing someone else's work and lying about it afterwards.

Are plagiarism and copyright infringement the same?

No! Plagiarism is not copyright infringement. While both terms may apply to a particular action, they are different wrongdoings. Copyright infringement is a violation of the rights of a copyright holder, when material protected by copyright is used without consent. On the other hand, plagiarism is concerned with the unearned increment to the plagiarizing author's reputation that achieved through false claims of authorship.

Summary

Plagiarism conceptualized as the use of someone's intellectual property without giving appropriate credit.

Lesson 5

Guidelines to avoid plagiarism

It's hard to defend plagiarism.

Objective

At the end of this chapter, the student should be able to:
- ➤ *list guidelines to avoid plagiarism*
- ➤ *acknowledge references or create a biblliography*

Plagiarism hurts everyone involved. Plagiarists do not acquire the skills that legitimate work would teach them, and risk failure and expulsion. Students who have worked hard for their grades have to compete with plagiarists for job and college admissions. Teachers are also affected as they have to take time out of the education process to deal with plagiarism.

Changing the words of an original source is not sufficient to prevent plagiarism. If you retained the essential idea of an original source, and have not cited it, then no matter how drastically you may have altered in context or presentation, you have still plagiarized it. Even though it may not be our intention to do so, once we fail to take the necessary steps to credit the author we are guilty of such an act.

The Guidelines to avoid plagiarism are:

1. **Acknowledgement of references in text and bibliography**
   An example is the use of referencing format.

   The American Psychological Association (APA) has established a style that uses in all of the books and journals that it publishers. The CSEC Business Study Subject Panel requires that citations of references are done using the APA study.

   Your job when citing a source is to make it possible for the readers to review the sources of your quotes. You do this by providing the reader with a short citation in parentheses in the body of your text and a list of references used (this is often called bibliography).

3. Obtaining approval for other persons' work

Most cases of plagiarism can be avoided by citing sources. First, *Seek permission to use copyrighted information of other person's work.* When approval is obtained a citation is necessary wherein a credit has been given back to the source of information. To cite a source, you are required to acknowledge that certain material has been borrowed; and provide your audience with the information necessary to find that source.

Summary

Guidelines to avoid plagiarism:

1. *Acknowledgement of references in text and bibliography, for example, use of referencing formats*

2. *Obtaining approval for other persons' work*

L esson 6

Acceptable Standard of Work

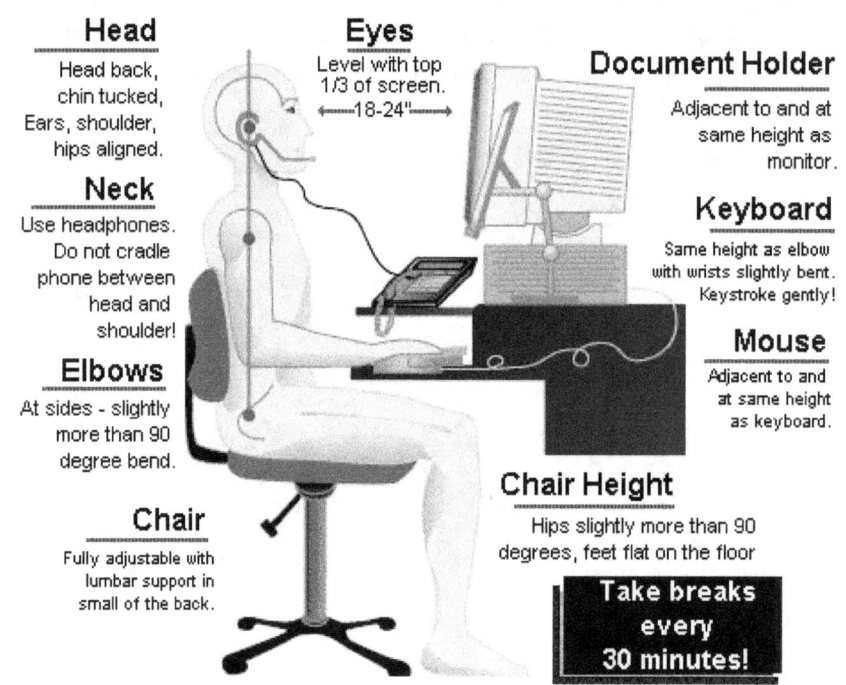

Head

Head back, chin tucked, Ears, shoulder, hips aligned.

Neck

Use headphones. Do not cradle phone between head and shoulder!

Elbows

At sides - slightly more than 90 degree bend.

Chair

Fully adjustable with lumbar support in small of the back.

Eyes

Level with top 1/3 of screen. ←18-24"→

Document Holder

Adjacent to and at same height as monitor.

Keyboard

Same height as elbow with wrists slightly bent. Keystroke gently!

Mouse

Adjacent to and at same height as keyboard.

Chair Height

Hips slightly more than 90 degrees, feet flat on the floor

Take breaks every 30 minutes!

Objective

At the end of this chapter, the student should be able to:
➤ *plan and order priorities to **ensure** acceptable standards of work*

Organization of work station

A work station is the environment in which an administrative assistant prepares documents.

Employees may be characterized by their work stations. In other words, working environment can depict how organised the worker is in executing task.

The layout of a work station can affect the way in which a person works either adversely or favourably. A cumbersome work station can cause confusion and frustration, while a tidy environment can enhance one's productivity level. Therefore, the work station should be such that the preparation of documents can be done with competence and ease.

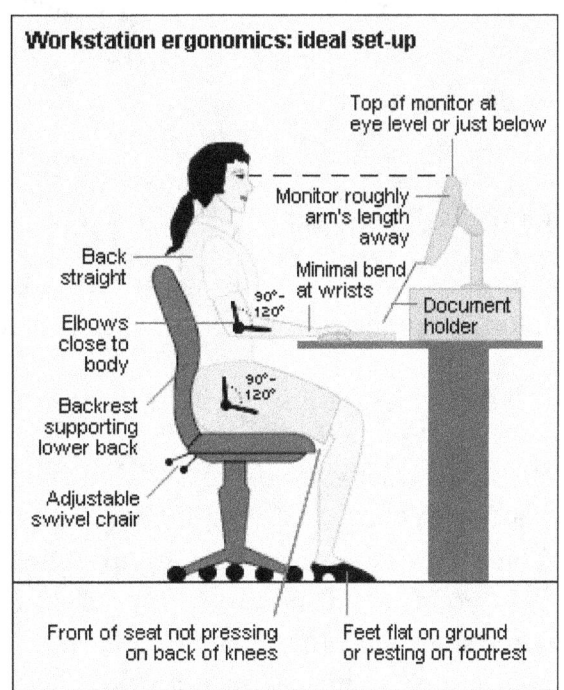

Organization of work

In order to accomplish a goal, constructive planning for that event is crucial as it allows for satisfactory results. Tasks should be carried out in a systematic order to ensure that they are completed on time and are mailable. **Mailable** refers to documents that are error-free, attractive and ready to be submitted.

The following tips could enhance your competence:

- Keep your work environment free of unnecessary clutter.
- Practise effective *time management* and *follow-up procedures*.
- Ensure that you are comfortably seated.
- Keep the copy you are typing from at an angle that can be easily seen.
- Endeavour to be accurate.

Submission of assignments

For the effective accomplishment of goals, you need to plan ahead of the time execution. Take the following tips into consideration:

- Keep all necessary items at hand to avoid frequently having to leave the work station.
- Prepare a *'things to do'* list with projects that you have to complete. As you work, check tasks on the list to ensure completion on time.
- Complete assignments that are of utmost importance first.
- It is good to get up from your desk once in a while since tasks can sometimes become monotonous and a break will rejuvenate you to continue working. Stretching will also help to prevent strain on your muscles.

Execution of effective time management

- Your work is a reflection of yourself.
- Make sure that all assignments are neat and well organized. Ensure that your information is accurate relevant, sufficiently detailed and well researched.
- Make certain that your is free from errors in grammar, spelling and punctuation.
- Always be punctual. Use an electronic or paper diary to record all assignments. Aim to complete work assignments well in advance of deadlines. Avoid distractions

Summary

Organization of work and work station

Submission of assignments;
execution of effective time management;
Follow-up procedures

Lesson 7
Desirable habits and work attitudes

Objective

At the end of this chapter, the student should be able to:

➤ *demonstrate awareness of desirable habits and work attitudes*

Work ethics in any line of work are critical for the success of the facility, regardless if it is on the private sector or public sector. When you observe that appear to be very knowledgeable and confident in their field of endeavors, we should know that they weren't born with these skills. These skills were developed because of hard work and dedication. Along with these developed technical skills, they have developed work habits and attitude that have assisted them to reach their respective levels of efficiency.

A habit is a settled or regular tendency or practice, particularly one that is hard to give up while an attitude is a settled way of thinking or feeling, typically reflected in a person's behaviour. As a student being prepared for employment in the business field, you must try to develop *positive habits and work attitudes*. This will lead to a favourable working relationship with your colleagues and enhanced professionalism.

The Elements of desirable habits and work attitudes are the following:

a) **Individual responsibility without supervision**

b) **Willingness** - These types possess the trait of awareness that knowledge-sharing of work is for the good of the organization. An example of the negative side of this scenario is the employee who won't share knowledge or methods for the fear of losing his position or possible job replacement. The layman's term for this is "false job security."

c) **Meeting deadlines**

d) **Team spirit** - This is proof-positive that the employee isn't power-driven or territorial within his domain or work area. We have all witnessed through the years where an individual does his job adequately, but doesn't work well with a group. Sometimes these folks are looking for individual recognition or looking to be promoted. The fear of group efforts doesn't give him or her high visibility of individual recognition from upper recognition.

e) **Cooperation-**-*is the process of working together to the same end*

f) **Recognition of diversity**

g) **Courtesy-**Willingness or generosity in providing something needed:

h) **Punctuality and regularity** -*These two traits reflect an employee's ability to manage their time and overcome work obstacles.*

i) **Good grooming**

j) **Personal integrity-***Personal integrity is the quality of being honest with yourself and others, and living a life that is aligned with your moral principles, not just liberty. It requires examining your beliefs and value system, and taking conscious steps to behave in ways that are consistent with your personal moral code.*

k) **Respect for others**

Summary

Elements of desirable   habits and work attitudes:

a) Individual responsibility without supervision.
b) Willingness
c) Meeting deadlines
d) Team spirit.
e) Co-operation
f) Recognition of diversity
g) Courtesy
h) Punctuality and regularity
i) Good grooming
j) Personal integrity
k) Respect for others

Exercise IX.7

Name: _____ Date: _____

Level: _____

Score: _____

Direction: True or False

1. Behavior is your actions but does not include your attitude. - True or False

2. A future employer usually evaluates a prospective employee's attitude before hiring them. - True or False

4. Work ethics includes which of the following?
        a. Attitude   b. values
        c. behavior   d. integrity
        e. all of the above

4. Displays loyalty, displays honesty, displays trustworthiness, and self-discipline all fall into which category in work ethics?

    a. Organization   b. Character

    c. Communication   d. Productivity

    e. All of the above

5. Teamwork involves which of the following:

    a. not respecting the rights of others

    b. being a team worker

c. respects some areas of confidentiality

d. demonstrates unmannerly behaviors

6. Initiative involves which of the following

    a. being independent   b. being ambitious

    c. being perceptive   d. being resourceful

    e. all of the above

7. Nonverbal communication deals with

    a. using time wisely   b. having a realistic expectation of
one's self

    c. attending class every day   d. eye contact and body language

    e. all of the above

8. Respects the rights of others, respects confidentiality, and cooperation falls under which category in work ethics?

    a. Initiative   b. Teamwork

    c. Productivity   d. Organization skills

    e. all of the above

9. The first step in the six-step problem solving method is to _____
the problem.

    a. Solve   b. manage   c. ignore   d. identify

10. Attendance at school and in class is routinely stressed. How does going to school regularly now impact your possible success in a career ten years from now?

   a. Attending school everyday helps you establish the habit of having good attendance.
   b. Being in attendance indicates you value the work being assigned and your responsibility in completing the work.
   c. Being in attendance helps you learn and master basic academic skills that may be beneficial on a job site.
   d. All of the above

Bibliography And Web Sites

http://www.computerhope.com
http://www.threesl.com
http://www.mit.edu/course
http://www.securityinabox.org
http://www.gcflearnfree.org
http://www.wikihow.com
http://www.cessi.org
Health Ergonomics

http://www.uhs.umich.edu/computerergonomics#arrange

http://www.learntyping.org/beginnertypinglesson1.htm
http://www.a1websitepro.com/blog

India Typing
http://indiatyping.com/index.php/typing-tips/typing-speed-calculation-formula

Related MARC fields or documents:
http://www.itsmarc.com/crs/mergedprojects/helpauth/helpauth/types_of_headings.htm

Typing Master
http://www.typingmaster.com/forum/topic20-regarding-typing-test-statistics.aspx

Retrieved blogs of Answer by Thushara Indika January 31, 2015
http://www.answers.com/Q/What_are_the_features_of_presentation_software

http://classjump.com/s/smallk/documents/KEYBOARDINGSKILLS.pdf

http://listdose.com/top-10-disadvantages-of-using-computers-for-long-hours/
http://classjump.com/s/smallk/?what=classes&class=160170

Revised October 23, 2012 http://www.coyotecommunications.com/tech/cellphone.shtml

Retrieve an Article r on January 9, 2015 at WIKI How to do anything
http://www.wikihow.com/Edit-a-Document-Using-Microsoft-Word%27s-Track-Changes-Feature

WIKIPEDIA The free encyclopedia
http://en.wikipedia.org/wiki/Proofreading
WIKIHOW
http://www.wikihow.com/Create-a-Graph-in-Excel

GCF Learnfree.org
http://www.gcflearnfree.org/office
[http://en.wikipedia.org/wiki/Paper_size#The_international_standard:_ISO_216]
[http://en.wikipedia.org/wiki/Memorandum]
[http://www.wikihow.com/Write-a-Memo]
[http://www.theofficeguide.com/copy-paper/]
[https://www.google.com.ph]
http://encyclopedia.thefreedictionary.com/Index+cards
http://en.wikipedia.org/wiki/Paper_size#The_international_standard:_ISO_216

Office online
https://support.office.com/en-us/article/Change-page-size-paper-size-or-orientation-

http://systemerrorblog.blogspot.com/2012/11/style-of-business-letter.html

https://support.office.com/en-us/article/Using-Word-for-an-email-merge-0f123521-20ce-4aa8-8b62-ac211dedefa4

Retrieve on Dec 3, 2015 Office on line
http://classjump.com/s/smallk/documents/EDPM13-3.pdf
https://support.office.com/en-us/article/Create-and-use-your-own-template-a1b72758-61a0-4215-80eb-165c6c4bed04
http://www.thefreedictionary.com/Legal+documents
http://en.wikipedia.org/wiki/
How-To Geek
http://www.howtogeek.com/howto/12916/center-pictures-and-other-objects-in-office-2007-2010/
Block Quotations in APA Style by Timothy McAdoo
http://blog.apastyle.org/apastyle/2013/06/block-quotations-in-apa-style.html
http://www.businessdictionary.com/definition/agreement.html

for creating brochure
http://www.vtaide.com/gleanings/BrochureMSWord.htm

Southern Silicon Valley retrieved on January 10, 2015

http://www.southernsiliconvalley.com/what-is-an-electronic-filing-system.htm

http://www.businessdictionary.com/definition/file-recovery.html#ixzz3OyhFSqLZ

http://www.threesl.com/pages/news/webletter-May12/Source_Documents.php

The Mayfield Handbook of Technical and Scientific writing

http://www.mit.edu/course/21/21.guide/websites.htm

https://www.police.qld.gov.au/programs/cscp/eCrime/security.htm

DREAMSTIME http://www.dreamstime.com/royalty-free-stock-photography-check-mark-symbol-image17822097

https://securityinabox.org/comodofirewall_main

Some of the technical terms that you will encounter, as you read through these chapters, are defined below:

A

Android : A Linux-based open-source operating system for smartphones and tablet devices, developed by Google.

APG : Android Privacy Guard: FOSS app for Android smartphones which facilitates OpenPGP encryption. It can be integrated with K9 Mail.

.apk file : The file extension used for Android apps.

App Store : The default repository from which iPhone applications can be found and downloaded.

Avast - A freeware anti-virus tool

B

Basic Input/Output System (BIOS) - The first and deepest level of software on a computer. The BIOS allows you to set many advanced preferences related to the computer's hardware, including a start-up password

BlackBerry : A brand of smartphones which run the BlackBerry operating system developed by Research In Motion (RIM).

Blacklist - A list of blocked websites and other Internet services that can not be accessed due to a restrictive filtering policy

Bluetooth - A physical wireless communications standard for exchanging data over short distances from fixed and mobile devices. Bluetooth uses short wavelength radio transmissions.

Booting - The act of starting up a computer

C

CCleaner - A freeware tool that removes temporary files and potentially sensitive traces left on your hard drive by programs that you have used recently and by the Windows operating system itself

CD Burner - A computer CD-ROM drive that can write data on blank CDs. *DVD burners* can do the same with blank DVDs. *CD-RW *and *DVD-RW drives* can delete and rewrite information more than once on the same CD-RW or DVD-RW disc.

Circumvention - The act of bypassing Internet filters to access blocked websites and other Internet services

Clam Win - A FOSS Anti-virus program for Windows

Cobian Backup - A FOSS backup tool. The most recent version of Cobian is closed-source freeware, but prior versions are released as FOSS.

Comodo Firewall - A freeware firewall tool

Compute r is an electronic machine or device that accepts data, processes and produces information

Cookie - A small file, saved on your computer by your browser, that can be used to store information for, or identify you to, a particular website

Cryptonite : A FOSS app for file encryption on Android smartphones.

D

Digital signature - A way of using encryption to prove that a particular file or message was truly sent by the person who claims to have sent it

document header- Text that is included at the top of a document before any other text and usually includes important information.

Domain name - The address, in words, of a website or Internet service; for example: www.securityinabox.org

E

EDGE, GPRS, UMTS : Enhanced Data Rates for GSM Evolution, General Packet Radio Service, and Universal Mobile Telecommunications System – technologies which allow mobile devices to connect to the internet.

Emerging technology (as distinguished from a conventional technology) is a field of technology that broaches new territory in some significant way, with new technological developments

Encryption - A way of using clever mathematics to *encrypt*, or scramble, information so that it can only be *decrypted* and read by someone who has a particular piece of information, such as a password or an *encryption key*

Enigmail - An add-on for the Thunderbird email program that allows it to send and receive encrypted and digitally signed email

Eraser - A tool that securely and permanently deletes information from your computer or removable storage device

F

F-Droid : An alternative repository from which many FOSS Android applications can be found and downloaded.

Firefox - A popular FOSS Web browser that provides an alternative to Microsoft Internet Explorer

Firewall - A tool that protects your computer from untrusted connections to or from local networks and the Internet

Free and Open Source Software (FOSS) - This family of software is available free of charge and has no legal restrictions to prevent a user from testing, sharing or modifying it

Freeware - Includes software that is free of charge but subject to legal or technical restrictions that prevent users from accessing the source code used to create it

G

Gibberbot : A FOSS app for Android which facilitates secure chats over XMPP protocol (used also by Google Talk). It is compatible with Off-the-Record and, when used in conjunction with Orbot, can route chats through the Tor network.

Google Play : The default repository from which Android applications can be found and downloaded.

GNU/Linux - A FOSS operating system that provides an alternative to Microsoft Windows

Global Positioning System (GPS) - A space-based global navigation satellite system that provides location and time information in all weather, anywhere on or near the Earth, where there is an (almost) unobstructed sky view.

Guardian Project : An organisation which creates smartphone apps, mobile devices operating system enhancements and customisations with privacy and security in mind.

H

Hacker - In this context, a malicious computer criminal who may be trying to access your sensitive information or take control of your computer remotely

I

iPhone : A brand of smartphones designed by Apple which run the Apple's iOS operating system.

Information technology (IT) is the application of computers and telecommunications equipment to store, retrieve, transmit and manipulate data, often in the context of a business or other enterprise.

Internet Protocol address (IP address) - A unique identifier assigned to your computer when it is connected to the Internet

Internet Service Provider (ISP) - The company or organisation that provides your initial link to the Internet. The governments of many countries exert control over the Internet, using means such as filtering and surveillance, through the ISPs that operate in those countries.

Infrared Data Association (IrDA) - A physical wireless communications standard for the short-range exchange of data using infrared spectrum light. IrDA is replaced by Bluetooth in modern devices.

J

Java Applications (Applets) - Small programs that can run under many operating systems, are cross-platform. They are frequently used to provide improved functionalities within web pages.

Jailbreaking : The process of unlocking features on an iPhone which are otherwise blocked by the manufacturer or mobile carrier in order to gain full access to the operating system.

K

K9 Mail : A FOSS e-mail client for Android smartphones, which enables OpenPGP encryption when used with the APG app.

Keylogger - A type of spyware that records which keys you have typed on your computer's keyboard and sends this information to a third party. Keyloggers are frequently used to steal email and other passwords.

KeePass - A freeware secure password database

L

LiveCD - A CD that allows your computer to run a different operating system temporarily.

M

Malware - A general term for all malicious software, including *viruses*, *spyware*, *trojans*, and other such threats

Mnemonic device - A simple trick that can help you remember complex passwords

N

NoScript - A security add-on for the Firefox browser that protects you from malicious programs that might be present in unfamiliar webpages

O

Obscuracam : A FOSS app for Android smartphones, which protects identity of people by facilitating editions such as face-blurring to photographs.

Orbot : A FOSS app for Android smartphones which enables apps such as Orweb and Gibberbot to connect to the Tor network.

Orweb : A FOSS web browser for Android smartphones which, when used in conjunction with Orbot, facilitates browsing over the Tor network.

Off the Record (OTR) - An encryption plugin for the Pidgin instant messaging program

P

Peacefire - Subscribers to this free service receive periodical emails containing an updated list of circumvention proxies, which can be used to bypass Internet censorship

Physical threat - In this context, any threat to your sensitive information that results from other people having direct physical access your computer hardware or from other physical risks, such as breakage, accidents or natural disasters

Pidgin - A FOSS instant messaging tool that supports an encryption plugin called *Off the Record (OTR)*

Proxy - An intermediary service through which you can channel some or all of your Internet communication and that can be used to bypass Internet censorship. A proxy may be public, or you may need to log in with a username and password to access it. Only some proxies are secure, which means that they use encryption to protect the privacy of the information that passes between your computer and the Internet services to which you connect through the proxy.

Proprietary software - The opposite of Free and Open-Source Software (*FOSS*). These applications are usually commercial, but can also be *freeware* with restrictive license requirements.

R

RiseUp - A email service run by and for activists that can be accessed securely either through webmail or using an email client such as *Mozilla Thunderbird*

Rooting : The process of unlocking features on an Android Phone which are otherwise blocked by the manufacturer or mobile carrier in order to gain full access to the operating system.

Router - A piece of networking equipment through which computers connect to their local networks and through which various local networks access the Internet. *Switches* , *gateways* and *hubs* perform similar tasks, as do wireless *access points* for computers that are properly equipped to use them

S

Secure password database - A tool that can encrypt and store your passwords using a single master password

Secure Sockets Layer (SSL) - The technology that permits you to maintain a secure, *encrypted* connection between your computer and some of the websites and Internet services that you visit. When you are connected to a website through SSL, the address of the website will begin with ***HTTPS*** rather than ***HTTP*** .

Security certificate - A way for secure websites and other Internet services to prove, using encryption, that they are who they claim to be. In order for your browser to accept a *security certificate* as valid, however, the service must pay for a *digital signature* from a trusted organization. Because this costs money that some service operators are unwilling or unable to spend, however, you will occasionally see a *security certificate* error even when visiting a valid service.

Security policy - A written document that describes how your organization can best protect itself from various threats, including a list of steps to be taken should certain security-related events take place

Security cable - A locking cable that can be used to secure a laptop or other piece of hardware, including external hard drives and some desktop computers, to a wall or a desk in order to prevent it from being physically removed

Server - A computer that remains on and connected to the Internet in order to provide some service, such as hosting a webpage or sending and receiving email, to other computers

SIM card - A small, removable card that can be inserted into a mobile phone in order to provide service with a particular mobile phone company. SIM cards can also store phone numbers and text messages.

Skype - A freeware Voice over IP (VoIP) tool that allows you to speak with other Skype users for free and to call telephones for a fee. The company that maintains Skype claims that conversations with other Skype users are encrypted. Because it is a closed-source tool, there is no way to verify this claim, but many people believe it to be true. Skype also supports instant messaging.

Smart phone is a pocket-sized handheld networked device that is a phone, a portable media players, a digital camera, a video camera, and a handheld computer.

Source code - The underlying code, written by computer programmers, that allows software to be created. The source code for a given tool will reveal how it works and whether it may be insecure or malicious.

Spybot - A freeware anti-malware tool that scans for, removes and helps protect your computer from spyware

Steganography - Any method of disguising sensitive information so that it appears to be something else, in order to avoid drawing unwanted attention to it

Swap file - A file on your computer to which information, some of which may be sensitive, is occasionally saved in order to improve performance

T

Textsecure : A FOSS app for Android which facilitates encrypted sending and storage of text messages.

Thunderbird - A FOSS email program with a number of security features, including support for the Enigmail encryption add-on

Tor - An anonymity tool that allows you to bypass Internet censorship and hide the websites and Internet services you vist from anyone who may be monitoring your Internet connection, while also disguising your own location from those websites

TrueCrypt - A FOSS file encryption tool that allows you to store sensitive information securely

U

Undelete Plus - A freeware tool that can sometimes restore information that you may have deleted accidentally

Uninterruptable Power Supply (UPS) - A piece of equipment that allows your critical computing hardware to continue operating, or to shut down gracefully, in the event of a brief loss of power

V

VautletSuite 2 Go - A Freeware encrypted email program

Voice over IP (VoIP) - The technology that allows you to use the Internet for voice communication with other VoIP users and telephones

W

Whitelist - A list of websites or Internet services to which some form of access is permitted, when other sites are automatically blocked

Windows Phone : A smartphone operating system developed by Microsoft.

Wiping - The process of deleting information securely and permanently

X

Your-Freedom - A freeware circumvention tool that allows you to bypass filtering by connecting to the Internet through a private proxy. If Your-Freedom is configured properly, your connection to these proxies will be encrypted in order to protect the privacy of your communication.

ELECTRONIC DOCUMENT PREPARATION AND MANAGEMENT

Sample Reference Manual Checksheet

NAME:_____

Elements	Tick if you have Completed	Tick if checked by Teacher	Tick if you made corrections	Tick if error free and Mailable	Final score after all corrections must be entered by teacher
Two- page letter indented or blocked style					
Circular letter or form with tear off slip					
A Report or Specification or Play					
Ruled Tabulation with Main heading, multiple column heading, Oblique/vertical sort					
Notice of a meeting with an agenda for a meeting					
A Chairman's Agenda or Minutes of a meeting					
An invitation with menu or A programme for an event					
A Flow Chart or Organizational Chart					
A Lease or Hire Purchase Agreement or Will with an endorsement					
A Contract of employment					
A Chairman's agenda					
Minutes of a meeting					

Manuscripts - shoulder, and paragraph headings & footnotes					
An invitation with menue					
A programme for an event					
Flow Chart OR organisation chart					
A play or Poem					
A lease					
A Will					
Total score					

Basic PC shortcut keys

Below is a list of some of the most commonly used basic shortcut keys that work with almost all IBM compatible computers and software programs. It is highly recommended that all users keep a good reference of these shortcut keys or try to memorize them. Doing so will dramatically increase your productivity.

Shortcut Keys	Description
Alt + F	File menu options in current program.
Alt + E	Edit options in current program
Alt + Tab	Switch between open programs
F1	Universal Help in almost every Windows program.
F2	Rename a selected file
F5	Refresh the current program window
Ctrl + N	Create a new, blank document in some software programs
Ctrl + O	Open a file in current software program
Ctrl + A	Select all text.
Ctrl + B	Change selected text to be Bold
Ctrl + I	Change selected text to be in Italics
Ctrl + U	Change selected text to be Underlined
Ctrl + F	Open find window for current document or window.
Ctrl + S	Save current document file.
Ctrl + X	Cut selected item.
Shift + Del	Cut selected item.
Ctrl + C	Copy selected item.
Ctrl + Ins	Copy selected item
Ctrl + V	Paste
Shift + Ins	Paste
Ctrl + K	Insert hyperlink for selected text
Ctrl + P	Print the current page or document.
Home	Goes to beginning of current line.
Ctrl + Home	Goes to beginning of document.
End	Goes to end of current line.
Ctrl + End	Goes to end of document.
Shift + Home	Highlights from current position to beginning of line.
Shift + End	Highlights from current position to end of line.
Ctrl + Left arrow	Moves one word to the left at a time.
Ctrl + Right arrow	Moves one word to the right at a time.
Ctrl + Esc	Opens the START menu
Ctrl + Shift + Esc	Opens Windows Task Manager
Alt + F4	Close the currently active program
Alt + Enter	Open the Properties for the selected item (file, folder, shortcut, etc.)

PC shortcut keys for Special Characters

There are many special characters that can be created using keyboard shortcuts. Below are some of the more common and popular special characters and the keyboard shortcuts to create them.

Shortcut Keys	Special Character
Alt + 0224	à
Alt + 0232	è
Alt + 0236	ì
Alt + 0242	ò
Alt + 0241	ñ
Alt + 0228	ä
Alt + 0246	ö
Alt + 0252	ü
Alt + 0248	ø
Alt + 0223	ß
Alt + 0198	Æ
Alt + 0231	ç
Alt + 0191	¿
Alt + 0176	° (degree symbol)
Alt + 0177	± (plus/minus symbol)
Alt + 0153	™
Alt + 0169	©
Alt + 0174	®
Alt + 0128	€ (Euro currency)
Alt + 0162	¢ (Cent symbol)
Alt + 0163	£ (British Pound currency)
Alt + 0165	¥ (Japanese Yen currency)

Microsoft Word shortcut keys	
Below is a listing of all the major shortcut keys in Microsoft Word. See the computer	
Note: If you have a tablet computer that does not have Function keys (F1-F12) on its	
Shortcut	**Description**
Ctrl + 0	Adds or removes 6pts of spacing before a paragraph.
Ctrl + A	Select all contents of the page.
Ctrl + B	Bold highlighted selection.
Ctrl + C	Copy selected text.
Ctrl + D	Open the font preferences window.
Ctrl + E	Aligns the line or selected text to the center of the screen.
Ctrl + F	Open find box.
Ctrl + I	Italic highlighted selection.
Ctrl + J	Aligns the selected text or line to justify the screen.
Ctrl + K	Insert link.
Ctrl + L	Aligns the line or selected text to the left of the screen.
Ctrl + M	Indent the paragraph.
Ctrl + P	Open the print window.
Ctrl + R	Aligns the line or selected text to the right of the screen.
Ctrl + S	Save the open document. Just like Shift + F12.
Ctrl + T	Create a hanging indent.
Ctrl + U	Underline the selected text.
Ctrl + V	Paste.
Ctrl + X	Cut selected text.
Ctrl + Y	Redo the last action performed.
Ctrl + Z	Undo last action.
Ctrl + Shift + L	Quickly create a bullet point.
Ctrl + Shift + F	Change the font.
Ctrl + Shift + >	Increase selected font +1pts up to 12pt and then increase font +2pts.
Ctrl +]	Increase selected font +1pts.
Ctrl + Shift + <	Decrease selected font -1pts if 12pt or lower; if above 12, decreases font by +2pt.
Ctrl + [	Decrease selected font -1pts.
Ctrl + / + c	Insert a cent sign (¢).

Ctrl + ' + \<char>	Insert a character with an accent (grave) mark, where \<char> is the character you want. For example, if you wanted an accented è you would use Ctrl + ' + e as your shortcut key. To reverse the accent mark use the opposite accent mark, often on the tilde key.
Ctrl + Shift + *	View or hide non printing characters.
Ctrl + \<left arrow>	Moves one word to the left.
Ctrl + \<right arrow>	Moves one word to the right.
Ctrl + \<up arrow>	Moves to the beginning of the line or paragraph.
Ctrl + \<down arrow>	Moves to the end of the paragraph.
Ctrl + Del	Deletes word to right of cursor.
Ctrl + Backspace	Deletes word to left of cursor.
Ctrl + End	Moves the cursor to the end of the document.
Ctrl + Home	Moves the cursor to the beginning of the document.
Ctrl + Spacebar	Reset highlighted text to the default font.
Ctrl + 1	Single-space lines.
Ctrl + 2	Double-space lines.
Ctrl + 5	1.5-line spacing.
Ctrl + Alt + 1	Changes text to heading 1.
Ctrl + Alt + 2	Changes text to heading 2.
Ctrl + Alt + 3	Changes text to heading 3.
Alt + Ctrl + F2	Open new document.
Ctrl + F1	Open the Task Pane.
Ctrl + F2	Display the print preview.
Ctrl + Shift + >	Increases the selected text size by one.
Ctrl + Shift + <	Decreases the selected text size by one.
Ctrl + Shift + F6	Switches to another open Microsoft Word document.
Ctrl + Shift + F12	Prints the document.
F1	Open Help.
F4	Repeat the last action performed (Word 2000+)

F5	Open the Find, Replace, and Go To window in Microsoft Word.
F7	Spellcheck and grammar check selected text or document.
F12	Save As.
Shift + F3	Change the text in Microsoft Word from **uppercase** to **lowercase** or a capital letter at the beginning of every word.
Shift + F7	Runs a Thesaurus check on the selected word.
Shift + F12	Save the open document. Just like Ctrl + S.
Shift + Enter	Create a soft break instead of a new paragraph.
Shift + Insert	Paste.
Shift + Alt + D	Insert the current date.
Shift + Alt + T	Insert the current time.

In addition to the above shortcut keys, users can also use their mouse to perform some common actions. Below some are examples of mouse shortcuts.

Mouse shortcuts	Description
Click, hold, and drag	Selects text from where you click and hold to the point you drag and let go.
Double-click	If double-clicking a word, selects the complete word.
Double-click	Double-clicking on the left, center, or right of a blank line makes the alignment of the text left, center, or right aligned.
Double-click	Double-clicking anywhere after text on a line will set a tab stop.
Triple-click	Selects the line or paragraph of the text that the mouse triple-clicked on.
Ctrl + Mouse wheel	Zooms in and out of document.

Microsoft Excel shortcut keys

Below is a listing of all the major **shortcut keys** usable in **Microsoft Excel**. See the**computer shortcut page** if you are looking for shortcut keys used in other programs.

Shortcut	Description
F2	Edit the selected cell.
F3	After a **name** has been created, F3 will **paste** names.
F4	Repeat last action. For example, if you changed the color of text in another cell, pressing F4 will change the text in cell to the same color.
F5	Go to a specific cell. For example, C6.
F7	Spell check selected text or document.
F11	Create chart from selected data.
Ctrl + Shift + ;	Enter the current time.
Ctrl + ;	Enter the current date.
Alt + Shift + F1	Insert New Worksheet.
Alt + Enter	While typing text in a cell, pressing Alt + Enter will move to the next line, allowing for multiple lines of text in one cell.
Shift + F3	Open the Excel formula window.
Shift + F5	Bring up search box.
Ctrl + 1	Open the Format Cells window.
Ctrl + A	Select all contents of the worksheet.
Ctrl + B	Bold highlighted selection.
Ctrl + I	Italic highlighted selection.
Ctrl + K	Insert link.
Ctrl + S	Save the open worksheet.
Ctrl + U	Underline highlighted selection.
Ctrl + 1	Change the format of selected cells.
Ctrl + 5	Strikethrough highlighted selection.
Ctrl + P	Bring up the print dialog box to begin the printing process.
Ctrl + Z	Undo last action.
Ctrl + F3	Open Excel Name Manager.
Ctrl + F9	Minimize current window.
Ctrl + F10	Maximize currently selected window.
Ctrl + F6	Switch between open workbooks or windows.
Ctrl + Page up	Move between work sheets in the same document.
Ctrl + Page down	Move between work sheets in the same document.
Ctrl + Tab	Move between Two or more open Excel files.
Alt + =	Create a formula to sum all of the above cells.
Ctrl + '	Insert the value of the above cell into the cell currently selected.
Ctrl + Shift + 1	Format number in comma format.
Ctrl + Shift + 4	Format number in currency format.
Ctrl + Shift + 3	Format number in date format.
Ctrl + Shift + 5	Format number in percentage format.

Ctrl + Shift + 6	Format number in scientific format.
Ctrl + Shift + 2	Format number in time format.
Ctrl + Arrow key	Move to next section of text.
Ctrl + Space	Select entire column.
Shift + Space	Select entire row.
Ctrl + -	Delete the selected column or row.
Ctrl + Shift + =	Insert a new column or row.
Ctrl + Home	Move to cell A1.
Ctrl + ~	Switch between showing Excel formulas or their values in cells.

Chat slang

Chat slang is a method of typing long words and phrases as short one-

r u smart bcoz i need some1 smart

If you are looking for chat shorthand words such as "cya", "lol", "ty", etc. see

Slang	Full word
@	at
@teotd	at the end of the day
1	one or won
14aa41	one for all and all for one
2	to, too, or two
2b or not 2b	to be or not to be
2dA	today
3sum	threesome
4	for, four, or the prefix or suffix: fore)
411	information
4ever	forever
86	out of, or over
aaaaa	American association against acronym abuse
aaf	as a friend
aak	asleep at keyboard
aamoi	as a matter of interest
aar, aar8	at any rate
aas	alive and smiling
aatk	always at the keyboard
aayf	as always, your friend
ab	ass backwards
abithiwtidb	a bird in the hand is worth two in the bush
abt2	about to
acd	alt control delete
ack	acknowledgement
adad	another day, another dollar
adbb	all done bye bye
adih	another day in hell
adip	another day in paradise

afagay	a friend as good as you
afahmasp	a fool and his money are soon parted
afaic	as far as I'm concerned
afaiu	as far as I understand
afap	as far as possible
afayc	as far as your concerned
afc	away from computer
afdn	any f***ing day now
afiaa	as far as I am aware
afiniafi	a friend in need is a friend indeed
afz	acronym free zone
agkwe	and God knows what else
aiamu	and I'm a monkey's uncle
aih	as it happens
aimb	as I mentioned before
aimp	always in my prayers
aise	as I said earlier
aisi	as I see it
alol	actually laughing out loud
alot or allot	a lot
altg	act locally, think globally
amap	as many as possible
ambw	all my best wishes
aml	all my love
and	any day now
anfawfows	and now a word from our web sponsor
aoas	all of a sudden
aob	abuse of bandwidth
asafp	as soon as freakin possible
aslmh	age,sex,location,music,hobbies
atb	all the best
atst	at the same time
atw	all the web, or around the web
ayk	as you know
aysos	are you stupid or something
aytmtb	and you're telling me this because?
ax	ask
b	be, bee
b/c	because
b4u	before you
b4uki	before you know it
bag	busting a gut
bai	bye
bak	back at my keyboard
bau	business as usual
bb	bye-bye or bulletin board
bb4n, bbfn	bye bye for now

bbbg	bye bye, be good
bbias	be back in a sec
bbiaw	be back in a while
bbn	bye bye now
bbsd	be back soon darling
bbsl	be back sooner or later
bbt	be back tomorrow
bc	because
bcoz	because
bdn	big d**n number
bf	boyfriend
bfd	big f***ing deal
bg	big grin. See bg definition for alternative meanings.
bif	before I forget
bion	believe it or not
bioyn	blow it out your nose
bitd	back in the day
bk	big kiss
bka	better known as
bm	bite me
bmota	bite me on the ass
bohica	bend over, here it comes again
bout	about
br	bathroom
brt	be right there
bs	big smile, bull sh**
btdt	been there done that
bthoom	beats the heck out of me
btsoom	beats the sh** out of me
btwbo	be there with bells on
bw	best wishes
bwd	backward
bwdik	but what do I know
by	busy
bykt	but you knew that
c-t	city
c	see
'cause	because
cb	call back, chat brat
cfv	call for vote
cid	consider it done
cmiw	correct me if I'm wrong
cos, coz	because
craft	can't remember a f***ing thing
crat	can't remember a thing
csl	can't stop laughing
cul, cul8r	see you later

cus	because
cuz or cuzz	because
cwyl	chat with you later
cyt	see you tomorrow
da	the
dat	that
deti	don't even think it
df	dear friend
dga	don't go away (or anywhere)
dgara	don't give a rat's a**
dgt	don't go there
dhyb	don't hold your breath
diaf	die in a fire
diku	do I know you?
dis	this
dkdc	don't know, don't care
dltm	don't lie to me
dnc	does not compute
doin	doing
dos	those
dqydj	don't quit your day job
drib	don't read if busy
dunno	don't know
dust	did you see that?
duz	does
duznt	doesn't
dyjhiw	don't you just hate it when...
dyofdw	do your own f***ing dirty work
dystsott	did you see the size of that thing?
e123	easy as 123
eak	eating at the keyboard
em	them, excuse me
eso	equipment smarter than operator
evar	ever
ewi	emailing while intoxicated
ez	easy
faql	frequently asked questions list
fav	favorite
fawc	for anyone who cares
fe	fatal error
fitb	fill in the blanks
fo	f*** off
foc	free of charge
foe	for
fofl	falling on floor laughing
ftasb	faster than a speeding bullet
fttb	for the time being

fwd	forward
fya	for your amusement
g or <g>	grin
ga	go ahead
gbh	great big hug
gd	good
ggn	gotta go now
go2	go to
gok	God only knows
gonna	going to
gth	go to hell
gtsy	good to see you
gud	good
h2	how to
hagd	have a good day
hai	hi
hhoj	ha ha, only joking
hhtyay	happy holidays to you and yours
hih	hope it helps
hlp	help
hua	heads up ace
hugz	hugs
huh	have you heard
huya	head up your a**
i1dr	I wonder
iae	in any event
ianac	I am not a crook
ianae	I am not an expert
iat	I am tired
ibrb	I'll be right back
ibt	in between technology
ibtd	I beg to differ
icbw	I could be wrong
iccl	I couldn't care less
idgaf	I dont' give a f***
idgi	I don't get it
idky	I don't know you
idl	ideal
idm	it doesn't matter
idst	I didn't say that
idts	I don't think so
ifu	I f***ed up
igtp	I get the point
ihaim	I have another instant message
ihno	I have no opinion
iimad	if it makes a difference
iir	if I remember

iiwm	if it were me
ik	I know
imnsho	in my not so humble opinion
ims	I'm sorry
in4ml	informal
inmp	it's not my problem
inpo	in no particular order
INNW	if not now, when?
ioh	I'm outta here
iss	I said so
istm	it seems to me
istr	I seem to remember(recall)
iswym	I see what you mean
itm	in the money
ium	if you must
iyss	if you say so
j/c	just checking
j/w	just wondering
jad	just another day
jam	just a minute
joo or j00	you
k	ok
kbd	keyboard
kewl or kool	cool
kfy	kiss for you
kir	keep it real
kiss	keep it simple, stupid
kk	ok
kma	kiss my a**
kok	knock
kotc	kiss on the cheek
kotl	kiss on the lips
kthx	ok, thanks
kwim	know what I mean
kthxbai	ok, thanks, bye
kthxbye	ok, thanks, bye
kutgw	keep up the good work
kypo	keep your pants on
l8	late
laf or laff	laugh
laq	lame a** quote
lil	little
lola	laugh out loud again
ltic	laugh til I cry
lul or lulz	lol
luv	love

m	am
mai	my
mfd	multi function device
mhbfy	my heart bleeds for you
mhoty	my hats off to you
mite	might
mkop	my kind of place
mmk	ok
moar	more
mof	matter of fact
moos	members of the opposite sex
moss	members of the same sex
mte	my thoughts exactly
mubar	messed up beyond all recognition
mwbrl	more will be revealed later
n	and or in
n/t	no text
n2m	not to mention
nagi	not a good idea
naz	name, address, zip
ncg	new college graduate
ne1	anyone
nething	anything
ng	new game
nim	no internal message
nimby	not in my backyard
nimq	not in my queue
nmp	not my problem
no1	no-one
noyb	none of your business
nrg	energy
ntk	nice to know
ntn	nothing
ntymi	now that you mention it
nw	no way!
o	oh
oaus	on an unrelated subject
oars	oh no, not again
obtw	oh by the way
oh	over heard
oll	online love
omdb	over my dead body
omik	open mouth, insert keyboard
ootb	out of the blue
ot	off topic
ott	over the top
ottomy	off the top of my head

ousu	oh you, shut up
owtte	or words to that effect
p&c	private and confidential
pans	pretty awesome new stuff
pcm	please call me
pdq	pretty darn quick
pd	public domain
pimp	peeing in my pants
pita	pain in the a**
pls	please
plz	please
pmfji	pardon me for jumping in
po	piss off
poof	good bye
ppl or peeps	people
ptl	praise the lord
pza	pizza
ql	quit laughing
r	are
r&d	research and development
r&r	rest and relaxation
rbay	right back at ya
rbtl	read between the lines
re	regarding
rfd	request for discussion
rite	right
rlf	real life friend
rlh	run like hell
rmlb	read my lips baby
rn	right now
rsn	real soon now
rtfaq	read the faq file
rtk	return to keyboard
ruok	are you ok?
ruup4it	are you up for it?
ryo	roll your own
s or <s>	smile
scnr	sorry, could not resist
sep	someone elses problem
sez	says
sfete	smiling from ear to ear
sh	sh** happens
sitd	still in the dark
slirk	smart little rich kid
smaim	send me an instant message
sme	subject matter expert

smem	send me email
snafu	situation normal, all f***ed up
so	significant other
sok	it's ok
some1	someone
sorg	straight or gay
soz	sorry
spk	speak
srlsy	Seriously
sro	standing room only
sry	sorry
ssdd	same sh** different day
str8	straight
stra	stray
stys	speak to ya soon
sum	some
sum1	someone
suyf	shut up you fool
sux, sux0r	suck
swak	sealed with a kiss
swdyt	so what do you think
ta	the
tafn	that is all for now
tah	take a hike
tarfu	things are really f***ed up
tas	taking a shower
tbc	to be continued
tdtm	talk dirty to me
teh	the
tfn	thanks for nothing
thanx	thanks
thnq	thank you
tho	though
thot	thought
thx	thanks
tia	thanks in advance
tiail	think I am in love
tic	tongue in cheek
tlgo	the list goes on
tm	trust me
tna	temporarily not available
tom	tomorrow
tot	tons of time
tp	team player
tptb	the powers that be
ttg	time to go
ttly	totally

ttt	that's the ticket
tvm	thank you very much
twimc	to whom it may concern
u	you
u2	you too?
uok	are you ok?
ur or ure	your or you're
usu	usually
uve	you've
vbg	very big grin
vbs	very big smile
vm	voice mail
vrbs	virtual reality bull sh**
vsf	very sad face
wad	without a doubt
wai	what an idiot
wan2	want to
wanna	want to
w/o	without
w84m	wait for me
wat	what
wc	who cares
wdys	what did you say
wdyt	what do you think
wf	way fun
wfm	wait for me, works for me
wiifm	what's in it for me
wknd	weekend
woulda	would of
wn	when
wog	wise old guy
wrt	with regards to, or with respect to
wt	without thinking
wtsds	where the sun don't shine
wu	what up?
wut	what
wwy	where were you?
wycm	will you call me?
wyp	what's your problem?
wyrn	what's your real name?
wys	whatever you say
wyt	whatever you think
wywh	wish you were here
x-i-10	exciting
xlnt	excellent
xme	excuse me
y	why

ya	yet another
yafiygi	you asked for it you got it
ydkm	you don't know me
ygbk	you gotta be kidding
yhm	you have mail
yic	yours in Christ
ykw	you know what
YM	you mean
ynk	you never know
yr	your, yeah right
yoyo	you're on your own
ysyd	yeah, sure you do
yttt	you telling the truth?
yup	Yes
yur	your or you're
yyssw	yeah, yeah, sure sure whatever
zzz	sleeping, tired, bored

When chatting or typing anything on the Internet, unless you're

TERMINOLOGY	to be encoded on Glossaries	Example
orientation	layout of paper used in document production	Landscape, protrait
Central Processing Unit (CPU)		
processor		
memory		
input devices		
output devices		
software		
hardware		
motherboard		
power supply		
computer		
Spelling		
Punctuation		
Capitalisation		
Transposition		
grammar		
paragraphing		
hyphenation		
margins		
tabulation		

_____

Table of contents

	Section Title Page				Contents								
	Title page Label	Pix-2	Objective	Obj explanation	Description/Definition	Discussion	Samples	Steps/How to	Summary	Activities	Exercises	Answers	References

		Section Title Page				Contents								
		Title page Label	Pix-2	Objective	Obj explanation	Description/Definition	Discussion	Samples	Steps/How to	Summary	Activities	Exercises	Answers	References
Section IV	**Use of Application Software**													
	(Objectives 1,6)													
	Features of formatting	1	1	3	1	1								
	Various Types of Documents	1		2	1	1								
	Documents with Tabulation	1	2											
	Creating Database	1		3	1	1	1	1		1				
	creating Simple Presentation	1		2	1	1	1	1		1				
Section V	**Business Document Preparation**													
	(All 9 objectives)													
	1 Paper size and Orientation	1	3	2	1									
	2 Types of Stationery Document	1	3	2	1									
	3 Stationery Document Preparation	1	2	1										
	4 Styles of Letters	1												
	5 Envelopes and Labels	1	2	2										
	6 Correspondence and various media	1	2	2										
	7 Various styles of Memoranda	1	2	2										
	8 Meeting Documentation	1												
	9 Manipulating Graphics	1		1										
Section VI	**Specialized Document Preparation**													
	(All 3 objectives)													
	Creative Displays	1	3	2	1	1	1	1	1	1		1		
	Types of documents	1	2	3										
	Creating Templates b											1		

	Section Title Page				Contents								
	Title page Label	Pix-2	Objective	Obj explanation	Description/Definition	Discussion	Samples	Steps/How to	Summary	Activities	Exercises	Answers	References
Section VII Electronic Communication													
(All 6 objectives)													
• Types of Electronic Communication	1	3	3	1	1	1	1	1	1	2			
• Features of e-mail	1	2	2	1	1	1							
• Electronic Communication Media													
• Communication technologies													
• File Organization Methods	1	1	2	1	1	1	1	1	1				
Selection of Communication Media													
Section VIII Document Management													
(Objectives 1, 2, 5, 6, 7)													
1 Manual and electronic filing system	1	3	3	3	5	5			2				
2 Types of document	1	2	1	5	5	5	5		5				
3 Electronic Filing system	1 -model	1	3	5	5	5	5	5	5	10	10	10	10
4 Integrity of Files	1	2	1	1	1	2	1		4				
5 Security of Files	1	2	1	2	3	3	1		3				
6 Retention of Files	1	1	3										
7 Tracing of Documents	1	1	1		1								
Section IX Ethics													
• Concepts of Intellectual Property	1	2	2	1	1	1	1	1	1				
• Intellectual Property Laws	1		1	1	1	1	1	1	1				
• Ethical standard with respect to Intellectual Property	1		1										
• Concept of plagiarism													
• Guidelines to avoid plagiarism													
• Acceptable standard of work													
Desirable habits and work attitudes s													
Bibliography and websites													
Glossary Glossary													
Index Index